ONLINE
INVESTING
HACKS™

Other resources from O'Reilly

Related titles

Excel Hacks

Spidering Hacks

Google Hacks

Windows XP Hacks

Mac OS X Panther Hacks

Hacks Series Home

hacks.oreilly.com is a community site for developers and power users of all stripes. Readers learn from each other as they share their favorite tips and tools for Mac OS X, Linux, Google, Windows XP, and more.

oreilly.com

oreilly.com is more than a complete catalog of O'Reilly books. You'll also find links to news, events, articles, weblogs, sample chapters, and code examples.

oreillynet.com is the essential portal for developers interested in open and emerging technologies, including new platforms, programming languages, and operating systems.

Conferences

O'Reilly brings diverse innovators together to nurture the ideas that spark revolutionary industries. We specialize in documenting the latest tools and systems, translating the innovator's knowledge into useful skills for those in the trenches. Visit *conferences.oreilly.com* for our upcoming events.

Safari Bookshelf (*safari.oreilly.com*) is the premier online reference library for programmers and IT professionals. Conduct searches across more than 1,000 books. Subscribers can zero in on answers to time-critical questions in a matter of seconds. Read the books on your Bookshelf from cover to cover or simply flip to the page you need. Try it today with a free trial.

ONLINE INVESTING HACKS™

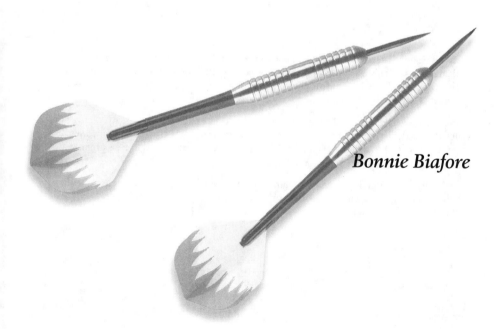

Bonnie Biafore

O'REILLY®

Beijing · Cambridge · Farnham · Köln · Paris · Sebastopol · Taipei · Tokyo

Online Investing Hacks™
by Bonnie Biafore

Copyright © 2004 O'Reilly Media, Inc. All rights reserved.
Printed in the United States of America.

Published by O'Reilly Media, Inc., 1005 Gravenstein Highway North, Sebastopol, CA 95472.

O'Reilly books may be purchased for educational, business, or sales promotional use. Online editions are also available for most titles (*safari.oreilly.com*). For more information, contact our corporate/institutional sales department: (800) 998-9938 or *corporate@oreilly.com*.

Editor:	Rael Dornfest	**Production Editor:**	Sarah Sherman
Series Editor:	Rael Dornfest	**Cover Designer:**	Hanna Dyer
Executive Editor:	Dale Dougherty	**Interior Designer:**	David Futato

Printing History:

June 2004:	First Edition.

RepKover™ This book uses RepKover™, a durable and flexible lay-flat binding.

ISBN: 0-596-00677-2
[C]

Contents

Credits

About the Author

Bonnie Biafore is the author of several books about personal finance, investing, and project management. She wrote the NAIC Stock Study Handbook, for which she earned a Distinguished Award from the Society of Technical Communications. She writes a monthly column about online investing called "WebWatch" for *Better Investing* magazine. As a consultant, she manages projects for clients and wins accolades for her ability to herd cats. Bonnie is annoyingly attentive to detail and always digs into the software she uses to get the most out of it. Now, she enjoys explaining the details of making things work to anyone who will listen or read. You can learn more at her web site, *http://www.bonniebiafore.com*.

Contributors

The following people contributed their hacks, writing, spreadsheets, and knowledge to this book:

- Amy B. Crane (*http://www.amybcrane.com*) helps people make sense of personal finance, mutual funds, and investing through her writing for magazines, books, and the Web. The author of *The NAIC Mutual Fund Handbook*, she writes a monthly mutual fund column for *Better Investing* magazine and articles on consumer finance issues for Bankrate.com. She teaches mutual fund classes at regional and national investing conferences, and has developed curriculum and taught online investing classes. A graduate of Furman University, Amy lives and invests in Erie, PA.

- Martha Sippel (*http://www.azuwrite.com*) abandoned her corporate lifestyle to become an independent consultant who creates solutions with the user in mind. She likes to create user interfaces for web applications and web sites. A native of Colorado and an information architect with 28 years of experience in technical communication, she was a geologist in her former career. Martha is a senior member of the Society for Technical Communication, where she has authored articles and presented at regional and international conferences.

- Doug Gerlach (*http://www.douglasgerlach.com*) is the author of several books on investing and a recognized authority on online investing. He is featured in television and radio, as well as in publications, including *The Wall Street Journal*, *ComputerWorld*, *HomePC*, *Barron's*, *New York Magazine*, *Los Angeles Business Review*, *Fidelity Focus*, *The St. Petersburg Times*, CNNfn's *Digital Jam*, Extra Help Channel's *In The Money*, and ZDTV's *The Money Machine*. He has founded several financial web sites, including Investment-Clubs.com, a clearinghouse for investment club information; DRIPCentral.com, a resource for direct investing; ArmchairMillionaire.com, a site committed to teaching "common sense saving and investing" strategies; and the now-defunct Investorama.com. He is also the cocreator of the NAIC web site.

- Saul Seinberg is an attorney specializing in intellectual property law for a large computer company. He has been active in the study of investments since wrangling a job as an order clerk on the floor of the American Stock Exchange back in its precomputer days when orders were transmitted to floor brokers by hand signals. A firm believer in the use of fundamentals to identify quality and growth companies, and technical analysis to determine when to buy, hold, or sell them, Saul resides in Colorado, near Boulder, and enjoys his adopted state's many recreational opportunities. He also applies his investment techniques to the use of covered call options to supplement and boost portfolio performance. Saul is a lifetime member of both AAII and NAIC who looks forward each day to the market's many opportunities and challenges.

- Ellis Traub (*http://www.financialliteracy.us*) is the founder of Inve$tWare Corporation, which sells fundamental analysis tools (Take $tock and the Investor's Toolkit). A popular speaker at both local and national events, he is the author of *Take $tock* (Dearborn Trade Publishing) in addition to many articles for *Better Investing* magazine and *Bits*, the NAIC Computer Group's newsletter. His latest endeavor is a non-profit foundation, Financial Literacy for Youth (*http://www.financialliteracy.us*), dedicated to teaching kids everything they need to know about money before leaving high school.

- Jim Thomas is an individual investor and has been a member of NAIC for nine years. He started programming computers in 1969 and uses Excel spreadsheets on a regular basis to help with monitoring and evaluating investments.

- Bob Adams (*http://bobadams.homestead.com/bobsite.html*) is an investor, a teacher, and a frequent speaker at local and national investor conferences. A strong believer in the teachings of the National Association of Investors Corporation (NAIC), he maintains a web site where he posts files and information used in his teaching and tools for making investing decisions. Credit for many of the innovations contained in his investment tools goes to the conference attendees who offered suggestions or encouragement.

- Gordon Gerwig (*http://www.spredgar.com*) is an avid individual investor and a member of the American Association of Individual Investors (AAII). He is a candidate for Level II of the Chartered Financial Analyst (CFA) exam administered by the Association of Investment Management and Research (AIMR). He has worked in the financial services industry as a financial advisor for both Morgan Stanley and American Express. He has passed the Certified Financial Planner (CFP) exam.

Acknowledgments

This book wouldn't have a purpose without the efforts of financial companies and investment aficionados everywhere. Keep up the good work.

My thanks go to Rael Dornfest for making sure that the hacks are helpful and fun, and to Jim Thomas for being even more attentive to detail than I and making sure that the hacks are accurate. In addition, I want to thank my contributors not only for their hacks and tools, but for everything I learned from them. My portfolio will thank them.

Preface

In the past, many people stayed at the same job and lived in the same town their entire lives. Children often went to the same college as their parents and entered the same line of work. Even naming one's male offspring was easy: add Junior to the father's name. Financial decisions were simple as well—companies offered pension plans that managed employees' retirement funds for them. The local bank was *the* place for the family checking account, a savings account, and any required loans and mortgages. The bank manager knew customers and recommended the best products for their needs.

Now, it's more, faster, and more complicated. Every aspect of our lives requires more decisions made in less time. Workers change jobs every few years, either voluntarily or due to layoffs. Families move from one city to another, or from one house to another. Children's names are now a major outlet for parental creativity, and even deciding how to combine each spouse's last name can be a significant negotiation.

And our finances seem to be the most demanding. People have to fend for themselves. Company-funded pension plans are as scarce as hens' teeth. Instead, employees contribute their own money to 401(k) retirement plans and IRA accounts, and have to decide how to invest for retirement. Going to college is practically a requirement for survival, while the costs of college strain the most affluent budgets. The choices for every aspect of personal finance and investing are overwhelming: dozens of account types (the burgeoning tax code ensures an ever-expanding list of options), hundreds of financial institutions located in every state of the union and some that operate entirely online, thousands of savings vehicles, stocks, mutual funds, and other types of investments. Each of these choices requires careful study, because the fine print has become finer even as our eyes become weaker.

The result? We need more education, more information, and more assistance with our financial lives, while companies work furiously to remove human interaction from their customer service processes. Fortunately, the Web has grown to fill the gap. Online investing isn't a new tool. Just about every investor has used the Web to perform at least some aspect of managing his finances. So why does online investing continue to generate a buzz? Because the Web changed everything. Financial information was once expensive, hard to obtain, and available only to those who knew enough to ask their brokers. Now, it's available to everyone, at all hours of the day, and much of it is free.

Competition in the financial world has driven banks, brokerages, insurance companies, and every other type of financial institution to vie for customers, while at the same time containing or reducing costs. In many instances, the solution is online services. Financial companies introduce web-based services with lower fees to keep existing customers happy and to attract new customers from a larger geographical area. In addition, these companies often publish educational articles, training courses, financial calculators, and other valuable financial tools to capture potential customers' attention. In most cases, you can take advantage of these tools regardless of whether you decide to become a customer.

The problem today is the magnitude of available information. With financial institutions and dot-com companies struggling to become the newest must-have financial bookmark, the education, information, or service you want is probably out there. But finding it is another matter. To make matters worse, the Web changes constantly: new sites with incredibly helpful new tools appear; old favorites drop the features you like or hide them somewhere; the URLs you diligently save as bookmarks stop working; and the user-interface changes make you wonder whether you're on the right page. The Web offers an opportunity to simplify our financial lives. We don't want its abundance and constant renewal to ruin our chances.

Why Online Investing Hacks?

The term *hacking* has a bad reputation. Many people picture geeky kids breaking into systems and wreaking havoc with computers as their weapons. However, among people who write code, the term *hack* refers to a "quick-and-dirty" solution to a problem or a clever way to complete a task. It is very much a compliment to be called a *hacker*: you're *creative* and have the technical wherewithal to get things done. But what could this possibly have to do with investing?

Knowing the key players in the online investment arena can provide a nucleus of tried and true financial web sites. They're not going away (although they might change their names as MarketGuide.com a.k.a. Multex Investor a.k.a. Reuters Investor has done). These sites continually improve their offerings with cleaner interfaces, more powerful tools, and a regularly updated library of educational information. Sometimes, these sites "improve" by starting to charge for what once was free, but that doesn't happen as often as you might think.

New investment features or brand-new web sites spring up every day. If you've been looking for a site with free long-term historical data or an online bond trading service that you like, the answer might be in this book or in tomorrow's Google search.

Then, there's financial and investment advice. There is no shortage of people desperate to help you make more money. However, advice from even the most helpful financial advisors is often targeted to the masses. You're left asking "Yes, but exactly how do I do that?" At that point, customized answers from financial advisors tend to come with big price tags.

Online Investing Hacks isn't meant to teach you everything you need to know about investing. It does provide pertinent and pithy introduction to the concepts and calculations you'll need, and points you to online and printed resources that can direct you further to the areas you want to know better. This book teaches you how to coax online tools and Excel spreadsheets into making your investments work specifically for you and your goals—in short, it shows you how to hack.

How to Use This Book

You can read this book from cover to cover if you like, but for the most part, each hack stands on its own. Each chapter addresses a different area of investing or step in the investing process. Chapter 2 digresses into hacking Excel in ways that you can apply throughout the remaining chapters. So feel free to browse, flipping to the hack or chapter that interests you the most.

How This Book Is Organized

Investing can seem like a broad topic to master, and the number of online investing resources exacerbate the situation. This book cuts the topic down to size by dividing the investment field into the subjects that investors need the most and focusing on tools that can really make a difference. This book is divided into nine chapters:

Chapter 1, *Screening Investments*
> The number of investments clamoring for your investment dollars is enough to make you slump in front of your computer drooling. A series of tests that investments must pass to earn your attention can filter the field down to a manageable number for further evaluation.

Chapter 2, *Hacking Excel for Financial Analysis*
> Excel offers numerous features that can make your investing faster and easier—if only you knew about them. This tour of Excel features can jet-fuel all your spreadsheet work.

Chapter 3, *Collecting Financial Data*
> Investment research can consume all the data you're willing to feed it. Find out where the best data is located, how much it costs, and when enough is enough.

Chapter 4, *Analyzing Company Fundamentals*
> Evaluating the fundamental measures of company performance can be the beginning of a beautiful financial relationship—quality companies can grow for decades, pulling their stock prices up with their sales and earnings. Learn the basics of fundamental analysis and dig into its details.

Chapter 5, *Technical Analysis*
> Stock prices follow somewhat predictable patterns, which traders use to buy and sell stocks for financial gain. Fundamental investors can follow these same patterns to choose advantageous times to buy or sell their holdings. If you're new to technical analysis, read the hacks in this chapter to learn about the most popular technical tools and find additional resources for your study.

Chapter 6, *Executing Trades*
> Your investment research won't do you much good until you actually buy or sell investments. Learn to choose appropriate types of trades to make the most of online transactions while avoiding problems.

Chapter 7, *Investing in Mutual Funds*
> Many investors think they don't have to worry about their mutual fund investments because funds have managers to produce the results they advertise. Choosing a good mutual fund for your portfolio can mean years of minor checkups and major investment returns. But that requires some good research up front and the occasional peek at performance.

Chapter 8, *Managing Your Portfolio*
> A portfolio is like a garden: it contains a lot of green and you want it to grow. Learn how to weed and feed your investment portfolio to get the results you want.

Chapter 9, *Financial Planning*

Success means achieving your goals without having to sacrifice too much. Planning helps. Picking the right investment strategies can be as important as picking the right investments. These hacks show you how to pull unconnected goals and investments into a solid financial plan.

Conventions

The following is a list of the typographical conventions used in this book:

Italic

Used to indicate new terms, URLs, filenames, file extensions, directories, commands and options, and program names, and to highlight comments in examples. For example, a path in the filesystem will appear as */Developer/Applications*.

`Constant width`

Used to show code examples, the contents of files, or the output from commands.

`Constant width bold`

Used for emphasis and user input in code.

`Constant width italic`

Used in examples and tables to show text that should be replaced with user-supplied values.

Color

The second color is used to indicate a cross-reference within the text.

You should pay special attention to notes set apart from the text with the following icons:

This is a tip, suggestion, or general note. It contains useful supplementary information about the topic at hand.

This is a warning or note of caution.

The thermometer icons found next to each hack indicate the relative complexity of the hack:

 beginner   moderate   expert

How to Contact Us

We have tested and verified the information in this book to the best of our ability, but you may find that features have changed (or even that we have made mistakes!). As a reader of this book, you can help us to improve future editions by sending us your feedback. Please let us know about any errors, inaccuracies, bugs, misleading or confusing statements, and typos that you find anywhere in this book.

Please also let us know what we can do to make this book more useful to you. We take your comments seriously and will try to incorporate reasonable suggestions into future editions. You can write to us at:

O'Reilly Media, Inc.
1005 Gravenstein Highway North
Sebastopol, CA 95472
(800) 998-9938 (in the U.S. or Canada)
(707) 829-0515 (international/local)
(707) 829-0104 (fax)

To ask technical questions or to comment on the book, send email to:

bookquestions@oreilly.com

The web site for *Online Investing Hacks* lists examples, errata, and plans for future editions. You can find this page at:

http://www.oreilly.com/catalog/0596006772

For more information about this book and others, see the O'Reilly web site:

http://www.oreilly.com

Got a Hack?

To explore Hacks books online or to contribute a hack for future titles, visit:

http://hacks.oreilly.com

Screening Investments

Hacks 1-6

Like fast-food meals, the scope of investing has gone super-sized. As an investor, you're confronted with more and more types of investments, each with numerous options that usually require a magnifying glass to peruse the fine print. Then, having decided on the type of investment, you must choose from overwhelming numbers of individual investments—more than 10,000 publicly held companies and in excess of 14,000 mutual funds, for example. With the explosive growth of online services, even choosing a place to stash your cash has gone from a drive to your local bank to a nationwide search for the best savings rates. Investors are barraged with advertising for financial products; hot tips from friends typically aren't so hot, and financial magazines and newsletters often omit the information you really want to know. So, how can you, as an independent investor, actually choose good investments that support your financial goals, and still have some fun and get some sleep? The answer is *screening*.

Screening means defining criteria for the financial product or investment you want, and filtering out the ones that don't fill the bill. For example, if you've decided that you want to add a small-cap mutual fund to your portfolio, you want a manager with at least five years at the helm, and if you only have $1,000 to invest, a fund screen containing all these conditions pares the field from 14,000 funds down to about 100 funds. If you further filter the list to funds with less than $100 million in assets (which means the fund manager can invest in small companies without influencing their stock prices), the fund world drops to less than 30 funds. You can add, subtract, or refine criteria until you have a manageable number of investments to evaluate in more detail.

Screening is just as prone to garbage in, garbage out (GIGO) as anything else. You must choose your criteria wisely to produce a list of suitable investments. Of course, this means that you must know what you need to reach your financial goals, as well as the characteristics of the investments that meet those needs. Therefore, before you put screening tools to work, you'll want to refer to these other chapters in this book to identify the criteria you should use:

- Chapter 4 explains the evaluation of stocks based on their fundamental financial measures and identifies key financial measures you can use to screen for individual stocks.

- Chapter 5 explains the evaluation of stocks based on technical measures of price and volume changes.

- Chapter 6 explains the evaluation of mutual funds, identifies key characteristics you can use to screen for mutual funds, and points you to the best mutual fund screens online.

- Chapter 8 discusses techniques for improving portfolio performance, managing portfolio risk, and identifies types of investments that support different financial goals.

Many web sites offer screening tools. Some are quite sophisticated, whereas others keep things simple. Yet, all of them reduce the number of options you must evaluate. Choosing a screening tool is a matter of personal preference. When you're a neophyte investor, you have enough to think about without figuring out how to use a complex tool. As you gain experience, you may develop a more discriminating list of criteria that only more advanced screening tools can satisfy. Even the most capable online screening tools are reasonably easy to check out, so give several a try before you select your favorite. Different web sites use different data sources, so screening tools don't always provide the same features or criteria. If you come up with tests that your screening tool of choice won't handle, simply use another tool.

Screen Savings Rates

HACK #1

With everyone after your savings dollars, take advantage of the fierce competition to find the best deals on interest rates using online tools.

Interest rates are near historic lows, so retirees and other savers who depend on income from their savings and investments are in a fix. The same interest-rate cuts that have fueled the home buying and refinancing boom are a disaster for savings-minded folks. Financial firms only raise their rates so far above the market averages to capture business, but even a fraction of a percent can help. In the past, finding better interest rates was a real chore, so many people simply took what their bank offered. Now, you can use online screening tools to find savings options that fit your timeframe at the highest possible interest rate.

In October of 2000, the average interest rate on money market accounts was running a bit over 4 percent. By early 2004, rates dipped so low that the rate on a typical money market account was below 1 percent. Table 1-1 shows how much this drop costs the typical saver.

Table 1-1. Impact of interest rates on money market returns

Initial deposit	How long	Contributions	Interest rate	Ending balance
$10,000	2 years	$100 per month	1.25%	$12,681.02
$10,000	2 years	$100 per month	4%	$13,325.43
$100,000	2 years	None	1.25%	$102,515.62
$100,000	2 years	None	4%	$108,160.00

Because *compounding* is so important to savers, higher interest rates increase the interest paid more dramatically over time than lower interest rates. You can see the difference in interest from a $10,000 nest egg, but the impact is far more dramatic on the $100,000 investment. Many people formulated their retirement budgets based on certain interest-rate expectations, which didn't come through. These same retirees must now make do with much less. It's hard enough to save, but the current anemic growth in account balances is enough to put off even the most dedicated saver. Rates will rise eventually, although no one can say when. For now, the predictions are for fairly stable rates in the absence of earth-shaking events on the international or national stage.

Interest rates are set by the Federal Reserve and are closely tied to the economy. During a recession, such as the economic downturn in 2000–01, the Fed is likely to lower—or ease—rates to stimulate economic activity. When times are good, the Fed might raise rates to rein in excessive growth and keep inflation low. Bond traders also influence interest rates as they trade existing federal, corporate, and mortgage bonds. Although you can't do much about the level of interest rates, one way to increase your savings return is to mine the Internet for the highest savings rates. Many personal finance sites enable you to screen for the best rates for a variety of accounts:

Checking Accounts
These transaction accounts don't earn much interest. If you're lucky, the interest you earn offsets the fees you pay. If you link accounts, a bank might waive your fees.

Savings Accounts
These accounts pay slightly more than checking accounts, but not by much. Many people use these accounts only for small emergency stashes. However, both savings and checking accounts at banks, savings and loans, and credit unions with balances up to $100,000 are insured.

Money Market Accounts

> Money market *deposit* accounts, offered by banks, savings and loans, and credit unions, are insured. Money market *fund* accounts, offered by brokers and mutual fund companies, are not insured, but usually pay slightly higher interest.

Certificates of Deposit (CDs)

> These debt instruments are offered by banks and brokerages and carry differing maturity dates, usually three months to five years. The longer the term, the better the interest rate is. As long as a CD is $100,000 or less and is issued by a bank, savings and loan, or credit union, it's insured. There are different flavors of CDs—for more information, see the article "Understanding CDs FAQ" at *http://www.bankrate.com/brm/ news/sav/20020805a.asp?prodtype=dep.*

The players in the savings game are banks (both online and bricks-and-mortar), savings and loans, credit unions, brokerages, and mutual fund companies. The Internet has made what used to be a primarily local game into a national one, with online-only, national, and regional financial institutions competing for your savings dollar. Before you begin screening to find the best rates, you must make a couple of decisions:

Do you want your savings dollars insured? Federal depository insurance means a lot to people who don't want to lose their savings in case of a bank failure. Although money market funds aren't insured, they have never lost money for their customers.

 When the net asset value of a money market fund drops below $1 per share, it's called *breaking the buck*.

Do you prefer to deal with a local bank, credit union, or savings and loan? Some people like to know that they can enter a bank branch and talk to someone when necessary. With all the mergers-and-acquisitions activity in the banking industry these days, more and more cities have branches of large national banks, as well as regional, state, and local players.

Are you willing to deal with an online-only bank, or do you feel more comfortable with a bricks-and-mortar institution? Internet-only banks frequently offer higher teaser savings rates to attract business, so if you have enough savings and don't mind banking online, this could be a solid option for you.

Most personal finance sites offer savings screening tools that enable you to screen by rates and locale. Bankrate.com (*http://www.bankrate.com/brm/rate/dep_home.asp*) is one of the best, although MSN Money (*http://money.msn.com/banking/home.asp*) and Interest.com (*http://www.interest.com/investing*) also offer helpful screening tools. You'll find a comparison of their good and bad points in Table 1-2.

> Not all cities are included in the screens. I was disappointed to find out that my hometown, Erie, PA.—the fourth largest city in Pennsylvania—wasn't included while other, smaller cities were. So if your hometown isn't included you may miss out on some better local rates. Check out savings rate boxes that run usually once a week in local newspapers to make sure you're not missing out on a great local deal.

Table 1-2. The best sites that screen for savings products

	Bankrate.com	MSN Money	Interest.com
Savings products screened	Money market, CDs, credit union savings	Interest checking, savings accounts, CDs, and money market	Interest checking, savings accounts, CDs, and money market
Best feature	Initially screens by best rate or by state	Prominently displays national averages for each type of account above the screen results	Screen is easy to use with all options centralized on one page
Worst feature	Must dig to find screen for money market accounts and credit unions	Must view MSN Partners' promotional slant (to skip this ad, screen by highest yield or lowest minimum balance)	Must search by city, and if the screen doesn't include your city, you must pick the closest one to you
Additional features	Extensive article archive for explanations of the ABCs of savings; weekly CD rate newsletter; and weekly analysis of interest rates	Four savings calculators (including "How long will it take me to reach my savings goals?") and a Savings & Debt Decision Center with practical tips for increasing your savings	A no-frills site that focuses on the basics

To find the best rates for a one-year CD using the Bankrate.com web site, follow these steps:

1. Select CDs/Savings in the product list and click Go.

2. Select the Select Best Rate option and click Go.

3. Select 1 Yr CD in the account list and click Go. Bankrate.com displays the 100 highest rates for the CD you chose, as illustrated in Figure 1-1.

4. To sort by a field, such as the minimum deposit required, select the option button underneath the column heading.

5. If you want to receive an email alert when rates reach your target, click Rate Alert near the top of the page.

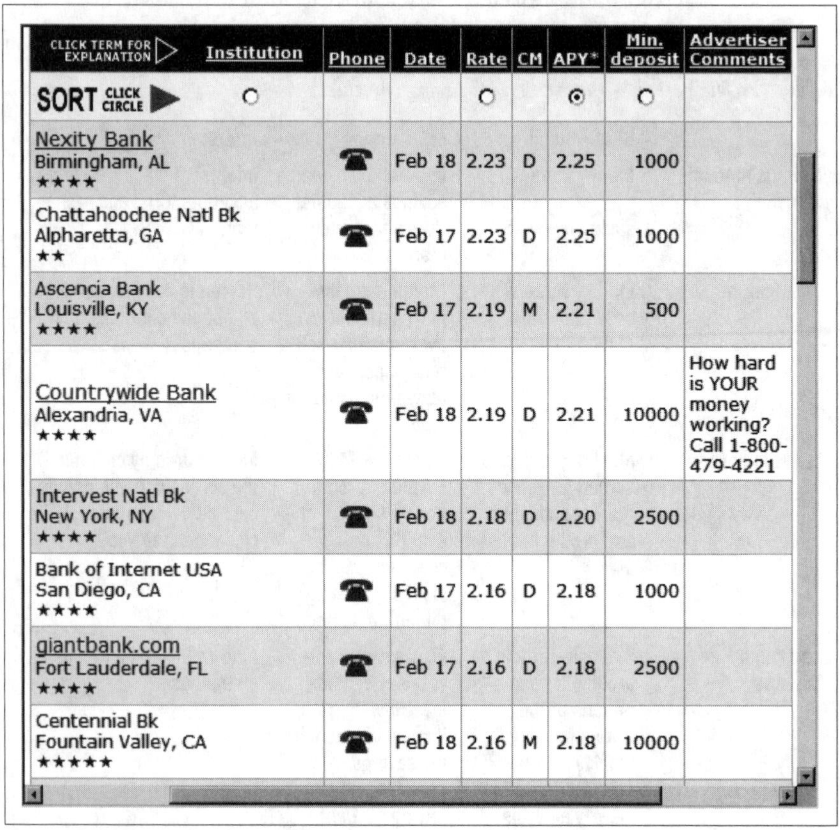

CLICK TERM FOR EXPLANATION ▷	Institution	Phone	Date	Rate	CM	APY*	Min. deposit	Advertiser Comments
SORT CLICK CIRCLE ▶	○			○		⊙	○	
	Nexity Bank Birmingham, AL ★★★★	☎	Feb 18	2.23	D	2.25	1000	
	Chattahoochee Natl Bk Alpharetta, GA ★★	☎	Feb 17	2.23	D	2.25	1000	
	Ascencia Bank Louisville, KY ★★★★	☎	Feb 17	2.19	M	2.21	500	
	Countrywide Bank Alexandria, VA ★★★★	☎	Feb 18	2.19	D	2.21	10000	How hard is YOUR money working? Call 1-800-479-4221
	Intervest Natl Bk New York, NY ★★★★	☎	Feb 18	2.18	D	2.20	2500	
	Bank of Internet USA San Diego, CA ★★★★	☎	Feb 17	2.16	D	2.18	1000	
	giantbank.com Fort Lauderdale, FL ★★★★	☎	Feb 17	2.16	D	2.18	2500	
	Centennial Bk Fountain Valley, CA ★★★★★	☎	Feb 18	2.16	M	2.18	10000	

Figure 1-1. Bankrate.com provides the best interest rates nationwide or within the state you specify

See Also

- Bauer Financial (*http://www.bauerfinancial.com/cdrates.html*) provides a weekly list of top CD rates from the national banks in the best financial condition.

- Amazing Rates (*http://www.amazingrates.com/startsearch.asp*) enables you to search what they say is the largest database for CD rates.

- NAIC's Mutual Fund Education and Resource Center (*http://www. better-investing.org/funds*) enables subscribers to screen for mutual fund money market accounts and compare them based on three-, five-, and ten-year total return and cost [Hack #67].

—Amy Crane

HACK #2 Screen Fixed-Income Investments

Find the perfect individual bond for the income-producing portion of your portfolio with online bond screening tools.

Investing in individual bonds [Hack #80] provides you with another safety net to preserve your principal while providing income. When you build your own bond portfolio you can customize it so the bonds mature exactly when you need the money. For example, if you want to create a bond portfolio that matures when your kids' college bills are due or when you retire—and you don't want the fees and additional risks of bond funds [Hack #64]—do some research and buy individual bonds. Online screening tools for individual bonds can help, but free tools that locate individual bonds are rare. The Yahoo! Finance's bond screener (*http://bonds.yahoo.com/search.html*) and BondsOnline's Fixed-Income Research Center (*http://www.bondsonline.com/asp/research/intro.asp*) enable you to search for bonds that meet your needs without paying for the privilege.

Consider Bond Variables Before Screening

Bonds generally have a predictable payment stream and repay the principal, so people often invest in bonds to collect consistent interest income, or to preserve and increase their capital. Whether you are saving for a new home, your child's college education, or you want to increase your retirement income, investing in bonds can help you achieve your objectives.

To fund financial objectives with a deadline, such as college tuition, select bond maturity dates to match. If you want the tax advantage, investigate bonds that are exempt from both Federal and State taxes. To preserve your principal and avoid bonds that default, use Treasury bonds or AAA-rated corporate bonds. Moody's indicates that only 18 of the 45,000 municipal bonds that they rated have defaulted since 1970 (1 in every 2,500). Although the chances of a bond defaulting are slim, you lose your entire investment when it happens, so evaluating bonds for their default potential is worth your time.

Bond characteristics determine bond investment value and whether a bond meets your financial objectives. Before you build a bond screen, identify the characteristics you want in a bond. Typical factors to consider when screening bonds for investment include:

- The bond's maturity and redemption features
- Credit quality (rating by Moody's or Standard and Poor's)
- Interest rate
- Price/yield ratio
- Tax status

Screening Bonds

Two web sites offer bond screening tools that allow you to screen by bond types, safety level, and maturity dates. BondsOnline.com (*http://www.bondsonline.com*) offers the most options, although Yahoo! Finance (*http://bonds.yahoo.com/search.html*) offers basic features that do most if not all of what you want. Table 1-3 summarizes the feature-sets of each.

Table 1-3. The best sites for bond screening

Features	BondsOnline.com	Yahoo! Finance
Bond products screened	CDs, Corporate, Municipal, Savings, Treasury, Zero Coupon	Corporate, Municipal, Treasury, Zero Coupon
Best feature	Screens by best rate or by state	Provides a simple search to find basic bond issues
Worst features	You have to sign up for 30 days to screen any bonds	You can't enter a minimum interest rate or yield
	The font is small	The bond screener displays only a limited amount of corporate bonds
	You might have to scroll to click the Search button	
Additional features	Provides extensive information in the Educated Investor Center and Fixed Income Research Center and Investor Tools	Provides context-sensitive help that includes basic information on the search fields and related topics

Yahoo! offers plenty of educational material and an easy-to-use, basic bond screening tool accessible from the Yahoo! Finance Bond Center at *http://bonds.yahoo.com*, as illustrated in Figure 1-2. Yahoo! Finance's simple screening tool allows you to find bonds based on type, dollar amount, maturity dates, and safety. Yahoo! Finance's bond calculators answer questions like "How will rate changes affect my bond's current value?" or "What is my return if I sell today?" The Composite Bond Rates link displays a chart comparing current and historical yields for Treasury, Municipal, and Corporate bonds.

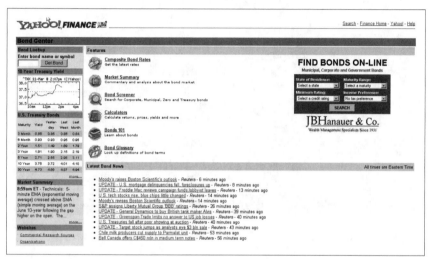

Figure 1-2. Yahoo! Finance's Bond Center provides extensive information on bonds

For more robust bond screening using more criteria, navigate to *http://www. bondsonline.com*. Click the Research Bonds checkmark icon at the top of the home page to navigate to the Fixed Income Research Center. You can sign up for a free month by providing a username, your name, email address, and phone number. BondsOnline.com automatically emails you a password that is good for 30 days. With this username and password, you can research Treasury, Municipal, Corporate, Zero Coupon, CDs, and Savings Bonds.

Let's use the BondsOnline.com web site to find the best $10,000 AAA-rated corporate bond with a minimum yield of 4.25 percent and a maximum maturity date of 2014. Follow these steps to create a bond screen:

1. Select Corporate Bonds from Prices/Quotes/Yields in the Fixed Income Research Center.

2. Enter the user ID and password you received from BondsOnline.com.

3. Type the name for your search in the Title field.

4. Type **2014** in the Maximum Maturity field.

5. From both the Moody's and Standard and Poor's (S&P) ratings drop-down lists under the Minimum heading, select AAA.

6. Type **10** under the Minimum heading in the Qty 000's field.

7. Type **4.25** in the Yield field.

8. Select Yield from the Sort By drop-down list.

9. Scroll down and click Search. BondsOnline.com displays the results from the highest to lowest yields, as shown in Figure 1-3.

	Ratings	Qty	Min	Ticker	Description	Coupon	Maturity	YTC/YTM		Price	
	Aaa/AAA	60		GE	General Elec Cap Corp 36966RHR0 Ge Capital Inter Nt MTN Non-Callable	5.250	06-15-2014	4.514		106.055	
	Aaa/AAA	220		GE	General Elec Cap Corp 36966RMH6 Ge Capital Inter Nt MTN Non-Callable	4.800	02-15-2014	4.450		101.183	
	Aaa/AAA	21	10	IBRD	International Bk For Recon & Dev 459056JL2 Bd Zero Cpn Ser 2 Non-Callable	-0-	02-15-2013	4.429		57.672	
	Aaa/AAA	22		GE	General Elec Cap Corp 36966RAM8 Ge Capital Inter Nt MTN Non-Callable	5.000	12-15-2012	4.395		104.339	
	Aaa/AAA	150		XON	Seariver Maritime Finl Hldgs Inc 81229 JAB4 Old Deb Defd Continuous Call Par Cal 04-11-04	-0-	09-01-2012	4.370		89.375	
	Aaa/AAA	630		AIG	American Intl Group Inc 026874AS6 Global Bd Rule 144a Make-Whole	4.250	05-15-2013	4.327		99.418	
	Aaa/AAA	20		GE	General Elec Cap Corp 36966RKB1 Ge Capital Inter Nt MTN Non-Callable	5.000	10-15-2014	4.307		105.84	
	Aaa/AAA	157	10	GE	General Elec Cap Corp 369622DX2 Otd Sub Nt Non-Callable	6.125	05-15-2012	4.251		126.481	

Figure 1-3. *BondsOnline.com results for a top-quality corporate bond search*

But wait, there's more! You can also specify call dates or non-callable bonds, and select the industry groups (industrial, financial, utility, government) that you want to include or exclude (or select all to include them all). You can choose how you want the information sorted and displayed, including whether you want a printable version or an HTML attachment emailed to you. You can choose to update your search anytime or in set hourly increments, and you can also choose whether to include new offers, price changes, or quantity changes. To check on specific bond issues, select specific CUSIP or Issuer numbers. These features make it easy to search for bonds that meet detailed criteria.

See Also

- The Bond Market Association's web site InvestinginBonds.com (*http://www.investinginbonds.com*) provides extensive bond information. The web site's Tax-Free versus Taxable Yield Comparison Calculator computes your tax consequence based on your income and state of residence, and then displays a chart showing the taxable yields you need to match the return from a tax-free municipal bond. It also displays your Federal and State tax rates.

- The Motley Fool has good basic information on bonds located at *http://www.fool.com/school/basics/basics05.htm*.
- Visit *http://www.publicdebt.treas.gov/sav/savprice.htm* to find out what your U.S. Savings bonds are worth.

—*Martha Sippel*

Screen Loan and Mortgage Rates

Getting a great loan or mortgage rate is one of the easiest ways to free up some serious cash to fund your investments.

Buying a house may be the largest one-time investment you ever make, and the total interest you pay on your house mortgage is most likely into six-figure territory. Of course, you can save some money with astute housing research and tough negotiating, but you can save thousands of dollars quite easily just by finding a mortgage with a great rate, up-front points you can live with, and low fees. HSH Associates, an independent publisher of mortgage and consumer loan information, is truly a one-stop shop for saving thousands on your mortgage and other consumer loans. Their web site (*http://www.hsh.com*) includes articles and pamphlets that explain what you need to know to pick the right loan or mortgage, and calculators that turn your newfound knowledge into hard numbers. The HSH Mortgage Survey provides data, updated weekly in most cases, for mortgages available around the country. If your credit rating isn't as good as it could be [Hack #98], HSH also provides data for mortgages for borrowers with less than perfect credit.

Unraveling Mortgage Costs

A lower interest rate on a loan or mortgage means you pay less interest on the money you borrow. Sure, lower rates on consumer loans save you money, but the amount you typically borrow to buy a house and the longer terms for mortgages make the savings from lower rates quite dramatic. If you refinance your mortgage after interest rates drop significantly, as they have over the last several years, the savings can be extraordinary. Table 1-4 shows examples of how much you can save by lowering your mortgage interest rate on a 30-year fixed-rate mortgage.

Table 1-4. Total savings on mortgage interest from lower interest rates

Refinanced mortgage amount	Interest saved when rate is reduced from 6 to 5 percent	Interest saved when rate is reduced from 9 to 5 percent
$100,000	$22,582.41	$96,408.36
$200,000	$45,164.81	$147,651.90
$400,000	$90,329.62	$295,303.81

Interest rates typically don't plummet in a short period of time, but drop over several years. Therefore, if you refinance from a 9 percent mortgage to one at 5 percent, the savings you achieve will be less than the amounts shown in Table 1-4 and decrease the longer you hold the original mortgage.

Of course, it's not just about interest rates. The real winner in a mortgage race depends on how long you own the house, your future financial situation, and, for some mortgages, the change in overall market rates—all of which are unknown when you have to choose your mortgage. It's frustrating, but you have to make your best guess and hope for the best.

The interest rate for a *fixed-rate mortgage* remains the same for the life of the loan, no matter where market interest rates go. To take advantage of lower rates, you can refinance and obtain a new mortgage with a lower rate, but there are always some expenses associated with a refinance. *Adjustable-rate mortgages* (ARMs) offer rates based on an index, such as the current rate for treasury bills. The interest rates for these mortgages increase and decrease as the corresponding index changes, so you obtain a lower rate automatically without refinancing when interest rates go down. Choosing an adjustable-rate mortgage is more complicated than picking its fixed-rate counterpart, because these mortgages include additional features that can affect how much you pay. For example, how much can the rate go up if rates begin to rise? When rates rise, how frequently does the mortgage rate increase and how much can it jump each time?

When interest rates are above average, adjustable-rate mortgages can save you money over the long term, because you'll pay less as the rates drop. However, be sure that you can afford the higher payments that the mortgage would require if rates jump up. When rates are very low, as they are now, fixed-rate mortgages are more attractive, because they lock in your low rate for the entire life of the loan.

If you can handle a higher monthly payment, a shorter term on a mortgage drastically cuts your total interest, because you don't borrow the money for as long a period. For example, a $100,000 15-year mortgage at 6 percent costs $63,943.96 *less* in interest than a 30-year mortgage at the same rate. The monthly payment increases from $599.55 to $843.86. If you're unsure of your ongoing ability to handle a higher payment, you can also save on mortgage interest by prepaying principal, which reduces the balance of money owed and shortens the life of the loan. Unlike a shorter-term mortgage, in which the monthly payment is required, you can prepay when you have extra cash and pay only the mortgage payment the rest of the time.

Most but not all mortgages allow prepayment of principal. If you plan to prepay, be sure to get a mortgage that you can prepay without additional fees.

The Pain of PMI

As a borrower, you might have to pay *private mortgage insurance* (PMI) if your down payment represents a smaller percentage of the house price than the lender requires. PMI is insurance that protects the lender if the borrower defaults on the mortgage. It can be quite costly. If you're close to the PMI percentage cutoff, look for lenders that accept lower PMI percentages or try to dig up more money for your down payment.

If you must use PMI to get your mortgage, keep tabs on your home equity level. When your equity in the house reaches the required percentage for down payment, you can cancel your policy. Many PMI policies don't include automatic cancellation provisions, which means that you must ask the lender to cancel your policy. Otherwise, the PMI company happily continues to accept the insurance premium that you no longer need to pay.

Mortgages come with all sorts of fees that can really add up, including *discount points* you can pay up-front to obtain a lower mortgage rate. After you find mortgage candidates, it's important to identify the mortgage that costs the least, taking interest and fees into account. In addition, when you pay fees and points up-front to refinance, you save money only if you own the house long enough that your cumulative interest savings exceed the fees and points you paid. For example, paying 2 points to drop a 6 percent rate to 5.5 percent means an up-front payment of $2,000 on a $100,000 mortgage. The lower rate saves you $31.76 a month, so you won't break even for 5 years.

To learn all the ins and outs of mortgages, you can read free articles online at the HSH web site or purchase their pamphlets (*http://www.hsh.com/catalog.html#3primer*). The cost of HSH pamphlets covers printing, shipping, and handling, so they are reasonably priced, particularly when you consider how much they may save you in the long run. The following articles and pamphlets highlight some of the information HSH provides:

The HSH Mortgage Glossary
Navigate to *http://www.hsh.com/library.html* and click the Mortgage Glossary link for this free online article that defines mortgage terms.

How to Shop for Your Mortgage
Navigate to *http://www.hsh.com/hmk_toc.html* to purchase this 56-page pamphlet ($10), which educates homebuyers about mortgages and includes how-to advice for getting the best deal. The pamphlet describes the types of loans available today, explains the options and features you can get, outlines the steps to picking the right loan, identifies factors that can save or cost you money, and provides tips for reducing up-front fees. In addition, it includes worksheets for determining your loan qualifications and monthly payments. You can also obtain the pamphlet when you purchase the Homebuyer's Mortgage Kit ($20 for the pamphlet and one weekly survey of mortgage data).

Ten Best Ways to Improve Your Mortgage Experience
Navigate to *http://www.hsh.com/library.html* and click the link for this free online article, which offers tips to make your mortgage process as smooth as possible.

A Homeowner's Guide to Prepaying Your Mortgage
Click the link on the HSH home page to purchase this pamphlet ($4), which explains the benefit of prepaying your mortgage and when it makes sense not to.

A Homeowner's Guide to Mortgage Refinancing
Click the link on the HSH home page to purchase this pamphlet ($4), which explains the costs and risks of refinancing your mortgage and how to refinance successfully.

A Homeowner's Guide to Private Mortgage Insurance
Click the link on the HSH home page to purchase this pamphlet ($4), which explains types of mortgage insurance, payment options, and cancellation procedures.

Learn How ARMs Work
Click the link on the HSH home page to read this free online article, which explains ARM features and how they work with indexes, why you would use an ARM, and who can benefit from them.

What to Do When Mortgage Rates Are Rising
Navigate to *http://www.hsh.com/library.html* and click the link for this free online article to learn ways to keep your mortgage rate low when interest rates are on the rise.

Screening Mortgages

Each weekly HSH Associates Mortgage Survey provides the current terms for all types of mortgages from more than 2,000 lenders nationwide. You can purchase one Mortgage Survey for $10 and receive a print version, or download a spreadsheet or plain-text file. To screen for mortgages, choose the email delivery option and the spreadsheet format (either Excel 5.0, which corresponds to Office 97, or Lotus 1-2-3).

> The HSH Homebuyer's Mortgage Kit ($20) includes one weekly HSH Mortgage Survey and the 56-page How to Shop for Your Mortgage pamphlet. The first time you use HSH, purchase the Homebuyer's Mortgage Kit. When you buy another house or refinance, purchase only the Mortgage Survey.

Every HSH Mortgage Survey includes the following fields:

Loan type
Amortization term
Lender name
City and state
Phone number
Down payment
Interest rate or initial interest rate for adjustable-rate mortgages
Discount points
Origination points
A.P.R.
Maximum loan amount
Application fee
Rate lock time
Lock-in period
Adjustment term (adjustable-rate mortgage)
Per-adjustment cap (adjustable-rate mortgage)
Life cap (adjustable-rate mortgage)
Index on which the rate is based (adjustable-rate mortgage)

> The A.P.R. (Annual Percentage Rate) is the effective mortgage rate that represents the total cost of the mortgage including fees and points. If you want to compare mortgages with varying fees and points, use A.P.R. to find the lowest cost mortgage.

After you receive your Mortgage Survey spreadsheet, you can use the features in your spreadsheet application, such as AutoFilter in Microsoft Excel, to filter out mortgages that don't meet your needs. For example, if your ready cash is limited, look for mortgages with no points and down payments less than 20 percent. If you simply want to find the 15-year fixed-rate mortgage with the lowest interest rate, filter for **CON** in the Type column (a conventional mortgage, not an ARM), **15** in the TERM column, and look for the lowest value in the A.P.R. column.

> The criteria you use for screening depends on your circumstances. If you don't know what to look for, read the How to Shop for Your Mortgage pamphlet first.

To filter an HSH Mortgage Survey using Excel for the lowest rate on a 15-year mortgage, follow these steps:

1. Open the Mortgage Survey in Excel.

2. Select the column ID for the Type column and choose Data → Filter → AutoFilter.

3. Click the AutoFilter arrow in the Type header cell and choose Custom from the drop-down menu.

4. In the Custom AutoFilter dialog box, keep equals as the test, and type **CON** for the test value.

5. To filter for 15-year mortgages, apply AutoFilter to the TERM column. In the Custom AutoFilter dialog box, select "is less than" in the test drop-down list and type **15** for the test value.

6. To sort the mortgages by interest rate, choose Data → Sort. In the Sort dialog box, select A.P.R. in the Sort By drop-down list, ensure that the Ascending option is selected, and click OK.

HSH Calculators

HSH Associates provides numerous online and downloadable calculators to identify what you can afford, calculate monthly payments and interest for potential mortgages, or determine how long it will take to recoup refinancing fees. Navigate to *http://www.hsh.com/calculators.html* and click the following links to crunch mortgage numbers:

Credit Grade Calculator
    If your credit is less than perfect, use this calculator to estimate your credit score before you start looking for an impaired credit mortgage.

> The HSH site separates mortgages into Perfect Credit and Bruised Credit categories. If your credit is less than perfect, you'll have to pay higher rates than someone with perfect credit, but HSH can still help you find the lowest possible rate.

The Payment & Amortization Schedule Calculator
> This calculator figures out the monthly payment, the amortization schedule using monthly or bi-weekly payments, and the total interest you would pay over the life of a mortgage. You can specify prepayments you plan to make to calculate how much you would save by prepaying your mortgage.

The Refinance Calculator
> Use this online calculator to compare an existing mortgage to a replacement mortgage, and calculate your new monthly payment and the number of months to recover the closing costs for the new mortgage.

The Income Qualification Calculator
> Find out much income you need to qualify for a specific monthly payment.

How Much House Can You Afford?
> Determine the house price you can afford based on your income, current credit payments, down payment, and mortgage terms.

The HSH Home Buyer's Calculator
> This downloadable tool is top-notch. What's more, it's free and runs on Windows 95 through Windows XP. Its 10 functions include calculating the loan amount for which you qualify, comparing the effect of different interest rates side by side, comparing refinance deals, comparing renting versus buying, estimating closing costs, and calculating the savings you can achieve by making biweekly payments or prepaying principal on your loan. It also includes a more robust version of the online Payment & Amortization Schedule Calculator. It includes additional features, such as sample text for closing credit accounts to clean up your credit reports, a Documentation List to help you collect the paperwork you'll need, and a Home Inspection form for evaluating houses. Because this program runs on your computer, data entry is easier and faster and you obtain results more quickly.

Fast and Free Stock Screening Tools

#4 Narrowing the stock field down to a handful of attractive candidates is easy with many of the online stock screening tools.

With over 10,000 publicly held companies available as investments, you need some help whittling the field down to a few companies for further study. Many companies aren't good investments. Some don't grow enough. Some don't grow at all. Others are growing, but cost too much to offer you a sufficient investment return. Others are growing and reasonably priced, but too risky for your peace of mind. Weeding out all these companies typically narrows your candidates significantly. In addition, you can narrow the field further if you're looking for companies in specific industries or with a particular market capitalization to satisfy your portfolio diversification objectives [Hack #74]. It doesn't do much good to identify desirable characteristics, unless there's an easy way to filter the list for stocks that possess those features. Fortunately, that's exactly what stock screening does, and free stock screening tools abound on the Web.

Stock screening tools are black and white. When you define a criterion, a company either meets it or doesn't. For example, if you screen for EPS growth rate of greater than 15 percent, a company growing at 14.9 percent won't show up. Overly rigorous screening criteria might weed out companies that you should consider. One way to correct this failing is to adjust your criteria until the screen returns eight to twelve stocks. Then, you can compare the companies' financial measures [Hack #6] to identify the three or four you want to study in depth.

Don't try to screen all the way to the final four stocks for your in-depth study and under no circumstance screen to only one stock! Keeping your criteria more flexible enables you to catch companies that don't quite fit your criteria but are worth consideration, such as high-quality companies that are currently overpriced. Besides, companies are more than their numbers [Hack #45]. For example, a stock screen can find companies with attractive historical earnings and sales growth, but it can't tell you which companies are positioned to continue their growth into the future.

The Best of the Bunch

Every comprehensive financial web site worth its salt offers stock screening tools, most at no charge. In fact, most of these sites provide several types of screening tools including predefined stock screens, easy-to-use screening forms on a web page, and sophisticated criteria builders that enable you to create highly customized screens [Hack #5]. Table 1-5 summarizes the features available for the best fast and free online screening tools.

Table 1-5. The best tools for screening stocks quickly

Screening feature	Quicken.com Full Screen	Morningstar Stock Screener	Yahoo! Finance Stock Screener
Industry	✓	✓	✓
Market capitalization	✓		✓
Investment style		✓	
Growth rates	One-, three-, and five-years revenue, EPS, and income	One-, three-, and five- years revenue, and five-years EPS	

Table 1-5. The best tools for screening stocks quickly (continued)

Screening feature	Quicken.com Full Screen	Morningstar Stock Screener	Yahoo! Finance Stock Screener
P/E ratio	✓	✓	✓
PEG ratio	✓	✓	✓
Dividend yield	✓	✓	✓
Debt ratio	✓		
Profit margin	✓		✓
ROE and ROA	✓	ROE only	
Percent institutional ownership	✓		
Test choices	Optional minimum and maximum values	Greater than or equal to	Small menu of choices

Quicken.com (http://www.quicken.com/investments/stocks/search/)

Quicken.com screening tools take the prize in the fast and free category. Popular Searches use predefined criteria to find frequently sought-after stocks, such as small-cap growth stocks or high-yield stocks. If you like handholding, the EasyStep Search feature walks you through the construction of a stock screen one step at a time. Each step includes an explanation of how you might use that criterion. Clicking the criterion label opens a window with a glossary definition for the measure. The Full Search screener offers 41 screening variables. On the results page, click Compare Stocks to display company financial measure side by side in a table or graphed in a chart [Hack #34].

Morningstar Stock Screener (http://screen.morningstar.com/StockSelector. html?ssection=StockScreener)

Morningstar offers a simple, customizable screening tool as well as several built-in screens with catchy names and attractive philosophies, such as Profitable but Unloved, Blue-Blood Blue Chips, and Classic Appeal. The customizable tool offers 17 variables with numerous values on drop-down lists. Whether you use built-in screens or create your own, you can choose different views of company data, including Snapshot for variables such as the stock sector and market cap, or Company Performance for growth rates, ROE, and debt ratio. To sort the results by a financial measure, simply click the column heading. When you use a built-in screen, you can select the Set Criteria tab to create a customized screen based on the criteria for the built-in screen.

Yahoo! Finance Stock Screener (http://screener.finance.yahoo.com/ newscreener.html)

The Yahoo! Finance Stock Screener comes in two varieties: the HTML version and the Java version. Click the Launch HTML Screener link to access a rudimentary and easy-to-use screening tool that offers 17 variables. Drop-down lists for each variable make it easy to specify criteria, but the screens you can create with this tool are elementary. On the Stock Screener page, click the Large Cap Value link or Bargain Growth link to open the stock screener with the preset screen in place, or click the More Preset Screens link to access the remaining 19 built-in screens such as Strong Forecasted Growth, which screens for companies estimated to earn at least 30 percent a year for the next five years. The built-in screens run the Java version of the stock screening tool **[Hack #5]** and open a window showing the screen criteria and results. You can modify the criteria to customize the screen and sort the results by clicking column headers.

> The basic online stock screening tool offered by MSN Money is far too simplistic to be of any value. However, MSN Money provides dozens of built-in stock screens (*http:// money.msn.com/investor/finder/predefstocks.aspx*), including some of the only free technical screens available online. In addition, you can download a plug-in to use their powerful customized screening tool **[Hack #5]**.

Using Quicken.com's Full Search Screening Tool

Let's use the Quicken.com Full Search tool to find some large-cap growth companies that also pay attractive dividends. The stock prices for companies like this are less volatile and hold up in down markets. However, with growth companies that pay dividends, they allow you to receive total return from both price appreciation and dividend yield.

1. Navigate to *http://www.quicken.com/investments/stocks/search/full/* to open the web page for the Full Search screening tool.

> You don't have to specify values for every criterion or for both minimum and maximums. If you don't care about a specific criterion or one end of a range, just leave the box blank.

2. To specify that you want large-cap companies, choose *at least* $5B on the Market Cap drop-down list. You can also type a value such as **25,000** in the Market Cap Min box, for example if you want companies with market capitalization of at least $25 billion.

3. To look for companies that offer a dividend yield [Hack #27] of at least 3 percent, type **3** in the Min box for Dividend Yield. To ensure that companies keep enough earnings to fund future growth, limit the dividend yield by typing a value such as **7** in the Max box.

4. To find companies that are growing at an above-average rate for their size, type **10** in the Min box for 5 yr. EPS Growth. The 5 yr. EPS Growth drop-down list includes options, such as "Above industry average" and "At least 15%." To look for companies expected to continue growing in the future, you can specify a minimum growth rate in the Earnings Growth Avg Est Next 5 Yrs criterion.

5. To search for companies that don't carry excessive debt [Hack #29], which can burden companies when times are bad, limit the debt-to-equity ratio to 30 percent by typing **30** in the Max box for LTD/Equity Ratio.

6. To ensure that the companies provide an adequate return on shareholders' investment in the company [Hack #30], type **15** in the Min box for Return on Equity.

7. To display the results, choose the type of data you want to see from the "Select which data to display" drop-down list. For example, choose Growth to display EPS, Sales, and Income growth rates for the past one, three, and five years. Click Show Results to view the companies that meet your criteria, as shown in Figure 1-4.

8. To sort the results, select the field to sort by in the Sort drop-down list. Select Asc or Desc to sort the companies in ascending or descending order, respectively.

9. To modify the search criteria, for example to further reduce the number of results, click the Full Search link in the left margin. Make the changes you want to the screen and click Show Results again.

> If your screens return too many companies, you can change several criteria before resubmitting your screen. However, when the number of stocks is close to what you want, tighten up the criterion that is most important to you, such as the dividend yield if you want current income or EPS growth if you want price appreciation.

H A C K #5 Build Industrial Strength-Stock Screens

When you have very exacting criteria for the stocks you want, define your own criteria with an industrial-strength screening tool.

Preformatted stock screening tools [Hack #4] are great for quick and easy filtering, but you're limited to the financial fields and the criteria tests that they

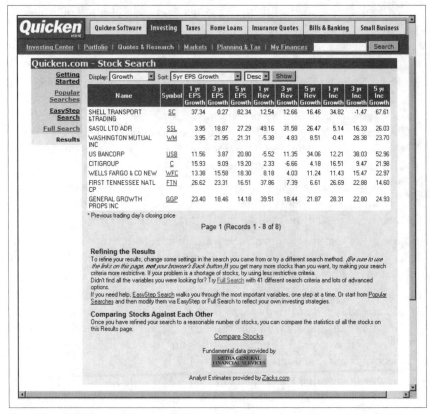

Figure 1-4. Sort the Quicken.com Full Search results, or change the criteria to tighten or loosen the search criteria

provide. When you want to define sophisticated screens, in which you combine tests or screen with numerous financial measures, you need a screening tool that provides access to dozens of financial measures, and includes arithmetic and logical operators for comparing multiple measures. You might expect to pay for a tool with this kind of power and, in some cases, you would be correct. However, the best industrial-strength stock screening tools are free.

The same web sites that bring you basic stock screens often provide more sophisticated screening tools for the overachievers in the audience. Although MSN Money's basic screener is lame, their Deluxe Screener rules. Reuters Investor doesn't offer much in the basic screen department either, but the Reuters Power Screener lives up to its name. Although Morningstar and Hoover's both offer industrial-strength screening tools, they don't offer enough additional features to justify the price tag they carry. In the for-a-fee category, stock screening software applications sometimes offer advantages over online tools that might make them worth the price.

*MSN Money Deluxe Screener (http://money.msn.com/investor/finder/
customstocks.asp)*

With the MSN Money Deluxe Screener, you can build screens from hundreds of financial measures and ratios. Selecting fields, operators, and values from pull-down menus or simply typing values in boxes makes it easy to define your criteria. In a criterion, you can specify a numeric value or compare a company's performance to the industry average **[Hack #23]**. In addition, you can define a criterion so that the screener prompts you for a value. For example, if you screen for different growth rates, use a prompt instead of creating multiple screens for each growth rate you use.

You can save the screens you build to run again. You can also export screen results to an Excel spreadsheet or comma-delimited file, and you can export the symbols for the resulting companies to MSN's Portfolio Manager. You can specify the financial measures that appear in the results table. To evaluate the screened companies with companies that don't appear in the results, type the ticker symbol for the missing company in the Compare With box.

- Best feature: when you type a ticker symbol in the Stock Matcher tool, it configures the screening tool with criteria based on the financial values for the company you specified and finds similar companies.

- Worst feature: for fundamental investors, this screen provides five-year revenue growth but not five-year EPS growth.

The MSN Money Deluxe Screener requires some software on your computer. To load the deluxe tool, click the Deluxe Stock Screener link at the bottom right of the web page and follow the instructions. A graph appears on the download web page to indicate that the installation was successful. When you click the Custom Search link in the navigation bar, the Deluxe Screener appears instead of the basic screening form.

Reuters Investor Power Screener (http://www.reuters.com/finance.jhtml)

For the screening connoisseur, the Reuters Investor Power Screener can't be beat, but be forewarned: it isn't as easy to use as the MSN Deluxe Screener. Reuters provides a tutorial for the tool if you need help. The Power Screener provides dozens of financial measures and ratios, although it lacks several that many fundamental investors would like to see. You can define your own variables by defining formulas with financial measures, and arithmetic or logical operators. For example, you can create a user-defined variable for the PEG ratio **[Hack #28]** by dividing the built-in variable for the P/E ratio by the built-in variable for EPS growth.

To define criteria, choose variables, operators, logical operators, and values, as shown in Figure 1-5. You can create criteria with multiple tests, such as a criterion that looks for companies whose sales and EPS growth rates are both greater than 15 percent. To save yourself a few steps, you can base your screen on one of the built-in screens and modify the criteria you want. When you click Run, the screen adds the criterion to the stock screen and shows you how many companies passed the existing set of criteria. Continue to add criteria until you have the number of results you want to work with. You can view either the screen criteria or the companies that meet those criteria by selecting the Screen Builder and Screening Results tabs, respectively.

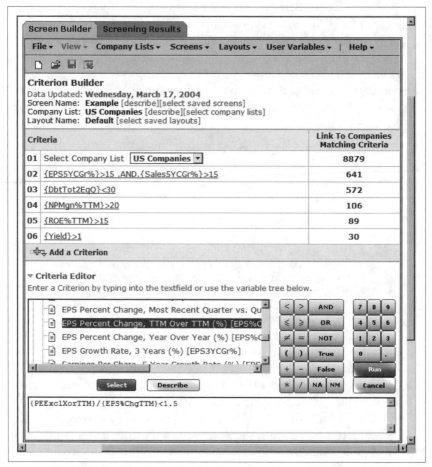

Figure 1-5. Use the Reuters Investor Criterion Builder to define screening criteria

You can save the screens you build to run again; save the results as a list of companies for future evaluation, or export the results to an Excel spreadsheet. In addition to choosing the financial measures that appear in the results table and the order in which they appear, you can choose to display statistics such as the average, maximum, or minimum values for columns. The modifications you make to the columns that appear can be saved as a layout, so different screens can display different fields for the results. You can also add individual companies to the results list.

- Best feature: it provides the most capabilities of the free industrial-strength screening tools.

- Worst feature: it's about as easy to use as the programming features on circa 1980 VCRs.

 To access the Power Screener, navigate to *http://www.reuters.com/finance.jhtml*, click Ideas & Screening in the navigation bar in the left margin, and then click PowerScreener in the navigation bar.

NAIC Stock Prospector (http://www.better-investing.org/about/software/ prospector.html)

Stock Prospector is a software application that runs on your computer. It searches the data available through NAIC Online Premium Services [Hack #20] or other data in NAIC's *.ssg* file format to find companies that meet your criteria. Features not available in online screening tools include weighted screens based on growth, value, quality, and safety; the capability of weighting and ranking individual criteria; advanced customization features; customizable reports; and more than 100 industry average measures for comparing companies to industries.

- Best feature: miniature Stock Selection Guide graphs that highlight key company performance and help you decide whether to evaluate a company further.

- Worst feature: it's not a biggie, but the software costs $59 and NAIC Online Premium Services costs an additional $25 per year.

AAII Stock Investor Professional (http://aaii.com/store/sipro/)

Stock Investor Professional contains both data and a screening tool. You receive a CD each month with the screening software and updated data for more than 2,000 data fields per company. The screening tool includes powerful features similar to those available with Stock Prospector. AAII provides additional data, such as percentile rankings and numbers from company cash flow and income statements.

- Best feature: you can screen for data fields not available with any of the other tools.
- Worst feature: data and software costs $247 per year ($198 for AAII members).

Using the MSN Money Deluxe Screener

Because the Deluxe Screener has more features than basic online tools, let's use an example of a high-quality growth screen to try it out. For example, to find companies that have been growing at a strong pace that also exceed the industry average in key financial measures, we can use the following criteria:

- Annual EPS growth rate greater than 12 percent
- Five-year revenue growth greater than 12 percent
- Net profit margin greater than 15 percent
- Five-year average return on equity (ROE) greater than 15 percent
- Debt to equity ratio less than the industry average
- Inventory turnover greater than industry average
- P/E ratio greater than 5 and less than 30

To work with the Deluxe Screener, follow these steps:

1. After installing the plug-in required on your computer, navigate to *http:// money.msn.com/investor/finder/customstocks.asp* and click Custom Search in the navigation bar to open the Deluxe Screener.

2. To start a new screen, choose File → New on the Deluxe Screener menu bar.

All references to commands in this numbered list refer to the Deluxe Screener menu bar, not your browser menu bar.

3. To define the Annual EPS growth rate criterion, click the first Field Name box and choose Growth Rate → Annual EPS Growth Rate. Click the first Operator box and choose >=. Click the first Value box once to select it, click a second time, and then type **12**.

4. To define the five-year revenue growth criterion, click the next Field Name box and choose Growth Rate → 5-Year Revenue Growth. Click the first Operator box and choose >=. Click the next Value box once to select it, click a second time, and then type **12**.

5. To define the net profit margin criterion, click the next Field Name box and choose Profit Margins → Net Profit Margin. Click the next Operator box and choose >=. Click the next Value box once to select it, click a second time, and then type **15**.

6. For ROE, click the first Field Name box and choose Investment Return → ROE: 5-Year Avg. Click the next Operator box and choose >=. Click the next Value box once to select it, click a second time, and then type **15**.

7. For the debt to equity ratio, click the first Field Name box and choose Financial Condition → Debt to Equity Ratio. Click the next Operator box and choose <=. Click the next Value box and choose Financial Condition → Industry Average Financial Condition.

8. For inventory turnover, click the first Field Name box and choose Mgmt. Efficiency → Inventory Turnover. Click the next Operator box and choose >=. Click the next Value box and choose Mgmt. Efficiency → Industry Average Inventory Turnover.

9. To screen a field for a range of values, you must define two criteria. To define the criteria for the P/E ratio, follow these steps:

    a. Click the first Field Name box and choose Price Ratios → Price Ratio: Current. Click the next Operator box and choose >=. Click the next Value box twice and then type **5**.

    b. Click the first Field Name box and choose Price Ratios → Price Ratio: Current. Click the next Operator box and choose <=. Click the next Value box twice and then type **30**.

10. The Deluxe Screener runs the search each time you complete a criterion and shows the results as illustrated in Figure 1-6. However, to refresh the search, click Run Search.

11. To save the screen, choose File → Save (in the Screener, not your browser). Type the name of the screen and optionally a description of the screen criteria. Click OK.

> To use a saved screen at a later time, choose File → Open, expand the My Saved Searches folder in the Finder Search box, select the screen you want to use, and click Open and Run or Open and Edit.

You can modify a screen in numerous ways and perform other administrative tasks before or after you save the screen, including the following:

- To sort the results, click the heading for the column you want to sort by. The sort order toggles between ascending and descending.

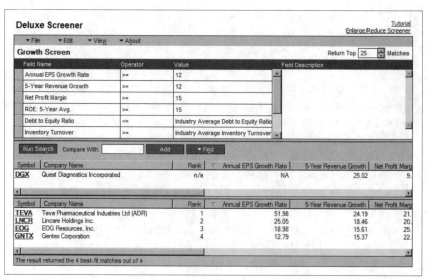

Figure 1-6. *View the screen criteria, screen results, and values for other companies all on the same page with the MSN Money Deluxe Screener*

- To modify the search criteria, make the changes you want to the criteria and click Run Search again.

- To change the columns of data displayed or the order in which they appear, choose View → Column Set Displayed → Customize Column Set. You can add or remove columns. To reorder the columns, select one in the Displayed Columns list and click Move Up or Move Down.

- To export the screen results to a spreadsheet, choose File → Export → Results to Excel. Click OK.

- To add the ticker symbols for the results to a portfolio in MSN Portfolio Manager, choose Edit → Add All Symbols to Portfolio Manager.

- To compare values with a company not in the screen results, type the company ticker symbol in the Compare With box and click Add. The company appears in the Comparison pane as shown in Figure 1-6.

To display the Comparison pane if it is not visible, choose View → Show Comparison Pane.

Weed Out Results
#6

After you obtain the results of a stock screen, use other features and software to further filter your list of candidates.

Because stock screens blindly follow the criteria tests and cut-off values you specify, they can omit companies that almost meet your criteria. By using looser screening criteria, you'll end up with more results, but you can use Excel or online features to compare financial measures and then decide for yourself which companies to keep. Downloading screen results to a spreadsheet gives you the most flexibility, because you can bring all of Excel's features into play to evaluate your contestants. However, if you use Quicken.com's stock screens, the Compare Stocks feature displays the financial measures for all the screen results in a table on the Web.

If you download results data to a spreadsheet, be sure to display all the columns of data you want to evaluate before you create the spreadsheet. Whether you use the MSN Money Deluxe Screener [Hack #5], the Reuters Investor Power Screener, or another stock screen that downloads results, add, remove, or rearrange columns in the results on the web page. For example, using the MSN Money Deluxe Screener, you choose View → Column Set Displayed → Customize Column Set on the screener's menu bar. Then, you can select columns and click Add, Remove, Move Up, or Move Down to modify the columns in your results.

Tinkering with Results in a Spreadsheet

With the data for the companies that pass your criteria stored in a spreadsheet, you can sort and filter based on any of the data in the spreadsheet with much more flexibility than that provided by online tools. Because you're playing directly on your computer, you don't have to worry about dropped Internet connections or slow web site response. If you use the MSN Money Deluxe Screener, choose File → Export → Results To Excel and then click OK. The spreadsheet opens in Excel with a default filename, so you'll have to choose File → Save As in Excel to save it to the folder you want on your computer.

> The exported results file opens in Excel as a comma-delimited file. Before you save the file, be sure to change the file type to an Excel workbook.

Sorting. With the online screening tools, you can typically sort by only one column at a time. Although you can sort using up to three columns in Excel, it's not much help, because sorting by multiple columns implies duplicate entries in the first and second sort column. Because these spreadsheets contain financial measures to at least one significant digit, you won't see much duplication, but the capability is there if you need it. To sort the results in Excel, follow these steps:

1. Select a cell in the spreadsheet. If you know which column you want to sort by, select the label for that column.

2. Choose Data → Sort.

3. In the Sort By box in the Sort dialog box, select the label for the column by which you want to sort in the drop-down list. For example, as a fundamental investor, you might sort by EPS growth. If you selected the label cell before you opened the dialog box, Excel selects that column automatically as the sort field.

4. Because higher growth rates are more desirable, select the Descending option, so the results appear from highest to lowest growth.

5. Click OK.

Filtering. Excel enables you to filter the rows that appear in your spreadsheet. If you run a stock screen that produces several dozen companies, you can turn Excel filters on and off quickly, or filter by more than one column at a time. For example, you can apply a filter to find the companies with great growth rates, then filter for companies with strength (low debt, good inventory turnover ratios, and more). Filtering rows is faster and more flexible than changing criteria in a stock screen, so it's a great way to see which companies keep showing up as you look for desirable characteristics.

Let's filter a results screen to see how it can help evaluate a number of potential investments. Follow these steps to define and refine filters:

1. Select a cell on the spreadsheet—any cell will do.

2. Choose Data → Filter → AutoFilter. Down arrows appear in each column heading in the spreadsheet.

3. To define a filter for a column, click its Down arrow. For example, to filter for companies with reasonable levels of debt, click the Down arrow in the Debt to Equity Ratio column. The AutoFilter drop-down list includes all the values that appear in cells in the column as well as other filter options.

4. To specify a filter test, choose (Custom...) from the drop-down list. The Custom AutoFilter dialog box appears.

5. Choose the comparison operator from the drop-down list in the first box. For example, to show companies with debt to equity ratios less than 30 percent, choose "is less than or equal to." In the box on the right, type **.3** (for 30 percent) for the value for the test.

6. Click OK. Only rows with companies that meet the debt to equity ratio filter criteria appear, as shown in Figure 1-7.

	A	B	C	D	E	F	G	H	I
1	Symbol	Company Name	Rank	Annual EPS Growth Rate	5-Year Revenue Growth	Net Profit Margin	ROE: 5-Year Avg	Debt to Equity Ratio	Industry Average Debt to Equity Ratio
3	GNTX	Gentex Co	15	12.79	15.37	22.8	15.9	0	0.72
4	NOK	Nokia Corp	14	13.13	17.62	12.2	26.1	0	0.41
5	ANF	Abercromb	12	14.97	15.58	12	34.1	0	0.28
6	JNJ	Johnson &	13	15.58	11.5	17.2	25.4	0.12	0.26
7	YDNT	Young Inno	11	18.6	16.86	17.3	14.9	0	0.5
9	AMRI	Albany Mo	6	20.89	72.06	15.9	14.3	0.18	0.23
10	ICUI	ICU Medic	9	21	22.29	20.8	13.8	0	0.5
11	EMBX	Embrex, In	8	22.29	10.5	20	23.6	0.12	0.23
13	MYL	Mylan Lab	5	26.41	14.84	23.9	13.4	0.01	0.25
14	ACS	Affiliated C	4	29.06	21.47	12.6	12.9	0.12	0.38
15	COLM	Columbia S	3	31.52	18.33	12.6	21.2	0.03	0.42
16	TEVA	Teva Pharr	2	51.98	24.19	21.1	17.8	0.19	0.32
17	TARO	Taro Pharr	1	80.34	36.61	19.4	14.6	0	0.32

oih_01 Screen Results.xls

INV50

Figure 1-7. Display only the rows that meet filter criteria you define in Excel

7. To apply another filter, click the Down arrow in another column. For example, these companies have grown quickly over the past several years, so let's filter out the lower revenue growth rates. Click the Down arrow for 5-Year Revenue Growth, and choose (Custom...) on the drop-down list. Choose "is greater than or equal to," and type **20** in the value box. The rows that appear in the spreadsheet show the companies that meet the filters set for both columns.

You can define a filter based on a range of values by defining the first test in the Custom AutoFilter dialog box to look for values greater than one value and the second test to find values less than another value.

8. To turn a column filter off, click the Down arrow in that column, and then choose (All) from the drop-down list.

To turn AutoFilter off completely, choose Data → Filter, and then click AutoFilter to clear the checkmark.

CHAPTER TWO

Hacking Excel for Financial Analysis
Hacks 7-13

Microsoft Excel is a versatile tool in your financial analysis arsenal. It can calculate, compute, and tally any financial measure you want to evaluate. In addition, Excel can digest data—downloading data from the Web to feed your analyses; validating the values you enter to ensure that they are appropriate; sorting, filtering, and highlighting financial values to hide poor results or emphasize the good; and categorizing or aggregating values to show portfolio composition. Excel can produce charts that make it easy to compare financial results or visualize trends. And if you manage to come up with requirements that Excel's built-in features can't satisfy, you can always write some code in Visual Basic for Applications (VBA).

Throughout this book, you'll find hacks that take advantage of Excel features and functions. This chapter explains how to use them. Excel includes functions that calculate commonly used financial measures, such as the internal rate of return of an investment or the monthly payment for a loan. As it turns out, investing uses several statistical functions to evaluate growth rates and trends, and others to assess risk. When you want to find data in your spreadsheets or process that data in some way, you can use additional functions in the Date & Time, Text, Logical, and Lookup & Reference categories. To reduce time, frustration, and errors as you build your own financial spreadsheets, examine the list of functions that Excel provides before concatenating long strings of nested functions to compute a result.

Fancy footwork with Excel functions can be exasperating, even if you can navigate around most programming languages. Using Excel itself, you won't find a development environment to help you construct complicated solutions. Don't even dare to hope for meaningful debugging features that help you correct the errors in your code. Figuring out which functions do what you need to do entails browsing through Excel Help or reading the function descriptions within the Insert Function dialog box—finding what you're after isn't particularly easy either way. If you do identify an inspired assortment of functions to do the job, those nested functions and the rolling waves of parentheses that accompany them can make your head hurt. Even the parentheses matching feature that Excel provides is small solace.

You can tame this beast, although the taming isn't totally painless. This chapter describes the features you'll find most helpful for financial analysis and investing. You'll also learn some tricks to simplify nesting and troubleshooting Excel functions.

Because Microsoft introduces new features in each version of Excel and includes different features in the versions for Windows and the Macintosh OS, you might not find some of the features in this chapter in your software. The hacks in this chapter identify the version of Excel that offers a feature, if it isn't available in Office 2000 and all later versions. Sometimes, features simply relocate to another menu in a newer version. If you don't see the feature you want, press F1 to open the Excel Help window and type the name of the feature, such as **Web Query**, in the Type Keywords box on the Index tab. You can also search Microsoft Office Online (*http://office.microsoft.com/*) or the Microsoft Knowledge Base (*http://support.microsoft.com/*).

HACK #7 Download Data Using Excel Web Queries

When a web site doesn't offer a downloadable file of the data you want, avoid manual data entry by using Excel's Web Query feature.

These days, you can find most of the data you need to analyze investments on the Web, and much of it for little or no cost. However, putting that data into a spreadsheet where you can use it is another matter. Some web sites include links to download spreadsheets, text files of prices, or other financial data to your computer. Other sites offer subscriptions to downloadable data. However, if you can accept with equanimity the inevitable web page changes and the subsequent rework of your Excel spreadsheets that those changes require, you can create your own tools to download data from the Web. Excel *web queries* are easy to use and capture data by taking advantage of tables in a web page's HTML source. You can use web queries to feed your financial formulas, and produce new investment studies or update portfolio management tables in a matter of seconds.

Web queries are available in Excel for Windows 2000 and later, or in Excel v.X for Macintosh.

Creating an Excel Web Query

Web queries are pretty slick. The only information a web query needs is the address (URL) of the web page and the tables on that page that contain the data that you want. When you specify the address of the desired web page in the New Web Query dialog box, the web page appears in the dialog box. In Excel XP and 2003, arrows point to each table on the page. After you select the tables to query, Excel extracts the labels and values from those tables and adds them to cells in a worksheet. With one shortcut command, you can refresh the data from the Web. To illustrate a web query, let's use an easy example—the price quote for a stock or mutual fund from Yahoo! Finance.

Web queries are tailored to the configuration of a specific web page. If the web site changes its URL or reformats data into different tables, you must recreate your web queries.

To add a web query to an existing worksheet in an Excel workbook, open the workbook and select the tab for the worksheet you want. To create a new web query in Excel XP, follow these steps:

1. Choose Data → Import External Data → New Web Query. The New Web Query dialog box opens, displaying the home page you use in Internet Explorer. The toolbar in the New Web Query dialog box includes an Address drop-down list, which is automatically populated with your URL History list from Internet Explorer. The toolbar has other frequently used browser commands, such as Back, Forward, and Refresh.

2. If you've recently accessed the web page you want to query, click the Address arrow to display your URL History list and select the desired web page. Otherwise, you can type the URL for the web page in the Address box and click Go. For example, to use Yahoo! Finance, type *http://finance.yahoo.com* in the Address box.

   You can browse in the New Web Query dialog box, so you don't have to enter the URL for a specific page. For example, after you navigate to the Yahoo! Finance home page, you can type the ticker symbol for the stock you want in the Enter Symbol(s) box and click Go—all on the Yahoo! Finance web page in the dialog box browser. The browser in the dialog box displays the quote page for the stock ticker you typed.

Make sure you click the Go button on the Yahoo! Finance Web page, not the Go button in the New Web Query toolbar.

3. In the New Web Query dialog box, the browser positions a yellow box with a black arrow next to every table on the web page. To select a table, position the mouse pointer over the yellow box to the left of the data you want. Excel outlines the table with a thick line so that you can verify the data that the query will return. If you picked the correct table, click the yellow box. It changes to a green box with a checkmark, as shown in Figure 2-1. Continue to click tables until you've selected all the ones you want.

> If you don't see yellow boxes in the browser, click the Show Icons button on the New Web Query toolbar.

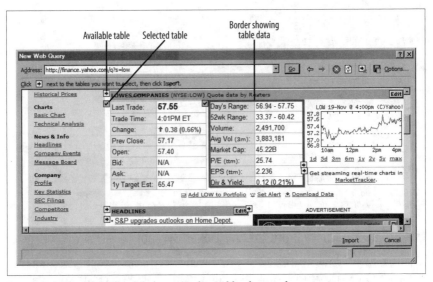

Figure 2-1. Visual feedback helps you select tables for a web query

4. Click Import. The Import Data dialog box appears.

5. To insert the results of the query into the current worksheet, select the Existing Worksheet option. By default, the address for the current selected cell appears in the box. Type another cell address to specify where you want to import the data on the worksheet.

   To create a new worksheet for the query, select the New Worksheet option.

6. Click OK to import the data into the worksheet.

Although the cells don't look like cells with super powers, they are associated with your web query. You can refresh the data from the associated web page by right-clicking any cell in the web query and choosing Refresh Data from the shortcut menu, as illustrated in Figure 2-2.

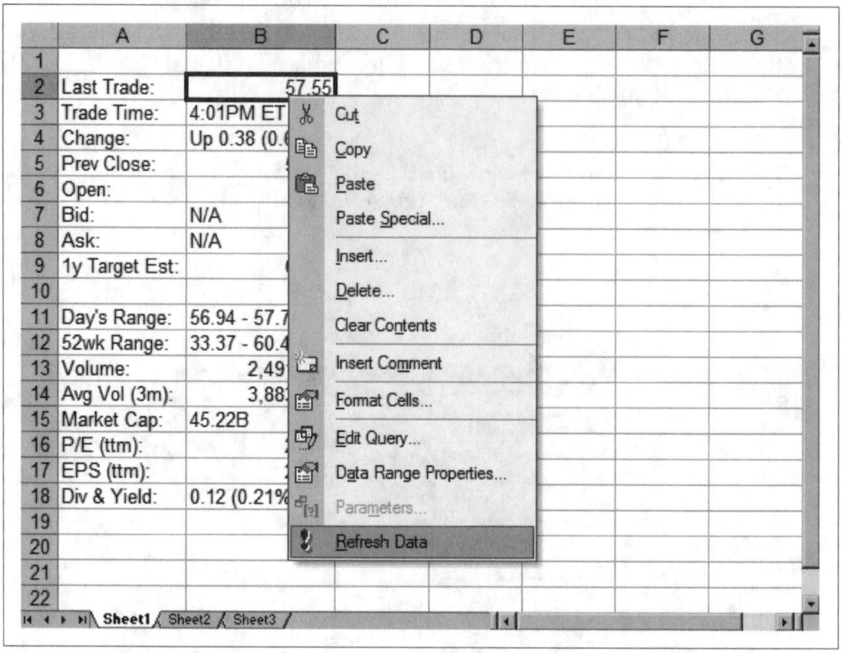

Figure 2-2. Refresh web query data with the Refresh Data command

Making a Web Query Work for Any Ticker Symbol

The web query you just created is pretty handy. You can update the quote for a stock you own or watch by refreshing its data. However, as you manage your investment portfolio, you must constantly evaluate new stocks and mutual funds. Creating a new web query for each investment prospect would become downright tiresome. Wouldn't it be cool if you could make this query download data for a new prospect by simply typing its ticker symbol into a worksheet cell? Well, you can, and it's easy when you follow these steps:

1. To customize a web query, first save it as a file. Right-click any cell for the web query in the worksheet and choose Edit Query from the shortcut menu. In the Edit Web Query dialog box, make sure that the tables you want show green boxes with checkmarks, and then click the Save As icon on the toolbar, shown in Figure 2-3. In the Save As dialog box, navigate to the folder in which you want to store the web query, type a name for the file in the File Name box, such as **Yahoo_Price_Quote**, and click Save.

Figure 2-3. Click the Save As icon to save a web query to a file for editing

2. Next, add the ticker symbol as a parameter to the saved web query file. Navigate to the saved web query file in Windows Explorer (*Yahoo_Price_Quote.iqy* in this example), right-click it, and choose Edit with Notepad from the shortcut menu. The third line in the file specifies the URL for the web page. The URL for a Yahoo! Finance quote page, like most web pages with data for a specific investment, includes the ticker symbol of the stock or mutual fund quoted. In Example 2-1, the ticker symbol low represents Lowe's.

Example 2-1. The URL for a web page with financial data often includes the investment's ticker symbol

```
http://finance.yahoo.com/q?s=low
```

3. To make the web query download the data for the ticker symbol you specify, replace the ticker symbol in the URL with **["symbol", "Enter Symbol"]**. The URL in the web query should look like the line in Example 2-2.

Example 2-2. Modify the URL in a web query to prompt for the ticker symbol

```
http://finance.yahoo.com/q?s=["symbol", "Enter ticker symbol"]
```

4. To save the web query, choose File → Save.

Now, use this new web query in a spreadsheet to retrieve data based on the ticker symbol you specify:

1. Type a ticker symbol in a worksheet cell—for example, use cell A2 on Sheet1.

2. To use the web query to import data, choose Data → Import External Data → Import Data.

3. In the Select Data Source dialog box, navigate to the folder that contains your saved web query file and double-click it.

4. In the Import Data dialog box, select an option to specify whether to use the current worksheet or create a new one. If you select the Existing Worksheet option, type the cell address that denotes the upper-left corner of the cell range where you want the data imported in the Existing Worksheet box.

5. Click Parameters. In the Parameters dialog box, select the Get the value from the following cell option, click the box immediately below the option, and then select the worksheet cell that contains the ticker symbol (in this example, A2).

> The Get the value from the following cell option does not accept named cells. You must either select the cell that contains the parameter value in the worksheet, or type the cell address using column and row references, such as A2.

6. If you want the web query to retrieve new values automatically from the Web when you enter a new ticker symbol, check the Refresh automatically when cell value changes checkbox.

7. Click OK twice to import the data. In this example, when you type a new ticker symbol in cell A2 and press Enter or an Arrow key to navigate away from the ticker symbol cell, the web query refreshes the web query cells with values for the new ticker symbol.

> When a web query uses parameters, you can use the same web query text file to import data for multiple companies into different areas of a worksheet. To reuse a web query text file, select the cell in the upper-left corner of the cell range into which you want to import data, and then repeat Steps 1 through 7.

Hacking the Hack

After your web query successfully grabs the data you want from the Web, you can feed those values into a data summary worksheet or into formulas on other worksheets. You could name the cells within the web query cell range, but that could throw your calculations off if the query returns values in a different order. By using a function such as VLOOKUP instead, you can find the text label that identifies the value you want regardless of the cell [Hack #11]. For example, suppose you want to use values from a price query to compare the current price to the 52-week high and low prices. In Figure 2-4, the Current Price and 52-week range cells use VLOOKUP to find values based on labels, as the formula bar shows.

Take a look at the worksheets in Figure 2-4 to see how this works. To obtain the current price from the Yahoo! price web query, find the row that has the exact label Last Trade: in column A on the Price Query worksheet. Then, retrieve the value in that row from column B. The formula to perform these tasks is in cell B3 on the Price Check worksheet and is also shown in Example 2-3.

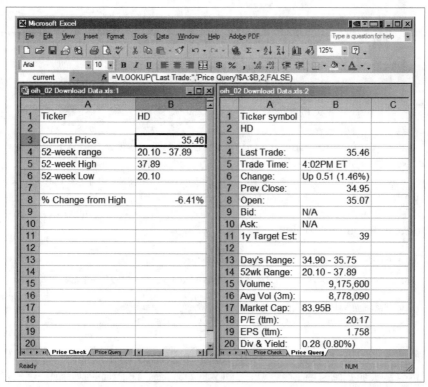

Figure 2-4. The VLOOKUP function finds values based on labels, not cell addresses

Example 2-3. Use VLOOKUP to find a value in one column based on the label in another column

```
Current Price = VLOOKUP("Last Trade:",'Price Query'!$A:$B,2,)
```

In Example 2-3 and other examples of Excel formulas throughout the book, the text to the left of the equals sign identifies the information being calculated or retrieved by the Excel formula. To enter the formula in a cell in a spreadsheet, enter the formula beginning with the equals sign (=).

To find the 52-week price range, use 52wk Range: as the lookup_value, as shown in Example 2-4.

Example 2-4. Another example of VLOOKUP

```
Price Range = VLOOKUP("52wk Range:",'Price Query'!$A:$B,2,)
```

Web queries come with a built-in name that represents the cell range that contains the result of the web query. To view or modify this name, right-click within the web query results and choose Data Range Properties from the shortcut menu. If you specify the web query name as the table_array parameter of the VLOOKUP function, the cell range adjusts automatically to match the web query results.

Finally, you can use some nested text functions to extract the high and low values out of the 52-week price range, as shown in Example 2-5—for instance, to calculate the percentage change from the stock's high price to its current value. You can use functions such as RIGHT, LEFT, LEN, and FIND to parse the prices out of the price range [Hack #9]. The VALUE function converts the text to a numeric value.

Example 2-5. Text functions extract information from text strings

```
High Price = VALUE(RIGHT(price_range,LEN(price_range)-FIND("- ",price_range)-
1))
Low Price = VALUE(LEFT(price_range,FIND("- ",price_range)-1))
Percent Change = (Current Price - High Price)/High Price
```

HACK #8 Make Good and Bad Values Stand Out

In an Excel spreadsheet, you can highlight red flags and green-light results with formatting.

Studying investments generates a lot of numbers. You need the information, but you can also get lost in the forest as you scrutinize every tree. Excel charts [Hack #13] are good for emphasizing trends in sets of numbers, such as sales and earnings growth, or P/E ratio changes, but Excel can also highlight important values in numerical tables. Excel's conditional formatting changes the colors in worksheet cells based on the value in a cell or the results of a formula. By associating good results with green and bad results with red, you can draw attention to desirable values and red flags, making the big picture visible at a glance.

You can implement this highlighting feature in several ways. In some cases, you might compare company results to a guideline, such as a debt to equity ratio less then 33 percent. For other measures, you might compare results to the industry average or to other measures for the same company, hoping for improvement but watching for deterioration, as illustrated in Figure 2-5.

	A	B	C	D	E
1	Lowe's				
2	LOW				
3	Home Improvement				
4					Conditional Formatting
5	EPS Growth Rate	25%		Compares to market cap guidelines	Formula Is =$B$5>IF(MarketCap<500,0.15,IF(MarketCap<5000,0.1,0.07))
6	EPS growth compared to industry			Compares to industry average growth	Formula Is=EPSGrowth>IndustryGrowth
7	Industry Average Growth Rate	9%			
8	Market Cap (mil.)	45,455			
9	Debt to Equity Ratio	48%		Compares debt to equity to guidelines based on industry	Formula for green (light gray) Is =OR(AND($A$3="Utility",DebtEquity<0.85),AND($A$3<>"Utility",D ebtEquity<0.33))
10	P/E Ratio	28.1			
11	PEG Ratio	1.1		Compares to guideline	Cell Value Is, Between, 1, 1.5
12					

Figure 2-5. Use conditional formatting to rate company results against guidelines, benchmarks, or other company results

Figure 2-5 uses gray patterns instead of colors so you can see them in this book. However, you can use color shading as well.

This technique works well for any of the financial measures described throughout this book. Here are some examples of key measures and comparisons you can highlight:

EPS growth rate compared to industry average growth rate

EPS growth rate compared to desirable growth rate based on size

Debt to equity ratio compared to industry average

PEG ratio compared to guideline

If you use green, yellow, and red highlighting to flag good, neutral, and bad financial results, a sea of green quickly indicates that a company or fund is doing the right things. Using highlighting to compare several companies side by side can help identify the most promising candidate.

Applying Conditional Formatting

Conditional formatting can be based on the value in a cell. For example, conditional formatting can apply green highlighting when the value for the P/E to Growth ratio (PEG) is less than one. You can also use a formula to control conditional formatting. For example, you can turn the cell for a company's sales growth green when its value is greater than the value in the cell for the industry average sales growth. For any given cell, you can define up to three conditions, each with its own format. To apply conditional formatting, select the cell you want to format and choose Format → Conditional Formatting.

Here's an example of highlighting a cell based on the value in the PEG ratio cell:

1. To highlight PEG ratios less than one with green, for Condition 1, select Cell Value Is in the first drop-down list, select "less than" for the condition test in the middle drop-down list, and type **1** for the test value in the third box.

2. To specify the formatting when the condition is met, click Format, select the Patterns tab, click a green square, and then click OK.

3. To add another condition, for instance to highlight PEG ratios between 1 and 1.5, click Add. For Condition 2, select Cell Value Is in the first drop-down list, select "between" for the condition test, and type **1** and **1.5** in the third and fourth boxes, which represent the lower and upper limits of the range. To highlight this condition with yellow, follow the instructions in Step 2 but click a yellow square.

4. To add the last condition to flag PEG ratios greater than 1.5, click Add. Select Cell Value Is in the first drop-down list, select "greater than" for the condition test, and type **1.5** for the test value. Set the formatting to red.

5. To apply this conditional formatting, click OK.

What if you want to use a formula to highlight a cell? Suppose you want to compare a company's EPS growth to industry average growth, as demonstrated in Figure 2-5. To do this, select the company EPS growth rate cell (B5 in the example) and choose Format → Conditional Formatting. This time, select Formula Is for Condition 1. In the formula box, type = **B5 > B7** where B7 is the cell for the industry average EPS growth rate. As before, choose the formatting you want to apply when the condition is met. In this example, a second condition could flag EPS growth that is below industry average.

Hacking the Hack

Although you can define only up to three conditions for one cell, you can cram multiple tests into one condition by defining formulas with logical tests. For example, you can define one test that gives the green light to debt to equity ratios less than 85 percent when the company is a utility, and less than 33 percent for any other industry. In the spreadsheet in Figure 2-5, the formula to accomplish this is:

```
=OR(AND($A$3="Utility",DebtEquity<.85),AND($A$3<>"Utility",DebtEquity<.33))
```

Make Nested Functions Work in Excel

Getting nested functions to work is easy when you trick Excel features into mimicking functions and subroutines.

You're either a genius or a fool if you select an Excel spreadsheet cell, type an equals sign, pound out a multilevel nested function start to finish—and expect everything to work just the way you planned. It's easier to write code in even the most cryptic of programming languages. There, you often have a development environment that provides tips for function parameters; you can code and separately test subroutines and objects, or you can construct code stubs to gradually build up a working program. At first glance, Microsoft Excel appears to offer no more than the Insert Function command, which shows you the parameters only for a top-level function. However, you can simulate subroutines and stubs in out-of-the-way worksheet cells, and check the accuracy of your formulas every step of the way.

Suppose you want to create a formula that indicates whether you should change your diversification in growth, value, and bond investments, and you want to perform the following actions:

- Calculate the formula only if the investment value is a valid number (not text or blank).

- Display a warning when the investment is a valid number and is more than 25 percent of your total portfolio.

- Use only half the investment value in the calculation if the investment is in a blend-style mutual fund, because the fund splits its investments between growth and value.

- Extract the second word in the fund-style cell to determine the style.

Using Named Cells

Instead of using cell references, such as B24, which can make formulas quite inscrutable, assign descriptive *names* to individual worksheet cells, ranges of cells, formulas, or constants. Names are like variables and make formulas easier to read, as illustrated in Example 2-6.

Example 2-6. Names make Excel formulas easy to decipher

```
= balance * interest_rate
```

Names are also more portable. You can reference a name in an Excel worksheet throughout the entire workbook, and move formulas to other cells or even to other worksheets within the workbook without changing the name references they contain. If you're going to use a value more than once, it's much easier to calculate that value in a named cell and refer to the name.

Creating Stubs

For logical functions, it's easy to build a *stub* to check your logic before you plug in calculations. For example, the Excel IF function uses three parameters: the test condition, the result when the test is true, and the result when the test is false, shown in Example 2-7.

Example 2-7. The Excel IF function with its three parameters

```
= IF(test_condition, result_if_true, result_if_false)
```

You can type in a test condition along with hardcoded strings or cell references to show the true and false results, as shown in Example 2-8.

Example 2-8. An example of the IF function

```
action = IF(ISNUMBER(investment),test_diversification,"Investment isn't a
number.")
```

 In this example, investment and test_diversification are name references to cells C2 and sheet2!A2, respectively.

Here's how the parameters work:

Test condition
For the first parameter, specify a condition test that checks if the investment is a number: **ISNUMBER(investment)**.

Result if test is true
If the test condition is true (the investment is a number), you want to test for diversification. For this parameter, you simply type the name of the cell that performs the diversification test.

Result if test is false
If the investment cell doesn't contain a number, you want to display a warning. For this parameter, then, type the string: **Investment isn't a number**.

To test the formula, type the string **Check diversification** in the test_diversification cell. When you type a valid number in the investment cell, the action cell should display the string Check diversification. When you type a string or leave the investment cell blank, the action cell should display Investment isn't a number.

This formula is done! Because it works and refers to other cells, it won't change, regardless of future calculations. For example, you can replace the text in the test_diversification cell with the formula that actually tests your portfolio diversification. Example 2-9 shows another example of simplifying logical tests using strings and cell references.

Example 2-9. Named cells and text strings simplify the diversification test

```
= IF(InvestPercent > 0.25,"Check diversification","Leave it alone")
```

Creating Excel Subroutines

To create a true subroutine in Excel—one that you can call with parameters—you must use macros and Visual Basic for Applications (VBA). However, you can mimic the behavior of a subroutine using intermediate calculations in several cells, where each cell uses the results of other cells. By combining this divide-and-conquer approach with named cells, each intermediate calculation is easy to decipher and test.

> You can nest functions only to seven levels in Excel. If you have a particularly deep nesting problem, you can sidestep this limitation by calculating portions of your problem in other cells.

The three components of the test for diversification show how this subroutine technique works. In this example, we'll develop the lower level tasks first:

1. Determine the fund style.

   Processing text strings can breed nesting levels in a jiffy. The Excel function to pull the second word out of the fund style cell is Mid(string, start_num,number_of_chars). By breaking each parameter down into separate calculations, you can avoid nesting functions altogether. For example, you can use three cells to calculate the parameters and a fourth cell to extract the string, as demonstrated in Example 2-10.

Example 2-10. Simplify a formula by calculating parameters in separate cells

```
string_length = LEN(Style)
space_to_end = FIND(" ",Style,1)
final_length = string_length - space_to_end
extract_style = MID(Style,space_to_end+1,final_length)
```

In Example 2-10, Style is the name of the fund style cell. In the MID function, the start_num parameter should specify one position to the right of the space in the string, so that the function extracts the word and not the preceding space. To do this, the example uses space_to_end+1 for the start_num parameter. The number_of_chars parameter is the length of the second word, which is the length of the entire string minus the length of the string up to and including the space, which is calculated in final_length.

2. Calculate the amount of the investment to use.

   Example 2-11 shows another simple logical test. However, it only looks simple because all the functions used to extract the text that describes the fund style from the string are somewhere else.

Example 2-11. A simple logical test that refers to other cells.

```
invest_final = IF(extract_style="Blend",Investment*0.5,Investment)
```

3. Calculate the percentage that the investment represents of your total portfolio.

   The calculation in Example 2-12 also looks simple, because of the work done in other cells. In addition, this cell feeds the condition you test for diversification.

Example 2-12. A simple formula that refers to other cells with additional calculations

```
invest_percent = invest_final/portfolio
```

To edit a formula, select the cell that contains the formula and press F2. Excel highlights the cells referenced by the formula, color coding them to match the cell references in the formula. As you edit formulas, you can press Ctrl-Z to undo a change or Ctrl-Y to redo an edit (Command-Z and Command-Y, respectively on a Macintosh).

Hacking the Hack

If you plan to use the top-level formula more than once—for instance, to evaluate each holding in your portfolio—you won't want to name dozens of cells or create separate formulas for each application of the formula. Not only does it take too much time, it's mind-numbingly tedious as well. However, after you get your calculations working properly, it's easy to go back and paste the intermediate calculations into the top-level formula. You can then copy the complete formula to other cells. To incorporate subroutine calculations into a top-level formula, start at the top and work your way down, replacing cell references with the contents of the cell, as shown here.

The original top-level formula is:

```
=IF(ISNUMBER(Investment),test_diversification,"Investment isn't a number.")
```

You can replace the named cell references with the formulas in those cells or, for references to values, the cell address, as shown in the following steps:

1. Select the test_diversification cell and select the formula without the equals sign in the formula bar.

2. Press Ctrl-C to copy the formula to the Windows Clipboard. Be sure to press Esc to break out of edit mode in the test_diversification cell.

> If you don't press Esc to stop editing, Excel will add every cell you select and every character you type to the formula in that cell.

3. To replace the test_diversification cell reference with the formula, select the action cell whose formula is shown in Example 2-9 and choose Edit → Replace. Click the Replace With box and press Ctrl-V to paste the formula in it. Type **test_diversification** into the Find What box, click Replace, and then click Close.

4. Next, replace the cell reference Investment with its cell address, C2. The resulting formula looks like this:

```
=IF(ISNUMBER(C2),IF(InvestPercent> 0.25,"Check diversification",
    "Leave it alone"),"Investment isn't a number.")
```

At this point, you can repeat Steps 1 through 4 to replace the cell reference InvestPercent with the formula in that cell. Then, repeat Steps 1 through 4 until you either replace all cell references with their corresponding calculations or run out of nesting levels. If you replace every intermediate calculation, the diversification formula looks like the one in Example 2-13.

Example 2-13. The diversification test as a nested function
```
=IF(ISNUMBER(C2),IF(IF(MID(B2,FIND(" ",B2,1)+1,
    LEN(B2)-FIND(" ",B2,1))="Blend",C2*0.5,C2)
    /Portfolio> 0.25,"Check diversification","Leave it alone"),
    "Investment isn't a number.")
```

> In Example 2-13, you can leave the Portfolio cell reference in place, because each holding calculation uses the total portfolio value.

Prevent Growth Calculations from Blowing Up

Excel's regression functions are great for calculating compound growth rates unless there's a zero or negative value in the mix; conditional statements prevent these values from destroying your calculations.

Arguably, the two most important metrics for the long-term, fundamental investor are the strength of a company's earnings growth and the stability of that growth over time. Growth is usually expressed as an annualized, compounded rate, because that makes it easier to compare growth rates between companies. Stability is most often measured using the *coefficient of determination* or *R-Squared* [Hack #35]. You can handily generate both of these metrics using functions in Excel as long as the values you want to evaluate are positive. However, introduce a zero, a negative number, or a null value into the data and the calculation generates an error message of one sort or another, because it is, in fact, mathematically impossible to calculate a compound annual growth rate from either a zero or a negative value. Because companies do have bad years and data does contain zeros and negative numbers, you can use any of several workarounds to prevent errors when you calculate growth.

Calculating Growth Between Start and End Dates

One way to overcome these error messages is to calculate the growth rate by distributing the change in value between a beginning date and an end date. To estimate the average compound annual growth rate (CAGR) [Hack #26], use the formula in Example 2-14.

Example 2-14. Formula for estimating CAGR

```
% CAGR = ((Ending Value / Initial Value) ^ ( 1 / # of years) - 1) * 100
```

Here, Ending Value is the value at the end date, Initial Value is the value at the beginning date, and # of years is the number of years over which the growth takes place. For example, if the value five years ago was $2.00 and it is now $4.50, the estimated compound growth rate is shown in Example 2-15.

Example 2-15. Calculating estimated CAGR

```
Estimated compound growth rate = ((4.50 / 2.0)^(1/5) -1) * 100
                               = 17.6%
```

The drawbacks to this method are:

- It doesn't calculate accurately when the beginning value is either negative or zero
- It doesn't show variations in growth during the intervening periods

Value Line, a popular data provider, addresses the first drawback by using the average of the most recent three years as the ending value and the average of the previous fifth, sixth, and seventh year (or tenth, eleventh, and twelfth) for the initial value in the equation. This solution handles the first drawback as long as the earlier years are not all zero or negative, but doesn't resolve the second.

Protecting Regression Calculations

Regression analysis is a method of calculating the trend in a series of data with which you can accurately calculate compound annual growth rates and growth stability. It forecasts the performance of one variable (y or earnings, in this case) against one or more known values (x or the years). Example 2-16 shows the mathematical formula for calculating a data trend, where n is the number of periods and m is the slope of the straight line that lies closest to all the data points.

Example 2-16. Formula for regression growth calculation

$$m = \frac{n(\sum xy) - (\sum x)(\sum y)}{n(\sum (x^2)) - (\sum x)^2}$$

Excel calculates this formula in the LINEST and LOGEST functions—LINEST calculates simple or linear growth, which represents how much of an increase occurs between the data points corresponding to each year. To calculate the desired *compound* growth rate, you apply the LOGEST function, which uses the logarithmic values of y in Example 2-16. Logarithmic values of y transform the calculation into exponential regression, which calculates the percentage increase for each year—the annualized compound growth you want. However, while LINEST behaves when zeros and negative values are present in the data, LOGEST does not, generating a #NUM! error because of the logarithms.

Null values or blank cells in the data range generate a #VALUE! error.

To see these limitations, set up an Excel spreadsheet with the numbers 1 through 10 representing years in the range A1:A10. For each year, enter a corresponding sample earnings value in column B. To simplify the formula, create a named range, years, for the year cells and another, earnings, for the earnings cells. Then use the formulas in Examples 2-17 and 2-18 to calculate simple and compound growth rates.

Example 2-17. Excel function for calculating linear growth

```
Simple growth = LINEST(earnings,years)
```

Example 2-18. Excel function for calculating compound annual growth (CAGR)

```
CAGR = LOGEST(earnings,years)
```

If all the earnings cells are positive numbers, both functions produce a result. Now, see what happens when you enter a zero or negative value in any of the cells in column B. Immediately, the LOGEST function generates an error. Although the LINEST function doesn't generate an error, its result is meaningless for evaluating growth. We need a way to make the LOGEST function ignore zero, negative, or null numbers.

The solution to taming the LOGEST function lies in replacing the LOGEST function with your own Excel formula for calculating growth. In your implementation of LOGEST, you can feed logarithms of earnings values to the LINEST function to find the compound annual growth rate, and also introduce conditional IF statements to eliminate offending data from the calculation. By using Excel's *array formulas*, which perform multiple calculations and can return either a single result or multiple results, and including functions that test the validity of each mathematical step, you can eliminate negative, zero, or null data from the calculation and bypass the need for an error intercept.

The array formula in Excel is shown in Example 2-19.

Example 2-19. An array formula that uses the LINEST function for calculating CAGR

```
{=EXP(LINEST(IF(Earnings>0,LN(Earnings),0)IF(Earnings>0,Years,0)))-1}
```

> The brackets at the beginning and end of this formula indicate an array formula, but you don't type them into the formula bar. Excel adds them automatically when you create an array formula by typing the basic formula in the Excel formula bar and then pressing Ctrl-Shift-Enter.

When the earnings data is positive, the LOGEST formula in Example 2-18 returns the same value as CAGR in Example 2-19. However, when you insert a zero or negative value in the earnings column (column B in Figure 2-6), the formula in Example 2-19 doesn't generate an error message, as demonstrated in cell D14 in Figure 2-6. Instead, it effectively eliminates anomalous data and goes on without it, calculating the compounded growth rate of the remaining values.

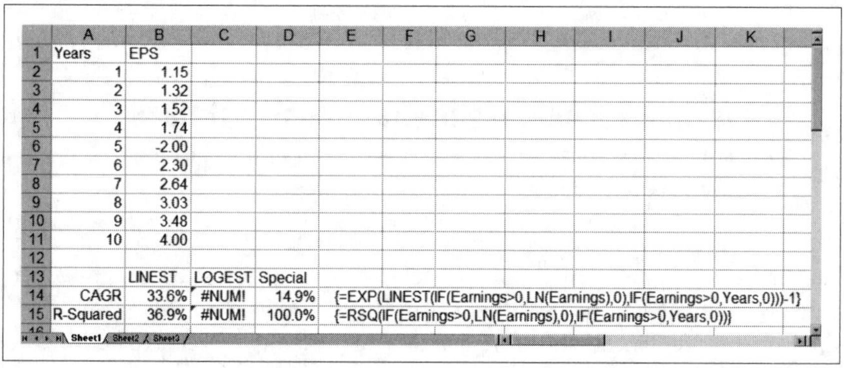

	A	B	C	D	E	F	G	H	I	J	K
1	Years	EPS									
2	1	1.15									
3	2	1.32									
4	3	1.52									
5	4	1.74									
6	5	-2.00									
7	6	2.30									
8	7	2.64									
9	8	3.03									
10	9	3.48									
11	10	4.00									
12											
13		LINEST	LOGEST	Special							
14	CAGR	33.6%	#NUM!	14.9%	{=EXP(LINEST(IF(Earnings>0,LN(Earnings),0),IF(Earnings>0,Years,0)))-1}						
15	R-Squared	36.9%	#NUM!	100.0%	{=RSQ(IF(Earnings>0,LN(Earnings),0),IF(Earnings>0,Years,0))}						

Figure 2-6. *Use a custom formula to calculate growth while handling anomalous data*

Calculating R-Squared Without Mishap

Using R-Squared to measure stability is a tangential issue, but is subject to the same drawbacks for anomalous data as when you use LOGEST in Excel. When all data is positive, you can use the formula for R-Squared as shown in Example 2-20.

Example 2-20. Excel formula for R-Squared

```
R-Squared = INDEX(LOGEST(earnings,years,,TRUE),3)
```

However, this formula for R-Squared generates the same error message as the LOGEST formula for growth when earnings include zero, negative, or null numbers. Once again, you can feed logarithms of earnings values to the RSQ function to obtain an R-Squared value without an error message as shown in Example 2-21.

Example 2-21. Custom formula for R-Squared

```
R-Squared = {RSQ(IF(Earnings>0,LN(Earnings),0),IF(Earnings>0,Years,0))}
```

As with the custom CAGR formula, your calculation of R-Squared now eliminates inappropriate data values and returns a result based only on positive data.

These workarounds can hide a variety of ills. A company whose earnings or revenues are zero or negative in more than one or two years is not a particularly desirable investment, regardless of the growth and stability indicated by these calculations.

—Ellis Traub and Bonnie Biafore, with Excel formulas by Jim Thomas

HACK #11 Flexible Techniques for Referencing Data

A number of Excel functions can help you summarize data or retrieve specific values to use in a formula.

Excel is a natural choice for processing financial data; not only does it calculate numeric results from values in cells, but it also acts as a lightweight database management system that sorts, filters, and validates those same cell values. However, when you store a great deal of data in Excel, cell addresses might be hard to handle. If you move data around, formulas that use cell addresses might stop working properly. Worksheets are more flexible when you retrieve data using Excel functions that search for labels associated with the data you want. In addition, formulas are hard to understand and even harder to troubleshoot, because cell addresses don't convey their purpose. You can make formulas easier to understand by using data retrieval functions to pull values into a summary worksheet with named cells that identify the financial measures that they represent.

Essentially, Excel worksheets are tables with cells at the intersection of each column and row. Typically, when you store data in a range of cells, the first column on the left side of the range includes labels that describe the rows, and the first row of the cell range includes labels that describe the columns. You can use Excel functions to search these labels for text and retrieve data in nearby cells.

Searching Labels in a Column

Suppose you want to use the five-year average tax-adjusted return to evaluate a mutual fund [Hack #65]. If the worksheet arrangement is unlikely to change, the easiest method is to use a cell address, such as C6. However, if the number of rows or their order changes, formulas that reference cell addresses might grab the wrong data. To overcome the problem of changing rows, use the row labels to find the data you want.

In the worksheets in Figure 2-7, the five-year average tax-adjusted return can be in either cell C6 or C7. Although one table includes more rows than the other, column A in both tables contains row labels.

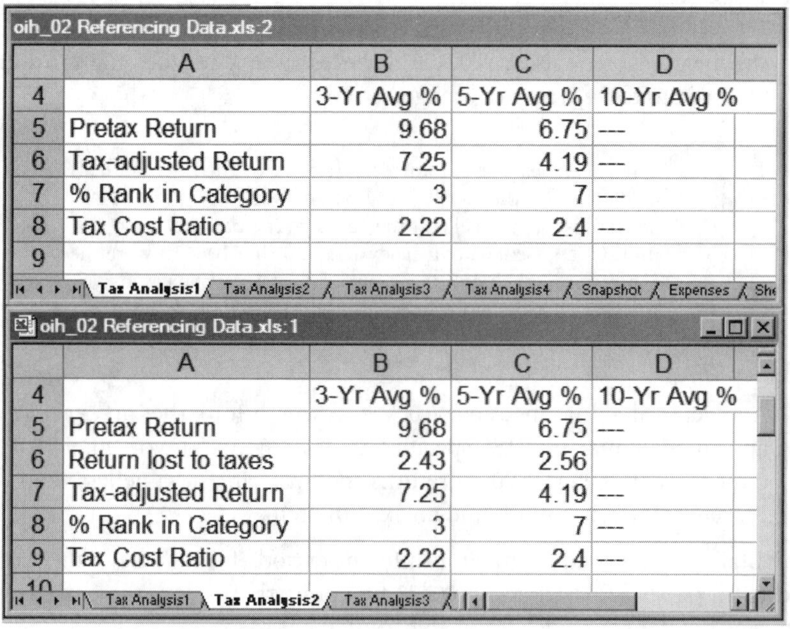

oih_02 Referencing Data.xls:2			
A	B	C	D
4	3-Yr Avg %	5-Yr Avg %	10-Yr Avg %
5 Pretax Return	9.68	6.75	---
6 Tax-adjusted Return	7.25	4.19	---
7 % Rank in Category	3	7	---
8 Tax Cost Ratio	2.22	2.4	---
9			

⤸ ⤸ ⤸⤸\ **Tax Analysis1** ⟋ Tax Analysis2 ⟋ Tax Analysis3 ⟋ Tax Analysis4 ⟋ Snapshot ⟋ Expenses ⟋ She

oih_02 Referencing Data.xls:1			_□×
A	B	C	D
4	3-Yr Avg %	5-Yr Avg %	10-Yr Avg %
5 Pretax Return	9.68	6.75	---
6 Return lost to taxes	2.43	2.56	
7 Tax-adjusted Return	7.25	4.19	---
8 % Rank in Category	3	7	---
9 Tax Cost Ratio	2.22	2.4	---
10			

⤸ ⤸ ⤸⤸\ Tax Analysis1 \ **Tax Analysis2** ⟋ Tax Analysis3 ⟋

Figure 2-7. Excel functions search labels to help you find data

Excel's VLOOKUP function searches column A for Tax-adjusted Return and retrieves the value from the same row, but from the five-year average column—C in this example. The VLOOKUP function finds the lookup value in the leftmost column of a range of cells and returns a value from the same row, but from a column that you specify as well. The VLOOKUP function uses four parameters, as shown in Example 2-22.

Example 2-22. The VLOOKUP function uses labels in one column to locate value in other columns

```
VLOOKUP(lookup_value, table_array, col_index_num, range_lookup)
```

Here's how the VLOOKUP parameters work:

lookup_value
  The value you want to find in the leftmost column of a cell range.

table_array
  The range of cells that contains both the labels and data. You can specify the cell range using cell addresses, such as A4:D8, or named ranges.

col_index_num

> The column you want to retrieve a return value from. For example, if
> col_index_num equals 3, VLOOKUP retrieves the value from the third col-
> umn in the table_array cell range.

> The col_index_num parameter is relative to the range of cells
> as defined by the table_array parameter. In Figure 2-7, A4:
> D9 represents the cells in the table_array parameter, so col-
> umn C represents a col_index_num of 3. If K10:N18 were the
> table_array, then col_index_num of 3 retrieves the value from
> column M of the worksheet.

range_lookup

> A logical value that instructs VLOOKUP to search for either an exact or an
> approximate match. FALSE specifies an exact match; if you enter TRUE or
> omit the parameter, VLOOKUP returns the next largest value less than the
> lookup_value if it doesn't find an exact match.

To obtain tax-adjusted returns for different periods from those in the worksheets in Figure 2-7, type the VLOOKUP functions that follow the equals sign
into a cell in your spreadsheet, as in Example 2-23.

Example 2-23. Using VLOOKUP to find a three-year and five-year return

```
3-Yr Avg Tax-adjusted Return = VLOOKUP("Tax-adjusted
Return",FundData,2,FALSE)
5-Yr Avg Tax-adjusted Return = VLOOKUP("Tax-adjusted
Return",FundData,3,FALSE)
```

> In Example 2-23, FundData represents a named range, which
> represents cells A4:D8 in the first worksheet and cells A4:D9
> in the second worksheet.

In Example 2-23, VLOOKUP looks in column A for the label Tax-adjusted
Return, which it finds in row 6 in the first worksheet and in row 7 in the second. For the five-year return, it retrieves the value from the third column,
column C, in the row in which it found Tax-adjusted Return. In either worksheet, VLOOKUP returns the value 4.19.

Searching Labels in a Row

The HLOOKUP function is like the VLOOKUP function turned on its side. Instead
of searching a column for the lookup_value and grabbing a value from
another column, HLOOKUP searches for the lookup_value in the top row of a
range of cells and returns a value from another row that you specify, but
from the same column that contains the lookup value. Suppose your data

can have different numbers of columns, as illustrated in Figure 2-8. For example, most of the companies you study have ten years of data, but some up-and-coming companies don't go back that far. In Figure 2-8, the five-year average tax-adjusted return appears in the same row, but shows up either in cell C6 or F6.

oih_09 Referencing Data.xls:1

	A	B	C	D	E	F
4		3-Yr Avg %	5-Yr Avg %	10-Yr Avg %		
5	Pretax Return	9.68	6.75	---		
6	Tax-adjusted Return	7.25	4.19	---		
7	% Rank in Category	3	7	---		
8	Tax Cost Ratio	2.22	2.4	---		
9						
10						

‖ ◂ ▸ ▸‖\ **Tax Analysis1** ⟨ Tax Analysis2 ⟨ Tax Analysis3 ⟨ Snapshot ⟨ Expenses ⟨ Sheet2 /

oih_09 Referencing Data.xls:2   _ □ ×

	A	B	C	D	E	F
4		1-Yr Avg %	2-Yr Avg %	3-Yr Avg %	4-Yr Avg %	5-Yr Avg %
5	Pretax Return	11.52	10.75	9.68	7.85	6.75
6	Tax-adjusted Return	8.63	8.05	7.25	5.88	4.19
7	% Rank in Category	3	2	3	5	7
8	Tax Cost Ratio	2.01	2.19	2.22	2.31	2.4
9						
10						

‖ ◂ ▸ ▸‖\ Tax Analysis1 ⟨ Tax Analysis2 ⟩ **Tax Analysis3** ⟨ Snap ‖◂‖

Figure 2-8. HLOOKUP finds data that appears in different columns

Example 2-24 demonstrates how to use HLOOKUP to find the five-year return.

Example 2-24. Use HLOOKUP to find data when the number or order of columns changes

```
5-YrAvg Tax-adjusted Return = HLOOKUP("5-YR*",FundData,3,FALSE)
```

In Example 2-24, the lookup_value includes an asterisk (*): 5-Yr*. The asterisk is a wildcard character that matches any sequence of zero or more characters. If you want to match any single character, use a question mark (?).

The formula in Example 2-24 searches the cells in the first row of the FundData named range, A4 through F8 in this example, for a label that begins with 5-Yr. In the first worksheet in Figure 2-8, this formula finds the label in the third column and retrieves the value in the third row of the cell range. In the second worksheet, the formula finds the label in the sixth column and retrieves the value in the third row. In both worksheets, the formula in Example 2-24 returns 4.19.

Retrieving Values When Rows and Columns Change

What if both rows and columns are dynamic, as demonstrated in Figure 2-9? In this example, the five-year average tax-adjusted return might show up in cell C6, C7, F6, or F7.

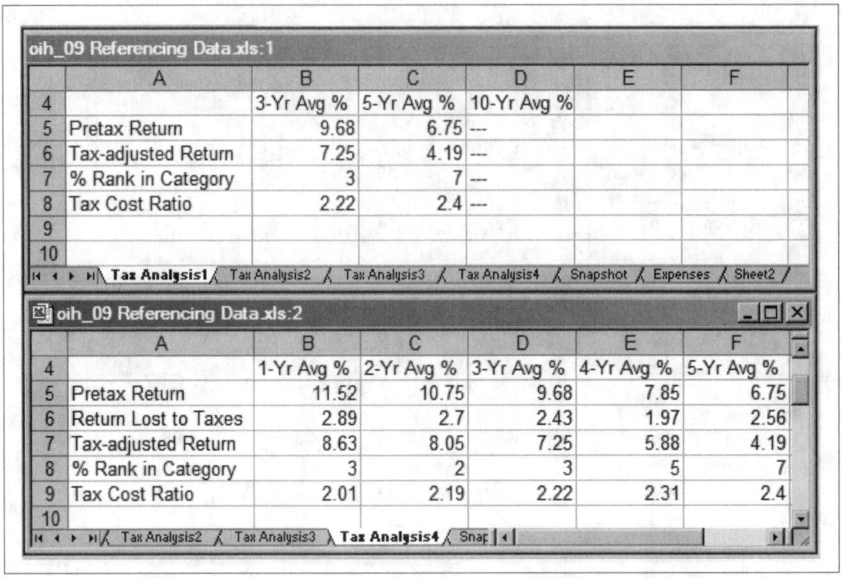

Figure 2-9. *Use MATCH with a LOOKUP function to find values that show up in different rows and columns*

A combination of Excel's MATCH function with VLOOKUP or HLOOKUP can handle changes in the number or order of both rows and columns. The MATCH function returns the relative position of the value you're looking up in an array of cells, as shown in Example 2-25. It's perfect for calculating the col_index_num parameter for the VLOOKUP function or the row_index_num parameter for the HLOOKUP function.

The formula in Example 2-26 searches the first row of the FundData named range for a label that begins with 5-Yr and returns the relative position in the cell range of the column that contains the matching value.

Example 2-25. *The MATCH function finds the relative position of a lookup value*

```
MATCH(lookup_value,lookup_array,match_type)
```

Example 2-26. *Putting the MATCH function to work.*

```
MATCH("5-Yr*",Index(FundData,1,0),0)
```

Using the first worksheet in Figure 2-9, MATCH finds the matching label in column C, the third column in the range, so it returns 3. By using the MATCH function to feed the col_index_num parameter for the VLOOKUP function, as demonstrated in Example 2-27, you can retrieve a value without knowing either the row or column.

Example 2-27. Using MATCH and VLOOKUP to find data without specific columns or rows

```
VLOOKUP("Tax-*",FundData,(MATCH("5-Yr*",Index(FundData,1,0),0)),FALSE)
```

Retrieving Data Near a Label

What if your data is presented in a column with a heading above and the value directly below, as shown in Figure 2-10?

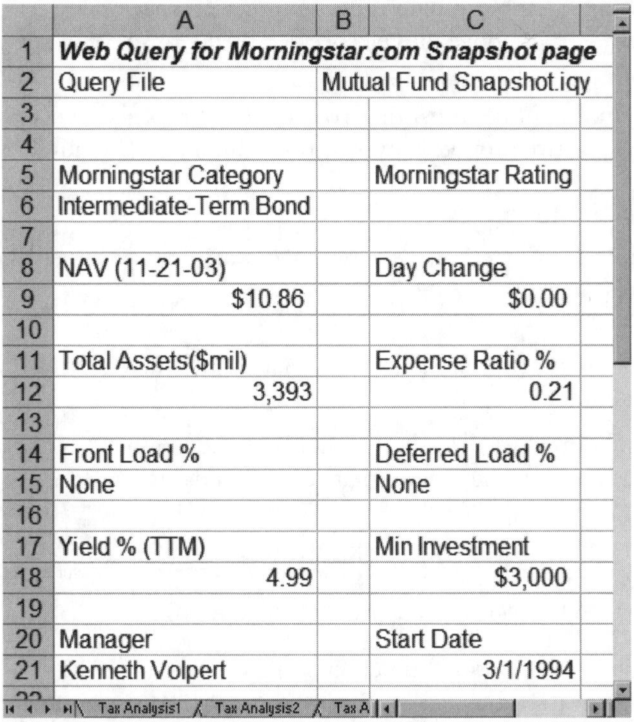

	A	B	C	
1	Web Query for Morningstar.com Snapshot page			
2	Query File		Mutual Fund Snapshot.iqy	
3				
4				
5	Morningstar Category		Morningstar Rating	
6	Intermediate-Term Bond			
7				
8	NAV (11-21-03)		Day Change	
9	$10.86		$0.00	
10				
11	Total Assets($mil)		Expense Ratio %	
12	3,393		0.21	
13				
14	Front Load %		Deferred Load %	
15	None		None	
16				
17	Yield % (TTM)		Min Investment	
18	4.99		$3,000	
19				
20	Manager		Start Date	
21	Kenneth Volpert		3/1/1994	

Tax Analysis1 / Tax Analysis2 / Tax A

Figure 2-10. The OFFSET function finds data in a cell that is a number of rows and columns away from the starting point

In this case, you can use the MATCH function to locate the cell that contains the label you want and then apply the OFFSET function to specify the cell that contains the value you want. The OFFSET function returns a value from a cell that is a specified number of rows and columns from another cell, and uses five parameters, which are listed in Example 2-28.

Example 2-28. The OFFSET function with its parameters

```
OFFSET(reference,rows,cols,height,width)
```

Here's what the OFFSET function parameters do:

reference
> The cell you want to measure the offset from. For example, if your labels and data are in cells A8:C21, as in Figure 2-10, you can measure from the top left of the cell range by setting reference to A8.

rows
> The number of rows that you move up or down to access the data cell. A positive number moves down in the worksheet; a negative number moves to a row above the cell specified by the reference parameter.

cols
> The number of columns that you move left or right to access the data cell. A positive number moves to the right; a negative number moves to the left.

height
> The number of rows that you want to return. height must be a positive number.

width
> The number of columns that you want to return. width must be a positive number.

The formula in Example 2-29 demonstrates the combination of MATCH and OFFSET to retrieve the value that corresponds to Yield % (TTM) in Figure 2-10.

Example 2-29. Use MATCH and OFFSET in concert to retrieve data near a label

```
Yield = OFFSET(A8,MATCH("Yield % (TTM)",A8:A21,0),0,1,1)
```

In Example 2-29, the MATCH function searches cells A8:A21 for a label that exactly matches Yield % (TTM). In this example, MATCH returns the value 10 because the label appears in the tenth row starting at the reference cell, A8. Next, look at the OFFSET function using 10 as the rows parameter. OFFSET(A8,10,0,1,1) starts at cell A8, and moves down 10 rows to row 18 in Figure 2-11. Using 0 as the cols parameter, OFFSET retrieves the value from the same column, A in this case. A height of 1 and a width of 1 returns a single cell, A18 in this case, which is equal to 4.99.

In Example 2-29, the MATCH function returns the value 10 because it finds the label in cell A17. However, using the value 10 to specify the rows in the OFFSET function returns the value from cell A18. How does the same value of 10 in each of these functions take you to two different cells?

The MATCH function starts numbering rows at 1, so cell A8 is in row 1 of the cell range, and cell A17 is in row 10. The OFFSET function starts numbering at 0, so cell A8 is in row 0, cell A9 is in row 1, and row 10 represents cell A18.

HACK #12 Add Conditional Commentary

You can use the Excel IF function to display reminders or recommend appropriate steps to take based on the values for a company's financial results.

When you learn something new, some points don't sink in the first time, particularly when the topic is as broad as investing. For a while, you must refresh your memory each time you look at a financial measure—"Why should I care about this?" or "Is this number good or bad?" Suppose you build a fancy spreadsheet for evaluating investments. Then, after a well-deserved vacation, you come back with no clue as to why you calculated the inverse sales to popularity ratio—at least you think that's what you were supposed to calculate—nor do you remember how to use your masterpiece of a worksheet. Just like comments in code, instructions and notes in your worksheets aren't a symptom of a compulsive disorder. They are a valuable aid to you, the author, helping you to remember what you were trying to do. If you share your work with others and prefer not to provide informal technical support, comments and notes are indispensable.

For financial analysis, you might want different notes depending on the values for financial measures. For example, you can display one note when earnings are growing faster than sales, and another note when earnings are not only growing slower than sales, but also growing slower than desirable for the size of the company. In Excel, you can use the IF function to display messages, and you can nest IF functions up to seven levels to provide different messages for numerous tests. The Excel IF function works much like IF statements in programming languages and uses the parameters shown in Example 2-30.

Example 2-30. The Excel IF function and its three parameters

```
IF(logical_test,value_if_true,value_if_false)
```

Here's how the IF parameters work:

logical_test
      A value or expression, such as F12 > E12, that evaluates to true or false
value_if_true
      The value that the IF function returns if the logical test is true
value_if_false
      The value that the IF function returns if the logical test is false

How do you use this to display instructions? One way is to compare financial measures for the logical_test parameter, and then return a different text string depending on whether the ratio passes the test. For example, suppose you want a reminder to investigate why earnings are growing faster than sales. Companies can grow earnings faster than sales in a couple of ways:

- When companies buy back shares, EPS is the net earnings of the company divided by a smaller number of shares, which makes EPS increase without any corresponding increase in sales. The result is EPS growing faster than sales.

- By cutting costs, companies make more profit on their sales, which also increases EPS without a corresponding increase in sales.

Example 2-31 shows an IF function that displays instructions for this situation. If sales are growing faster than earnings, the IF function displays the message OK for now. However, if earnings are growing faster than sales, the function displays the instruction Check for a stock buy-back program or cost-cutting efforts.

Example 2-31. An IF function provides instructions based on EPS and sales growth

```
= IF(sales_growth > EPS_growth,"OK for now",
      "Check for a stock buy-back program or cost-cutting efforts.")
```

In some situations, you might want to run more tests, and you can nest IF functions to run more than one test. For example, you might want to expand Example 2-31 to check whether the company is growing faster than the industry average in addition to comparing sales and earnings growth. In Example 2-32, the function displays the warning Below average competitor, find another company? when EPS grows slower than the industry average. When EPS growth is at or above the industry average, the function moves on to the next test, represented by the nested IF function in the top-level value_if_false parameter.

Example 2-32. Nest IF functions to make more than one comparison

```
= IF (EPS_growth < ind_avg_growth,
      "Below average competitor, find another company?",
```

Example 2-32. Nest IF functions to make more than one comparison (continued)

```
IF(sales_growth > EPS_growth,"Above average growth",
"Check for a stock buy-back program or cost-cutting efforts."))
```

Using named cells, such as EPS_growth, instead of cell addresses, such as C14, makes these formulas easier to decipher. If you want to build an IF formula that nests more than two levels, simplify your work by using the techniques described in "Make Nested Functions Work in Excel" [Hack #9].

HACK #13 Create Financial Charts in Excel

Excel charts make it easy to visualize financial data so that you can make better financial decisions.

With some financial data, historical trends are as important as the values in any given year. You can spot trends in a series of values effortlessly with a line graph. A pie chart handily illustrates your portfolio asset allocation, whereas a stacked area chart can emphasize the changes in your asset allocation over time. Regardless of the type of financial data you want to visualize, it's easy to build a chart from data in Excel spreadsheets using Excel's Chart Wizard. You don't even have to get the chart right the first time. After the Chart Wizard adds the chart to a worksheet, you can right-click the chart and choose commands from the shortcut menu to configure and format every aspect of the chart until it looks exactly the way you want.

Using the Excel Chart Wizard

The Excel Chart Wizard walks you through each step of chart configuration and provides options to make your financial data as comprehensible as possible. If the chart doesn't turn out the way you want, you can choose from several methods to correct the chart after the fact.

You can simplify the chart creation process before you start the Chart Wizard by setting up your data in a way that Excel understands. The Chart Wizard is easier to use when you structure your data in the Excel worksheet following these rules:

- Enter row titles in the left column of the data area.
- Enter column titles in the top row of the data area.
- Don't type data into the upper-left cell of the data area. Otherwise, Excel might try to plot the data below that cell as a data series.
- If the row or column titles are numbers, such as years, precede the number in the cell with a single quote (') to prevent Excel from plotting the title values in the chart.

After you finish structuring the data, create a chart with the Chart Wizard by following these steps:

1. Select the cells that contain the data you want to graph, the cells that contain the chart title, and the row and column titles, as shown in the portfolio allocation worksheet in Figure 2-11. You don't have to select cells with total values for charts.

	A	B	C	D	E
1	Allocation				
2		Dollar value	Portfolio %	Target %	
3	Cash	9,247.83	7%	10%	
4	Equity Income	12,762.91	10%	15%	
5	International	25,552.10	20%	15%	
6	Large	22,371.24	17%	15%	
7	Medium	39,342.04	31%	30%	
8	Small	18,590.44	15%	15%	
9					
10		127,866.56	100%	100%	
11					

allocation

Figure 2-11. *Select the data cells you want to graph before you start the Chart Wizard*

2. To start the Chart Wizard, choose Insert → Chart or click the Chart Wizard button on the Standard toolbar.

In each step of the wizard, you can click Finish to use default settings for the remaining options.

3. Select the type of chart you want to use by selecting a category, such as Column, in the Chart Type list, and then clicking the image of the chart variation you want under the Chart Sub-type heading. Click Next.

If you want to use a less common chart type or a custom chart type that you've created, select the Custom Types tab, select either the User-defined option or the Built-in option, and then select a type of chart in the Chart Type list. Because there are no subtypes for custom charts, a sample of the selected chart type appears on the right side of the dialog box.

4. In the next screen, the Chart Wizard evaluates the cells that you selected in Step 1 of this procedure and makes assumptions about the cells that comprise the data range and data series. The Data Range field defines the entire range of cells that contain data and titles. A data series is one category of data, such as the portfolio percentages in Figure 2-11. A data

series can also be within a row, such as EPS numbers for several years when the income statement for each year is in its own column. When you select the Data Range tab, you can preview the chart using the data range and data series that Excel assumed.

The wizard selects the Series in Rows option when the numbers within a row are of the same format. When the number format changes within a row but is the same within a column, the wizard selects the Series in Columns option. If the wizard picks the wrong option, simply select the correct one.

5. If the chart doesn't graph the data you want, select the Series tab so that you can specify the correct cell ranges.

In the example in Figure 2-12, the dollar values in column B throw the chart off. It uses the values in column A for category names, plots the dollar values in column B, and the allocation percentages in columns C and D. However, the magnitude of the dollar values overwhelms the much smaller percentages, so the percentage bars aren't visible, and they are the columns to graph in this case. To remove a data series from the chart, select it in the Series list (Allocation Dollar value in this example), and then click Remove. The Chart Wizard automatically graphs the remaining two data series, Allocation Portfolio % and Allocation Target %.

> To add a new data series, click Add. To name the data series, type text or a cell reference in the Name box. To specify the cells that contain the values for the series, type a cell range in the Values box.

6. If the wizard doesn't select the correct cell range for the labels for the X-axis, specify the cell range that contains the categories you want to use as X-axis labels in the Category (X) axis labels box. For example, if your worksheet headings are very long or quite abbreviated, you can type concise yet meaningful headings elsewhere in the worksheet and select those cells for the X-axis labels. With focus in the Category (X) axis labels box, you can also drag the mouse over cells in the worksheet to specify a cell range. Click Next.

7. The next wizard screen contains tabs that contain chart options for configuring the chart. The tabs vary depending on the type of chart. For example, charts with X- and Y-axes include the following tabs:

   a. Titles. Type text for a title for the chart, an overall heading for the X-axis categories, and an overall heading for the values on the Y-axis, if desired. If the chart includes secondary groupings on either axis, you can add labels for those as well.

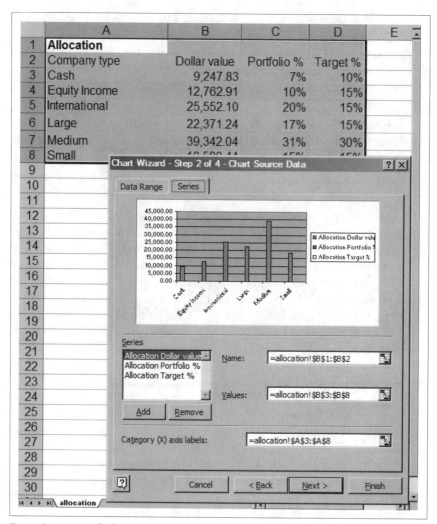

Figure 2-12. Specify the values you want to graph on the Series tab

   b. Axes. Choose options to show category labels for the X-axis and the Y-axis. For the X-axis, you can specify whether to use a time scale or the category labels.

   c. Gridlines. Specify whether the chart includes major or minor gridlines for the X-axis and the Y-axis.

   d. Legend. Specify whether to display a legend and, if so, where to position it relative to the chart.

e. Data Labels. Specify whether to show the series name, the category name, and the value at each data point. If you display more than one field in the label, you can specify the separator between the fields.

f. Data Table. Specify whether to show the table of data in addition to the chart.

8. Click Next to advance to the last step. Choose an option to either create a new worksheet for the chart or add the chart to the current worksheet. Creating a chart in the current worksheet is preferable, because you can easily move, manipulate, and resize the chart. Creating a separate chart worksheet limits the movement of the chart and the editing commands that are available to you. In addition, updating the chart to reflect changes to data requires several steps.

9. Click Finish to create the chart, as illustrated in Figure 2-13.

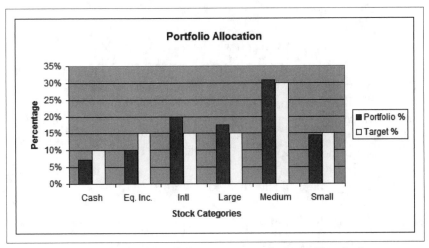

Figure 2-13. Excel charts convey information more easily than tables of values

Getting Charts Right

If the resulting chart is totally off base, you can delete the chart and start over. However, when a chart is mostly correct, it's usually easier to fix the problems in the existing chart. There are two ways to access chart commands:

- If you like the Chart Wizard, you can use it to modify it. Select the chart on the worksheet and then click the Chart Wizard button on the Standard toolbar. The wizard starts with the chart's options selected. Make the changes you want to the options in the wizard and click Finish when you're done.

> Make sure you click the Chart Wizard button on the Stan-
> dard toolbar to modify a selected chart. If you select a chart
> on the worksheet and choose Insert → Chart, the wizard
> ignores the selected chart, sets the default options, and cre-
> ates a new chart.

- Right-click the chart and choose one of the following chart commands from the shortcut menu:

  Chart Type
  > Select a different type of chart or variation.

  Source Data
  > Modify the data range, the data series, or category label cell ranges.

  Chart Options
  > Change settings for the chart options for the selected chart type.

  Location
  > Change the worksheet on which the chart is located.

In addition to these chart commands, you can also format the elements of a chart with commands on the chart's shortcut menu. To format an element, such as the chart title, axis headings, axis labels, chart area, data series, and more, right-click the element in the chart and then choose a format command from the shortcut menu. For example, to format the Y-axis, right-click the Y-axis and choose Format Axis from the shortcut menu. You can format the lines and tick marks, the scale and number format for the values on the axis, and the font and text alignment for the labels.

Matching Charts to Objectives

The Chart Wizard doesn't care which type of chart you use, and the wrong variation of chart might not convey your data very well. Here's a quick guide to chart types and when to use them.

Column Chart Clustered
> Good for showing values or quantities over time and comparing values between different series, such as comparing the portfolio allocation against the target percentages.

Column Chart 100% Stacked
> Compares the percentage each value contributes to a total. Good for showing the change in portfolio allocation over time or highlighting increases or decreases in different types of company expenses.

Creating Logarithmic Graphs

In investing, growth is important. When you plot growing numbers on a linear scale, it's hard to see how fast those numbers are increasing because the curvature of the line changes continuously. However, when you plot increasing numbers on a logarithmic scale, a steady compound growth rate appears as a straight line at an angle, with steeper angles indicating faster growth. This makes the growth rate easy to identify and compare to other growth rates.

To change a chart to a logarithmic scale, follow these steps:

1. Right-click the Y-axis and choose Format Axis from the shortcut menu.

2. Select the Scale tab, check the Logarithmic Scale checkbox, and click OK. Excel sets the units, and minimum and maximum values for you.

3. To specify the starting value for the Y-axis, right-click the Y-axis and choose Format Axis again. This time, select the Category (X) axis checkbox, type the starting number, such as **.1**, in the Crosses At box, and click OK.

4. To add a trend line to the chart, right-click any element that graphs the data points, such as bars in a column chart or lines in a line graph, and choose Add Trend line from the shortcut menu. Click the Exponential box and click OK.

Line Chart

> Good for showing trends over time or categories, such as the historical trends in sales and earnings growth. For discrete data points, you can use either a column or line chart. Line charts are better for plotting continuously over time.

Area Chart

> Similar to a line chart except that the areas under the lines are filled to emphasize the values. Good for showing trends in a presentation.

Pie Chart

> Good for showing percentages that contribute to a whole, such as a snapshot of portfolio allocation. However, pie charts show only one data series. To show two data series, such as current and target allocation, you can use the doughnut chart.

Stock Chart

> Good for showing stock prices and volume, similar to the stock charts you obtain online. Variations include High-Low-Close, Open-High-Low-Close, Volume-High-Low-Close, and Volume-Open-High-Low-Close.

CHAPTER THREE

Collecting Financial Data
Hacks 14-24

People may think that love makes the world go around, but in the financial world, it's data. Regardless of the different types of investments, analysis methods, and stages of building a portfolio, you need data to evaluate the investments you make.

In simpler times, the individual investor was stuck with hardcopy financial reports, a calculator, and tedious pencil pushing. Now, the Web has opened new avenues for data. Data subscriptions for comprehensive financial measures aren't free, but offer valuable interpretations that make the data more useful. Whether you receive a CD or download files from the Web, data subscription services typically update data on a regular schedule, such as weekly or quarterly.

Free online data is prevalent as well, although it's often in very raw form. Some financial information is practically a commodity on the Web. You can't swing a subpoenaed CEO without hitting a web site that offers financial news [Hack #21] and price quotes [Hack #16]. The stock pages on comprehensive financial web sites, such as MSN Money and Reuters Investor, offer company overviews, SEC filings, historical price files, competing companies, industry news, and industry averages for financial measures. These sites deliver mutual fund data as well.

However, hardcore analysis of individual stocks eventually boils down to financial statements, and that's when some people get queasy. So, before we fill our computer hard disks with financial data, let's look at the origins of financial statements, what they do, and how to read them.

Fathoming Financial Statements

Financial data isn't as black and white as you might think. Accounting rules are as open to interpretation as laws are. Although the Securities and

Exchange Commission (SEC) requires companies to report information in specific formats and at specific times, companies have some leeway in how they present their financial data—and they use that leeway to portray their performance in the best possible light. Data providers analyze the data that companies report and tweak it in various ways to better reflect company performance or to make it easier to compare competitors—all in an effort to add value for their clients and earn their subscription fees.

After the 1929 stock market crash and the Great Depression, Congress stepped in to try to prevent similar catastrophes. The Securities Act of 1933 requires companies to publish financial information about the securities they sell to the public. The Securities Exchange Act of 1934 directs the operation of securities markets and brokerage firms, defines the rules for purchasing securities on margin, and outlines access to financial information. These two acts are the basis for the contents, disclosure requirements, and frequency of reporting for today's financial statements.

The SEC oversees compliance with these acts. Companies must provide unaudited financial information for each quarter, called 10-Qs, within 45 days of the end of the quarter. Annual reports, called 10-Ks, must be audited by independent third parties and are due within 90 days of the end of the fiscal year.

Three financial statements work together to paint a picture of company performance: the income statement, the balance sheet, and the statement of cash flows. Quarterly and annual reports include more than financial statements, as you'll learn in Chapter 4, but the financial statements provide key information about company performance.

The Income Statement

The income statement covers a period of time, typically a quarter or an entire year, and shows how a company makes money, how it spends money, and how much is left over at the end. This financial report is the source for information about growth over time—both for revenue as well as expenditures. Look at a company's income statement and find that it begins with revenues at the top, as demonstrated by an EdgarScan income statement in Figure 3-1. Revenues are whittled away by various expenses until you're left with net income at the bottom.

Numbers might seem black and white to you, but accountants can be quite creative (really!) to produce the most favorable picture of a company's net earnings.

	A	AQ	AR	AS	AT
	HOME DEPOT INC				
1					
2					
3	Filing Period	2003/05/04	2003/08/03	2003/11/02	2003/02/02
4	Filing Type	10-Q/1	10-Q/2	10-Q/3	10-K
5					
28	Income				
29	Total Operating Revenue	$15,104,000,000	$33,093,000,000	$49,691,000,000	$58,247,000,000
30					
31	Cost of Goods Sold	$10,275,000,000	$22,659,000,000	$34,064,000,000	$40,139,000,000
32	Interest Expense	$18,000,000	$34,000,000	$48,000,000	$37,000,000
33	Income Before Tax	$1,442,000,000			$5,872,000,000
34	Operating Income	$1,448,000,000	$3,514,000,000	$5,337,000,000	$5,830,000,000
35					
36	Net Income	$907,000,000	$2,206,000,000	$3,353,000,000	$3,664,000,000
37					
38	Common Shares Outstanding	2,267,500,000	2,297,916,667	2,296,575,342	2,333,757,962
39	Earnings Per Share: Basic	0.4	0.96	1.46	1.57
40	Earnings Per Share: Diluted	0.39	0.96	1.46	1.56

Figure 3-1. An income statement shows income and expenses for a period of time

First, a company subtracts items like the *cost of sales* and *selling, general, and administrative (SGA) expenses.* These are the costs for the company to manufacture the products it sells, to operate its stores, to pay salaries to its employees, and to pay the rent each month. These fixed costs are the company's direct operating expenses; the money that's left over is its operating profit.

Next, the company subtracts non-cash items such as depreciation and amortization, which don't appear in the simplified income statement in Figure 3-1. For example, depreciation is an accounting convention that enables companies to obtain a tax break as their equipment and facilities age and become less productive. Further down the income statement, the company deducts any interest paid on its debts as well as taxes. Eventually, you reach the company's net income.

 Net income, before any extraordinary expenses, is usually carried forward to the first line of the cash flow statement, listed as "Cash flows from operating activities."

The Balance Sheet

The balance sheet is a snapshot, typically at the end of a quarter or a year, of what a company owns and owes, illustrated with an EdgarScan spreadsheet in Figure 3-2. The property a company owns is an *asset,* and may include equipment, land, product inventory, accounts receivable, cash, or other items of this nature. The money a company owes to others is a *liability*, and may include debt, accounts payable, unpaid expenses, estimates of future expenses, such as pensions, or money received for services that haven't been provided yet. When you subtract liabilities from assets, you obtain the amount of equity that shareholders hold in the company.

	A	AQ	AR	AS	AT
1	HOME DEPOT INC				
2					
3	Filing Period	2003/05/04	2003/08/03	2003/11/02	2003/02/02
4	Filing Type	10-Q/1	10-Q/2	10-Q/3	10-K
5					
6	Assets				
7	Cash	$4,264,000,000	$5,209,000,000	$4,944,000,000	$2,188,000,000
8	Receivables	$1,386,000,000	$1,379,000,000	$1,432,000,000	$1,072,000,000
9	Inventory	$9,264,000,000	$8,621,000,000	$9,002,000,000	$8,338,000,000
10	Other Current Assets	$319,000,000	$313,000,000	$297,000,000	$254,000,000
11	Current Assets	$15,309,000,000	$15,567,000,000	$15,697,000,000	$11,917,000,000
12	Net Property Plant & Equipment	$17,654,000,000	$18,263,000,000	$18,876,000,000	$17,168,000,000
13					
14	Total Assets	$33,747,000,000	$34,612,000,000	$35,374,000,000	$30,011,000,000
15					
16	Liabilities				
17	Accounts Payable	$6,397,000,000	$5,875,000,000	$6,380,000,000	$4,560,000,000
18	Income Tax Expense	$535,000,000	$1,301,000,000	$1,977,000,000	$2,208,000,000
19	Current Liabilities	$10,925,000,000	$10,389,000,000	$10,972,000,000	$8,035,000,000
20	Common Equity	$118,000,000	$118,000,000	$119,000,000	$118,000,000
21	Deferred Tax	$362,000,000	$362,000,000	$686,000,000	$362,000,000
22	Long Term Debt	$1,321,000,000	$1,327,000,000	$847,000,000	$1,321,000,000
23	Total Debt	$1,321,000,000	$1,327,000,000	$1,355,000,000	$1,321,000,000
24					
25	Total Liabilities	$13,069,000,000	$12,679,000,000	$13,113,000,000	$10,209,000,000
27					
28	Shareholders' Equity	$20,678,000,000	$21,933,000,000	$22,261,000,000	$19,802,000,000

Figure 3-2. The balance sheet shows a snapshot of assets, liabilities, and shareholders' equity

Shareholders' equity is the corporate equivalent of the equity you hold in your house. When you purchase a house, you pay a specific price for it, which is initially comprised of your down payment and the mortgage you obtain. At any given time, your equity in the house is the current value of the house minus the balance on your mortgage. Similarly, shareholders' equity is the monetary value that remains after you subtract company liabilities from company assets. It has nothing to do with how much money shareholders actually pay to buy their shares in the company. This financial report is called a balance sheet, because the amount of total assets balances with the sum of total liabilities and shareholders' equity.

Balance sheets don't always paint a perfect picture of a company's financial situation. Because these reports don't show the fair market value of assets and liabilities, some items can be grossly over- or understated. For example, land might appreciate dramatically in value over time, but that increase in value doesn't appear until the land is sold and its value is measurable. The often-significant value of a brand name doesn't appear on a balance sheet, which might understate a company's worth. Conversely, the potential obligations from lawsuits, such as those in the tobacco industry, might lead to an overly optimistic picture of company worth.

The Statement of Cash Flow

Because of the creativity of accountants and the idiosyncrasies of balance sheets, the income statement and balance sheet reports can hide important information. Therefore, many experts prefer cash flow as the most telling measure of corporate health. The concept of cash flow is easy to understand. For example, your personal balance sheet might look good—a million in assets, such as your home and retirement plan, and $400,000 in liabilities for your mortgage and car loan. That's $600,000 in net worth! However, if you don't have readily accessible cash to pay your mortgage, you have a cash flow problem.

The purpose of the statement of cash flow is to follow the cash coming into and flowing out of a company—which is hard to fake with any amount of legal accounting creativity [Hack #39]. The statement of cash flows starts with the net income from a company's income statement and ends with the cash on the balance sheet. This is illustrated in Figure 3-3 with a statement of cash flow from the Reuters Investor web site.

Cash comes from three different sources. Cash from operating activities is the money that a company generates from its business operations. When a company generates cash from its ongoing operations, the business is sustainable. Cash from investing activities represents transactions, such as buying or selling buildings, or investing company cash in the stock market. On an income statement, selling an asset shows up as a gain or loss, which *temporarily* enhances or reduces the company's earnings. Cash from financing activities represents cash from outside sources, such as debt borrowed from banks or money raised by selling more shares to investors.

A company can finance investments (read: borrow money) [Hack #29], which is great when those investments help a company grow. Young companies often have no other source of cash. However, when mature companies raise cash to pay for ongoing operations by borrowing money, watch out. That could

	Annual	Quarterly

QUARTERLY CASH FLOW STATEMENT (Indirect Method)

In Millions of U.S. Dollars (except for per share items)	N/A Ending	39 Weeks Ending 11/02/03	26 Weeks Ending 08/03/03	13 Weeks Ending 05/04/03	52 Weeks Ending 02/02/03
Net Income/Starting Line	–	3,353.0	2,206.0	907.0	3,664.0
Depreciation/Depletion	–	786.0	505.0	248.0	903.0
Deferred Taxes	–	–	–	–	173.0
Non-Cash Items	–	–	–	–	–
Changes in Working Capital	–	2,002.0	1,910.0	1,616.0	62.0
Cash from Operating Activities	–	**6,141.0**	**4,621.0**	**2,771.0**	**4,802.0**
Capital Expenditures	–	(2,508.0)	(1,671.0)	(756.0)	(2,749.0)
Other Investing Cash Flow Items, Total	–	318.0	276.0	181.0	(185.0)
Cash from Investing Activities	–	**(2,190.0)**	**(1,395.0)**	**(575.0)**	**(2,934.0)**
Financing Cash Flow Items	–	–	–	–	–
Total Cash Dividends Paid	–	(436.0)	(276.0)	(138.0)	(492.0)
Issuance (Retirement) of Stock, Net	–	(778.0)	67.0	12.0	(1,674.0)
Issuance (Retirement) of Debt, Net	–	(7.0)	(6.0)	(4.0)	1.0
Cash from Financing Activities	–	**(1,221.0)**	**(215.0)**	**(130.0)**	**(2,165.0)**
Foreign Exchange Effects	–	26.0	10.0	10.0	8.0
Net Change in Cash	–	**2,756.0**	**3,021.0**	**2,076.0**	(289.0)
Cash Interest Paid	–	–	–	–	50.0
Cash Taxes Paid	–	–	–	–	1,951.0

Figure 3-3. *The statement of cash flow isn't as susceptible to accounting creativity*

be a red flag that the company can't generate enough cash from operations to maintain financial stability.

Company cash isn't quite the same as greenbacks in your wallet. With the advent of discounted cash flows and leveraged buyouts, accounting rules now disconnect revenues and expenses from cash. In effect, a dollar of revenue does not equal a dollar of cash. To sort out this tangle of ephemeral finance, here are some questions you can ask to evaluate a company's health based on its statement of cash flow:

Does the net income on the income statement closely equal the cash from operating activities? If it does, the company's earnings are primarily from operations, and the business can support itself.

Are net income and cash from operations growing at about the same rate?
When cash from operations grows slower than net income growth, cash flow problems may arise.

Are accounts receivable [Hack #31] *increasing faster than sales?*
This indicates that a company can't collect what it is owed, which not only hurts cash flow, but may indicate problems with product quality or obsolescence.

Are inventories [Hack #31] *growing faster than sales or cost of goods sold?*
Buying supplies and producing inventory require cash, so increasing inventory decreases cash flow and may indicate problems with products.

Did cash increase or decrease? Decreasing cash might lead to additional financing activities, which eventually negatively impacts the value of stock shares.

Is cash flow from operations negative over time? Negative cash flow may indicate a rapidly growing company—without financing, the company can grow only as fast as it can generate cash from operations. However, it's a bad sign when a company isn't growing quickly but still can't generate cash.

 Although taking on debt to fuel growth is a reasonable strategy for a company, it's risky for shareholders. If the fast growth stalls and the company falters, the debt holders get paid before shareholders receive any money.

Is the company increasing cash by selling assets? This can be a double whammy. First, selling assets to raise cash might mean a company can't borrow money anymore, which means banks don't like what they see. Second, assets often produce growth, so selling assets means the company will be less able to generate cash in the future.

Download Mutual Fund Data

#14 Regardless of the web site you choose as your source of mutual fund data, you can use Excel web queries to download the data you need to evaluate mutual fund performance.

Mutual fund companies feed their features and statistics to the companies that provide you with mutual fund reports, so you won't find much of a difference between mutual fund numbers from web site to web site. However, each web site tweaks its presentation of data to make it easier to find data. After you decide which web site you prefer, use Excel web queries [Hack #7] to download data into a spreadsheet, refreshing the data whenever you want or grabbing data for another mutual fund.

Picking the Data Behind Door Number One or Door Number Two

Two web sites duke it out as the top dogs of mutual fund data, and they both offer data from Morningstar. Whether you choose Morningstar (*http://www.morningstar.com/Cover/Funds.html*) or Yahoo! Finance (*http://biz.yahoo.com/funds/*) depends on the analysis you want to perform and the comparisons you want to make. In fact, because the data that these sites offer is so similar, you can download data from either site, collecting the data from the site that makes it easier to get what you want.

It's no surprise that Morningstar.com offers Morningstar data. Morningstar offers two versions of its data—one for free and the other by subscription. You can analyze mutual funds quite well with Morningstar's free data, so we'll focus on that data in this hack. When you evaluate mutual funds, the salient features boil down to expenses, turnover, manager tenure, and total returns (tax-adjusted, load-adjusted, or as is). As it turns out, you can't get everything you want for a thorough mutual fund study from one site, so Table 3-1 summarizes what each site offers.

Morningstar's paid subscription includes much more than a few more fund statistics [Hack #20]. You can receive analyst reports, including in-depth studies of stocks and mutual funds, plus analyst picks and pans. The Premium membership also offers some cool portfolio tools such as the Portfolio X-Ray® [Hack #77], which analyzes your portfolio allocation and diversification for the individual stocks, bonds, and investments held by the mutual funds you own.

Table 3-1. *Morningstar.com and Yahoo! Finance each offer presentations of Morningstar mutual fund data*

Mutual fund data	Morningstar.com	Yahoo! Finance
Category	Morningstar category	Morningstar category
Expenses	Expenses are broken down into twelve items with the category average for the total expense ratio	Expenses are broken down into seven items with the category average for six of them
Manager tenure	Manager start date	Manager start date
Turnover	Annual holding turnover percentage	Annual holding turnover percentage
Total return summary	Trailing returns for one-year, three-year, five-year, and ten-year periods, and short-term average returns	Trailing returns for one-year, three-year, and five-year periods, and some short-term average returns
Annual total returns	Seven years of annual total returns with comparisons to average returns for the category and a comparable index	Ten years of annual total returns with comparisons to average returns for the category and a comparable index
Tax-adjusted returns	Tax-adjusted returns for three-year, five-year, and ten-year periods; the tax cost ratio; and potential capital gains exposure percentage	No tax-adjusted returns

Building a Mutual Fund Data Workbook

For analysis, mutual funds require less data than stocks call for, but there's enough data that you don't want to copy it all manually. You can use Excel web queries to capture the mutual fund data you want and then evaluate that data in a mutual fund analysis spreadsheet [Hack #71].

You can heave all your mutual fund data onto the same Excel worksheet if you want to store all the data for one mutual fund in the same place. Because Morningstar.com and Yahoo! Finance distribute mutual fund data across several web pages, your worksheet holds several web queries. You can also create each web query on a separate worksheet, as demonstrated in Figure 3-4.

Follow the instructions in "Download Data Using Excel Web Queries" [Hack #7] to define web queries for mutual fund data. To navigate to the starting point for the web queries, follow these instructions:

The Morningstar Mutual Funds Page
  Navigate to *http://www.morningstar.com/Cover/Funds.html*. Type the fund ticker symbol in the box immediately below the top toolbar and click Quotes/Reports.

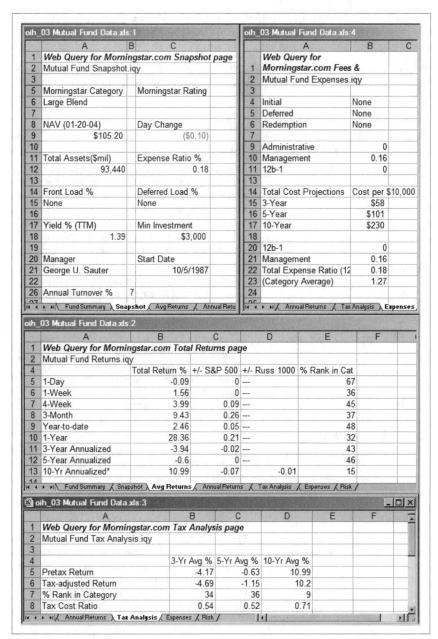

Figure 3-4. Segregating web queries on different worksheets helps organize data

Yahoo! Finance Mutual Funds Center

Navigate to *http://biz.yahoo.com/funds/*, type the fund ticker symbol in the Enter Fund Symbol box, and then click Get Quote.

The sample Excel mutual fund workbook includes seven worksheets, each containing a different type of mutual fund data. Cells in the Fund Summary worksheet contain the ticker symbols that feed into the parameters for the web queries on the other worksheets. Table 3-2 includes instructions for specifying the tables to query to collect the mutual fund data you want.

Table 3-2. Define web queries for each type of mutual fund data

Mutual fund data	Web site to use	Instructions
Snapshot	Morningstar.com	In the New Web Query dialog box, select the Snapshot tab. Click the yellow table indicator to the left of the Morningstar Category label to obtain the category, minimum investment, and fund manager's start date. Scroll down to the Portfolio Analysis section and click the yellow table indicator to the left of the Annual Turnover % label to obtain the annual turnover.
Average returns	Morningstar.com	Select the Total Returns tab. In the Trailing Total Returns section, click the yellow table indicator that points to the Total Return % label to obtain total returns over a number of periods for the fund and indexes with similar investment strategies.
Annual returns	Yahoo! Finance	On the Quotes & Info page for a mutual fund, click the Performance link under the Fund heading in the navigation bar. In the Annual Total Return (%) History section on the Performance page, click the yellow table indicator that points to the Year label to obtain the annual returns for the last ten years for the fund and the fund category.
Tax analysis	Morningstar.com	Select the Tax Analysis tab. In the Tax Analysis section, click the yellow table indicator that points to the 3-Yr Avg % label to capture Morningstar's tax analysis measures.
Expenses	Morningstar.com	Select the Fees & Expenses tab. In the Fees and Expenses section, click the yellow table indicators to the left of the Initial, Total Cost Projections, Administrative, and 12b-1 labels.
Risk	Morningstar.com	Select the Risk Measures tab. In the Volatility Measures section, click the yellow table indicator to the left of the Standard Deviation label. In the Modern Portfolio Theory Statistics section, click the yellow table indicator that points to the Standard Index label.

Be sure to check the Refresh automatically when cell value changes checkbox when you specify the cell for the query parameters so that the web queries retrieve data from the Web each time you type a new ticker symbol in the ticker symbol cell on the Excel summary worksheet.

Choose Your Favorite Flavor of Data

HACK #15

Mixing financial data from different sources can lead to fiscal indigestion, so you should evaluate data differences and then stick to only one source for all your stock analyses.

Accounting might seem tedious, unambiguous, and best performed by quiet folks wearing thick glasses, but in reality it's a creative field with plenty of room for interpretation. Generally Accepted Accounting Principles (GAAP) are merely a set of guidelines that have evolved over the years to help accountants present financial information fairly and consistently from company to company. Truth be told, there's wiggle room in those rules and companies take advantage of that fact. Once in a while, a company goes much too far. The data providers that distribute financial data don't necessarily fabricate, but they do use the gaps in GAAP to manipulate data to suit their clients' needs. Sometimes, these data differences can make good companies look so-so and bad companies look better than they are. To get a true picture of a stock's potential, you must understand the pros and cons of the style of data reporting, and then use the same standard to analyze each company's performance.

Types of Financial Data

Data can be manipulated more than once, and I'm not talking about cooking books like twice-baked potatoes. Companies can change how they report their own data, whereas data providers often modify the data that companies report to add value for their clients.

When companies report their financial data, it is called *as reported* data. However, as reported data comes in two flavors: *original* and *restated*. Original data is simply financial data as a company originally reported it at the end of a financial period. However, original data is re-reported sometimes. The *Financial Accounting Standards Board* (FASB), a private and independent accounting organization that sets the standards for financial accounting and reporting, requires companies to modify past financial reports to reflect current accounting practices.

Companies seem to reorganize all the time—spinning off business units, acquiring small fry in their industry, or shutting down poorly performing operations. Restated data is no more than an educated guess of what past performance might have looked like if the company always ran in its current configuration. For example, if a company acquires a competitor, original data might show a big jump in sales and earnings for the year in which the acquisition takes place. Restated data shows the combined income and expenses for both companies going back in time, so you don't see a jump.

Data providers have created ways to make financial numbers more appetizing to their clients. Data providers preprocess as reported data to make it easier to analyze company performance and compare the performance of competitors. In turn, they charge for their data—anywhere from modest sums to substantial fees. If you decide to pay for financial data, you should know what value is added and then decide if it's worth the money. Two widely used flavors of modified data are *standardized data* and *normalized data*.

If you've ever tried to compare financial data from different annual reports, you know already that companies have an endless supply of names for different types of income and expenses. Data providers create standardized data by placing income and expense items into standard categories, so that you can more easily compare companies side by side. In addition, data providers often extract data that is buried in the footnotes of financial reports and add those values to the same standard categories where you can see them. The advantage to standardized data is that you don't have to wade through the minutiae of annual reports to determine whether one company's flip-flop carry-forward earnings (don't try to find this in a financial glossary) is the same as another's earnings from ongoing operations.

> Although data providers do some of the dirty work for you, reading company annual reports and 10-K reports is worth the effort. You can glean important *qualitative* information from these reports and learn more about a company's problems, opportunities, hopes, and dreams.

Normalized data removes the impact of nonrecurring gains and losses. If you're about to ask what the heck that means, a nonrecurring gain or loss is the income or expense from an act a company does once—or at least not every year. For example, it costs money to acquire another company, but those costs typically appear in only one year. When an acquisition occurs, you usually see a distinct dip in profit and earnings in as reported data, which reflects the costs of the acquisition. Should you worry about a dip in earnings due to an acquisition? Usually no. Should you get excited about a spike in earnings from selling a valuable asset? No. Should you care about the underlying trend in sales and earnings growth year after year? Absolutely. With one-time events eliminated, you see a picture of a company's ongoing performance without static, so normalized data can be invaluable for analyzing company fundamentals.

> If you don't like the price tag that comes with normalized data, you can always research nonrecurring events in company reports and remove the irrelevant data yourself.

Choosing a Data Source

Depending on what you want to do and how much you're willing to spend, there's data to meet your needs [Hacks #19 and #20]. Table 3-3 shows the best-known data providers, the type of data they offer and how much they charge.

Table 3-3. Different styles of data come with different levels of convenience and price

Data provider	Data style	Price	Notes
Company reports	As reported, original or restated	Free	Provides fiscal year prices. Companies do not revise old annual and quarterly reports to reflect stock splits after the data of the report, so you must recalculate per share numbers.
Value Line	Original, normalized	$598 per year	Reports net profit but not pretax profit. The table with years of data is based on the calendar year, not the fiscal year. Includes value of intangibles in book value.
Standard & Poor's printed stock reports	As reported, original and restated	Free through libraries and with an account with some brokers; $2-$5 per report elsewhere	Excludes value of intangibles in book value. Provides calendar year prices.
Standard & Poor's Component (electronic files)	Restated, standardized	$25 per year through NAIC Online Premium Services	Includes value of intangibles in book value. Provides either calendar year or fiscal year prices.
Reuters	As reported, restated, normalized	$99 per year or $198 per year from AAII	Includes value of intangibles in book value. Provides fiscal year prices.

Obtain Price Quotes

#16

You must know the going price for an investment so that you can make an informed decision to buy, sell, or hold.

Stock price is an essential ingredient in a sound investment. Finding a company with terrific growth and impeccable quality isn't enough—an exorbitant stock price puts your potential return into the financial toilet. Before you buy a stock, you should check the current price to see if it's a good value. When you give a stock the green light, you must also know the current price to calculate how many shares you can afford to buy. If you're selling an investment because you need a specific amount of money, you must know the current price, so that you sell only as many shares as necessary. To make investing more fun, there's more than one current price from which to choose. No matter whether you're a day trader who wants real-time quotes or a buy-and-hold investor who can handle delayed prices, you can find the type of price quote you want online without paying a dime.

Current price is a matter of perspective. Depending on your investment timeframe, current could mean right now, a few minutes ago, or at market close yesterday. Your choice of price quote is based on the trade you plan to make [Hack #54]:

Ask price
> The price that owners are asking for their shares. It doesn't mean that a potential buyer will pay that price.

Bid price
> The price that buyers are bidding to purchase shares. It doesn't mean that a seller will accept that price.

> When you place a market order to buy or sell a stock, you accept the current ask or bid price, respectively, for your trade. You can set your selling or buying price by using limit orders or stop orders and specifying the purchase or sales price you want.

Delayed quote
> The prices you see typically by default are delayed by 15 to 20 minutes, which means they are the prices at which trades executed 15 to 20 minutes earlier. When you buy for the long-term, a delayed quote is fine, because the small price perturbations during a few minutes are peanuts compared to the long-term change in price. After the stock exchange closes, delayed quotes show the closing price until the exchange opens the following business day.

Real-time quote
> The price at which the last trade executed. If you day-trade and attempt to earn a profit from small changes in stock price, you need all the help you can get. You must know the most up-to-date price, which is a real-time quote.

Real-time quotes also show you the current price during after-hours trading sessions. Before you set up a market order that you want to execute when the market reopens the next day, you should check the real-time quote to see if the stock price is behaving erratically. If you don't, you might be surprised by the price at which your trade executes in the morning.

If you have an account with a brokerage—which is almost a certainty if you're reading this book—chances are you can obtain delayed or real-time quotes on your brokerage's web site. Most brokerage web sites also include a link to obtain a real-time quote when you initiate an order to buy or sell. However, you can get price quotes from plenty of other web sites. Use the information in Table 3-4 to obtain price quotes from the stock or fund pages at the most popular financial web sites. Download price quotes into a spreadsheet [Hack #7] to feed investment analysis or portfolio management tasks .

Table 3-4. The most popular financial web sites offer all types of price quotes for free

Web site	Bid and ask	Delayed quote	Real-time quote
Quicken.com *http://www.quicken.com*	On Full Quote tab	Last Trade on Full Quote tab	Only available with a Quicken brokerage account
Yahoo! Finance *http://finance.yahoo.com*	On Summary page	Last Trade: on Summary page	Click Real-Time Mkt/ECN link to obtain real-time quotes from participating institutions
Reuters Investor *http://www.investor.reuters.com*	On Quote page if you are a registered user	Last: on Quote page if you aren't a registered user	Last: on Quote page if you are a registered user
MSN Money *http://moneycentral.msn.com*	On Quote Detail page	Last: on Quote Detail page	On Real-Time Quotes page

For each stock exchange from which you want to obtain free real-time quotes, you must accept and electronically sign agreements in which you accept the stock exchange's terms and conditions for providing real-time data.

Download Historical Price Files

Historical prices are necessary if you're to successfully evaluate fundamental and technical measures for a stock.

Fundamental and technical analysts (for the difference between the two, see Chapters 4 and 5) don't have much in common other than the evaluation of historical prices to determine whether a stock is a buy, hold, or sell. Those who study fundamental measures use historical prices to identify typical P/E ratios and dividend yields for stocks. Because fundamental investors buy for the long term, they want historical prices going back several years. Conversely, technical analysts study the vagaries of price movement to try to determine where the price might go next. Technical analysis tends to the short term, so price charts might cover a few months or even a few hours. Smart investors combine the best of both of these methodologies to buy quality growth companies at good prices. Whether you want prices for days, months, or years, you can download a price spreadsheet from Yahoo! Finance.

When you open a web page for a stock at Yahoo! Finance (*http://finance.yahoo.com*), it's easy to download the historical prices you want by following these steps:

1. Click the Historical Prices link in the navigation bar in the left margin to open the Historical Prices page.

2. Specify the start and end dates for your price history.

3. Select the Monthly option to download for each month: the opening price on the first trading day of the month, the closing price on the last trading day, and the highest and lowest prices during the month. You can also select the Daily, Weekly, or Dividend Only options.

4. To retrieve the prices, click Get Prices. As illustrated in Figure 3-5, Yahoo! Finance displays the Open, Close, High, and Low prices for the periods you chose. However, for a true indication of a stock's price history, you want the prices adjusted for stock splits and dividends, which is provided by Adj Close in the last column.

5. To download a spreadsheet of these prices, scroll to the bottom of the page and click Download to Spreadsheet. Depending on the browser you use, the steps may be different. If you use Internet Explorer, when the File Download dialog box appears, click Save. In the Save As dialog box, navigate to the folder in which you want to save the historical price file. By default, the filename is *table.csv*, so be sure to type a meaningful name in the File Name box. For example, you might use *INTC_Price0311* for Intel's prices downloaded in November 2003.

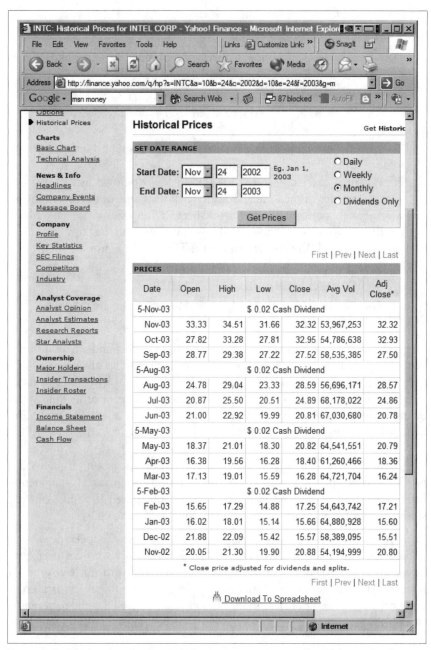

Figure 3-5. You can download actual closing prices or prices adjusted for stock splits from Yahoo! Finance

By using a filenaming format, you can control the order in which your price files appear in Windows Explorer. For example, by starting the filename with the stock ticker followed by the year, and then the month (*<ticker><yyyy> <mm>*), all the price files for a stock appear in chronological order. To group price files by year, start the filename with the year and month, and append the ticker symbol to the end.

6. To open the price file in Excel, choose File → Open and navigate to the folder that contains the price file. In the Open dialog box, select Text Files (*.prn; *.txt; *.csv) in the Files of Type drop-down list, so you can see the *.csv* files in the folder. Double-click the name of the price file you want. Excel opens the file as a worksheet. If you want to save the file as an Excel workbook, choose File → Save As and be sure to select Microsoft Excel Workbook (.xls) in the Files of Type drop-down list.

HACK #18 Download Financial Statements

Download financial statements to study financial ratios without tedious manual data entry.

To puzzle out how a company has performed in the past and where it might be heading, financial ratios can't be beat. The problem has always been data entry. Evaluating trends in financial measures requires at least three years of values, but who wants to manually transcribe three years of income statements, balance sheets, and cash flow statements into a spreadsheet? Sure, financial data providers offer data files of financial information—with a price tag attached [Hack #20]. And, you can always use Excel web queries to grab data from web pages [Hack #7]. However, EdgarScan (*http://edgarscan. pwcglobal.com*) provides the key information from financial statements, extracted from the filings that the company submits to the SEC, already stored in Excel spreadsheets that you can download at no charge.

The Global Technology Centre at Price Waterhouse Coopers developed EdgarScan, and it's a mother lode of data for investors who dig deep into financial ratios. EdgarScan spreadsheet files contain up to thirteen years of financial statements (both annual and quarterly) for companies. If a company has been in business less than thirteen years, it provides the data that is available.

Financial statements can be quite complex. EdgarScan aggregates some numbers into higher-level categories. If Edgar-Scan data doesn't contain the measures you need, use other sources for data [Hacks #19 and #20].

Financial Statements from EdgarScan

EdgarScan scans the filings in the SEC EDGAR database for financial data and stores them in standard categories, so you can locate and compare numbers. Although you can view this data on the EdgarScan web site, downloading it as an Excel spreadsheet means you can slice and dice ratios for one company, or compare values between competitors. EdgarScan spreadsheets include columns for quarterly (10-Q) and annual (10-K) filing for the last thirteen years; samples are shown in Figures 3-1, 3-2, and 3-3.

To download an EdgarScan spreadsheet, follow these steps:

1. Navigate to *http://edgarscan.pwcglobal.com/servlets/edgarscan* to access the EdgarScan web page.

2. Type the name or ticker symbol in the box and click Search.

> To limit the companies or filings that EdgarScan returns, click the Advanced link next to the Search button. You can search by company name, ticker symbol, industry, and SIC code, and limit the filings to a specific type of SEC filing, filings submitted during a range of dates, or filings that contain keywords or phrases.

3. If EdgarScan finds more than one company that matches the name or ticker you typed, it displays links for each result. Click the link for the company that you want.

> A company page includes three links that help you research a company. Click (business) to read the description of the business from the most recent 10-K. To jump to the company's summary page at Yahoo! Finance, click the ticker symbol link, such as (HD). The third link takes you to a web page that lists all the companies in the same industry, as defined by the *Standard Industry Classification* (SIC) code.

4. To download an EdgarScan spreadsheet, scroll below the company summary table and click Excel Spreadsheet. In the File Download dialog box, click Save. In the Save As dialog box, navigate to the folder in which you want to store the file, type a name for the file in the File Name box, and click Save.

Links to recent filings, 10-Ks, and 10-Qs display the SEC filing on the screen. Click links to jump to the sections you want to read. If you want to work offline, you can download filings as text files, HTML files, or rich text files. If you can't call to mind what an SB-2MEF filing is (or any of the other SEC form identifiers), click the glossary of form types link at the bottom of the page.

You can also download SEC filings from the EdgarScan web
site into Excel using web queries [Hack #7].

EdgarScan includes a feature called the Benchmarking Assistant, which displays a graph of values for one financial measure at a time. You can choose from several categories of measures and almost 100 financial measures in all. In general, a linear graph of values isn't useful, because you want to see the growth year over year [Hack #26]. However, you can check trends in key financial ratios by displaying a graph of a measure in the Ratios category in the Benchmarking Assistant, demonstrated in Figure 3-6. For example, you can check whether debt is increasing by graphing the debt to equity ratio [Hack #29]. You can specify the number of years of data that you want to see or display the data in vertical bar, horizontal bar, or pie chart format. If you want to review the financial statement associated with a value, click a bar or slice of pie in the graph. If you want to download the chart to an Excel spreadsheet, click the Excel Chart button below the chart.

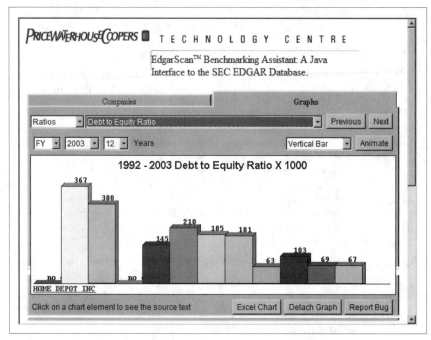

Figure 3-6. The EdgarScan Benchmarking Assistant graphs financial ratios

The Best Data for Free

#19

Data that helps you evaluate investments doesn't have to cost an arm and a leg—or anything at all for that matter.

SEC filings, such as the 10-K and 10-Q forms, provide data *as reported* by the company. Without any value-added manipulation [Hacks #15 and #20], you have to judge for yourself whether data truly reflects a company's performance. Many web sites provide information suitable for your initial research and qualitative evaluations. In addition, you can use Excel web queries [Hack #7] to extract data directly from web pages into a spreadsheet for processing and ratio analysis. The only time free data falls short is when you want to feed an investment analysis program [Hacks #38 and #53] that runs on your computer. These programs require data in a specific format, and it's just too much trouble to format free data to fit their specifications.

When you want to put financial ratios (see Chapter 4) to the test, you need data from financial statements—and lots of it. For almost effortless downloads of financial statement data, there's only one free alternative: Edgar-Scan [Hack #18].

Many web sites provide easy access to SEC filings, such as the 10-K and 10-Q reports. In most cases, you can view the filings on the screen or download them as Adobe PDF, HTML, or rich text format files. If the web site uses HTML tables to display the SEC filing, you can use Excel web queries to extract the data to a spreadsheet. The best web sites in this category not only offer access to SEC filings, but also include a comprehensive financial dossier for each company with an intuitive interface that makes it easy to find what you're looking for. Consider the following web sites when you want to view company data or use web queries to download tabular data:

- The Reuters Investor web site (*http://www.investor.reuters.com*) gets *my* vote for the most comprehensive and most navigable stock page around. The navigation bar in the left margin starts with an overview, proceeds to basic information, such as quotes, price charts, a company profile, and a list of officers and directors, and then provides additional links under the News, Finances, Sentiment, and Analysis categories. Most of the links are available at all times so it's easy to find the information you want. To access the company financial statements, click Financial Statements under the Financial Info heading. If you would rather see ratios that are already calculated and shown side by side with industry and index averages, click Ratios under the Finances heading. Ratios are distributed among several categories.

- Yahoo! Finance (*http://finance.yahoo.com*) is right up there with Reuters Investor. In addition to the navigation bar, the Summary page includes links to other information you might want. You can access links to SEC filings by clicking SEC Filings under the Company heading. To view the filings on the screen, click Income Statement, Balance Sheet, or Cash Flow under the Financials heading. The Competitors link shows a few measures for the company you're studying compared to values for its closest competitors and the industry averages. The Industry link takes you to a page with information about the industry to which the company belongs. Yahoo! Finance is also the best site for downloading historical price files **[Hack #17]**.

- MSN Money (*http://money.msn.com*) is another strong contender. The navigation bar includes many links to financial information. However, unlike Reuters Investor, some additional links are available only when you navigate to a specific web page. If you're a visual person, you'll appreciate the graphs of financial data that MSN Money displays.

If you're looking for SEC filings and nothing but SEC filings, the obvious source is the SEC, right? Well, yes and no. The SEC web site (*http://sec.gov/edgar/searchedgar/webusers.htm*) does provide links to download any SEC filing for any company for the past ten years. The interface, however, isn't very user-friendly. Free EDGAR (*http://www.freeedgar.com*) offers all the same filings as the SEC site, but you can obtain the filings much more easily. Type in a ticker symbol, click Search, and then click the VIEW FILINGS link on the Search Results page, and you're there. As described in "Download Financial Statements" **[Hack #18]**, EdgarScan provides not only SEC filings but SEC filing information in standardized formats and downloadable files.

In addition to the reports that the SEC requires, companies publish annual and quarterly reports. Annual reports strive to please the shareholders rather than a government agency—the reports are often printed on fancy paper with many colors and pictures. In reality, the appearance of the annual report reveals a company's philosophy. Of course, the contents of an annual report can do that as well. The Public Register's Annual Report Service offers annual reports for over 3,000 companies, available in Adobe PDF format or hardcopy. You can also obtain annual reports, quarterly reports, SEC filings, and other types of investor information directly from the web site of the company you're evaluating—just type the company name into the Search box at Google (*http://www.google.com*). On the company web page, look for an Investor Relations, Financial Reports, or similar link.

HACK #20 The Best Data for a Fee

Some data is worth the price you pay for it, making it significantly easier to evaluate company performance.

Data providers that charge for their data typically earn their keep by manipulating the numbers reported by companies [Hack #15] in one of two ways. They create standardized data by assigning the reported values for income and expense items into the most appropriate standard categories. In addition to saving you time in calculating or categorizing reported numbers, standardized data definitely saves you from deciphering the more enigmatic income or expense categories used. Normalized data removes the impact of one-time events so that a company's ongoing performance is more visible.

Data for a fee often includes business summaries and analyst opinions to help you identify strengths and weaknesses more quickly. In addition, data providers present quantitative and qualitative data for each company in the same layout, so you'll know just where to look.

Data for a fee ranges from almost free to "this better be good." If you're using a stock analysis program [Hacks #38 and #53], you must choose a data source that provides data in a format that your program can read.

When you're in the market for data that makes your job easier, consider one of the following sources:

- Value Line (*http://www.valueline.com*) offers data for 1,700 stocks in the Value Line Investment Survey Standard Edition, and an additional 1,800 companies in the Small and Mid-Cap Edition. Each Value Line report is a heady synopsis of 15 years of normalized data with an analyst's summary and opinion of the company's prospects for the next three to five years. Value Line also rates each company for timeliness (the prospect of a near time price increase), safety, technical factors, financial strength, price stability, and earnings predictability [Hack #35]. The cost is $538 for a one-year subscription to the online version of the Standard Edition.

  On the down side, the table of data on a Value Line report shows data based on a calendar year instead of the company's fiscal year. In addition, only the CD provides data files that you can import into spreadsheets.

- Stock Investor Pro is a combination of a stock screening software program [Hack #5] and regularly updated data for over 8,000 companies sold by the American Association of Individual Investors (AAII) (*http://www. aaii.com*). You receive a CD once a month with updated data for 1,500 financial measures for each company. You can use these data files to feed spreadsheets or stock analysis programs. You can also obtain online weekly updates. For AAII members, the price is $198 a year. Nonmembers pay $247 per year.

Value Line, Stock Investor Pro, and the S&P Compustat files all include the value of intangibles in book value [Hack #28]. With intangibles such as the value of a brand name included in book value, you see a clearer picture of whether a company is over- or undervalued based on its assets.

- Standard & Poor's Compustat (*http://www.compustat.com*) is a database of restated, standardized financial data for 10,000 actively traded U.S. companies. However, as an individual investor, you won't want to pay the institutional-caliber fees. You can obtain downloadable files of Compustat data through NAIC's Online Premium Services (*http://www. better-investing.org*). The cost for a one-year subscription to Online Premium Services is $25 for club members. The service is bundled into the $39 cost of a one-year individual NAIC membership. In addition to downloadable files in SSG format that you can use to feed spreadsheets for software programs, each stock page in Online Premium Services includes helpful links to NAIC articles about the company, the conference call calendar, and a price chart.

NAIC's Online Premium Services wins the prize for most economical data for a fee. However, as your portfolio grows in size, the cost of the most expensive data becomes a minute fraction of the money you'll make each year.

Download News

HACK #21   Business news is all over the Web and easy to obtain electronically; the trick is receiving what you need to know without reaching information overload.

If you were to log on to every investing web site that you found interesting, you would find yourself quickly overwhelmed. Most of these sites offer delivery of headlines, company news, and industry trends—all useful, yet potentially more information than you want flooding your email box. Savvy investors want to know what's going on in the overall market, which includes news and analysis of business and industry trends, not just the scoop on the latest company earning release. It's just as important to know why something is happening as it is to know what is happening. In fact, informed analysis is what sets the best sites apart from the run-of-the-mill. This hack reviews the best free and for-a-fee sites for breaking news, company news, market news, and industry news.

News Delivery

Web sites that offer news also offer a choice of delivery options. You can choose to go to the news or request a web site to send the news to you. Table 3-5 provides the pros and cons for news delivery via email, PDA, or cell phone.

 Although it's easy to sign up to receive news, sign up only for what you really need. Otherwise, you'll ignore most of it, which defeats the purpose of readily available information.

Table 3-5. The pros and cons of electronic delivery options

	Pros	Cons
Email	This option is the easiest to set up. To avoid inbox overload, you can set up your email program to deliver headlines to individual mailboxes.	Some news outlets limit the number of days free subscribers can access old articles Don't sign up for too much or you won't have time to sleep.
PDA	This option makes the news extremely portable—either synch your PDA to your computer and read articles and headlines at your leisure, or use a wireless PDA and locate a wireless hotspot while you're on the go.	Takes more effort to set up and maintain. Some sites offer content directly to your PDA; with many others, you must go through a third party such as AvantGo.
Cell phone	This option is very convenient.	Not all cell phone providers offer this option and not all cell phone models support it It usually costs extra, and the more you use it, the more it costs. In most cases, you must go through a third-party provider such as AvantGo.

The Best Free News Services

The Web includes many sites that offer comprehensive news coverage and in-depth analysis. Different web sites excel in each category of news.

Headlines

For overall news, the *New York Times* (*http://www.nytimes.com*) is hard to beat. Although it offers some coverage focused on the New York City metro area, its business and technology news covers markets, company news, business news, and industry trends across the country. Many online subscribers receive daily headlines delivered via email. You can customize the news you want to see and how many headlines you receive from each section. A weekly Your Money section comes out every Monday focusing on personal finance, retirement, and business trends. Read what interests you right away, because free subscribers have free access to the archives only for five days. The *Times* offers a paid alert service, called the Times News Tracker. For $29.95 per year, you can set up ten customized email alerts for keywords, ticker symbols, or *Times* topics. You also receive a 90-day archive for subjects covered by your alerts plus breaking news email alerts.

Company news

Yahoo! Finance (*http://finance.yahoo.com*) brings together news and analysis provided by individual companies as well as major news providers, such as Reuters, the Associated Press, Dow Jones Newswire, Business Week Online, and the Motley Fool. To receive news, you must first create a portfolio of stocks and funds. Stock investors obtain the most headlines, although funds generate occasional headlines. If you want overall market news, enter the symbols for the major indexes, which Yahoo provides. After you set up your portfolio, edit your company news preferences. Yahoo! receives and hosts news, commentary, financial alerts, and financial data from more than 40 providers. Select the types of news you prefer and whether you want all headlines, or the headlines only for the past day, week, or month.

Market news

MSN Money (*http://money.msn.com/investor/home.asp*) provides a variety of market news and statistics, broken down by topic, breaking news, industry news, and MSNBC news. When the market's open, check the daily market report, which provides hourly updates on the financial markets. Search the calendar for information on upcoming earnings reports, economic reports, stock splits, and other events. MSN distributes six newsletters, which update you on daily market events, tax articles, and information about the influence of government and business.

Industry analysis

Polson Enterprises (*http://www.virtualpet.com/industry/howto/search.htm*) lays out an extremely organized procedure for researching an industry, including regulatory and legal issues of industries, trade organizations and publications, and overall information. Each step is full of links and information that help you produce useful research. Polson also points you to references, other industry research sites, and links for researchers and librarians.

For the inside scoop on a company, listen to its latest conference call. The majority of publicly held companies host quarterly conference calls for investment analysts, which last from an hour to an hour and a half and usually feature presentations by top corporate officers, including CEOs and CFOs, with an analyst question-and-answer period at the end. With regulators and the public clamoring for more disclosure, many companies now place old conference calls on their web sites or invite individual investors to listen in. To listen to old calls or obtain dates for upcoming calls, go to Best Calls (*http://www.bestcalls.com*) or the company's web site. For $49 a year, you can track conference calls at Best Calls and receive alerts via email.

News for a Fee

With so much free news available, news for a fee has to really shine to earn its price tag. Like free news, news for a fee is plentiful, but the price tag doesn't guarantee that it's better than free news. Two sites stand out as worth the cost:

- The *Online Wall Street Journal*, the nation's premier business newspaper (*http://online.wsj.com*), costs $79 per year for the online-only version, and $39 for subscribers to the print edition on top of their regular subscription rate. The online edition offers its entire print content and more. You receive the day-to-day business news, as well as the scoop on business and industry trends, and news on specific companies. The Journal staff provides excellent, in-depth analysis of business trends, and how politics and the economy impact business. A nice bonus is access to *Barron's Online*, which is a weekly investing newspaper also published by the *Journal*. You can read news online at the Journal web site, or receive headlines and alerts delivered via email. Use AvantGo (*http://www.avantgo.com*) to receive headlines and news on your PDA or cell phone.

- Morningstar Online [Hack #67] (*http://www.morningstar.com*) costs $12.95 per month, $119 per year, or $199 for two years. Morningstar's forte is analysis of over 2,000 mutual funds and 1,000 companies. Their analyst reports are updated a couple of times a year with special updates for big news. In addition, you can read columns and newsletters such as the Stock Strategist, Five Star Investor, and Fund Spy.

See Also

- The Crow River Investment Club (*http://www.bivio.com/crowriver/files/ Index.htm*) maintains an excellent and extensive list of links to the best company, business, economy, and industry news and analysis. Click the Research link and then click the link for the type of information you want.
- CBS MarketWatch (*http://www.cbsmarketwatch.com*)
- CNN/Money (*http://money.cnn.com*)
- SmartMoney (*http://www.smartmoney.com*)
- Wall Street Executive Library (*http://www.executivelibrary.com/ Research.asp#industry*)

—Amy Crane

HACK #22   Locate the Competition

Before you can buy the best company in an industry, you must determine which companies represent the competition in that industry.

To find the best company in an industry, you must compare competitors within that industry to find the strongest contenders, and then evaluate those contenders to reduce the field, eventually to the one with the best combination of growth, quality, and level of risk for your portfolio. Like other aspects of investing, finding competitors isn't as easy as you might think. Most financial data providers and web sites categorize companies by sector and industry—but they typically define their own set of sectors and industries, and they might classify companies differently even if the sectors and industries are a close match. Sectors represent broader categories, such as healthcare, whereas industries are more specific, such as biotechnology, healthcare facilities, major drugs, and medical equipment and supplies. There are plenty of web sites that provide sector and industry classifications, but some have features that simplify the search for competition. After you find a web site that you like, use that same site every time, so that your classifications are consistent.

When you want to obtain industry information along with competing companies, Yahoo! Finance (*http://finance.yahoo.com*) and Reuters Investor (*http:// investor.reuters.com*) are both good choices. To find competition and industry information at Yahoo! Finance, type a ticker symbol in the Enter Symbols box and click Go. On the left side of the stock web page, click Competitors in the navigation bar to see a comparison of financial measures for the company, its direct competitors, and the industry, as shown in Figure 3-7. To view information about the company's associated industry, click the Industry link in the navigation bar or in the middle of the web page.

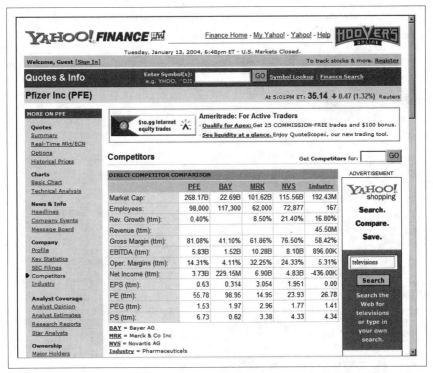

Figure 3-7. Yahoo! Finance shows direct competitors and provides links to industry information

On the Reuters Investor web site, you can find competitors by sector and industry whether or not you have a company in mind. For example, if you're interested in investing in a sector, such as Financial, follow these steps:

1. Click Industries in the navigation bar.

2. Click the sector, such as Financial, and then click the industry within that sector, such as Consumer Financial Services, as demonstrated in Figure 3-8. An industry web page appears that includes industry statistics, key developments, news, and top companies in the industry.

3. To see a list of companies in the industry, click Company List in the navigation bar on the left side of the page.

4. To rank the companies in the industry by any of 15 measures, such as growth history or profit margins, click the Company Ranks link in the navigation bar.

Figure 3-8. Reuters Investor includes sector and industry links, which you can click to get competitors and industry information

When you start with a company in mind on the Reuters Investor site, type the ticker symbol in the Name or Ticker box and click Go. To obtain industry information, click Company Profile in the navigation bar, and then click Industry Overview on the right side of the Profile page. The same page as displayed in Step 2 appears.

Quicken.com has several features that simplify the comparison of competitors. On the Quicken.com home page (*http://www.quicken.com*), type the ticker symbol for the company you're studying in the Enter Symbol box and click Go. On the navigation bar on the stock web page, click the Compare to Industry link. The heading for Section 2 of the comparison web page shows the industry in which Quicken.com classifies the company. The table in Section 2 shows several of the company's competitors, their ticker symbols, and their market cap, which is useful if you're looking for companies of a specific size for diversification. If you want to see all of the companies in that industry, click the Show All Competitors link below the table. You can also add other companies to the competitor list by typing ticker symbols separated by commas in the Enter Symbol box. Quicken.com also makes it easy to view company fundamentals side by side [Hack #34].

Difficult Classifications

Some companies are hard to classify. For example, large diversified companies often contain numerous business units that span several industries, each facing its own set of competitors. PepsiCo, Inc. makes Pepsi and other soft drinks in its beverages division, produces snack foods in its Frito-Lay division, and turns out other types of food in its Quaker Foods division. Although Coca-Cola is PepsiCo's prime competitor for the beverage business, Frito-Lay and Quaker Foods compete with food companies, not soft drink makers.

Nearly all data providers classify both companies as beverage companies, but a strict side-by-side comparison of fundamentals might not be completely valid. Sometimes, companies like PepsiCo publish summaries of financial results for their different divisions. For example, PepsiCo reports sales and operating profits for its divisions, which you can use as a starting point for analysis and comparisons.

Obtain Averages for an Industry and the Competition

HACK
#23

Some web sites place industry average values next to a company's financial measures for convenient comparison; you can obtain averages for a company's direct competitors with carefully configured stock screen results.

Each industry has its peculiarities: utility companies have learned to operate under debt loads that would crush companies in other industries; grocery stores can thrive with profit margins that leave no room for error; software companies enjoy high profit margins that other companies envy and that all software companies must attain to stay in the game. To understand whether a company is performing well or is down with the dogs, you must compare its financial measures with those of the overall industry to which it belongs. And, because most industries include companies of different sizes or subspecialties, it's a good idea to compare a company to its direct competitors. In most cases, a quick online comparison is enough. However, if you want to download values for more thorough investigation, you can play games with stock screening tools to produce downloadable spreadsheets and calculate averages for the competition yourself.

If you want to compare industry and sector averages to the values produced by a company, Reuters Investor (*http://investor.reuters.com*) makes it easy. To access a stock page, type a ticker symbol in the Symbol box and click Go. On the stock page, click Ratios in the navigation bar. By default, valuation ratios, such as the P/E ratio and institutional ownership, appear in the Ratio Comparison table, but you can view other types of ratios by clicking other ratio category links under the Ratio heading in the navigation bar: Dividend, Growth Rate, Financial Condition, Profit Margin, Management Effectiveness, and Efficiency. In the table, the first column shows the company numbers with additional columns for average values for the industry, sector, and the S&P 500 index.

To find strong competitors in an industry, you want to see above industry average performance. In most cases, a quick inspection of key ratios on these pages can tell you whether a company meets this criterion.

> For a quick reminder of how to use different ratios to analyze company performance, click the Learn about Dividend Ratios link below the table.

Yahoo! Finance (*http://finance.yahoo.com*) has a great concept for comparing a company to its competitors and its industry. When you open a stock page for a company and click the Competitors link in the navigation bar, the Direct Competitor Comparison table shows values for the company you're studying next to values for its closest competitors and the industry averages. Unfortunately, only a few of the measures shown are really helpful in finding the best of the bunch. For example, you can compare competitors using revenue growth, gross margin, and operating margin [Hacks #26 and #32], which are shown as percentages. You can also use the P/E ratio and the PEG ratio [Hacks #27 and #28] to compare companies.

Calculate Competitors' Averages Using Stock Screen Results

You can capitalize on the spreadsheets that industrial-strength stock screens produce to calculate average values for the competition. By screening for stocks in a specific industry, limiting the field to companies with similar annual revenue, or specifying other criteria, the results can reflect your view of a company's closest competitors. Before downloading the spreadsheet, add columns for all the industry figures you want to compare, such as annual revenue and EPS growth, pre-tax profit margin, return on equity, return on assets, inventory turnover, debt to equity ratio, and P/E ratio. To learn the importance of these measures, see Chapter 4. After you download the spreadsheet containing the companies and financial fields you want, use Excel functions to calculate the averages for a set of competitors.

Reuters Investor PowerScreener [Hack #5] provides the most useful set of financial fields for comparing competition. Defining stock screen criteria isn't as
easy to build with PowerScreener as with other screening tools. However,
for calculating competition averages, you need only one or two criteria. To
create a competition screen, follow these steps:

1. Navigate to *http://investor.reuters.com.*

2. Type the ticker symbol for the company you are studying in the Quote
   box in the menu bar and click Go.

3. To locate the industry and market cap for the company, click the Snapshot link in the navigation bar. The Key Ratios & Statistics table provides values that you can use for your competition screen, as illustrated
   in Figure 3-9. The industry is located at the top of the figure. Market cap
   is listed under the Share Related Items heading.

4. To access PowerScreener, click the Ideas & Screening link in the navigation bar and then click the PowerScreener link that appears under the
   Ideas & Screening heading in the navigation bar.

5. To define your first criterion, click Add a Criterion at the bottom of the
   Screen Builder table.

6. To screen for the industry, follow these steps:

   a. Expand the Descriptive folder, select Industry [IndDescr] in the
      variable list, and then click Select.

   b. In the Select a value dialog box that appears, check the checkbox
      for the industry to which the company you're studying belongs. For
      example, to find competitors for Pfizer, which belongs to the Major
      Drugs industry, check the Major Drugs checkbox.

   c. Click Go to add the criterion to the screen.

   d. Click Run in the Screen Builder table to execute the screen using the
      industry criteria. The table shows how many companies match the
      screen criteria.

7. To screen for companies of a similar size, follow these steps:

   a. Click Add a Criterion.

   b. To screen for market cap, you want to find companies in a similar
      size range: small-cap, mid-cap, or large-cap. Typical guidelines for
      these ranges are less than $600 million for small-cap, $600 million
      to $6 billion for mid-cap, and more than $6 billion for large-cap.
      Pfizer's market cap is almost $300 billion—more of a giant-cap, but
      we'll use large-cap in this example.

   c. Expand the Share Related Items folder, select Market Capitaliza-
      tion ($ millions) [MktCap] in the variable list, and then click Select.

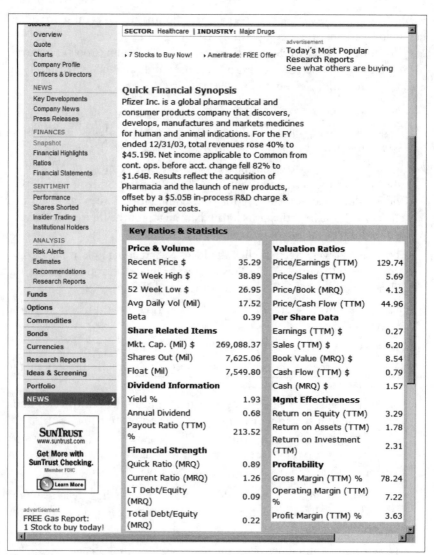

Figure 3-9. *The Reuters Investor Snapshot contains key ratios you can use to find competitors*

   d. Click the > button to the right of the variable list.

   e. To type the criterion value, click within the criterion window at the bottom of the Screen Builder table, and type **6000**.

   f. Click Run in the Screen Builder table to execute the screen using the industry criteria. The table shows how many companies match the screen criteria.

8. To save the screen, choose File → Save As → Screen. Type the name of the screen in the Save Screen As dialog box, and click OK.

9. To view the results of the screen, select the Screening Results tab.

10. To add fields to the results table, choose View → Add/Remove/Arrange Columns. In the All Variables list, expand the categories you want and select variables to add them to the Current Variable List. Click OK to display the columns in the results, as shown in Figure 3-10.

Because this screen returns companies in the same industry, select Industry in the Current Variable List and click Remove.

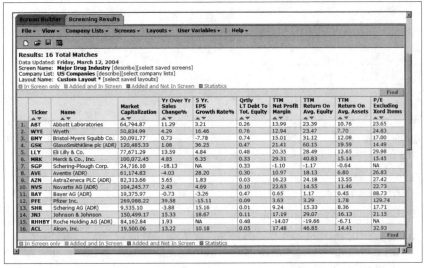

Figure 3-10. Select variables in the Reuters Investor PowerScreener to add columns to the screen results

For example, the results in Figure 3-10 include columns containing the following information:

Company Ticker Symbol
Company Name
Market Capitalization
Sales Percent Change, Year Over Year (this is the sales growth rate)
Earnings Per Share, 5 Year Compound Annual Growth Rate
Long Term Debt to Equity
Net Profit Margin

Return on Average Common Equity (this is ROE using an average value for shareholders' equity)

Return on Assets

Price to Earnings Ratio

11. To save the collection and order of the columns in the table as a layout, choose File → Save As → Layout. In the Save Layout As dialog box, type the name of the layout, such as Industry Comparison, and click OK.

12. To save the results to a spreadsheet, click the Export to Spreadsheet icon, shown in Figure 3-11, below the PowerScreener menu bar, or choose File → Export To Spreadsheet. If the Export to Spreadsheet dialog box appears, click OK. In the File Download dialog box, click Save. In the Save As dialog box, specify the folder and filename for the spreadsheet, and click Save.

Figure 3-11. Click the Export to Spreadsheet icon to save the screen results to a spreadsheet

With the spreadsheet of results downloaded to your computer, open the spreadsheet in Excel and follow these steps to calculate average values for the competition:

1. Select a cell below a column of results, such as D22 for Yr Over Yr Sales Change % in Figure 3-12.

2. Choose Insert → Function.

3. Select the Statistical category, select Average, and then click OK. By default, Excel selects the cells above the current cell and adds that range to the Number1 box in the Function Arguments dialog box. If the range isn't correct, simply select the correct cells on the worksheet, cells D5: D20 in this example.

4. Click OK.

 To format the results to only one decimal place, choose Format → Cells. Select the Number tab and select 1 in the Decimal Places box.

5. Copy this cell across the row to calculate the averages for the other columns.

oih_03 Industry Results.xls

	Ticker	Name	Market Cap	Yr Over Yr Sales Change%	5 Yr. EPS Growth Rate%	Qrtly LT Debt To Tot. Equity	TTM Net Profit Margin	TTM Return On Avg. Equity	TTM Return On Avg. Assets	P/E Excluding Xord Items
ABT	Abbott Laboratories		64794.87	11.29	3.21	0.26	13.99	23.39	10.76	23.65
WYE	Wyeth		50834.99	4.29	16.46	0.76	12.94	23.47	7.7	24.83
BMY	Bristol-Myers Squibb Co.		50091.77	0.73	-7.78	0.74	15.01	31.12	12.08	17
GSK	GlaxoSmithKline plc (ADR)		120485.3	1.08	36.25	0.47	21.41	60.15	19.59	14.49
LLY	Eli Lilly & Co.		77671.29	13.59	4.84	0.48	20.35	28.49	12.65	29.98
MRK	Merck & Co., Inc.		100072.5	4.85	6.35	0.33	29.31	40.83	15.14	15.45
SGP	Schering-Plough Corp.		24716.1	-18.13	NA	0.33	-1.1	-1.17	-0.64	NA
AVE	Aventis (ADR)		61174.83	-4.03	28.2	0.3	10.97	18.13	6.8	26.83
AZN	AstraZeneca PLC (ADR)		82313.66	5.65	1.83	0.03	16.23	24.18	13.55	27.42
NVS	Novartis AG (ADR)		104245.8	2.43	4.69	0.1	22.63	14.55	11.46	22.73
BAY	Bayer AG (ADR)		19375.97	-0.73	-3.26	0.47	0.65	1.17	0.45	88.73
PFE	Pfizer Inc.		269088.2	39.58	-15.11	0.09	3.63	3.29	1.78	129.74
SHR	Schering AG (ADR)		9535.1	-3.88	15.16	0.01	9.24	15.33	8.36	17.71
JNJ	Johnson & Johnson		150499.2	15.33	18.67	0.11	17.19	29.07	16.13	21.15
RHHBY	Roche Holding AG (ADR)		84162.84	1.93	NA	0.48	-14.07	-19.66	-6.71	NA
ACL	Alcon, Inc.		19500.06	13.22	10.18	0.05	17.48	46.85	14.41	32.93
	Average Values			5.5	8.5	0.3	12.2	21.2	9.0	35.2

oih_03 Industry Results

Figure 3-12. Use Excel features to calculate competition averages and highlight above-average performance

Hacking the Hack

Use other Excel features to emphasize the values that are better than the average for the competition. For example, you can apply conditional formatting to cells [Hack #8]. Follow these steps to shade values that are better than the industry average:

1. To highlight sales growth that is higher than the competition's average growth, select the first sales growth cell (D5 in this example) and choose Format → Conditional Formatting.

2. Select Formula Is for Condition 1.

3. In the formula box, type = **D5 > D$22** where D22 is the cell for the industry average sales growth rate.

4. Click Format, select the Patterns tab, click the colored square for the highlighting you want to apply when the condition is true, and click OK.

5. Back in the Conditional Formatting dialog box, click OK to apply the formatting to the cell.

6. To copy the formatting to the other cells in the column, click the Format Painter icon on the Standard toolbar, shown in Figure 3-13, and select the other company cells in the column.

Figure 3-13. Click the Format Painter icon to apply formatting to other cells

As long as you want to highlight cells whose values are higher than the competition's average, you can copy this formatting to cells in other columns. However, for some measures, such as long-term debt to equity and the P/E ratio, a number lower than the average is preferable. For these cells, follow Steps 1 through 6, but replace > with < in the formula.

HACK #24   Create Alerts

Instead of checking your portfolio every five minutes, use online automated alerts to notify you when something interesting happens to your investments.

Whether your portfolio is small or large, the market's daily gyrations can be nerve-racking. The thought of a favorite stock tanking in a matter of seconds leads many investors to compulsively check their portfolios 10, 20, or even 50 times a day. Instead of constantly interrupting your work, you can set up a group of portfolio alerts to notify you when something's going on with an individual stock or your entire portfolio. Several popular financial sites offer alerts for free, but you can access outstanding alert functionality when you subscribe to Morningstar's Premium service. In addition, some brokers offer automated alerts as part of their online brokerage services.

Alerts tell you when events occur so that you don't have to check for them. For example, you can set alerts that trigger when an individual stock's price or volume increases or decreases more than a specific percentage value; when a company announces quarterly earnings, distributes a dividend, or announces a stock split; or when analysts downgrade or upgrade a stock rating.

Although long-term investors don't care about daily price variations, it is important to know that a company's stock price has shot way up or down. You probably don't want to receive alerts every hour or even every day about stock prices—unless it's a company you're watching very closely. Stock prices are notoriously volatile, to the point that a 10 percent increase or decline in a day is a regular event for many stocks. Set price alerts at a big enough percentage change so that the alert means something. For example, 15 or 20 percent changes usually don't happen without a catalyst, such as a bad earnings announcement that catches everyone off guard or a takeover offer.

Volume alerts tell you when the amount of trading in a stock increases, which typically occurs when significant news is reported about a company. A sharp increase in trading volume in a stock can be positive or negative. Investors who use technical analysis (see Chapter 5) analyze volume and daily prices for clues to future stock price movements.

Some investors like to know about upcoming events, such as earnings announcements, dividend payouts, or stock split announcements. For example, earnings announcement alerts remind you to review the fundamental performance of your holdings.

 Be judicious about the alerts you define. If you set up numerous alerts for every stock in your portfolio, you'll quickly start to ignore the barrage of alerts you receive, defeating their purpose.

Free Alert Services

Before you can set up an alert or group of alerts, you must set up a portfolio at a site that offers an alert service. Fortunately, the best free alert services are available from the following popular web sites, so there's a good chance that you already have a portfolio [Hack #73] set up with one of them. If you don't, you can navigate to the following web pages to create one:

- Quicken.com (*http://www.quicken.com/investments/portfolio*)
- MSN Money (*http://money.msn.com/investor/dlportmgr/dpmNewAccount.asp*)
- Yahoo! Finance (*http://finance.yahoo.com*)

Quicken.com's alert service provides the easiest interface of the three and offers a wide variety of alerts. However, Quicken.com won't email individual alerts during the trading day—instead, they email your entire portfolio, which includes any alerts you've set at the end of the trading day. To set up alerts at Quicken.com, complete the following steps:

1. Go to *http://www.quicken.com/investments*.

2. If you haven't done so already, create a portfolio at Quicken.com [Hack #73].

3. On the Portfolio web page, click the My Alerts link at the top of the page.

4. On the My Alerts web page, click the Customize My Alerts link at the top of the page.

5. Specify the alerts you want from the following options:

   a. Price Change Exceeds: specify a percentage change. You can specify one percentage for all stocks or specify different percentages for each stock in your portfolio.

   b. Volume Exceed Average By: specify a percentage change. You can specify one percentage for all stocks or specify different percentages for each stock in your portfolio.

   c. Price Drops Below: specify the price at which you want to be notified for each stock. Although price drops are often overreactions to bad news, it's important to check that price drops aren't due to undesirable fundamental changes in a company's situation.

   d. Price Rises Above: specify the price at which you want to be notified for each stock. This type of alert is useful for watching a target sell price.

> Alerts set to specific stock prices require some maintenance. You must adjust price alerts if a stock splits. In addition, if the stock price increases or decreases significantly over time, you must adjust the price alerts accordingly. Otherwise, you might receive an alert because a stock priced at $110 increased to $111, which happens frequently.

   e. Section 2 Announcements: check the checkboxes in this section to receive notification for dividend payouts, stock splits, earnings announcements, analyst upgrades or downgrades, or the announcement of expected earnings.

   f. Section 3 Overall Account Value: you can specify the Drops Below price, the Rises Above price, or an intra-day percentage change for your entire portfolio.

> To receive alerts about companies you want to watch but don't yet own, create a separate portfolio of those stocks you. Keeping watch-list stocks separate means that the portfolio statistics for your real portfolio reflect its performance.

6. Click Finished to save your alerts.

7. To set up delivery of your portfolio with alerts for the end of the trading day, click E-mail my Portfolio. Confirm that the email address displayed is the one to which you want your portfolio sent, and click Sign Me Up!

With a portfolio open at MSN Money you can click the Summary Alerts link to set up price alerts using dollars or percentages, and to specify a volume alert for all the stocks and funds in your portfolio. To create alerts for a specific stock, type its ticker symbol in the Symbol box and define the alerts you want. You can specify one or two times during the day to receive alerts—you aren't notified immediately when a stock hits the alert price, percentage, or volume. You must also specify the number of shares for a volume alert, which means you must dig to identify the average daily volume for your companies. In addition, you can checkboxes to set up alerts for the following events:

Analyst upgrade or downgrade

Featured on CNBC

Stocks in Play from Briefing.com

Morningstar Mutual Funds upgrade or downgrade

Positive or negative earnings surprise

Reuters Research alert

Stock split announcement

Alerts on the Go

Stay in touch with your portfolio when you're on the go by using services that work with cell phones, PDAs, pagers, and other wireless devices. Yahoo! Finance enables you to obtain stock price alerts at specific times of the day via your cell phone or alphanumeric pager. Go to *http://mobile.yahoo.com/ wireless/alert*. With a subscription to AvantGo (*http://www.avantgo.com*), which is free, you can receive portfolio and business news from My Yahoo!, the Wall Street Journal Online, and other sites, delivered to your PDA. AvantGo also provides an updated list of wireless hot spots at *http://avantgo. jiwire.com*. MSN Mobile delivers alerts once or twice a day to cell phone subscribers. Find out if this is available to you by visiting *http://mobile.msn.com/ signup/Signup2.aspx*.

Yahoo! Finance has a very basic alert service for dollar and percentage price increases and declines. If your stock triggers an alert, you'll be notified by email. Although Yahoo! Finance doesn't offer as many types of alerts, choose Yahoo! Finance's alerts to know immediately when a stock price hits its target.

Alerts for a Fee

Morningstar's Portfolio Manager (*http://www.morningstar.com*) offers an outstanding alert system that belongs to their Premium Membership features [Hacks #67 and #77]. If you're interested in several of the premium features, the cost ($12.95 per month, $119 per year, and $199 for two years) might be acceptable to you. You can use a 14-day free trial offer to explore the site and the alerts before you pull out your credit card.

Unlike the free sites, Morningstar offers numerous separate alerts for stocks and funds. Fund investors typically receive short shrift when it comes to alerts, but you might get dizzy at all the fund alerts that Morningstar offers. Table 3-6 summarizes the vast array of alerts for stocks, funds, and your overall portfolio.

Table 3-6. Morningstar alerts

General alerts for stocks	Morningstar-analysis stock alerts	General alerts for funds	Morningstar-analysis fund alerts
Price up/down more than 10%	Change in Stock Grade for Profitability, Financial Health and Growth	Daily news articles	Change in Fund Star Rating
Price up/down 5% or more on heavy volume		Name change	Change in Style Box
	New Analyst Report, Stock Star Rating or Stock Fair Value Estimate	Ticker change	Change in Morningstar Category
Volume more than twice 30-day average		Capital gains distribution	
New 52-week high		Dividend distribution	
New 52-week low		Fund opens/closes to new investments	
Daily news articles		Manager change	
Name change		Expense ratio change	
Ticker change		1- and 3-month return top or bottom 10% of category	
Stock split			
Stock dividend distribution			
Change in this year's or next year's EPS estimate			
Reported EPS beats/ misses estimates for 2nd straight quarter			
Above or below average quarterly revenue growth			

Analyzing Company Fundamentals

Hacks 25-45

If you've ever browsed the financial section at a bookstore, you know there are almost as many theories on how to invest in stocks as there are stocks in which to invest. These stock investing methodologies break down into two camps, *fundamental analysis* and *technical analysis*, which are discussed here and in the next chapter.

Fundamental analysis is the art and science of examining the fundamental measures of a company to identify its underlying strengths and weaknesses. It is financial Darwinism at work, based on the notion that strong companies will survive—and the strongest will thrive. An investor who focuses on fundamentals digs into company financial statements, operating history, competitive pressures, and overall management expertise, as if he were Warren Buffett buying a business outright. (This makes perfect sense, because a shareholder does actually purchase a piece of a company when she buys shares of company stock.) As a fundamental investor, you collect data, research the business, study financial measures, and crunch numbers to amass enough knowledge about a company to develop your own outlook for the future of its stock.

Fundamental investors look for long-term, buy-and-hold stocks for their portfolios—companies that will outperform their peers and the overall market for at least several years—by analyzing three types of criteria: *growth*, *quality*, and *value*.

Investing in Growth

When companies increase their earnings over time, the companies become more valuable. Higher earnings can lead to more assets owned, more money to invest in producing additional growth, higher dividends paid out, and higher shareholders' equity in the company. As the value of a company increases, investors are willing to pay more to own it, so the price of the company's stock increases as well.

Investing in growth companies is easier than you might think. Once you know what to look for, growing companies are easy to recognize and easy to track. With growth companies as investments, you don't have to worry too much about whether the stock market is up or down, where a company is in its business cycle, or whether a company's turnaround strategy is successful. You can review financial performance when a company publishes a new quarterly report every three months to see if it's still on track. As long as the company continues to grow earnings at a healthy pace, its stock price should increase as well.

 Investing in growth companies is not a zero-sum game; as these companies grow, the size of the growth company pie grows larger, which means that every investor who invests in growth companies can make money.

So, what does financial growth look like? When you're looking for investments, a small amount of growth doesn't quite cut it. First, growth companies have to increase their sales and earnings faster than the combined growth of the economy and inflation. The growth companies you want to own also tend to grow faster than most of their industry competitors. Consistency is also good. If a company has grown consistently through thick and thin, it's more likely to weather future storms with equal aplomb. If you don't like the roller coaster at the amusement park, you'll like it even less when it's your money on the ride.

Just like children, companies don't grow at the same pace over the years. When companies are young and offer revolutionary new products with no competition, their growth can be explosive. The problem with these shooting stars is their risk. New technology can transform products from revolutionary to revoltingly passé. Tastes can change. Competition can eat a young company's lunch. And, trying to keep a place at the table can chew through cash flow. As companies expand, their growth usually slows down. Bureaucracy, competition, and the drag of the past all take their toll. However, larger companies also have more resources, and that often means less risk and years of consistent growth—a fundamental investor's dream. Unfortunately, some companies can't keep up with the times. When products and services aren't modernized or rejuvenated, growth can stall or even turn into decline, and that's a clear sign to find another investment. Table 4-1 shows the guidelines suggested by the National Association of Investors Corporation (NAIC) for growth rates for companies of different sizes.

Table 4-1. *Minimum suggested growth rates by company size*

Company size in annual sales	Suggested minimum growth rate
Small, less than $500 million	15 percent
Medium, from $500 million to $5 billion	10 percent
Large, greater than $5 billion	7 percent

Companies can grow their businesses in several ways, such as introducing new products, increasing their share of the market, building new stores, expanding into new territories, or acquiring competitors. Sure, some companies skyrocket to fame with a hot new product, but consumer tastes change as quickly as hemlines. The key to long-term growth is great management—a leadership team able to maintain quality while controlling costs, introduce new products and services without getting stuck with obsolete inventory, and beat the competition no matter how intense.

To choose good growth stocks and monitor their performance, you need to examine the growth rates of financial factors over time. Simple percentages are easy to calculate [Hack #25] and are good for rough estimates. Compound growth rates [Hack #26] take a little more work, but they can help you evaluate both quantity and quality

Starting with Simple Percentages

On October 27, 1997, the Dow Jones Industrial Average fell 554 points, the largest one-day point drop in history, even surpassing the decline on "Black Monday" a decade earlier when the Dow fell 508 points on October 18, 1987. While both tumbles sparked a bit of panic for many investors, was the 1997 plunge worse than that dark day in 1987? Hardly. To get some perspective on both events, consider the percentage change in the Dow's performance for each day. In 1997, that 554-point fall turned out to be a 7 percent decline for the day, whereas in 1987, the 508 point drop cut a whopping 23 percent out of the Dow. Clearly, 1987's "Black Monday" was far worse for investors.

Percentages are just as helpful in many other areas of investment analysis, whether you're calculating the rate of return on an investment, comparing the growth rates of several companies, or considering the performance of your overall portfolio. For example, let's say you bought stock in Amgen at $24 per share and now it's selling for $48 a share. You've doubled your money, and the gain on your investment is easy to calculate—it's 100 percent. Pretty sweet, right?

Before you get too excited about your investment prowess, there's another factor to consider. That 100 percent gain is the *overall appreciation* of the stock's price. It does not take into account the all-important element of *time*. If you bought your Amgen stock last year, doubling your money in roughly twelve months is a largely laudable accomplishment. However, if you bought the stock a decade ago, you might have failed miserably compared to the overall market. As it turns out, Amgen's stock price closed at $8.83 a share in 1992 (adjusted for splits). Ten years later in 2002, the stock ended the year at $48.34 a share, which is an overall appreciation over the decade of 447.5 percent. Over the same period, the Standard & Poor's 500 index increased from 435 to 879, an overall appreciation of only 102.1 percent.

The Value of Compounded Growth

To obtain a measure of stock performance that you can compare to other investments or your investment guidelines, you can calculate the return that you've earned on an *annualized* basis. *Annualized return* is also known as *compounded annual return*, *compound annual growth rate* (CAGR), or *dollar-weighted return*, because it includes the effects of compounding over time on the initial value.

Most likely, you were introduced to compounding when you were first taught how interest is calculated on a bank savings account. The interest rate (APR) advertised by banks is the annual interest rate they pay on the balance in the account. However, the yield (APY) paid by the account is based on keeping your money in the account for a full year without removing any of the interest paid each month. The yield is higher than the interest rate because you earn interest on your deposit as well as on the interest paid by the bank.

A 100 percent increase in a stock's price over ten years comes out to slightly more than 7 percent a year when calculated as CAGR.

Let's use CAGR to evaluate your hypothetical investment in Amgen. On an annualized basis, a 447.5 percent increase over ten years comes out to compounded annual return of 18.5 percent—not too shabby compared to the 7.2 percent annualized growth of the S&P 500 index.

Occasionally, the same method of calculating growth rates is applied to periods shorter than one year. While it can be useful to look at annualized rates of return, these can be wildly inflated if the stock, mutual fund, or other investment has seen a significant short-term fluctuation in one direction or another. If the share price of your new stock popped shortly after your purchase, your annualized rate of return might turn out to be several hundred (or thousand!) percent. However, you would be seriously disappointed if you expected your actual returns for an entire year to be anywhere near that result.

Insisting on Quality

When you invest in companies for the long haul, buying quality is critical. Sure, you might make some fast money buying a dicey company on a hot streak, but it's just as easy to lose most if not all of your original investment if the company runs into trouble. Quality growth companies make for a more relaxed approach to investing—not only can you assume less risk to earn your return, but you spend less time studying stocks because their past performance can be a good indication of what you can expect in the future.

Just as with consumer products, the quality of a company isn't just about numbers. Quality can be the number of skilled executives on the management team, the steady introduction of successful new products, revamping older products for new uses, dealing with problems that arise, and making the most of opportunities.

However, fundamental analysis does use financial measures and ratios to quantify quality. Strong, consistent growth is one good sign of quality. Many companies have turned in one spectacular year of growth, but the pickings are much slimmer when you demand a steady track record of strong growth for five or more years. You can also see quality in the financial strength of a company, the amount of money invested in research and development, steadily increasing profit margins, and above-average return on equity. Depending on the industry, different ratios might hold the key to quality. Regardless of the ratios you evaluate, you want to see trends moving in the right direction and numbers that compare favorably to those of the competition or the industry average.

Buying Good Value

Low price isn't a green light to buy. Low-quality, slow-growth stocks are dogs no matter how little you pay for them. On the other hand, the best-quality growth stocks can bark as well if you pay too much. By buying quality growth stocks at reasonable prices, you're well on your way to investors' nirvana—high returns with moderate risk. Sometimes, finding this magical combination takes time and patience. Simple really—as long as you have some discipline.

If you find a stock you really like but the price is simply too high, all you have to do is watch and wait. Chances are the price will come down. The stock market tends to go through cycles, from the irrational exuberance of the late 1990s, when people would pay hundreds of dollars for a share of stock in a company with no earnings whatsoever, to the irrational fear of the early 2000s, when investors kept their money in money market funds while quality growth companies were selling at almost bargain-basement prices.

Despite what you might have heard about the *efficient market theory*, which says that markets digest all the available information to appropriately price stocks, bonds, and other types of securities, the truth is that in the short term, the stock market overreacts, particularly to bad news. In fact, bad news for one company can drag the prices of its competitors down with it. When you follow a stock and are confident in its future, these quirky price drops become your buying opportunities.

HACK #25 Calculate Percentage Change for Growth and Return

It's basic math, but measuring the percentage change in price for a company is the first step to uncovering future winners.

Growth stock investors want companies that can increase their earnings and sales faster than their competition. To invest in growth stocks, you must be able to identify growth, which means you must be able to quantify the growth companies have generated in the past.

You can calculate the total percentage change in a company's price, earnings per share, revenues, or any other value, over a period of time. The percentage change acts as a quick test of a stock's performance before moving on to slightly more complicated compound growth rate calculations [Hack #26]. For instance, your goal might be to find companies that double their earnings every five years. A 100 percent increase over five years is a compound annual growth rate of approximately 15 percent a year. Example 4-1 shows how to derive this result.

Example 4-1. Comparing a percentage increase to a 15 percent annual growth rate

```
Ending value CAGR (year 1)    = Initial value * 1.15
Ending value CAGR (year 2)    = Ending value (year 1) * 1.15
                              = Initial value * 1.15 * 1.15
                              = Initial value * (1.15 ^ 2)
Ending value CAGR (year 5)    = Initial value * (1.15 ^ 5)
                              = Initial value * 2.0114
Growth factor for five years = (1.15^5) = 2.0114
```

Therefore, instead of calculating the compound annual growth rate right off the bat, calculate in your head whether earnings per share have increased 100 percent (doubled) in the past five years to learn quickly whether it's worth your while to continue your research.

Here's an example. Lincare generated Earnings per Share (EPS) of $.71 in 1997 and $1.73 five years later in 2002. Doubling the $.71 from 1997 results in EPS of $1.42, which is less than Lincare's 2002 EPS of $1.73. Because Lincare's EPS has more than doubled in the last five years, you know that the company has exceeded the 15 percent a year criterion and it makes sense to continue your research.

In addition to EPS, you can calculate the percentage increase of revenues, pre-tax profits, share price, long-term debt, shares outstanding, or dividends. Measuring the changes in these values is key to understanding a company's performance.

Taking Dividends and Commissions into Account

When you're calculating the percentage increase for the value of a stock or even an entire portfolio, you can more accurately estimate the change by considering the value of dividends, commissions, and other sales costs. The commissions and sales costs you pay to buy and sell stocks reduce your return, while the dividends you receive increase it. The formulas in Examples 4-2, 4-3, and 4-4 provide the percentage increase including dividends and sales costs paid for a single investment.

Example 4-2. Initial investment including commission

```
$ Initial Investment = ((# of Shares) * ($ Share Purchase Price))
+ $ Sales Costs
```

Example 4-3. End value including dividends and commissions

```
$ End Value = ((# of Shares) * ($ Current Share Price)) + $ Dividends
- $ Sales Costs
```

Example 4-4. Percentage change with dividends and commissions

```
% Change = ((End Value / Initial Investment) - 1) * 100
```

If you want to calculate growth taking into account the element of time, read "Calculate Compound Annual Rates of Growth" **[Hack #26]** and "Calculate Investment Return Over Different Time Periods" **[Hack #81]**.

—*Douglas Gerlach*

Calculate Compound Annual Rates of Growth

Compound annual growth rates are the key to comparing the growth rates of different investments.

To consider the rate of growth of a value over time, you must determine its *compound annual growth rate* (CAGR), also known as the annualized growth rate, which gives you an idea of how the value changed over the years—not the actual year-to-year changes, but the growth rate as if the value had grown at a consistent rate each year. Whether you use a formula or a built-in Excel function to calculate CAGR, a spreadsheet makes the calculations easy.

Estimating Compounded Annual Growth Rates

Example 4-5 shows the formula for estimating CAGR when you have the values only for the beginning and ending periods in question.

Example 4-5. Formula for estimated CAGR

```
% CAGR = ((Ending Value / Initial Value) ^ ( 1 / # of periods) - 1) * 100
```

This formula isn't much more complicated than the formula for percentage change, but it's a snap to calculate in a spreadsheet. Here's a walkthrough of the calculation:

The caret symbol (^)
> Raises the value to the left (Ending Value / Initial Value) to the power or exponent on the right.

The exponent
> Equals one divided by the number of periods that you're evaluating.

> Make sure to use the number of periods, not the number of years. For example, when you calculate CAGR based on five years of sales, you evaluate only four annual periods. The first year of sales provides the starting point. The remaining four years are the periods you evaluate for growth.

Percentage calculation
> Finally, subtract one to convert the results from an annualized growth factor to an annualized growth rate, and then multiply by 100 to display the result as a percentage. For example, when you have 150 percent of what you started with after one year, the annual growth factor is 150 percent, but the annual growth rate is 50 percent.

CAGR is handy for evaluating many measures on a company's financial statements. If you're looking at growth stocks, knowing how quickly those companies have been able to grow revenues, pre-tax profits, and earnings per share on an annual basis in the past can give you an idea of how well the company might perform in the future. A company with low growth in the past isn't likely to suddenly surge in the next couple of years.

From EdgarScan (*http://edgarscan.pwcglobal.com*), you can download a spreadsheet of historical company data extracted from the company's SEC filings. Eliminate the columns of quarterly data and calculate the compound annual growth rates for selected items, as illustrated by Home Depot growth calculations in Figure 4-1.

oih_04 Home depot growth.xls	A	B	C	D	E	F	G	H
1	HOME DEPOT INC							
2								
3	Filing Period	1997	1998	1999	2000	2001	2002	
4	Filing Type	10-K	10-K	10-K	10-K	10-K	10-K	5-Yr CAGR
5								
6	Income							
7	Total Operating Revenue	$24,156	$30,219	$38,434	$45,738	$53,553	$58,247	17.3%
8	Income Before Tax	$1,898	$2,654	$3,804	$4,217	$4,957	$5,872	21.2%
9	Net Income	$1,160	$1,614	$2,320	$2,581	$3,044	$3,664	21.3%
10	EPS: Diluted	0.52	0.71	1	1.1	1.29	1.56	19.9%

oih_04 HD growth / oih_04 Home depot data

Figure 4-1. CAGR shows the annual growth rate required to increase the initial value to the ending value

The formula in cell H7 for five-year compound annual growth for total operating revenue looks like this:

```
=(F7/B7)^(1/5)-1
```

Use Format → Cells to format the cell as a percentage to one decimal point.

For Home Depot, operating revenues exceed $58 billion a year, so you can see that the company has produced very strong growth in revenues, net income before and after taxes, and earnings per share. Compared to the 7 to 10 percent you might expect for a large company, Home Depot is certainly performing quite well.

Calculating Growth with the LOGEST Function

You can also use the LOGEST function [Hack #35] in Excel to calculate annual growth rates. This function applies the least squares method, so that instead of calculating the growth rate based only on the initial and ending values, it takes into account all the values to provide an annual rate of growth that best fits the historical trend.

In Figure 4-2, the LOGEST function is added to Column I in the compound annual growth rate spreadsheet. The formula in cell I7 is shown in Example 4-6.

Example 4-6. Excel function for growth using LOGEST

```
=LOGEST(B7:G7)-1
```

The formula is copied down the column, and the resulting value is formatted as a percentage to one decimal point.

oih_04 Home depot growth.xls								_	□	X
	A	B	C	D	E	F	G	H	I
1	HOME DEPOT INC								
2									
3	Filing Period	1997	1998	1999	2000	2001	2002		
4	Filing Type	10-K	10-K	10-K	10-K	10-K	10-K	5-Yr CAGR	5-YR CAGR LOGEST
5									
6	Income								
7	Total Operating Revenue	$24,156	$30,219	$38,434	$45,738	$53,553	$58,247	17.3%	19.7%
8	Income Before Tax	$1,898	$2,654	$3,804	$4,217	$4,957	$5,872	21.2%	24.3%
9	Net Income	$1,160	$1,614	$2,320	$2,581	$3,044	$3,664	21.3%	24.8%
10	EPS: Diluted	0.52	0.71	1	1.1	1.29	1.56	19.9%	23.5%

oih_04 HD growth / oih_04 Home depot data

Figure 4-2. The LOGEST function takes annual variations into account when calculating the compound annual growth rate

You can see the variations that come from the use of the LOGEST function to calculate the compound growth rate, such as 24.8 percent growth for net income using LOGEST and 21.3 percent using the estimated formula in Example 4-5. The LOGEST approach is better in that it uses the intermediate values to produce its result. Regardless which method you choose, use it consistently for each stock you compare.

Hacking the Hack

Consistency counts when considering historical growth, which is one element that's not accounted for when calculating annual growth rates by either method. Consider two companies, one whose revenues and earnings fluctuate wildly from year to year and another whose performance is very consistent. The companies might have the same starting and ending values, and thus the same CAGRs—but the less consistent company might be less attractive because its unpredictability might indicate less skilled management or other risks.

Fortunately, there's a way to measure the consistency of a company's past growth [Hack #35]. With a spreadsheet, you can calculate the *R-Squared* (or

R2) *value* of past trends. This statistical measure indicates how closely the historical data would match a straight line if plotted on a chart.

For instance, a company whose earnings grew at exactly the same rate from year to year would have an R-Squared of 1.00. In the real world, this never happens, but many companies turn in stable growth year after year, which you can measure by the R-Squared value of their revenues or earnings. In Figure 4-3, Column J includes the R-Squared values for Home Depot's historical data.

	A	B	C	D	E	F	G	H	I	J
	oih_04 Home depot growth.xls									
1	HOME DEPOT INC									
2										
3	Filing Period	1997	1998	1999	2000	2001	2002			
4	Filing Type	10-K	10-K	10-K	10-K	10-K	10-K	5-Yr CAGR	5-YR CAGR LOGEST	R-squared
5										
6	Income									
7	Total Operating Revenue	$24,156	$30,219	$38,434	$45,738	$53,553	$58,247	17.3%	19.7%	0.98
8	Income Before Tax	$1,898	$2,654	$3,804	$4,217	$4,957	$5,872	21.2%	24.3%	0.95
9	Net Income	$1,160	$1,614	$2,320	$2,581	$3,044	$3,664	21.3%	24.8%	0.96
10	EPS: Diluted	0.52	0.71	1	1.1	1.29	1.56	19.9%	23.5%	0.96

Figure 4-3. Excel's R-Squared function indicates the consistency of numbers

In Excel the LOGEST function returns the R-Squared value for a set of numbers in an array [Hack #35]. The formula in Example 4-7 extracts R-squared from the array. To obtain the array of results, you must enter the formula as an array formula. To do this, type the formula in the Excel formula bar and then press Ctrl-Shift-Enter to complete the entry. Excel adds the braces around the formula to indicate that it is an array formula.

Example 4-7. Excel function for calculating R-Squared

```
={INDEX(LOGEST(B7:G7,,,TRUE),3)}
```

In Home Depot's case, the R-Squared results are between .95 or .98, which shows that the company's performance has been remarkably consistent over the five years evaluated.

> Some investors reject companies whose EPS R-Squared values are below 0.90 with the rationale that these companies have not been consistent enough to provide confidence in their future performance.

If you choose to display data in a chart [Hack #13], you can add a trendline calculated by the least squares method and display the R-Squared value [Hack #35].

See Also

You can find online CAGR calculators at the following sites:

- MoneyChimp.com at *http://www.moneychimp.com/calculator/discount_rate_calculator.htm*
- CPAdvantage.com at *http://www.cpadvantage.com/onlinefinancialcalculators/cagrcalculation.aspx?LNC=_4_2* also calculates CAGR, but the user interface isn't as simple as MoneyChimp's

—Douglas Gerlach

HACK #27 Calculate Price and Dividend Ratios

Calculate price and dividend ratios to help you figure out the current value of a stock.

Of all the ratios used in stock valuation, probably none is as popular as the *price/earnings ratio* (sometimes known as the P/E ratio or *multiple*). The P/E ratio compares the current price of a stock to the amount of money the company has earned. One interpretation of the P/E ratio is the measure of how much investors are willing to pay for each dollar of earnings the company generates. Not only does it help you judge whether a stock's price is reasonable, it can indicate the confidence investors have in a company's future. The more investors are willing to pay for a dollar of earnings, the higher their expectations for future performance. If investors won't pay much for a dollar of earnings, they have little confidence in the company. The P/E ratio is calculated with the formula in Example 4-8.

Example 4-8. Formula for a basic P/E ratio

```
P/E Ratio = $ Current Share Price / $ Current Annual EPS
```

You can use a P/E ratio in your stock analysis in a couple of ways. First, you can compare the P/E ratios of two or more similar stocks to determine which stock is a better value. You can also use the P/E ratio as a proxy for a stock's value. You can't directly compare the prices of stocks. Is a $32 share of Intel stock really more expensive than a $27 share of Microsoft? However, if you compare the P/E ratios of both companies, you can see whether you'd have to pay a premium for one or the other. For example, at $32 a share, Intel's P/E ratio is about 45. Microsoft at $27 sports a P/E ratio of 29. Both stocks carry high P/E ratios, but in this example, Intel is quite a bit more expensive than Microsoft.

P/E ratios can vary greatly by industry (banks often trade at lower P/E ratios than other industries, for instance), size of company (a larger company might have a lower P/E ratio than a similar but smaller business because it's easier for the smaller company to produce faster growth in the future), and reputation (popular, stable companies often command a premium P/E ratio in the marketplace).

You can also use the P/E ratio of a stock to determine if the current price of a company is reasonable based on its history. By comparing the current P/E ratio to the stock's average, average high, and average low P/E ratios of the past few years as demonstrated in Figure 4-4, you can see whether the stock is a bargain or overpriced. If the stock has sold usually at a P/E ratio of 35 in the past and now sells for a multiple of 28, it might be undervalued or the lower P/E ratio could be a red flag. P/E ratios drop for two reasons: either company earnings are growing faster than the stock price or investors are paying less for the stock for some reason. For example, they might be concerned about the effect of government regulations on future earnings. Do your research to determine why the P/E ratio has changed.

	A	B	C	D	E	F	G	H
60		PRICE/EARNINGS	Hi Price	Lo Price	EPS	Hi P/E	Lo P/E	Avg P/E
61		1992	16.47	12.53	0.44	37.9	28.8	33.3
62		1993	17.06	11.50	0.51	33.5	22.5	28.0
63		1994	14.63	10.25	0.59	25.0	17.5	21.3
64		1995	13.81	9.56	0.60	23.2	16.1	19.6
65		1996	14.13	10.06	0.67	21.2	15.1	18.2
66		1997	20.97	11.50	0.78	26.9	14.7	20.8
67		1998	43.22	20.09	0.99	43.7	20.3	32.0
68		1999	70.25	38.88	1.28	54.9	30.4	42.6
69		2000	64.94	41.44	1.40	46.4	29.6	38.0
70		2001	59.98	41.50	1.49	40.3	27.9	34.1
71		10-YR AVERAGE	20.73			35.3	22.3	28.8
72		5-YR AVERAGE	30.68			42.4	24.6	33.5

Figure 4-4. A company's P/E ratio history in a spreadsheet

Column F in the Excel spreadsheet in Figure 4-4 calculates a company's high P/E ratios for the last ten years by dividing a year's high price (column C) by the company's EPS (column E) for that year. For example, Example 4-9 shows the Excel formula for cell F61, the 1992 high P/E ratio.

Example 4-9. Excel function for calculating a high P/E ratio

```
High P/E Ratio (cell F61) = IF(E61<=0,"n/a",C61/E61)
```

The formula uses a conditional clause to ignore the calculation when the company has zero or negative EPS figures. When a company has no earnings or loses money, the resulting P/E ratio is meaningless and doesn't offer any help in valuing the company. The low P/E ratios in column G are calculated in the same way.

Column H uses the annual high and low P/E ratios to determine an average annual P/E ratio, as shown in Example 4-10.

Example 4-10. Excel function for calculating an average P/E ratio

```
=IF(E61<=0,"n/a",AVERAGE(F61:G61))
```

You can calculate average high and low P/E ratios for multiple years to spot longer-term trends, too. The spreadsheet in Figure 4-4 contains five- and ten-year averages. The ten-year average uses the function in Example 4-11.

Example 4-11. Excel function for calculating ten-year average high P/E ratio

```
=AVERAGE(F61:F70)
```

You can quickly scan the columns to identify trends in a stock's P/E ratios: are they stable, increasing, or declining? Investigate the causes of any changes. For example, is tough competition cutting into the company's profit margins and resulting in lower earnings growth? Although lower earnings increase the P/E ratio if the price stays the same, you'll rarely find the price unchanged for long when earnings growth slows or declines.

You can compare the current P/E ratio to the historical trends and averages [Hack #36], and gain a better sense of whether the stock is over- or undervalued at its current price. For example, when the current P/E ratio is higher than the average as shown in Figure 4-4, you're paying a premium for the stock. You must be particularly careful when P/E ratios trend down. That's often a sign that the price is dropping, and you don't want to buy as the price continues to fall.

Dividend and Yield

The true measure of a publicly traded company's success will always be the profits it earns through the years. By reinvesting these profits back into its business, a company funds further expansion without the need to borrow money or sell additional shares to the public. For mature companies, however, there can come a time when management simply can't find enough uses for all of the money it earns each year. A company might then decide to start paying out a portion of these profits to investors as *dividends*.

A regular stream of dividend payments is important to investors who depend on their portfolios to deliver current income on which they can live. That's why stocks that pay high dividends are sometimes known as *income stocks*. For other investors, a dividend contributes to the overall return they receive from their investment and adds some security to the investment as well.

Analyzing the dividends that are paid by two different companies isn't as easy as figuring out how much each will pay to investors in a year. You need the market value of each stock to determine the *dividend yield*. The dividend yield is useful when comparing two or more stocks, but you can also use it to compare an investment to what you might earn in interest in a bank account or to the yield on a bond. Example 4-12 shows the formula for the yield represented by dividends paid.

Example 4-12. Formula for the yield represented by dividends paid

```
% Dividend Yield = ($ Annual Dividend Paid  / $ Market Value per share) * 100
```

A stock's yield is usually calculated using its *indicated dividend*, the total that would be paid per share over the next 12 months if each dividend were the same as the most recent dividend.

> A stock's dividend yield does not include the return you receive from the increase in stock price. Comparing dividend yield to bond or bank account yields makes the most sense for high-dividend stocks whose prices tend to be stable.

The Payout Ratio

Since dividends are, by definition, a portion of a company's profits that are paid to its shareholders, what happens to the dividend when a company earns fewer profits or even begins to lose money? Eventually, the company will have to stop paying dividends—a decision that is not popular with investors who might be counting on those regular cash payments. On the other hand, a company might pay too much of its income as dividends, leaving it with inadequate working capital to expand its business, pay down debt, or invest in other ways that might greatly benefit the company.

One way to examine a company's dividend policy is to calculate its *payout ratio*. The payout ratio is the amount of the company's annual earnings that is paid out as dividends to its investors. You can calculate it with the formula in Example 4-13.

Example 4-13. Formula for the payout ratio

```
% Payout Ratio = ($ Annual Dividend / $ Annual EPS) x 100
```

Most companies are quite concerned with protecting their dividends, because canceling or reducing dividend payments is never well received by shareholders. In addition, shareholders often pressure companies to increase their dividends on a regular basis. Many companies take pride in the number of years that they have regularly paid dividends to shareholders, as well as how often they have been able to increase those payments. Investors tend to interpret this historical record as a sign that a company is stable and safe.

The payout ratio can help you understand just how safe a company's dividend might be. High payout ratios are double-edged swords. For investors seeking current income, a consistently high payout ratio means more money to live on. In addition, a long history of paying steadily increasing dividends is often a sign of quality management and dependable performance. However, a company with a high payout ratio doesn't retain much of its earnings to grow its business, so the dividend might represent most, if not all, of the return you earn. Therefore, for younger investors who want to grow their portfolios, a high payout ratio might not be beneficial. High payout ratios can also lead to financial problems, if the company doesn't retain enough of its earnings to operate effectively.

High payout ratios are fine in industries that don't require a lot of additional capital. However, companies like Intel, which spends billions of dollars to build just one new plant, or Pfizer, which spends over $5 billion a year in research and development, require plenty of money to grow their businesses, and paying out a lot of dividends is detrimental.

> Because different industries have different capital requirements, it's a good idea to compare the payout ratio of a company to the industry average. If a company payout ratio is below average, investigate further to see if that is an indication of problems or that the company has investment plans. For high payout ratios, check financial strength ratios very carefully to make sure the company can afford to pay out that much of its earnings.

Dividend payout ratios can increase when company earnings fall. If you see the payout ratio increasing from year to year as earnings decrease, don't be surprised if the company slashes its dividends. If the payout ratio is over 100 percent, annual net income isn't enough to cover the total cost of dividends in that year. In that situation, companies must come up with the cash in some other way, such as borrowing from the bank or tapping into their own reserves. A company might do this to maintain its dividend payment record during a short dry spell, but over time, of course, a company simply can't continue to pay dividends if the cost exceeds what it earns in a year.

The Excel spreadsheet in Figure 4-5 continues the price and dividend ratio study by calculating the payout ratio and yield. To calculate the payout ratio, use the following formula in cell J61:

```
=IF(E61<=0,"n/a",I61/E61)
```

The IF clause makes sure that the EPS are positive. If a company is losing money, its dividends might be reduced down the road. You should do more homework to evaluate the cause and scope of the company's problems.

	A	B	C	D	E	I	J	K
60		PRICE/EARNINGS	Hi Price	Lo Price	EPS	Div	% Payout	% Hi Yield
61		1992	16.47	12.53	0.44	0.05	12.0%	0.4%
62		1993	17.06	11.50	0.51	0.07	12.7%	0.6%
63		1994	14.63	10.25	0.59	0.09	14.5%	0.8%
64		1995	13.81	9.56	0.60	0.10	16.8%	1.0%
65		1996	14.13	10.06	0.67	0.11	15.8%	1.0%
66		1997	20.97	11.50	0.78	0.14	17.3%	1.2%
67		1998	43.22	20.09	0.99	0.16	15.7%	0.8%
68		1999	70.25	38.88	1.28	0.20	15.6%	0.5%
69		2000	64.94	41.44	1.40	0.24	17.1%	0.6%
70		2001	59.98	41.50	1.49	0.28	18.8%	0.7%
71		10-YR AVERAGE	20.73				15.6%	
72		5-YR AVERAGE	30.68				16.9%	

Figure 4-5. Calculate yield and payout ratios in a spreadsheet

If you examine the company's annual payout ratio over several years, you can spot negative trends, such as increasing payout ratios from decreasing earnings that could forebode a coming crisis in the company's operations. You can also calculate an average payout ratio over five years to estimate how much a company might pay in dividends in the future.

Going Beyond the P/E Ratio

Because there are several flavors of earnings per share [Hack #15] (such as excluding extraordinary items, as reported, and normalized), make sure you know what kind of EPS figures are used to calculate a P/E ratio, particularly when comparing several companies.

The P/E ratio is calculated using earnings from the last four reported quarters. These *trailing* earnings are indicated with *TTM*, which stands for *trailing twelve months*. Some data providers calculate P/E ratios using EPS from the last two reported quarters plus the projections for the next two quarters. The *projected P/E ratio* uses estimated EPS for the next four quarters. The projected P/E ratio is helpful when you evaluate companies with very high EPS growth rates, because current P/E ratios for fast-growing companies are almost always high. The projected P/E ratio compares the current price, which typically incorporates expectations of future earnings, with those future earnings.

After you've determined the annual P/E ratio for the last five or ten years, you can refine your analysis with one additional calculation. *Relative value* (RV) is the ratio of what investors are paying today for a stock compared to what they have paid on average in the past. Relative value is calculated with the formula in Example 4-14.

Example 4-14. Formula for relative value

```
% Relative Value = (Current P/E Ratio / Average P/E Ratio) * 100
```

Relative value is expressed as a percentage. Generally, a stock with a relative value less than 100 percent is undervalued; if RV is much greater than 100 percent, a stock is probably overvalued. Most long-term investors consider a relative value between 90 percent and 110 percent as an indication of fair value. If RV is much less than 70 percent, the company might be going through a tough patch, and investors have bid down the share price because of their reduced expectations. In this case, the very low RV is a signal of trouble, not of a bargain price. However, by 2002 and 2003, many good companies carried RVs below 70 percent, because investors were being careful on account of the ongoing bear market.

Conversely, when RV is above 150 percent, investors are paying a significant premium for a stock. This can indicate that the stock has reached a price peak, and the only direction it can go from there is down. For companies with below-average growth rates, selling might be in order. However, for higher-growth companies, an RV of 150 is quite common.

One last wrinkle: you can also calculate projected relative value by substituting the projected P/E ratio for the current P/E in the relative value calculation in Example 4-14. This can be useful in comparing several stocks when analysts and investors see weakness in the next year for a particular company or industry.

Viewing Price and Dividend Ratios and Trends

With P/E ratios and dividend ratios, the more you compare, the better you can evaluate the current value of stock price. Comparing the current P/E ratio to historical values, P/E ratios of other companies, or average P/E ratios for the industry can indicate whether a stock is overpriced. Comparing dividend yields and payout ratios to those of other companies or the industry average can help you determine whether the ratios are signs of safety or trouble. You can compare ratios and view historical trends on several web sites. Each one has its own benefits, so you might choose to use one or all in your stock studies.

Historical price and dividend charts. With   BigCharts   (*http://bigcharts. marketwatch.com*), you can create charts that show historical prices, P/E ratios, dividends, and yields, as shown in Figure 4-6. For example, Home Depot's P/E ratio has cycled from values below 20 to as high as 75 twice in the past 25 years.

Type a ticker symbol in the Symbol box at the top of the page and click Interactive Charting.

1. In the Time drop-down list, choose All Data.
2. In the Frequency drop-down list, choose Monthly.

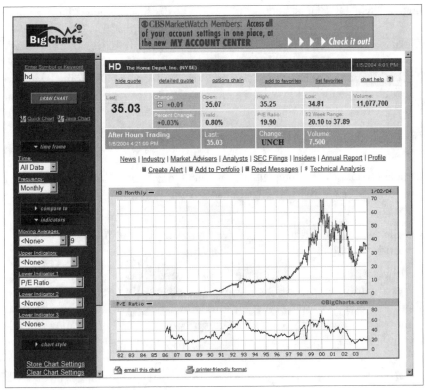

Figure 4-6. Using BigChart's interactive charting, you can see the historical variation in Home Depot's P/E ratio

3. Click the Indicators button.

4. In the Lower Indicators boxes, choose one of the following measures:

    P/E Ratio
    Displays the P/E ratio calculated using the rolling 52-week EPS

    P/E Ranges
    Shows high and low P/E ratios for the period you choose in the Frequency list

    Rolling Dividends
    Displays the rolling 52-week dividend as dollars per share

    Yield
    Shows yield calculated by dividing the 52-week rolling dividend by the stock closing price and multiplying by 100

5. Click the Draw Chart button.

Comparing historical price ratios. At Morningstar (*http://www.morningstar. com*), you can compare current and ten years of historical P/E ratios as well as three other stock valuation ratios: price/book, price/sales, and price/cash flow. The table also includes the valuation ratios for the S&P 500 index. Type a ticker symbol in the Ticker box on the Morningstar home page and then select the Valuation Ratios tab on the stock page. To see ten years of ratios, select the 10-Yr Valuation tab above the table. Select the Yields tab to see a graph of the earnings and dividend yield for the stock compared to other yields, such as the 30-year T-bond yield.

Comparing ratios to the competition. Quicken.com (*http://www.quicken.com*) provides an easy way to compare all sorts of financial measures and ratios to the competition.

On the Quicken.com home page, type a ticker symbol in the Enter Symbol box and click Go.

On the stock page, click Compare to Industry. You can check the checkboxes for the competitors you want to evaluate or type additional ticker symbols (separated by commas) in the "Enter tickers of the companies you want to compare" box. The table of competitors includes the market capitalization for each company, so you can choose competitors of similar size.

To add an index to the comparison, find its ticker symbol by clicking the "Don't know the symbol" link. Select the Index option, type **Index** in the Name box, and then click Search. You can cut one of the symbols from the Quicken Ticker Search window and paste it in the box on the "Compare to industries" page.

Under the Choose Information to Display heading, select the Fundamentals option. Click Compare. For each category of measures, Quicken.com displays a row for each company and index you chose with several measures in each row.

—*Douglas Gerlach*

Calculate Additional Valuation Ratios

Finding good companies is only half the battle; buying them at the right price is the other. A number of valuation ratios help you figure out if the price is right.

Although the P/E ratio can help you determine a stock's value, it can sometimes be misleading, particularly for companies that have recently issued a warning about their future earnings. Investors might have bid down the price of the stock based on those lowered expectations, resulting in an abnormally low P/E ratio for that company. In such a case, a low P/E ratio doesn't reflect the true value of the company based on its future growth. On the other hand, companies that grow very quickly often have extraordinarily high P/E ratios. However, if those companies can continue to grow at the same pace, the rapid increase in earnings over time brings those P/E ratios back to more common values. Other valuation ratios can confirm or challenge the value shown by the P/E ratio.

P/E to Growth Ratio

The *P/E to growth ratio* (PEG) is an indication of whether a company's growth can support the high P/E ratio that the stock price carries. The PEG ratio, shown in Example 4-15, compares a stock's current P/E ratio to its expected future EPS growth rate.

Example 4-15. Formula for the PEG ratio

```
PEG Ratio = (P/E Ratio) / % EPS Growth Rate
```

For long-term investors, it's best to look at EPS growth rate estimates as far in the future as possible. For example, you can find five-year analyst EPS estimates at Yahoo! Finance (*http://finance.yahoo.com*), Quicken.com (*http://www.quicken.com*), NAIC's Online Premium Services datafiles (*http://www.better-investing.org*), and MSN Money (*http://www.money.msn.com*), which is shown in Figure 4-7.

The rule of thumb for PEG ratios is that a stock with a PEG of 1.0 is reasonably valued—its P/E ratio is the same as its EPS growth rate. A company with a PEG of 0.5 is potentially a real bargain, while a PEG of more than 1.5 is getting into nosebleed territory on the valuation map.

Screening for stocks with low PEG ratios is a common technique for turning up potentially undervalued stocks. To learn more about screening and online screening tools, see Chapter 1.

As with most financial measures, there are a few caveats when applying the PEG ratio. It doesn't work well when you're evaluating industries valued on their assets and not their operations; these include financial institutions, real estate operations, airlines, and oil drillers. For companies in industries such as these, the price/book value ratio is helpful.

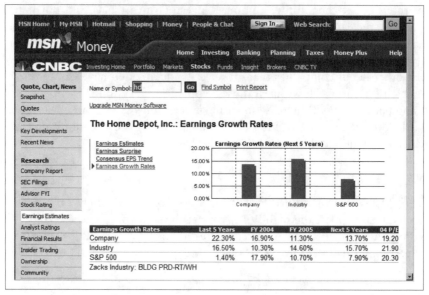

Figure 4-7. MSN Money provides analyst earnings estimates for the next one to five years

Price/Book Value Ratio

The *price/book value ratio,* also know as the price/book ratio, is one of the oldest analysis ratios used by investors and analysts. Popularized by Benjamin Graham in the years following the 1929 stock market crash, and later championed by his disciple Warren Buffett, the price/book ratio is the keystone of the *value approach* to the stock market.

The logic behind evaluating the price/book ratio is straightforward. Accounting practices are conservative when it comes to depreciating assets such as real estate on a company's ledgers. As a result, an established company might own property worth millions on the market but include that same property on its books on a fully depreciated basis with a value of $0. This hidden value means that a company with a low price/book ratio might be purchased for less than the total net worth of the company's assets.

Book value is also known as shareholders' equity, which is found at the bottom of a company's balance sheet. For an explanation of a balance sheet, read the introduction to Chapter 3. However, when investors speak of book value, they usually mean book value per share, which is nothing more than shareholders' equity divided by the number of shares outstanding. Historical book value/share is often included in analyst reports such as S&P Reports and on sites such as MSN Money.

Before you apply the price/book ratio, you must calculate *book value*, which in simple terms is the net worth of a company. Example 4-16 shows the formula to calculate book value.

Example 4-16. Formula for book value

```
Book Value = Total Assets - Total Liabilities
```

In its 2002 10 K filing to the SEC, Amgen reported total shareholders' equity of $18,286 million and 1289.1 million shares outstanding, so its book value per share at the end of 2002 was $14.18.

After you isolate book value per share, you can calculate the price/book ratio using the formula in Example 4-17.

Example 4-17. Formula for price/book ratio

```
Price/Book Ratio = $ Current Price / $ Book Value per Share
```

At year-end 2002, Amgen's stock closed at $48.34, so its price/book ratio was 3.4, close to the average price/book ratio of the S&P 500 of around 3.0.

When the price/book ratio is less than one, the share price for the stock is less than the book value for one share, which means you can purchase the company for less than its net worth. Some value investors consider a price/book ratio less than two as an undervalued opportunity.

Price/book ratios vary by industry. Today, many high-tech companies can generate hefty profit margins without lots of hard assets and factories (think Microsoft), and thus their book values are comparatively low. Although price/book ratios for manufacturing firms and utilities are higher than those of some high-tech companies, this doesn't mean that these companies are overvalued. You can compare a company's price/book ratio and other ratios to industry averages and market indexes at MSN Money (*http://money.msn.com*), as shown in Figure 4-8.

Price/Sales Ratio

You can use the *price/sales ratio* (PSR) as another way to look at a stock's value. PSR is particularly useful for companies that don't have any earnings (though you must always be extra careful when considering these emerging, speculative investments). The recent spate of accounting irregularities and write-offs has raised investors' awareness of how companies manipulate their reported earnings to present them in the most favorable light. The price/sales ratio provides a baseline for comparing companies with volatile or cyclical earnings, or whose management has made significant adjustments to reported earnings.

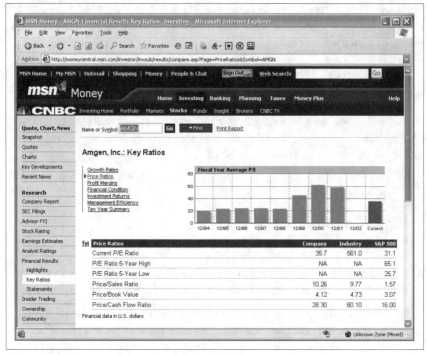

Figure 4-8. Compare a company's valuation ratios at MSN Money

Calculate the PSR using the formula in Example 4-18.

Example 4-18. Formula for price/sales ratio using per share values

```
Price/Sales Ratio = $ Current Price / $ Sales per Share
```

It's unusual to find sales per share in data sources, so you'll probably have to calculate it yourself by dividing the company's sales from the last four quarters by the number of outstanding shares at the end of the last quarter.

Because it's usually easier to find a stock's market capitalization, which is equal to the share price multiplied by the number of shares outstanding, you can also calculate the PSR, as shown in Example 4-19.

Example 4-19. Formula for price/sales ratio using market capitalization

```
Price/Sales Ratio = Market Cap / Sales in Last 4 Quarters
```

Now that you know a company's price/sales ratio, what do you do with it? For companies without earnings, the P/E ratio is useless, so you can use the

PSR as a substitute when comparing a stock to its peers or to an industry average. During economic down cycles, you can look for companies with comparatively low PSRs in cyclical industries, such as heavy equipment manufacturers or automobile makers, hoping that those companies can increase sales when the economy kicks back into gear.

You can also compare a company's current PSR to its historical trends. Using data that EdgarScan (*http://edgarscan.pwcglobal.com*) extracts from a company's financial statements [Hack #18], along with closing prices from Yahoo! Finance (*http://finance.yahoo.com*), you can calculate the PSR for several years. A typical formula for PSR in cell E5 of Figure 4-9 is straightforward, as shown in Example 4-20.

Example 4-20. Excel function for PSR

```
=E2/(E3/E4)
```

The spreadsheet in Figure 4-9 includes data for Amgen for the past ten years and the calculated price/sales ratio based on closing prices for each year. With this history, you can evaluate the company's current PSR and see where it falls in terms of past trends. Keep in mind that the PSR of a company fluctuates during the year just like the P/E ratio does, so you might want to calculate the PSR based on annual high and low prices, or using trailing four quarter revenues to get a more complete picture of changes throughout the year.

	A	B	C	D	E	F	G	H	I	J	K
1	Filing Period	1993	1994	1995	1996	1997	1998	1999	2002	2001	2002
2	Annual Closing Price	$ 6.19	$ 7.37	$ 14.84	$ 13.59	$ 13.53	$ 26.14	$ 60.06	$ 63.94	$ 56.44	$ 48.34
3	Sales (Millions)	$1,374	$1,648	$1,940	$2,240	$2,401	$2,718	$3,340	$3,629	$4,016	$5,523
4	Shares Outst. (Millions)	1073.712	1058.624	1062.8	1058.8	1033.2	1018.4	1017.9	1037.4	1045.8	1289.1
5	Price-Sales Ratio	4.8	4.7	8.1	6.4	5.8	9.8	18.3	18.3	14.7	11.3

Figure 4-9. Calculating price to sales ratio in a spreadsheet

In reviewing Amgen's PSR trends over the past decade, you can see that the PSR rose from 4.8 at the end of 1993 to a peak of 18.3 in 1999 and 2000, and then began to decline to 11.3 at year-end 2002. Is this a significant downward trend?

To examine the company's PSR more closely, surf over to MSN Money (*http://money.msn.com*) and check Amgen's Key Ratios. Type the ticker (AMGN) in the Symbol box and click Go. In the left margin, click Financial Results, click Key Ratios, and then click Price Ratios. As shown in Figure 4-8, the average PSR for the S&P 500 is 1.5, while Amgen and the biotech industry values are 10. That makes sense, because investors are expecting great things in the future from this relatively new business of biotechnology, even though many of these firms aren't yet producing much in the way of sales or profits. Amgen's decline in PSR actually brings it closer to the average PSR of its peers, so it might not be a warning sign, but merely the result of a maturing company and industry.

> The price/sales ratio can help in screening for undervalued opportunities. Although PSRs do vary by industry, searching for stocks with PSRs below 1.0 might tip you off to companies that have been overlooked by the market. You can also create stock screens that look for ratios that compare favorably to industry average ratios. To learn more about stock screening, see Chapter 1.

Price/Cash Flow Ratio

In the wake of accounting scandals that have toppled companies such as Enron and WorldCom [Hack #39], cash flow analysis has become much more popular among investors. Like the price/sales ratio, the *price/cash flow ratio* helps you to examine companies without worrying about how they might have manipulated net earnings.

Cash flow is tricky to understand, so let's start with one common definition. Cash flow is the money that's left from revenues after the company has paid the direct costs of manufacturing its goods or providing its services. It's often referred to as its *operating profit* or *EBITDA*, which stands for Earnings Before Interest, Taxes, Depreciation, and Amortization. On income statements, described in Chapter 3, companies subtract their expenses from their revenue to calculate their net income. The net income number at the bottom of the income statement appears as the first entry in the cash flow statement, labeled as "Cash flows from operating activities."

You'll need to calculate cash flow per share before you can determine the price/cash flow ratio. Divide the cash flow at the end of a period by the number of outstanding shares, and then calculate the price/cash flow ratio, as shown in Example 4-21.

Example 4-21. Formula for price/cash flow ratio

    Price/Cash Flow Ratio = Price per Share / Cash Flow per Share

The price/cash flow ratio is most often used to compare a stock to its industry or to the market in general. Because depreciation is a noncash expense that lowers earnings, the price/cash flow ratio can be particularly useful in examining industries with huge depreciation expenses, such as the cable television industry, as well as cyclical industries, such as paper mills, steel manufacturers, and automakers. If a stock's price/cash flow ratio is lower than the industry average, the stock might be selling at a discount to its competition.

When screening, a price/cash flow ratio of less than 20 is a good starting threshold.

MSN Money provides the current price/cash flow ratio for a company along with averages for industries and the S&P 500 index, as illustrated in Figure 4-8.

Hacking the Hack

Some companies carry a large amount of intangible assets on their books. These intangible assets include goodwill (the premium paid by a purchaser when acquiring another company) and the value of patents and trademarks. Because it's often difficult to determine the true value of that kind of property, despite what the company reports in its financials, some investors prefer to consider *price/tangible book value* in place of price/book value when analyzing stocks. Tangible book value excludes assets, such as patents, trademarks, and goodwill.

The value of intangible assets at some companies is obviously quite significant, as in the case of the brand name of Coca-Cola, but for other companies, it can be difficult to put numbers on those assets. In its July 2002 bankruptcy filing, WorldCom claimed that it had assets of $104 billion, nearly half of which was goodwill, and the value of its intangible assets, such as brand names and customers. Many financial experts disputed those figures: there was no way that WorldCom's goodwill could possibly be worth $45 billion. By March of the following year, the company finally agreed, and its revised financial statements eliminated goodwill altogether—a whopping $45 billion of so-called assets down the drain. Those analysts who focused on the book value of tangible assets weren't surprised to see the write-down, which makes a good case for using tangible book value.

Some data sources, such as Standard & Poor's Stock Reports, provide tangible book value/share. Others, such as Media General Financial Services, who provide data to Quicken.com and other sites, remove intangibles from their calculation of book value but don't explicitly label it as such.

The bottom line is that it's a good idea when you compare companies to obtain data for each company from the same data source. If you use data from different sources, make sure you know how the data providers calculate ratios so that you don't make invalid apples-to-oranges comparisons.

See Also

- Morningstar, "Using the Price/Sales Ratio" (*http://news.morningstar. com/news/Ms/Stocks101/991202s101.html*)

- Morningstar, "Going by the Book" (*http://news.morningstar.com/news/ MS/Stocks101/bookvalue.html*)

- Motley Fool, "Introduction to Valuation" (*http://www.fool.com/School/ IntroductionToValuation.htm*)

- Smart Money, "Digging into the Numbers" (*http://university.smart-money.com/departments/strategicinvesting/stockpicking/index. cfm?story=digging*)

—Douglas Gerlach

Calculate Financial Strength Ratios

Examine a company's financial strength to avoid the 98-pound weaklings that can wreck your portfolio performance.

Examining a company's financial statements isn't a lot of fun (unless you're an accountant or attorney general), but there's plenty of worthwhile information to be derived from a closer look at the balance sheet and income statement. There's no need for a lot of number crunching, though—a handful of ratios can give you a good snapshot of a company's fiscal fitness.

Current Ratio

The most common test of a company's financial strength is its *current ratio* (also called the *working capital ratio*). The current ratio, shown in Example 4-22, assesses a company's ability to pay off debts that are due in the next twelve months from readily available assets, including cash on hand, accounts receivable, and inventory.

Example 4-22. Formula for the current ratio

```
Current Ratio = Current Assets / Current Liabilities
```

Current assets and liabilities come from a company's balance sheet, which is a financial statement required for each quarterly and annual SEC filing. Be sure to use Total Current Assets and Total Current Liabilities, not Total Assets and Total Liabilities, which include illiquid assets, such as plants and equipment, and long-term debt. Figure 4-10 calculates the current ratio using the balance sheet entries for current assets and liabilities.

Current ratios can vary significantly by industry, but acceptable values usually range from 2.0 to 7.0 for a typical manufacturing company. This means

	A	B
1	Current Assets:	
2	Cash and cash equivalents	$1,078,907,000
3	Investment securities	$94,881,000
4	Total inventories	$2,724,783,000
5	Prepaid expenses, deferred income taxes, & other receivables	$2,982,049,000
6	**Total Current Assets**	**$9,714,796,000**
7		
8	Current Liabilities:	
9	Short-term borrowings	$1,616,563,000
10	Trade accounts payable	$1,487,956,000
11	Salaries, dividends payable, and other accruals	$3,947,385,000
12	Income taxes payable	$69,696,000
13	Current portion of long-term debt	$211,557,000
14	**Total Current Liabilities**	**$7,333,157,000**
15		
16	**Current Ratio**	**1.32**
17	**Quick Ratio**	**0.95**

Figure 4-10. Calculating the Current Ratio and Quick Ratio in a spreadsheet

that companies have current assets somewhere between two and seven times their current liabilities, and shouldn't have any problems paying their bills if business drops off for a short period.

A current ratio below 1.5 could be a red flag that a company might face liquidity problems in the coming months. For example, if unexpected expenses arise or revenue drops, a company might have to borrow money or sell longer-term assets to pay the bills. If the current ratio is below 1.0, the company has *negative working capital*, which is usually a bad sign.

These rules of thumb don't apply to companies in industries that operate primarily on a cash basis with low levels of inventories and accounts receivable. For instance, the reported inventory at a restaurant chain such as McDonald's or retailers such as Wal-Mart or Amazon is usually quite low. These companies convert their inventories to cash quickly—sometimes even before they pay their suppliers. To these companies, selling their inventory before they've paid for it is like an interest-free source of capital. A low current ratio is a sign that these companies are operating at a high level of efficiency. Table 4-2 shows current ratios for companies in several industries.

Table 4-2. Current ratios vary by industry

Company	Industry	Current ratio
Microsoft	Software	4.0
Pfizer	Pharmaceuticals	1.5
Walmart	Retail	0.9

Table 4-2. Current ratios vary by industry (continued)

Company	Industry	Current ratio
Consolidated Edison	Utility	0.9
General Motors	Auto manufacturing	2.7

A downward trend in the current ratio can indicate that a company's balance sheet is deteriorating. You can compare the current ratio over a few years to watch for signs of trouble.

Quick Ratio

Because it can take some time for companies to convert warehouses full of goods into cash, you can use a more stringent test to measure a company's financial strength by using current assets minus inventories. The *quick ratio* (sometimes known as the *acid test* or *liquidity test*) reveals how well companies can generate cold cash in a short amount of time, and is calculated using the formula in Example 4-23.

Example 4-23. Formula for the quick ratio

```
Quick Ratio = (Current Assets - Inventory) / Current Liabilities
```

In Figure 4-10, the quick ratio in cell B17 is calculated by subtracting the Total Inventories in cell B4 from the Total Current Assets in B6, and then dividing the result by the Total Current Liabilities in cell B14, as shown in Example 4-24.

Example 4-24. Excel function for calculating a quick ratio

```
=(B6-B4)/B14
```

As with the current ratio, the quick ratio isn't really applicable to cash-based businesses. For most other companies, the quick ratio should usually be greater than 1.0, and the higher, the better (although the average will vary by industry).

Of course, moderation is valuable in business. An excessively high current and quick ratio might mean that a company is keeping too much money in short-term assets when it could be using it in other ways to grow the business and improve returns to shareholders.

Debt-to-Equity Ratio

There are several ways that a public company can raise cash to expand and grow its business. It can sell shares of stock, issue bonds with a promise of repayment somewhere down the road (and paying interest along the way), or it can borrow money directly from a bank or other financial institution. Each method has its advantages and disadvantages, so company management has to decide how best to raise the working capital they need to achieve their business objectives.

For instance, company debt, whether bonds or bank loans, always has to be repaid along with interest on the outstanding principal. If a company can borrow money at 8 percent, invest those funds in expanding their operations, and generate a return of 12 percent on the investment, the company comes out ahead. They have successfully *leveraged* their debt to grow faster than they otherwise would have been able to.

But what happens if a company can't generate a rate of return on the borrowed money equal to the interest rate on the debt? Or, business deteriorates and the company has trouble covering its interest payments? In these situations, companies might have to cut costs to the detriment of further growth or take resources away from business operations to pay interest and pay back principal. Either way, the debt decreases growth instead of increasing it.

For these reasons, investors should evaluate a company's total debt and determine whether it can successfully manage its debt load. The *debt-to-equity ratio* is the place to start.

The debt-to-equity ratio compares the total debt of a company to its shareholder's equity. You can find both figures on a company's balance sheet. Shareholders' equity, also known as book value, is at the very bottom of a balance sheet and is calculated by subtracting liabilities from assets. Shareholder's equity is the amount that owners have invested in a company plus the total of any retained earnings. You'll probably have to add up several figures to come up with a company's total debt. In Example 4-25, total debt is the sum of short-term borrowings, current portion of long-term debt, and long-term debt, which equals $6,144,525,000.

Example 4-25. An excerpt showing debt on a balance sheet

```
Current Liabilities:
        Short-term borrowings                         $1,616,563,000
        Trade accounts payable                        $1,487,956,000
        Salaries, dividends payable & accruals        $3,947,385,000
        Income taxes payable                             $69,696,000
        Current portion of long-term debt               $211,557,000
            Total Current Liabilities                 $7,333,157,000

    Long-Term Debt                                    $4,316,405,000
```

After you've calculated total debt and shareholders' equity, you can calculate the ratio, as shown in Example 4-26.

Example 4-26. Formula for the debt-to-equity ratio

```
Debt-to-Equity Ratio = Total Debt / Shareholder's Equity
```

Debt-to-equity is sometimes expressed as a decimal, but more often as a percentage. To calculate the ratio as a percentage, multiply the formula in Example 4-26 by 100.

The lower the debt-to-equity ratio, the greater a company's financial safety. Some investors completely avoid investing in companies that have any debt whatsoever. That's certainly an easy way around the question of "How much debt is too much?" But debt isn't always a bad thing. A general rule of thumb is that a debt-to-equity ratio greater than 40 or 50 percent requires closer scrutiny of the company's general financial health. If interest rates rise or revenues fall, these companies might have trouble paying their debts. If such a company also has low quick ratios and current ratios, it might have liquidity problems that drive it to overextend its credit line.

You should also consider whether a company's debt is growing or shrinking. A company might have a good reason for increasing its debt load, such as a national expansion plan to build new stores across the country. However, a company that borrows more and more to merely sustain its operations is usually a sign of trouble. On the other hand, a business that decreases its debt year after year is usually a good sign of increasing financial strength.

 The debt-to-equity ratio can vary greatly by industry, so it's best to compare a company to its peers before making a final determination.

Long-Term Debt-to-Equity Ratio

The debt-to-equity ratio considers all of a company's debt, including short-term borrowing and the portion of long-term debt that must be paid back within the next twelve months. The *long-term debt-to-equity ratio* includes only the debt that the company will pay off more than twelve months in the future, such as mortgages and business loans.

Long-term debt usually appears on its own line in a company's balance sheet, as illustrated in Example 4-25, so the calculation is very straightforward, as shown in Example 4-27.

Example 4-27. Formula for the long-term debt-to-equity ratio

```
Long-Term Debt-to-Equity Ratio = Long-Term Debt / Shareholder's Equity
```

The trouble with the long-term debt-to-equity ratio is that companies can change their mix of short-term and long-term debt to make their current or total debt-to-equity ratios look more attractive. For this reason, it's more prudent to evaluate a company's debt load with the debt-to-equity ratio.

Interest Coverage Ratio

Another important financial strength ratio is *interest coverage*, which tells you how easily a company can pay the interest on its debt in the next twelve months from current profits. If a company has no debt, this ratio is irrelevant. The ratio is calculated using the formula shown in Example 4-28.

Example 4-28. Formula for interest coverage ratio

```
Interest Coverage = (Earnings Before Interest and Taxes) / Interest Expense
```

A company's income statement will usually have a line for interest expense, as shown in Example 4-29. If the income statement doesn't list Earnings Before Interest and Taxes (EBIT), calculate EBIT by adding the interest expense back into earnings before taxes. In Example 4-29, add Interest expense to Income before Income Taxes to calculate EBIT of $2,507,000,000. In this example, the interest coverage is $2,507,000,000 divided by $41,000,000 for a result of 61.1.

Example 4-29. An excerpt from an income statement

```
       Interest expense                              $41,000,000
       Total Expense And Other Income             $5,532,000,000
       Income Before Income Taxes                 $2,466,000,000
```

Interest coverage is a good indicator of a company's short-term health. A high interest coverage ratio means that a company is not likely to default on loans and bond payments, whereas interest coverage below 1.0 means that a company is having trouble generating the cash to make its interest payments. Most investors consider an interest coverage ratio below 1.5 as a serious red flag. Companies with interest coverage in the range of 4.0 to 5.0 are usually in good shape. Blue-chip companies, such as the one in Example 4-29, easily make debt payments, so values higher than 5.0 don't tell you much more.

You should examine companies with falling interest coverage to determine the cause. It is not a good sign if the ability to cover interest payments decreases.

In many cases, you can find these financial strength values calculated for you already on web sites such as Yahoo! Finance (*http://finance.yahoo.com*) or MSN Money (*http://money.msn.com*). However, their figures might differ from values you calculate yourself using SEC filing data you download from a source such as EdgarScan (*http://edgarscan.pwcglobal.com*). The discrepancies might be due to how numbers are rounded or how current the data is. When you calculate the ratios yourself, you'll gain greater insight into their meaning.

See Also

- Bob Adams's "Analyzing the Annual Report" (*http://www.bobadams.homestead.com/bobsite.html*) includes many of these ratios, along with red flags that warn of trouble areas.
- Smart Money, "Digging into the Numbers" (*http://university.smartmoney.com/departments/strategicinvesting/stockpicking/index.cfm?story=digging*)

—*Douglas Gerlach*

HACK #30 Calculate Management Effectiveness Ratios

Management effectiveness ratios tell you whether company management uses shareholders' equity and company assets to produce an acceptable rate of return.

Even with the best products or services, companies have trouble delivering strong long-term growth unless their management makes sure that everything operates effectively and efficiently. Management effectiveness ratios compare financial measures from company financial statements to evaluate management performance. Of all the fundamental criteria that long-term investors consider, one of the most important is *return on equity* (ROE), which is a basic test of how well a company's management uses its money—are they increasing the overall value of the business at an acceptable rate? *Return on assets* (ROA) takes another view of management's effectiveness by illustrating how much profit the company earns for every dollar of its assets, such as money in the bank, accounts receivable, property, equipment, inventory, and furniture. One reason to consider ROA as well as ROE is that the latter can make high-debt companies look more effective than low-debt firms with the same earnings and assets.

Evaluating Return on Equity

Calculate ROE with the formula in Example 4-30.

Example 4-30. Formula for ROE

```
% Return on Equity = (Annual Net Income / Average Shareholders' Equity) * 100
```

Understanding Equity

The concept of *equity* is sometimes hard to grasp, so here's a brief lesson. Simply defined, shareholders' equity is the difference between the total assets and total liabilities of a company. It's an accounting convention that represents the assets that a business has generated in its lifetime from two sources:

- Capital invested in the company by its owners
- Profits generated by the company over the years that are retained and reinvested in the company (also called retained earnings)

Fundamental analysts consider company assets that don't have corresponding liabilities to be equity generated by the skill of company management. The higher and more consistent the returns that management generates on money invested in the company, the better off shareholders will be.

You can find net income, also known as net earnings, on a company's income statement, which is a financial statement required in an annual 10-K SEC filing. Shareholders' equity appears at the bottom of a company's balance sheet, which is also in the 10-K report.

Table 4-3 shows a simplified example of Home Depot's 2003 financial statements, created with data obtained from the Home Depot web site (*http://www.homedepot.com*). First, identify net income near the bottom of the income statement (listed as Net Earnings in this case).

Table 4-3. Home Depot financial statements

Income statement (in millions)	Balance sheet (in millions)
NET SALES 58,247	ASSETS
Cost of Merchandise Sold 40,139	Total Current Assets 11,917
GROSS PROFIT 18,108	Property and Equipment, at cost 20,733
Total Operating Expenses 12,278	Less Accumulated Depreciation & Amortization 3,565
OPERATING INCOME 5,830	
Interest Income (Expense):	Net Property and Equipment 17,168
Interest and Investment Income 79	Notes Receivable 107
Interest Expense (37)	Other Assets 244
Interest, net 42	TOTAL ASSETS 30,011
EARNINGS BEFORE PROVISION FOR INCOME TAXES 5,872	LIABILITIES AND STOCKHOLDERS' EQUITY
	Total Current Liabilities 8,035
Provision for Income Taxes 2,208	Long-Term Debt, excluding current installments 1,321
NET EARNINGS 3,664	
	Other Long-Term Liabilities 491
	Deferred Income Taxes 362
	STOCKHOLDERS' EQUITY
	Common Stock, par value $0.05; authorized:
	10,000 shares, issued and outstanding 2,362
	Shares at 2/ 2, 2003 118
	Paid-in Capital 5,858
	Retained Earnings 15,971
	Accumulated Other Comprehensive Loss (82)
	Unearned Compensation (63)
	Treasury Stock, at cost, 69 shares
	at 2/ 2, 2003 (2,000)
	Total Stockholders' Equity 19,802

Then, look at the balance sheet and find shareholders' equity at the very bottom. Home Depot calls it *Total Stockholders' Equity*.

Using the formula in Example 4-31, you can calculate Home Depot's ROE.

Example 4-31. Calculating Home Depot's ROE

```
Home Depot's ROE = $3,664 / $19,802
                 = 0.185 or 18.5 percent
```

Home Depot's ROE is 18.5 percent, and you might be thinking "So what?" Think about the value of your home, your portfolio, or your business. If you were to increase its value by 18.5 percent in a year, you would be doing quite well. That's a much better return than you would receive from a bank savings account, for instance.

Some professional investors invest only in companies with a ROE higher than 15 percent. This guideline assures that company management has so far been effective in building up the value of their company. Home Depot exceeds this by a comfortable margin.

As with many other financial ratios, you can learn more about a company by comparing its ROE to its historical trends, as well as to other companies in the same industry. First, take a look at how Home Depot's recent results compare to its past.

In a spreadsheet, it's easy enough to calculate ROE for the past five years, as shown in Figure 4-11. EdgarScan (*http://edgarscan.pwcglobal.com*) is a good source of historical SEC filings already formatted in Excel spreadsheets. Simply isolate net income and shareholders' equity from each annual 10-K filing and add the ROE calculations, as shown in Examples 4-32 and 4-33.

Example 4-32. Excel function for ROE

```
Annual ROE (cell B4) = B2/B3
```

	A	B	C	D	E	F	G
1		1999	2000	2001	2002	2003	Average
2	Net Income	$1,614	$2,320	$ 2,581	$ 3,044	$3,664	
3	Shareholder's Equity	$8,740	$12,341	$ 15,004	$ 18,082	$19,802	
4	Return on Equity	18.5%	18.8%	17.2%	16.8%	18.5%	18.0%

Figure 4-11. Calculate ROE for several years to look for trends

Example 4-33. Excel function for the five-year average ROE

```
5-year Average ROE (cell G4) = AVERAGE(B4:F4)
```

In Figure 4-11, the formula in cell B4 was copied to cells C4 through F4. The cells are formatted as a percentage to one decimal point.

With these calculations, you can evaluate Home Depot's past performance in detail. The company's ROE has been fairly stable over the past five years. The company recovered from a downward trend in 2001 and 2002, which is a good sign. It's not unusual to see some fluctuation in ROE from year to year, but well-managed companies produce fairly stable results over the long term. Steadily rising ROEs are desirable, but that can't go on forever. Eventually a company's ROE will stabilize or start to fall slightly, which might not be negative if a company is maturing or receding from extraordinary performance levels.

Calculating a company's long-term average ROE can help smooth out short-term fluctuations and help you evaluate the stability of the ROE. Home Depot's most recent results exceeded its five-year average, which is what you want to see. If ROE declines for three or more consecutive years, you should research the company to understand the reasons for the fall. For example, cyclical companies by their nature see lower earnings as they reach the bottom of their cycle, so their ROEs trend up and down with the economic cycle.

ROE is another measure that you should compare within a company's peer group. The MSN Money web site (*http://money.msn.com*) calculates return on equity for you, and shows average ROE for the company's industry and the overall market. Enter the ticker symbol of the stock that you're studying and click Go. On the stock page, click Financial Results, then Key Ratios in the navigation bar, and then click the Investment Returns link, as shown in Figure 4-12.

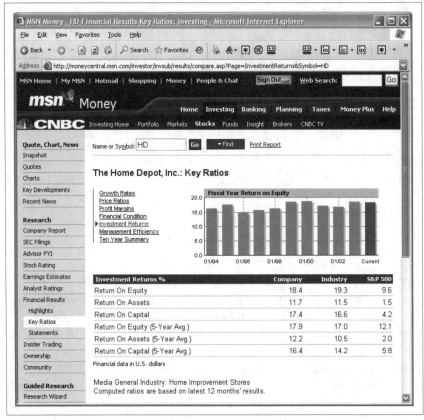

Figure 4-12. MSN Money offers ROE data and industry comparisons

In Figure 4-12, you'll notice a ten-year chart of a company's ROE where it's easy to see that the company's management has been doing its job well. In the table below the graph, you can also see that MSN Money calculates Home Depot's 2003 ROE as 18.4 percent. Small differences between this figure and the number calculated from SEC filings is likely due to rounding. Home Depot's ROE is somewhat below the industry average of 19.3 percent, but it's well above the S&P 500 average of 9.6 percent and the ROE guideline of 15 percent.

The Return On Equity (5-Year Avg.) a few lines down in the table is more telling. Here, Home Depot's performance is even better with an average ROE of 17.9 percent compared to the industry's 17.0 percent, and 12.1 percent for the S&P 500.

Five-Year Industry Averages for Return on Equity and Return on Assets (1998-2002)

Industries can have quite different average ROE and ROA. That's why it's imperative to compare a company to its peer group when looking at these figures.

	ROE	ROA
Aerospace/Defense	10.00%	3.00%
Application Software	14.10%	9.40%
Auto Manufacturers - Major	9.00%	1.40%
Beverages - Soft Drinks	23.60%	7.60%
Discount & Variety Stores	17.50%	7.10%
Drug Manufacturers - Major	30.20%	13.00%
Electric Utilities	8.70%	2.00%
Grocery Stores	12.60%	2.90%
Life Insurance	12.70%	0.70%
Major Airlines	3.30%	0.50%
Money Center Banks	14.80%	1.10%
Restaurants	17.00%	7.10%

Source: Media General Financial Services.

Evaluating Return on Assets

Because ROE only compares net income to shareholders' equity, a company that has raised working capital from bonds and borrowing might show a higher return on equity than a competitor without being any more effective at putting the shareholders' equity to work growing the company. Return on assets can help you understand how well a company uses debt as well as shareholders' equity.

You'll find a company's total assets on its balance sheet and can calculate ROA, as shown in Example 4-34.

Example 4-34. Formula for ROA

```
% Return on Assets = (Annual Net Income / Total Assets) * 100
```

Using the data from Home Depot's financial statements in Table 4-3, you can calculate its ROA, as shown in Example 4-35.

Example 4-35. Calculating Home Depot's ROA

```
Home Depot's ROA = $3,664 / $30,011
                 = 0.122 or 12.2 percent
```

Professional investors won't often consider stocks with ROA lower than 5 to 8 percent, so Home Depot's management has exceeded that standard. As with ROE, you should evaluate trends in ROA, and compare a company's ROA to its competitors and the market in general. A stable ROA over the years indicates that management is effectively managing its total resources to generate profits for the company. Looking at Home Depot's history in a spreadsheet (see Figure 4-13), you can see that the company's ROA has been consistent over the past few years.

	A	B	C	D	E	F	G
1		1999	2000	2001	2002	2003	Average
2	Net Income	$1,614	$2,320	$ 2,581	$ 3,044	$3,664	
3	Total Assets	$13,465	$17,081	$21,385	$26,394	$30,011	
4	**Return on Assets**	12.0%	13.6%	12.1%	11.5%	12.2%	12.3%

Figure 4-13. Examine ROA over a period of five years to check the company's trend and average

ROA varies significantly by industry, as shown in the sidebar on industry average ROE and ROA. An automobile manufacturer requires a huge amount of assets—factories, materials, and parts—to build those SUVs that are so popular. Software companies, on the other hand, don't need big manufacturing plants to turn out their products—after they develop a program, they just stamp out software CD-ROMs, package them, and ship them to customers. They might even outsource those tasks to reduce the employees and buildings they need.

To compare Home Depot's 12.3 percent average ROA to the industry, refer to MSN Money. Figure 4-12 shows that the company's ROA is better than the industry average of 10.5 percent and worlds better than the 2.0 percent average of the S&P 500.

—*Douglas Gerlach*

HACK #31 Calculate Turnover Ratios

Use turnover ratios to see if a company's management is using its assets effectively to generate profits.

Every company management team aims to deploy its assets to generate the most profits possible. It doesn't do any good for a company to own assets, such as factories, inventory, or even cash, if they're not being used to maximum advantage. There are three ratios that investors typically evaluate to measure the efficiency of company management: *asset turnover ratio*, *inventory turnover ratio*, and *receivable turnover ratio*.

Asset Turnover Ratio

The first ratio to consider is the *asset turnover ratio*, which assesses the sales that a company can generate for each dollar of assets it owns—the higher the asset turnover ratio, the better. Companies with high asset turnover ratios can thrive even with low profit margins.

The asset turnover ratio is calculated using the formula in Example 4-36.

Example 4-36. Formula for the asset turnover ratio

```
Asset Turnover Ratio = Total Revenue for Period / Average Assets for Period
```

Companies report the value of their assets on their balance sheets included in the financial statement section of their SEC 10-Q and 10-K filings. However, they report the value of those assets as they stood at the end of the year. You can calculate the average assets for the period by averaging the year-end values for total assets for the current and previous years.

> You can use total assets in place of average assets, mostly for the sake of simplicity. However, average assets better represent a company's efficiency.

The financial data spreadsheets available at EdgarScan (*http://edgarscan. pwcglobal.com*) provide a quick way to obtain the necessary values.

Let's look at Home Depot's asset turnover ratio. Table 4-4 shows pertinent Home Depot financials.

Table 4-4. *Home Depot measures from EdgarScan needed for calculating the asset turnover ratio*

Financial measure	Value in millions
2003 total operating revenue	$58,247.0
2003 total assets	$30,011.0
2002 total assets	$26,394.0

Using the assets from each period, the average assets are $28,202.5 million. Plug these values into the formula to determine Home Depot's asset turnover for the year, as shown in Example 4-37.

Example 4-37. *Formula for Home Depot's asset turnover ratio*

```
Home Depot's Asset Turnover Ratio = 58,247.0 / 28,202.5
                                  = 2.1
```

You can use the AVERAGE function to calculate the average assets, as shown in Example 4-38.

Example 4-38. *Excel function to calculate average assets*

```
Average Assets = AVERAGE(B2:C2)
```

MSN Money (*http://money.msn.com*) provides asset turnover and other turnover ratios for companies, industry turnover averages, and average turnover values for the S&P 500 index. As you can see in Figure 4-14, Home Depot's asset turnover ratio of 1.9 compares favorably to other companies in its industry, which has an average asset turnover ratio of 1.8.

> Companies with high asset turnover ratios tend to have lower profit margins (and vice versa). That doesn't mean that companies with higher or lower asset turnover ratios are better long-term investments. It's just an indication of a common business strategy of selling a high volume of goods at a small increase over cost.

Inventory Turnover Ratio

The *inventory turnover ratio* is an indicator of how quickly a company moves its inventory out of warehouses, factories, or stores, and into the hands of customers. The formula to calculate the ratio looks like Example 4-39.

Industry Average Efficiency Turnover Ratios (2002)

Efficiency ratios differ quite a bit between industries, so it's important to compare a company to its competition and industry averages. Retail stores, for instance, have higher asset turnover because they always have shelves and warehouses full of merchandise to stock their store's shelves.

Industry	Asset turnover ratio	Inventory turnover ratio	Receivables turnover ratio
Aerospace/defense	1.0	8.4	7.5
Application software	0.5	8.9	5.7
Auto manufacturers (major)	0.7	10.0	2.2
Beverages (soft drinks)	0.9	8.6	9.6
Discount and variety stores	2.5	2.5	53.8
Drug manufacturers (major)	0.8	3.0	6.8
Electric utilities	0.3	7.5	4.5
Grocery stores	2.1	7.2	35.5
Life insurance	0.2	n/a	n/a
Major airlines	0.6	21.6	11.0
Money center banks	0.1	n/a	n/a
Restaurants	1.2	33.0	30.9

Source: Media General Financial Services.

Example 4-39. Formula for inventory turnover ratio

```
Inventory Turnover Ratio = Total Revenue / Average Inventory
```

Total revenue appears on the income statement and inventory appears on the balance sheet. You must calculate the average value of inventory from the most recently reported inventory value and the value from the same period a year earlier. Using a spreadsheet of extracted financial data downloaded from EdgarScan (*http://edgarscan.pwcglobal.com*), you can quickly calculate the inventory turnover ratio for a company.

> Sometimes, the inventory turnover ratio is calculated by dividing the cost of goods sold by average inventory. Either method is acceptable—just make sure that you compute your ratios using the same method when comparing a company to its competitors or industry.

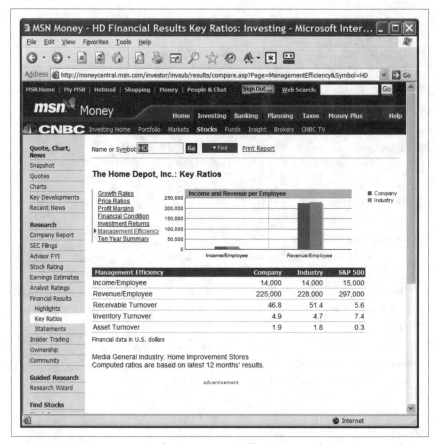

Figure 4-14. MSN Money provides management efficiency ratios for companies and their industries

Continuing the evaluation of Home Depot's efficiency ratios, Table 4-5 shows pertinent Home Depot financials for calculating the inventory turnover ratio.

Table 4-5. Home Depot measures from EdgarScan needed for calculating the inventory turnover ratio

Financial measure	Value in millions
2003 total operating revenue	$58,247.0
2003 total inventories	$8,338.0
2002 total inventories	$5,489.0

Using the assets from each period, the average inventory is $6,913.5 million. Using these values, Example 4-40 shows Home Depot's inventory turnover ratio for the year.

Example 4-40. Home Depot's inventory turnover ratio

```
Home Depot's Inventory Turnover Ratio = 58,247.0 / $6,913.5
                                       = 8.4
```

When it comes to evaluating the inventory turnover ratio, higher is better. As is standard practice, you should compare a company's inventory turnover to its competitors. Retail stores and grocery chains usually have higher rates of inventory turnover, because they sell a lot of low-cost products. Heavy equipment makers generally have lower turnover ratios, because bulldozers and cranes each sell for hundreds of thousands (or even millions) of dollars. You can see average inventory turnover ratios in the sidebar earlier in this hack.

> Financial companies don't have inventory like manufacturing or retail companies do, so this ratio doesn't apply to them.

You can quickly check a company's inventory turnover ratio at MSN Money (*http://money.msn.com*) and compare it to the industry average inventory turnover ratio and the average for the S&P 500 index. As shown in Figure 4-14, Home Depot's inventory turnover ratio of 4.9 compares favorably to other companies in its industry, which average 4.7.

Product inventories are the least liquid assets that a company owns, and unsold inventory quickly becomes a money-losing proposition. Last year's fashions become this year's bargain basement buys, outdated technology lands in the junk pile, and spoiled food goes into the garbage. This is why it's important for companies to manage their inventories closely. In the last decade, industries ranging from auto manufacturers to computer hardware makers have increasingly turned to methods that keep their inventory levels at a minimum, such as *just in time delivery* of parts and materials from suppliers, or building goods to order that are immediately shipped to customers, as Dell does with computers.

A low inventory turnover ratio is sometimes a signal that a company is out of step with customer demand for its products—its products are not succeeding in the marketplace, because of obsolescence or poor quality. However, companies sometimes stock up their warehouses to prepare for a new product rollout or for the holiday sale season, so you should dig deeper into the reasons.

Receivables Turnover Ratio

The third ratio to consider is the *receivables turnover ratio*. Accounts receivable (also known as receivables) are a company's uncollected income from customers, such as unpaid invoices. Higher receivables turnover ratios are preferable to lower ones, because companies run the risk of never collecting on open invoices if they delay too long. In addition, those receivables represent income, which most companies need to pay their own bills. Example 4-41 shows the formula for receivables turnover ratio.

Example 4-41. Formula for receivables turnover ratio

```
Receivables Turnover Ratio = Total Revenue / Average Receivables
```

The receivables turnover ratio reveals how many times a company has collected its receivables during a period. Unlike assets and inventories, receivables have a more immediate element of timeliness, and you use more recent values to calculate the receivables turnover ratio. Instead of averaging the receivables from the current and prior years, you calculate the average from the most recent two quarters.

Some analysts and data providers calculate average receivables by using two year-end values, whereas others use five quarters. As long as you use the same method when looking at competitors or industry averages, you can use any method to compute average receivables.

Continuing the evaluation of Home Depot's efficiency ratios, Table 4-6 shows pertinent Home Depot financials for calculating the receivables turnover ratio.

Table 4-6. Home Depot measures from EdgarScan needed for calculating the receivables turnover ratio

Financial measure	Value in millions
2003 total operating revenue	$58,247.0
2003 total receivables	$1,072.0
Third quarter 2002 total receivables	$1,379.0

Using these values, you can calculate Home Depot's receivables turnover ratio for the year, as shown in Example 4-42.

Example 4-42. Home Depot's receivables turnover ratio

```
Home Depot's Receivables Turnover Ratio = 58,247.0 / 1,225.5
                                         = 47.5
```

Is a receivables turnover ratio of 47.5 good? As with most retail stores, the bulk of Home Depot's customers pay with cash or credit cards that the company almost immediately turns into cash at the bank, so the company's ratio is quite good. You can see average inventory turnover ratios in the earlier sidebar "Industry Average Efficiency Turnover Ratios (2002)." As with the inventory turnover ratio, financial stocks don't report receivables, so the receivables turnover ratio isn't applicable for these companies.

You can also quickly compare the company to its industry at MSN Money, as shown in Figure 4-14. A low receivables turnover ratio compared to the competition is cause for concern. Home Depot doesn't compare as favorably with this ratio as it does with other efficiency ratios. Its receivables turnover ratio of 46.8 is slightly lower than the industry average of 51.4, but it is still high enough to safeguard the company from obsolete inventory.

Very high receivables turnover ratios, such as Home Depot's, indicate highly efficient companies that can usually delay paying their own bills while quickly collecting on money that's owed them. By doing this, companies obtain the equivalent of an interest-free loan. Averages vary by industry, so a 30-day payment period could be common practice or completely unattainable.

See Also

- In addition to MSN Money, you can also find management effectiveness ratios for companies and industries calculated at Reuters Investor (*http://www.investor.reuters.com*).

—Douglas Gerlach

Calculate Profitability Ratios

Calculate and evaluate a company's profitability to determine its chances of future success.

One of the cornerstones of successful long-term investing is identifying stocks whose profits are growing steadily. The idea behind this approach is that a company that consistently grows its earnings will eventually see its share price grow as well. Although companies can increase their earnings by selling more goods or services, they also must be mindful of how much of each dollar of sales represents profits on their books if they want to make as much money as possible (which is any company's goal, after all). There are several ways to assess a company's profitability, and each way reveals how well the company is run and whether the company is well-positioned for the future.

Key Profit Margins

Like canaries in a coal mine, profit margins serve as an early warning device. If profit margins begin to fall, earnings might begin to decrease, which often leads to drops in stock price. By watching for downward trends in profit margins, you can sell a company before its slipping performance hurts your portfolio. The key profitability ratios to examine are *gross margin, operating profit margin, net profit margin,* and *pre-tax profit margin.*

Gross margin. Start your analysis of a company's profitability by examining its *gross margin.* This figure reveals how inexpensively a company can manufacture or acquire the goods it sells to customers. To calculate a company's gross margin, you first need to identify its *gross profit,* which is the amount that a company makes from its core business after paying the *cost of goods sold* (the cost of raw materials and manufacturing), but before accounting for salaries, marketing, interest, and taxes. For a retail company, cost of goods sold is the amount it pays to suppliers for the products that stock its shelves. Using a company's income statement, you can calculate gross profit from these variables, as shown in Example 4-43.

Example 4-43. Formulas for gross profit and gross margin

```
Gross Profit = Total Revenue - Cost of Goods Sold (COGS)
% Gross Margin = (Gross Profit / Total Revenue) * 100
```

A company's gross margin gives you a good idea of the underlying profitability of a company's primary operations. Businesses strive to keep their gross margin as high as possible by keeping their raw material and manufacturing costs low, because a company with lower product costs has better control over the prices that it can charge its customers. Besides contributing to its overall profits, this higher level of efficiency can help the company combat pressure from competitors or weather tough times.

Operating profit margin. It's not enough for a company to have low gross margins, however. No matter how inexpensively they can make goods or acquire inventory for their shelves, they must also manage the expenses related to selling those products. The *operating profit margin* evaluates these costs and their impact on the company's overall profitability.

You calculate a company's *operating profit* (or *operating income*) by adding to the cost of goods sold the rest of the expenses involved directly in the business, and subtracting the result from revenues. These other expenses are known as *selling, general, and administrative expenses* (SG&A), and include the costs of administration, salaries, advertising, and marketing. Operating income is also known as earnings before interest, taxes, depreciation, and amortization (EBITDA) [Hack #29].

Calculate the operating profit margin by using the operating income from a company's income statement, as in Example 4-44.

Example 4-44. Formula for the operating profit margin

```
% Operating Profit Margin = (Operating Profit / Total Revenue) * 100
```

The operating profit margin goes beyond the question of whether the company can manufacture goods inexpensively to examine whether a company spends money wisely on the rest of its overhead expenses. If a company's SG&A expenses exceed the amount it can charge for those goods or if rising expenses reduce its operating profit margin below that of competitors, low manufacturing costs are ineffective. This is why companies sometimes move to protect their operating profit margin by downsizing—laying off staff, closing facilities, or eliminating less profitable product lines.

Pre-tax profit margin. Nothing is certain but death and taxes, as the old saying goes, but a company's management often doesn't have a lot of control over the taxes the company pays. Tax rates can change, and complicated tax credit schemes can affect the taxes a company must pay. To remove variations in profit margins due to these circumstances that management can't control, investors often put the most emphasis on a company's *pre-tax profit margin*.

Calculate the pre-tax profit margin using the formula in Example 4-45 and data from the income statement.

Example 4-45. Formula for pre-tax profit margin

```
% Pre-Tax Profit Margin = (Net Income Before Tax / Total Revenue) * 100
```

> For many companies, net income before taxes is the same as or quite close to operating income. Net income before taxes doesn't include noncash items, such as depreciation or income generated from financial investments, and usually doesn't include the effects of discontinued operations or extraordinary items that the company might have reported.

Net profit margin. Finally, the *net profit margin* tells you how much a company makes after it pays all its expenses and taxes. Net income after taxes is reported on a company's income statement, and the net profit margin is calculated like this:

```
% Net Profit Margin = (Net Income After Taxes / Total Revenue) * 100
```

The net profit margin is the bottom line of a company's profitability. After all is said and done, purchasing shares in a company that can't show a profit after paying expenses and taxes is purely speculation, not investing.

Analyzing Profitability

Let's take a look at Home Depot's profitability ratios based on its fiscal year ended on January 31, 2003. Using data extracted from its SEC 10-K filing by EdgarScan (*http://edgarscan.pwcglobal.com*), Table 4-7 shows the necessary figures from the income statement.

Table 4-7. Home Depot measures needed to evaluate profitability

Financial measure	Value in millions
Total operating revenue	$58,247
Cost of goods sold	$40,139
Operating income	$5,830
Income before tax	$5,872
Net income	$3,664

First, calculate the gross profit of $18,108 by subtracting the cost of goods sold from total operating revenue, and then determine the gross margin by dividing gross profit by total revenue, as shown in Example 4-46.

Example 4-46. Calculating Home Depot's gross profit and gross margin

```
Home Depot's Gross Profit = $58,247 - $40,139 = $18,108
Home Depot's Gross Margin = ($18,108 / $58,247) * 100 = 31.1%
```

Next, divide operating income by total revenue to determine the operating margin, 10.0 percent. Divide income before tax by total revenue to determine the pre-tax profit margin of 10.1 percent, as shown in Example 4-47.

Example 4-47. Calculating Home Depot's operating margin and pre-tax profit margin

```
Home Depot's Operating Margin = ($5,830 / $58,247) * 100 = 10.0%
Home Depot's Pre-Tax Profit Margin = ($5,872 / $58,247) * 100 = 10.1%
```

Finally, determine the net profit margin by dividing net income by total revenue, as shown in Example 4-48.

Example 4-48. Calculating Home Depot's net profit margin

```
Home Depot's Net Profit Margin = ($3,664 / $58,247) * 100 = 6.3%
```

With these margins in hand, you can turn to the task of interpreting them. The best candidates for a long-term growth stock portfolio are usually those companies whose profit margins outperform those of the competition. Supermarkets, for instance, have very slim net profit margins. Retail businesses that thrive on high-volume sales often have low margins because of their low markups and competitive pressures. On the other hand, software makers and pharmaceutical companies typically have quite high margins. As a result, it would be a mistake to compare a software company's margins to a grocery store's and conclude that the software developer is a better investment purely on the basis of profit margins. Comparing a grocery store to its competitors gives you a clearer picture of its overall health. Table 4-8 shows the average profit margins for selected industries.

Table 4-8. 5-year industry average profitability ratios from Media General Financial Services (1998–2002)

Industry	Gross margin	Pre-tax margin	Net margin
Aerospace/defense	16.0%	3.0%	1.8%
Application software	82.2%	24.8%	16.1%
Auto manufacturers (major)	29.1%	2.8%	1.7%
Beverages (soft drinks)	54.3%	14.8%	10.5%
Discount and variety stores	24.5%	5.2%	3.4%
Drug manufacturers (major)	72.4%	22.2%	16.7%
Electric utilities	42.3%	6.3%	-0.3%
Grocery stores	40.7%	-0.2%	-1.2%
Life insurance	N/A	6.3%	4.7%
Major airlines	51.3%	-9.3%	-7.1%
Money center banks	N/A	23.9%	17.1%
Restaurants	37.4%	8.2%	5.2%

If a company's profit margins trail the average profit margins of its industry by a significant amount, you should investigate further to determine the cause. Often, you can find explanations for shortcomings by reading the management discussion in the company's annual report, SEC Form 10-K or 10-Q, or by asking the company's investor relations representative directly. Successful companies always strive to maintain or even improve their margins in any number of ways. They can improve productivity, cut costs, or increase the volume of sales. In crisis mode, a company's tactics to protect its margins could include layoffs, closing factories, or eliminating unprofitable product lines. If these actions don't work, a company's margins could erode until their net profit margins reach negative territory—which is another way of saying that the company is losing money.

The MSN Money web site (*http://money.msn.com*) provides a quick way to compare profitability ratios for a company and its industry, as shown in Figure 4-15. Enter the ticker symbol and click Go, then Financial Results, and then Key Ratios. Click the Profit Margins link. In Home Depot's case, the company's profit margins are above average for the home improvement store industry.

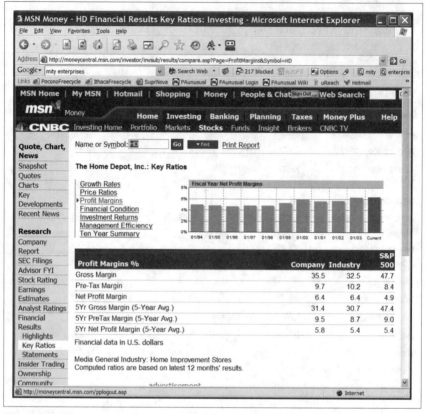

Figure 4-15. Examine a company's profitability ratios on the MSN Money web site

No two companies are alike, and that's particularly true for their profit margins. Minor differences between a company and its competitors aren't usually something you need to sweat about. If you see significant variances, though, you've probably found evidence of weakness or strength.

It's also important to compare a company's recent results to its historical averages. Stable profit margins are a sign of solid management expertise, an indication that the company is successfully squaring off against competition, managing its raw materials and manufacturing costs, and generally staying the course. Conversely, wildly erratic or declining margins are often indications of trouble.

EdgarScan's extracted financial data provides the numbers you need to calculate margins for several years. In the spreadsheet in Figure 4-16, you can easily trace the trends in Home Depot's margins over a five-year period. In addition, you can compare the most recent year's margins to the company's five-year averages. If the company's recent margins are below average, then it might be a sign that the company's future is not so bright, although Home Depot has nothing to worry about in this area.

	A	B	C	D	E	F	G
1		1999	2000	2001	2002	2003	Average
2	Total Operating Revenue	$30,219	$38,434	$45,738	$53,553	$58,247	
3	Cost of Goods Sold	$21,614	$27,023	$32,057	$37,406	$40,139	
4	**Gross Profit**	**$8,605**	**$11,411**	**$13,681**	**$16,147**	**$18,108**	
5	**Gross Profit Margin**	**28.5%**	**29.7%**	**29.9%**	**30.2%**	**31.1%**	**29.9%**
6	Operating Income	$2,670	$3,808	$4,191	$4,932	$5,830	
7	**Operating Profit Margin**	**8.8%**	**9.9%**	**9.2%**	**9.2%**	**10.0%**	**9.4%**
8	Income Before Tax	$2,654	$3,804	$4,217	$4,957	$5,872	
9	**Pre-Tax Profit Margin**	**8.8%**	**9.9%**	**9.2%**	**9.3%**	**10.1%**	**9.4%**
10	Net Income	$1,614	$2,320	$2,581	$3,044	$3,664	
11	**Net Profit Margin**	**5.3%**	**6.0%**	**5.6%**	**5.7%**	**6.3%**	**5.8%**

Figure 4-16. Looking at five years of Home Depot's profit margins clues you in to the stability of the company

When looking at a company's history, be aware of changes that might be caused by economic factors and not a specific weakness within the company. Cyclical businesses typically see their margins decline during down cycles, but they then recover along with the economy.

> Sometimes, even a company's strong performance can be cause for concern. Exceptionally high profit margins are good news for a company—at least for a while. However, high profit margins attract competition that might figure out how to provide similar products or services at a lesser cost, forcing the company to lower its prices, thereby putting pressure on its margins. When that happens, there's no place for a company's margins to go but down.

Hacking the Hack

After you've collected the data and calculated profit margins in a spreadsheet, it's easy to draw a picture to tell the story better. In Excel, insert a chart [Hack #13] and select the column type. For the data range, select cells A through F in rows 1, 5, 7, 9, and 11. Title the chart, and you'll end up with something that looks like Figure 4-17.

To select cells that are not contiguous, select the contents of the Data Range box in the Chart Wizard. Press and hold the Ctrl key and drag over the first set of cells. Continue to hold the Ctrl key and drag over each additional set of cells that you want to graph in the chart.

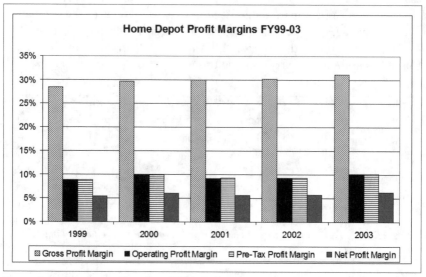

Figure 4-17. *It's easier to spot trends in a chart of profit margin, created in a spreadsheet*

See Also

- In addition to MSN Money, you can also find profit margins for companies and industries calculated at Reuters Investor (located at *http://www.investor.reuters.com*).

- Smart Money, "Digging into the Numbers" (*http://university.smartmoney.com/departments/strategicinvesting/stockpicking/index.cfm?story=digging*)

—*Douglas Gerlach*

HACK #33 Compare Year-to-Year Results

Buy-and-hold investing doesn't mean buy-and-forget. Compare a company's performance to the same period a year ago to look for signs of trouble with its fundamentals.

For long-term investors, comparing shorter-term financial results can raise red flags about a company's current condition. By comparing recent annual or quarterly results to the same period a year ago, you might receive early warning of a problem that could turn into a full-blown disaster over time. There is a wide range of figures you should evaluate on a company's income statement, balance sheet, and cash flow statement.

The formula for calculating percentage change is shown in Example 4-49.

Example 4-49. Formula for percentage change

```
Percentage change = ((Ending Value / Initial Value) - 1) * 100
```

Companies usually highlight changes in key figures in their quarterly and annual earnings releases. The financial tables that accompany these press releases include data for the most recent and comparable year-ago periods.

A good source of SEC filing data for public companies is Price Waterhouse Coopers Global's EdgarScan [Hack #18] (*http://edgarscan.pwcglobal.com*). Here you can download a single spreadsheet that has a company's annual and quarterly data going back ten years.

After you've downloaded the spreadsheet for a company, isolate any two columns (either for two years or two quarters) and calculate the percentage change in a third column. Copy the formula down the column, and you'll be able to spot any significant changes in particular data points, as illustrated in Figure 4-18. The percentage changes in column D use a formula such as the one shown in Example 4-50, formatted to display as a percentage to one decimal point.

Example 4-50. Typical Excel formula for calculating percentage change

```
Typical Excel Percentage Change Formula = ((C6 / B6) - 1)
```

In Excel, the formula does not multiply the result by 100, because you can apply formatting to show the value as a percentage.

When you compare quarterly results, use the same quarter from the current year and the prior year. For example, compare the fourth quarters for fiscal year 2003 and 2002. Many companies do better during specific times of the year. For example, bookstores and retailers do particularly well in the last calendar quarter because of holiday buying. Home improvement stores often do better during the summer months.

	A	B	C	D
1	HOME DEPOT INC			
2	Filing Period	2002/02/03	2003/02/02	
3	Filing Type	10-K	10-K	% Change
4				
5	Assets			
6	Cash	$2,477,000,000	$2,188,000,000	-11.7%
7	Receivables	$920,000,000	$1,072,000,000	16.5%
8	Inventory	$6,725,000,000	$8,338,000,000	24.0%
9	Other Current Assets	$170,000,000	$254,000,000	49.4%
10	Current Assets	$10,361,000,000	$11,917,000,000	15.0%
11	Net Property Plant & Equipment	$15,375,000,000	$17,168,000,000	11.7%
12	Total Assets	$26,394,000,000	$30,011,000,000	13.7%
13				
14	Liabilities			
15	Accounts Payable	$3,436,000,000	$4,560,000,000	32.7%
16	Income Tax Expense	$1,913,000,000	$2,208,000,000	15.4%
17	Current Liabilities	$6,501,000,000	$8,035,000,000	23.6%
18	Common Equity	$117,000,000	$118,000,000	0.9%
19	Deferred Tax	$189,000,000	$362,000,000	91.5%
20	Long Term Debt	$1,250,000,000	$1,321,000,000	5.7%
21	Total Debt	$1,250,000,000	$1,321,000,000	5.7%
22	Total Liabilities	$8,312,000,000	$10,209,000,000	22.8%
23	Retained Earnings	$12,799,000,000	$15,971,000,000	24.8%
24	Shareholders' Equity	$18,082,000,000	$19,802,000,000	9.5%
25				
26	Income			
27	Total Operating Revenue	$53,553,000,000	$58,247,000,000	8.8%
28	Cost of Goods Sold	$37,406,000,000	$40,139,000,000	7.3%
29	Interest Expense	$28,000,000	$37,000,000	32.1%
30	Income Before Tax	$4,957,000,000	$5,872,000,000	18.5%
31	Operating Income	$4,932,000,000	$5,830,000,000	18.2%
32	Net Income	$3,044,000,000	$3,664,000,000	20.4%
33	Common Shares Outstanding			
34	Earnings Per Share: Basic	1.3	1.57	20.8%
35	Earnings Per Share: Diluted	1.29	1.56	20.9%
36				
37	Cash Flow			
38	Capital Expenditures	$3,393,000,000	$2,749,000,000	-19.0%
39	Depreciation and Amortization	$764,000,000	$903,000,000	18.2%
40	Operating Activities	$5,963,000,000	$4,802,000,000	-19.5%
41	Investing Activities	($3,466,000,000)	($2,934,000,000)	-15.3%
42	Financing Activities	($173,000,000)	($2,165,000,000)	1151.4%
43	Cash at Year Start	$167,000,000	$2,477,000,000	1383.2%
44	Cash at Year End	$2,477,000,000	$2,188,000,000	-11.7%

Figure 4-18. Examine the year-over-year changes in a company's financials to spot potential problems

If you spot significant deterioration, you should dig deeper to determine the cause. Read the management's discussion in the annual report or SEC filings, check recent press releases and news, or ask investor relations representatives at the company directly for an explanation.

A negative percentage change doesn't necessarily represent deteriorating performance. For example, in Figure 4-18, the negative percentage change in cell D41 is an improvement. In addition, if one of the values in a calculation is positive and the other is negative, the resulting percentage calculation is meaningless.

Here are some key figures to consider when evaluating year-over-year changes:

Assets

If a company's current assets are growing, it may mean that the company is accumulating cash, a positive sign. On the other hand, if the receivables component of current assets is increasing, the company may be having trouble collecting on customer invoices, which wouldn't be good. Look at the changes in cash, receivables, and inventory to find an explanation for the changes. Home Depot's total asset growth of 13.7 percent is in line with the growth of most of its asset categories, with the exception of the decline in cash and the large growth in inventories and other current assets. The $84 million increase in *other total assets* makes up less than 0.2 percent of total assets of $30 billion, so the change doesn't have a large impact on the company's position. But the levels of cash and inventories do require a closer look.

Cash

Is the value of cash and cash equivalents (such as securities that can be readily sold) declining? If so, what are the reasons for the drop? Has the company been using its cash recently to expand operations? Or have profit margins or revenues been falling, which requires the company to use more of its cash position to fund operations? Home Depot's cash has declined 11.7 percent from the prior year, but the dollar value of cash on hand closely matches the increase in receivables. If the company has problems collecting on unpaid bills, it could be a sign of trouble. For now, however, the company is quite satisfied with having over $2 billion in cash and indicates that this amount will easily take care of its expansion plans for the next few years.

Inventory

Are inventories growing, shrinking, or stable? Too much inventory might mean that the company's resources are tied up in warehouses and not being sold to customers. The company might be ramping up for a future expansion, or it might have a dud product that consumers don't want. So what about Home Depot's 24 percent growth in inventory for the year? In its annual report, the company explains that upgrades in technology contribute to better inventory management, with stores averaging 8 percent more inventory at the end of the year than at the beginning. In a retail business, empty shelves mean no sales and disappointed customers, so better-stocked stores are a plus. Home Depot is also expanding the appliance departments in its stores and has become the third largest appliance retailer in the U.S. Refrigerators, stoves, washers, and dryers are more expensive than screws and tools, so this could also contribute to the increase in the value of its inventory. Since total revenues and profits are strong, this one-year change isn't a major cause for concern (although it might be a good idea to watch this item for any long-term changes).

Accounts Payable

If this liability is growing, is it because the company can't pay its bills on time or because they are rapidly growing their business? When a company grows, it buys more supplies, which leads to an increase in accounts payable. If accounts payable have increased without a corresponding increase in sales, check turnover ratios and cash flow for signs of a cash crisis. Maybe the company has negotiated better terms with its suppliers. If accounts payable have declined, have the company's sales also been falling? Home Depot's accounts payable grew 32.7 percent over the prior year, a bit higher than the increase in total inventories for the year. The company does have plenty of cash to pay its bills and is rapidly expanding its business, so the year-over-year change doesn't raise a big red flag.

Debt

Is the company paying down its long-term or short-term debt? Or have they borrowed more money from the bank, increasing their level of debt? If they've been borrowing money, find out if it has been to fund expansion or to simply pay their current bills. Home Depot is building more stores each year, so the 5.7 percent increase in total debt is likely due to their aggressive growth plans. By borrowing money, the company can build more stores and thus increase their profits at a faster rate. In its annual report, the company reports that their long-term debt-to-equity ratio at the end of the year was 6.7 percent and their credit quality is excellent, so the company is putting the borrowed money to good use.

Interest Expense

If interest expense is growing faster than sales and profits, determine the cause. If a company is borrowing additional money to finance operations or an expansion, then their interest expense might rise. But if the increase is due to higher interest rates on its debt, particularly in businesses that require a lot of capital to build plants or other high-cost items, interest expense increases could lead to decreased net profits in the future. Home Depot paid significantly more in interest in the most recent year, but even with the 32.1 percent increase, the company points out in its annual report that interest expense as a percent of sales was 0.0 percent for the year. Since their net income of $3.6 billion was nearly 100 times the $37 million they paid in interest, the increase isn't a significant concern at this point.

Revenues

A company must grow revenues over the long term in order to grow its profits. A company can increase its profit margins only so far by increasing productivity, lowering costs, or raising prices. Falling revenues can be a sign of trouble. However, small companies often grow faster than large companies, so revenue growth typically slows as small companies mature. The 8.8 percent gain in total operating revenue for Home Depot is well in line with expectations for a company of its size.

Pre-Tax Income

Changes in pre-tax profits can often be a warning sign of trouble. If pre-tax income has fallen, is it because of slowing revenue growth, increased expenses, or external factors such as an unfavorable economic climate? Home Depot grew its income before taxes 18.5 percent over the prior year, a strong showing for a large company.

Earnings Per Share (EPS)

EPS is probably the most closely tracked figure when investors research public companies. As a result, it's usually quite easy to find a company's explanation for its falling earnings or slowing growth. It's up to you, however, to determine whether the factors that contributed to the decline will continue to affect the company's future. Home Depot's EPS growth rate of 20.9 percent (on a diluted basis) is excellent for a company of its size.

Capital Expenditures

A decline in capital expenditures might mean that the company is stretching the usable life of its capital assets or is not currently funding expansion. However, reduction in this measure might indicate cash flow problems. In Home Depot's annual report for the year, management attributes the 19.0 percent decline in capital expenditures to a shift in the timing of spending for future store openings. The company opened nearly the same number of stores in the most recent year as they did in the prior year, and also expected to spend significantly more in capital expenditures in the next year, so this one-year slowdown isn't a big concern.

If you see a percentage change that appears to be out of range, it might not mean anything at all. A big change in a relatively small value isn't necessarily a cause for concern. For example, a large increase in interest expense in a company with very low debt might not raise red flags because, in this case, even a small amount of additional debt results in a large percentage increase in interest expense.

> No company is perfect. Sometimes a company will stumble and turn in financial results that aren't so favorable when compared to the prior year. This doesn't necessarily mean that the company is in big trouble—it could be a temporary problem that management will be able to remedy. If your research on the changes doesn't satisfy you, watch the company with additional care for the next several quarters. If things don't turn around, consider selling the stock [Hack #86] before that short-term predicament turns into a long-term problem.

Be aware of a company's exposure to general economic trends, as well. A cyclical company's financial statements will show a downturn as the economy contracts, but this might not indicate management's lack of expertise.

—Douglas Gerlach

HACK #34 Compare Several Competitors to Identify the Strongest Candidate

A beauty pageant with only one contestant isn't likely to find the most talented or congenial individual. Likewise with stocks—before you invest, judge your candidate against several of its peers.

Long-term investors often approach their stock selections with the mantra, "Invest in the best." High-quality, well-managed companies will frequently be the best buy-and-hold investments in your portfolio. By comparing several competitors in the same industry, you can identify the strongest contenders. Another reason to pay attention to a company's competition is that many financial ratios vary based on the characteristics of each industry. By comparing a company's financial ratios to those of the competition, you can identify the company's strengths and weaknesses, and perhaps find a better prospect for your portfolio.

There are two ways to compare a stock to its rivals:

- Compare a contender directly to one of its competitors, particularly if the challenger is a leader in its industry. If the stock you're studying doesn't measure up, then it might be best to pass over that company—and perhaps take a closer look at the challenger instead.

- Compare a stock's financial results to the averages for its industry. When a company compares unfavorably to the industry average, you can do more research to understand why the company differs from the norm. If the stock is of below average caliber in a number of areas, it's often better to look for another company. By researching a company's numbers that exceed industry averages, you can better understand just why the company is an industry leader.

The quickest way to compare a company with its competition, appropriately enough, is to visit Quicken.com (*http://www.quicken.com*). Armed with a stock you're studying, type the ticker symbol in the Enter Symbol box and click Go. On the stock's Quote page under the Company Data heading in the left navigation bar, click Compare to Industry. The Compare to Competitors page displays a list of several competitors. You can type additional ticker symbols in the ticker box in Section 1, or check the checkboxes in Section 2 for each competitor that you want to use. If you don't see a competitor that you want, click the Show All Competitors link underneath the competitor table.

Select the Fundamentals option in Section 3 for the master view—a whopping 70 different criteria for each company. After you choose the competitors you want to use, click Compare to view the information for each of them. The comparison table displays the measures for each competitor, one below the next, as shown in Figure 4-19. If you prefer graphical comparisons, click the View chart link at the top of a category.

There's a lot of information in the Quicken.com comparison table. To digest this information, the best approach is somewhat old-fashioned—print the table, then circle the company that leads for each criterion. The company that's circled the most wins!

Reuters Investor (*http://investor.reuters.com*) provides an easy way to compare a company against industry and sector averages, as illustrated in Figure 4-20. After you type a ticker symbol in the Symbol box and click Go, click Ratios in the navigation bar. By default, valuation ratios such as the P/E ratio appear in a table next to the average values for the company's industry, sector, and the S&P 500. In the navigation bar, you can view other ratios by choosing any of the seven ratio categories: Valuation, Dividend, Growth Rate, Financial Condition, Profit Margin, Management Effectiveness, and Efficiency.

Compare Several Competitors to Identify the Strongest Candidate

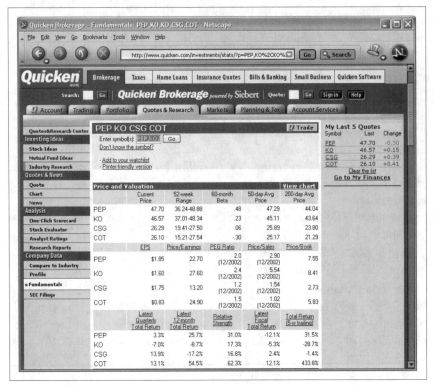

Figure 4-19. Quicken.com offers a wealth of comparative data for companies

In addition to the ratio comparisons, the Reuters Investor stock page includes a Risk Alert rating that's hard to ignore. Reuters assigns each company a low, medium, or high risk, based on the number of tests it passes or fails. However, the Risk Alert rating doesn't test a company's fundamental measures for risk. It uses estimate revisions, analyst recommendations, institutional selling, shorted shares, price deterioration, and price momentum. It's better to use your own judgment of a company's risk **[Hack #37]** after you've evaluated its fundamentals.

Be on the lookout for values that diverge significantly from the industry average. When a company is below the industry average, you must dig into the cause, whereas a positive variation can point out a company's strengths.

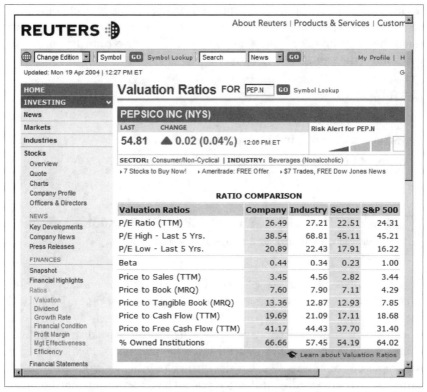

Figure 4-20. Reuters Investor provides industry comparisons for a large number of key ratios

In addition to industry averages, some data providers calculate sector averages. A sector is a broader classification, but might be too broad to make meaningful comparisons in many cases. For instance, the Utilities sector includes three industry groups: Electric, Natural Gas, and Water utilities. Because of the differences in those industries, comparing an electric utility to a water company or to sector averages won't necessarily help you determine the strongest stock in an industry.

To really dig into a company's position in its industry or to better understand its business, seek out trade publications and web sites aimed at people involved in that industry. Although content on these sites is sometimes restricted to subscribers, many sites have public articles and analyses that are quite informative. A finely tuned search at Google.com can turn up plenty of resources for particular industries and sectors. For instance, Bio.com (*http://*

www.bio.com) is a clearinghouse for information on the biotechnology sector. Silicon Investor (*http://www.siliconinvestor.com*) hosts discussion forums for technology investors, and Gas.com (*http://www.gas.com*) has links and news about the natural gas industry.

See Also

- Dow Jones Indexes (*http://www.djindexes.com*)
- Standard & Poor's Indexes (*http://www.spglobal.com*)
- Yahoo! Industry Center (*http://biz.yahoo.com/ic*)

—Douglas Gerlach

HACK #35   Measure Earnings Predictability in Excel

Calculating R-Squared for a company's earnings is one way to measure stock quality and risk.

Higher earnings increase the value of a company, which eventually increases a stock's price when investors realize the stock is worth more. How much the stock price increases depends on perception as much as reality. The stock market hates uncertainty, which is why investors usually pay more for companies that pump out consistently increasing earnings. Predictable earnings represent more safety—a greater chance of a higher stock price as the earnings increase steadily year after year. They also mean that company management is competent, successfully playing the problems and opportunities that every company is dealt. Although statistics are often maligned for twisting the meanings of numerical results, you can confidently apply the standard statistical function R-Squared to evaluate the predictability of a company's past earnings, and from that forecast its future earnings. Microsoft Excel makes this even easier with a built-in function that returns R-Squared as one of its results.

Getting the Earnings Data You Need

To measure earnings predictability, you need some earnings data. You should look for companies with at least five years of earnings, because you can't see meaningful trends with fewer years. To analyze earnings, use earnings per share (EPS), which illustrates how many dollars of earnings one share of stock generates. EPS is more meaningful than total earnings, because EPS can go up or down if a company issues more share, or initiates a stock buyback program. Issuing additional shares reduces the amount of earnings per share as well as the EPS growth rate (not good for existing shareholders), whereas buying back stock increases the EPS and EPS growth rate (good for existing shareholders).

You can obtain annual EPS figures from numerous online sources **[Hacks #18, #19, and #20]** and extract those numbers into a spreadsheet. Figure 4-21 shows EPS data for the past ten years for two companies: one grows consistently and the other one grows erratically.

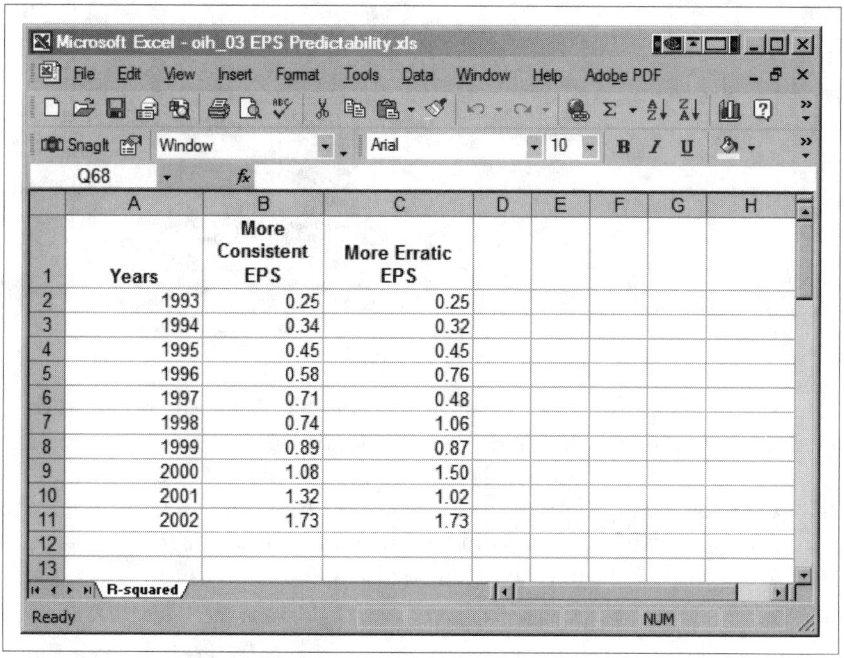

Years	More Consistent EPS	More Erratic EPS
1993	0.25	0.25
1994	0.34	0.32
1995	0.45	0.45
1996	0.58	0.76
1997	0.71	0.48
1998	0.74	1.06
1999	0.89	0.87
2000	1.08	1.50
2001	1.32	1.02
2002	1.73	1.73

Figure 4-21. Ten years of EPS data for two companies

In this example, the spreadsheet has three columns, with each row containing a calendar year and the EPS for each company. You could add additional company data in other columns. In practice, you might save a separate workbook for each company, with separate worksheets for the data and your financial analysis as described in "Find the Best Excel Tools for Fundamental Analysis for a Fee" **[Hack #42]**.

Looking at columns of EPS numbers doesn't show how quickly or consistently a company is growing. We are visual creatures, so graphs of EPS growth, such as the ones in Figure 4-22, are much more helpful. The data points in these graphs show the EPS for each of the last ten years. The thicker, straight line is an EPS growth trend line, which is called the least squares regression line, and is another statistical tool that Excel provides.

If you're looking at these EPS growth graphs closely, you might be concerned with the values on the Y-axes. The distance between 10 cents and 1 dollar is the same as the distance between 1 dollar and 10 dollars, but those

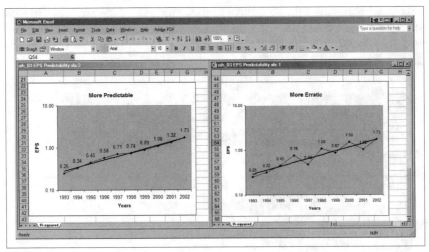

Figure 4-22. Graphs showing consistent and erratic EPS growth

values are different by an order of magnitude! Similar to interest paid on a bank savings account, EPS growth compounds on itself, and the earnings from the prior year fuel even higher earnings in the next year. Because of this, earnings ideally should grow exponentially. Fortunately, through the magic of mathematics, compounded growth plots as a straight line on logarithmic graphs like the ones in Figure 4-22.

Even if you have created charts in Excel [Hack #13] before, these charts use some Excel features that might be unfamiliar to you. To create a logarithmic chart of EPS growth, follow these steps:

1. Insert a line chart with markers at each data point by clicking Insert → Chart and clicking Line in the Chart Type list. Click the image of a line chart with markers at each data point and click Next.

2. Specify the cells containing EPS data by dragging the cursor over them (B2 through B11 for more consistent EPS in the example) and click Next.

3. To add the years as labels on the X-axis, select the Series tab and click the Categories (X) Axis Labels box. Drag the mouse pointer over the cells containing the years (A2 through A11 in the example). Type a name in the Name box to assign a more meaningful name to the series of data points. Click Next.

4. To display the values next to the data points, select the Data Labels tab and check the Value checkbox. Click Finish to add the basic chart to the active worksheet.

5. To change the chart to a logarithmic scale, hover the pointer over the Y-axis until the words Value Axis appear, right-click the Y-axis, and choose Format Axis from the shortcut menu.

6. Select the Scale tab, check the Logarithmic Scale checkbox, and click OK. Excel will set the units, and the minimum and maximum values for you.

7. To specify the starting value for the Y-axis, right-click the Y-axis again and click Format Axis. This time, check the Category (X) axis checkbox, type the starting value you want, such as **.1**, in the Crosses At box, and click OK.

8. To add a trend line to the chart, right-click the line between any two data points and choose Add Trendline from the shortcut menu. Click the Exponential box and click OK.

You can right-click other chart elements to format them, for instance to reposition the data labels, remove the legend, or clear the horizontal gridline.

Now that you can visualize earnings growth, you can quantitatively measure the quality of that growth using R-Squared.

Understanding the R-Squared Measure

R-Squared (a.k.a. the coefficient of determination in the statistical world) compares the least squares regression line to a set of actual data. What does that mean? R-Squared measures how closely a set of data maps to the straight line that fits those points the best. The closer the data fits the straight line, the more predictable the data is. The least squares regression line, represented by the trend lines in Figure 4-22, is a straight line that fits the data points the closest, because the total of all the gaps between the line and the actual points is the smallest value you can obtain.

You can read more about the math behind R-Squared and the least squares regression line at *http://www.stat. washington.edu/pip/courses/stat390/notes5_4.pdf*.

To analyze how consistently a company grows, use the least squares method to estimate an average historical growth rate (called a trend line) from a company's historical EPS. Then, you can calculate R-Squared to measure how predictable the annual EPS is when compared to that growth rate. If you're trying to choose between two companies of comparable growth, you can evaluate differences in quality by comparing R-Squared values. R-Squared ranges between zero and one: one indicates that the trend line is a perfectly reliable representation of past EPS, and zero means that the trend line is useless.

Using Excel to Calculate R-Squared

Microsoft Excel includes two functions, LINEST and LOGEST, that calculate regression lines and their associated R-Squared values. LINEST works with linear growth rates. Because EPS should grow exponentially due to the effect of compounding, you use LOGEST to compute R-Squared for EPS.

The LOGEST function computes the least squares regression line for a specified set of X and Y values and returns an array of values that describes the line. Using calendar years for the X values and EPS as the Y values, the LOGEST R-Squared measures EPS predictability—how well you can predict past EPS with a trend line, and thereby determining the confidence with which you can predict future EPS by extrapolating the EPS growth trend line into the future. Here's how the LOGEST function works.

To use LOGEST(Known-Y's, Known-X's, Const, Stats) to show EPS predictability, Excel uses the following four parameters:

Known-Y's
> The range of cells that contains the company's EPS for a number of years.

Known-X's
> The range of cells that contains the calendar years (or simply a sequence of digits) that correspond to the reported EPS. For example, you can use years such as 1993 through 2004 or the numbers 1 through 10 to represent ten years of data.

Const
> A logical value that specifies whether the line is forced through the origin. This constant has no effect on the R-Squared calculation, so you can omit this parameter.

Stats
> A logical value that specifies whether the function returns only the Y-intercept and slope coefficients or also returns additional regression statistics, such as R-Squared (which you should set to True for EPS predictability).

When the parameter Stats is False, LOGEST returns only the slope coefficient m and the Y-axis intercept constant b. When Stats equals True, LOGEST returns additional regression statistics, listed in Table 4-9.

Table 4-9. The LOGEST function provides a full set of regression statistics for a data set

Statistic	Description
se1,se2,...,sen	The standard error values for the slope coefficients.
seb	The standard error value for the constant b. Note that seb equals #N/A when constant is False.
r2	The R-Squared measure you use for earnings predictability.
sey	The standard error for the Y estimate.
F	The F measure, which determines whether the relationship between the variables occurs by chance.
df	The degrees of freedom you use to find F-critical values in a statistical table.
ssreg	The regression sum of squares is the sum of the distances between the points on the line and the average Y value.
ssresid	The residual sum of squares is the sum of the gaps between the points on the line and the actual data points.

In this example, you don't want all those other parameters. Fortunately, you can retrieve only the R-Squared result by using the INDEX function, which plucks a value out of an array. R-Squared is the third value in the LOGEST array, so you can use the following syntax to display R-Squared in a cell:

```
=INDEX(LOGEST(B2:B11,A3:A11,,TRUE),3)
```

Figure 4-23 shows two examples of combining LOGEST and INDEX to calculate R-Squared. The relatively consistent growth shown in Figure 4-22 generates an R-Squared of .98, very close to the perfect correlation of 1.0. On the other hand, the jumpy earnings growth shown in Figure 4-22 results in an R-Squared of .86, indicating less EPS predictability and lower quality of growth.

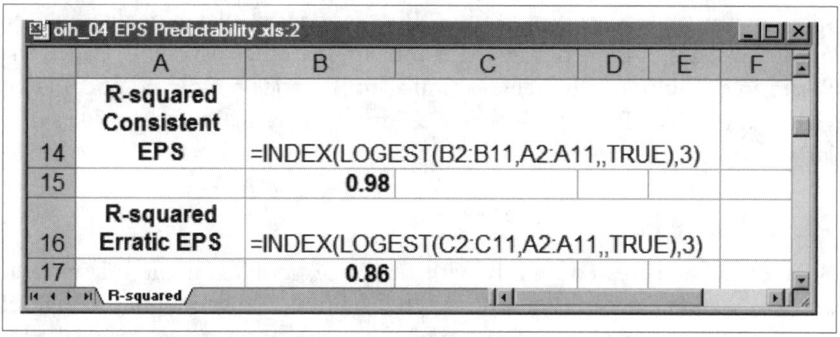

Figure 4-23. The Excel formula for calculating R-Squared

Hacking the Hack

Building a spreadsheet just to calculate R-Squared isn't useful if you plan to evaluate several other aspects of a company. To streamline your financial studies, follow the instructions in "Steps to Building a Financial Analysis Template" **[Hack #45]** to create a standard spreadsheet to hold all the tools that you use to evaluate a stock: graphs that show sales and EPS growth, financial ratios, and quantitative measures such as R-Squared. For example, you can run a macro, specify the file that contains company data, and watch Excel populate the functions and charts for your analysis.

Use Rational Values to Buy and Sell Wisely

#36 By determining the rational value of stocks, improve your investment results by keeping emotions out of your buy and sell decisions.

It's really tough for an investor to remain upbeat and hold investments whose prices are plummeting in the throes of a down market. And it's equally difficult to be realistic and patient (the cornerstones of successful investing) when the stock market is soaring. By assessing the *rational price* of a stock and the *rational value* of your portfolio, you can make sensible choices when others overreact.

Many shareholders fail to realize that there is a finite, absolute—though approximate—value for each share of stock. When viewed over a five-year period, the short-term ups and downs of a stock's price generally vary on either side of a value that's tied to the earnings of the underlying company. When you select successful companies capable of growing their earnings at a substantial rate, the underlying value of your shares should climb as well.

The relationship between a company's earnings and its stock's price is measured by the price to earnings ratio **[Hack #27]** and is calculated by dividing the price of a share of the stock by the company's earnings per share. Called the P/E ratio or multiple, this value is similar to the price per pound of coffee or gallon of gas. The P/E ratio is the price investors are willing to pay for a dollar's worth of the underlying company's earnings.

The Signature PE

Because it fluctuates constantly with the price, looking at the P/E ratio at any given moment isn't going to be that helpful. However, the average of those P/E ratios over a significant period of time can provide a typical, reasonable multiple of earnings to which the P/E ratio returns from higher or lower values, shown in Table 4-10. This value is called the *signature PE*.

Table 4-10. Using ten years of P/E ratios to identify the signature PE

Year	EPS	High price	Low price	High PE	Low PE
1993	0.39	5.60	4.10	14.4	10.5
1994	0.47	6.00	4.20	12.8	8.9
1995	0.58	7.50	5.30	12.9	9.1
1996	0.68	11.00	7.10	16.2	10.4
1997	1.04	14.50	9.40	13.9	9.0
1998	0.88	22.70	11.30	25.8	12.8
1999	1.04	28.40	19.50	27.3	18.8
2000	1.14	37.50	16.80	32.9	14.7
2001	1.28	36.10	23.00	28.2	18.0
2002	1.55	33.50	23.10	21.6	14.9
Median values				18.9	11.7
Average or signature PE					15.3

Until the end of the twentieth century, looking at the average P/E ratio over a five-year period seemed adequate because the average economic or business cycle ran its course in that length of time. However, the duration and amplitude of the most recent boom and ensuing bust have shown that we must consider an average P/E ratio over a longer period of time.

To arrive at a signature PE, the best approach is to calculate the high and low P/E ratios for the last ten years, calculate their medians to eliminate anomalous data above and below, then average the resulting values. Unlike an average, the median is the value with equal numbers of entries above and below. If there is an even number of values, the median is the average of the two middle values of the set of numbers.

Table 4-10 shows the calculation for the signature PE using the high and low prices and the earnings data for Aflac Inc. (AFL), the insurance company. When you consider that the signature PE represents a reasonable rate to pay for a dollar's worth of Aflac's earnings, it's easy to see in Table 4-10 that there were times—indeed entire years—when investors paid more than a reasonable P/E ratio and times when they paid less. By its definition, the average multiple paid for this stock was above the signature PE about half the time and below it the other half.

When the current P/E ratio is above the signature PE, the P/E ratio is likely to eventually decline; if the P/E ratio is below, it should sooner or later grow. Looking at the chart in Figure 4-24, you can see that, although the amplitude of the swing above or below might vary, the P/E ratios rise or fall to gravitate toward the signature PE.

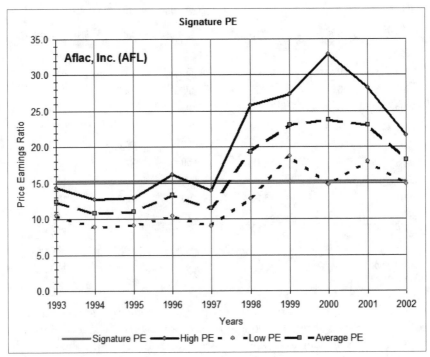

Figure 4-24. The P/E ratio varies above and below the signature PE

The Historical Value Ratio

How can you put the P/E ratio's tendency to return to the signature PE to practical use? There are several ways. When contemplating the purchase of a stock, look at the current P/E ratio and compare it to the signature PE. If the current P/E ratio is much above the signature PE, the stock is probably too pricey and will likely go down over time. If it's below, you might have a bargain.

> Before you snap up what looks like a bargain, you should question what others might know about the company that you don't. Something might be causing folks to sell and pushing the price below where it's traditionally been.

Dividing the current P/E ratio by the signature PE produces the *historical value ratio* (HVR). This is a way to quantify the comparison. If the HVR is more than, say, 110 percent, the rate for a dollar's worth of earnings is more than 10 percent above the typical rate. You probably should wait for the price to fall into a more reasonable range. If your HVR is below 90 percent, be careful. There might be a very good reason.

Rational Price and Rational Value

Probably the most useful purpose for the HVR is the calculation of a *rational price* and its derivative, *rational value*. The rational price of a stock is simply the price you would pay if the stock were selling at its signature PE, i.e., an HVR of 100 percent. If you've calculated the HVR for a stock, you can figure out the rational price by simply dividing the current price by the HVR. When the HVR is below 100 percent, the rational price for a stock is higher than the current price. When the HVR is elevated, the rational price is lower than the current price.

From this, it's easy to see that the rational value of your holdings in that company would be the product of the rational price and the number of shares you own. And the rational value of your portfolio would be the sum of the rational values of the stocks within it.

Relative value [Hack #27] is similar to rational value but utilizes the average P/E ratio of the most recent five years in lieu of the median over ten years. Looking at the chart in Figure 4-25, the elevated P/E ratios of the most recent five years show why using ten years of P/E ratio data is preferable. It would produce a more rational result than the more optimistic values of the past five years. However, you can use relative value as a quick-and-dirty method of arriving at the rational value. If you choose to use relative value, you must do your utmost to eliminate irrelevant, anomalous data from the five-year history before dividing the current price by the relative value to produce the rational price.

To see the benefit of using rational value to evaluate a portfolio, let's view a sample portfolio of 15 of the most widely held stocks at different points during the most recent bull and bear markets.

	B	C	D	E	F	G	H	I	J	K
4	Ticker	Signature PE	Shares	Price	Value	EPS	PE	HVR	Rational price	Rational value
5	AFL	15.4	200	10.10	2,019.00	0.69	14.7	0.96	10.55	2,109.80
6	AMGN	25.6	200	15.28	3,056.00	0.61	25.0	0.98	15.62	3,123.20
7	CSCO	42.0	200	6.18	1,236.00	0.17	36.4	0.87	7.14	1,428.00
8	GE	24.3	200	17.15	3,430.00	0.73	23.5	0.97	17.74	3,547.80
9	HD	32.6	200	12.14	2,428.00	0.43	28.2	0.87	14.02	2,803.60
10	HDI	23.8	200	9.34	1,868.00	0.48	19.5	0.82	11.42	2,284.80
11	INTC	24.1	200	17.73	3,546.00	0.72	24.6	1.02	17.35	3,470.40
12	JNJ	25.4	200	28.75	5,750.00	1.09	26.4	1.04	27.69	5,537.20
13	MRK	23.8	200	46.06	9,212.00	1.60	28.8	1.21	38.08	7,616.00
14	MSFT	31.2	200	12.19	2,438.00	0.24	50.8	1.63	7.49	1,497.60
15	ORCL	31.2	200	4.36	872.00	0.12	36.3	1.16	3.74	748.80
16	PEP	23.3	200	33.00	6,600.00	0.61	54.1	2.32	14.21	2,842.60
17	PFE	29.8	200	15.27	3,054.00	0.50	30.5	1.02	14.90	2,980.00
18	WAG	30.6	200	10.69	2,138.00	0.39	27.4	0.90	11.93	2,386.80
19	WMT	27.3	200	13.19	2,638.00	0.67	19.7	0.72	18.29	3,658.20
20					50,285.00	9.2%	above the rational value			46,034.80

Sheet1 \ Sheet2 / Sheet3 / Sheet4 /

Figure 4-25. Prices were just over their rational value in February 1997

Figure 4-25 shows that prices were relatively normal in February of 1997, priced a bit above the rational value. Investors were becoming a bit exuberant. If stocks were selling at a P/E ratio about what they had historically sold for, the portfolio's value would have been around $46,000, but investors were willing to pay $50,285.

Earnings and prices have been adjusted to compensate for splits.

In February of 2000, optimism was in full swing, near the peak of the period of *irrational exuberance* when the Greater Fool Theory dominated the decision making process. The market valued this portfolio at more than $132,000—more than 56 percent above the rational prices for its stocks, as shown in Figure 4-26. The increase in rational value from February 1997 was a natural result of earnings growth. The P/E ratios above the signature PEs as well as HVR values higher than 1.0 were telltale signs that the market was seriously inflated. Calculating the rational value is a good way to keep your feet on the ground in times like these.

	B	C	D	E	F	G	H	I	J	K	
		Signature							Rational		
22	Ticker	PE	Shares	Price	Value	EPS	PE	HVR	price	Rational value	
23	AFL	15.4	200	18.28	3,656.00	1.04	17.6	1.14	16.02	3,203.20	
24	AMGN	25.6	200	68.19	13,638.00	1.01	67.5	2.64	25.86	5,171.20	
25	CSCO	42.0	200	66.09	13,218.00	0.39	169.5	4.03	16.38	3,276.00	
26	GE	24.3	200	44.13	8,826.00	1.05	42.0	1.73	25.52	5,103.00	
27	HD	32.6	200	57.81	11,562.00	1.02	56.7	1.74	33.25	6,650.40	
28	HDI	23.8	200	34.06	6,812.00	0.86	39.6	1.66	20.47	4,093.60	
29	INTC	24.1	200	56.50	11,300.00	1.09	51.8	2.15	26.27	5,253.80	
30	JNJ	25.4	200	36.00	7,200.00	1.48	24.3	0.96	37.59	7,518.40	
31	MRK	23.8	200	61.56	12,312.00	2.45	25.1	1.06	58.31	11,662.00	
32	MSFT	31.2	200	44.69	8,938.00	1.71	26.1	0.84	53.35	10,670.40	
33	ORCL	31.2	200	37.13	7,426.00	0.24	154.7	4.96	7.49	1,497.60	
34	PEP	23.3	200	32.13	6,426.00	1.07	30.0	1.29	24.93	4,986.20	
35	PFE	29.8	200	32.13	6,426.00	0.83	38.7	1.30	24.73	4,946.80	
36	WAG	30.6	200	25.81	5,162.00	0.65	39.7	1.30	19.89	3,978.00	
37	WMT	27.3	200	48.88	9,776.00	1.28	38.2	1.40	34.94	6,988.80	
38					132,678.00	56.1%	above the rational value			84,999.40	

Figure 4-26. In February 2000, investors were paying irrationally high prices for stocks

By February of 2003 the bubble had burst, and the value of the portfolio, measured by what the now irrationally fearful market was paying for good quality stocks, had plummeted 27 percent from its high. Investors who had been willing to pay $132,000 for a portfolio rationally worth $84,999 were now paying only $97,884 for stocks rationally worth $112,613, as shown in Figure 4-27. The rational value of this portfolio, based on earnings growth, had continued to increase, even while those who didn't know any better were practically giving away their stocks. In times like these, when the hardiest of the long-term investors are suffering doubts and fears, it's helpful to look at the rational value to realize that the actual value of the portfolio should be considerably higher—and will be just as soon as the market comes back to its senses and pays a reasonable multiple of earnings for the stocks.

	B	C	D	E	F	G	H	I	J	K	
40	Ticker	Signature PE	Shares	Price	Value	EPS	PE	HVR	Rational price	Rational value	
41	AFL	15.4	200	31.25	6,250.00	1.55	20.2	1.31	23.87	4,774.00	
42	AMGN	25.6	200	54.64	10,928.00	1.29	42.4	1.65	33.02	6,604.80	
43	CSCO	42.0	200	13.98	2,796.00	0.44	31.8	0.76	18.48	3,696.00	
44	GE	24.3	200	24.05	4,810.00	1.44	16.7	0.69	34.99	6,998.40	
45	HD	32.6	200	23.45	4,690.00	1.56	15.0	0.46	50.86	10,171.20	
46	HDI	23.8	200	39.59	7,918.00	1.89	20.9	0.88	44.98	8,996.40	
47	INTC	24.1	200	17.26	3,452.00	0.49	35.2	1.46	11.81	2,361.80	
48	JNJ	25.4	200	52.45	10,490.00	2.27	23.1	0.91	57.66	11,531.60	
49	MRK	23.8	200	52.75	10,550.00	3.01	17.5	0.74	71.64	14,327.60	
50	MSFT	31.2	200	23.70	4,740.00	0.99	23.9	0.77	30.89	6,177.60	
51	ORCL	31.2	200	11.96	2,392.00	0.38	31.5	1.01	11.86	2,371.20	
52	PEP	23.3	200	38.32	7,664.00	1.97	19.5	0.83	45.90	9,180.20	
53	PFE	29.8	200	29.82	5,964.00	1.56	19.1	0.64	46.49	9,297.60	
54	WAG	30.6	200	28.14	5,628.00	1.02	27.6	0.90	31.21	6,242.40	
55	WMT	27.3	200	48.06	9,612.00	1.81	26.6	0.97	49.41	9,882.60	
56					97,884.00	-13.1%	below the rational value			112,613.40	

Figure 4-27. In February 2003, investors reversed themselves and were paying less than stocks were worth

Sure enough, only eight months from the depths of the market collapse, the market value of the portfolio had already exceeded the rational value from the previous February, as shown in Figure 4-28. What's more, the rational value had increased with the healthy increases in earnings that attended the end of the recession. This portfolio still has plenty of P/E ratio expansion to enjoy as its market value climbs to reach its current rational value.

Code

One of the best sources of data for this exercise [Hack #20] is NAIC's .ssg files, available through NAIC (Online Premium Service), or data available through AAII's Stock Investor Pro. When you open an .ssg file for any stock in Excel, the entire file is stored in column A, cells 1 through 531. You can set up an Excel template for these files using a defined array variable to calculate the HVR for a company.

Files in .ssg format contain the data you need in the following cells:

Annual high prices = $A$1:$A$10
Annual low prices = $A$11:$A$20
Annual earnings per share = $A$71:$A$80
Current PE = $A$92

	B	C	D	E	F	G	H	I	J	K
		Signature							Rational	
58	Ticker	PE	Shares	Price	Value	EPS	PE	HVR	price	Rational value
59	AFL	15.4	200	36.48	7,296.00	1.73	21.1	1.37	26.64	5,328.40
60	AMGN	25.6	200	61.76	12,352.00	1.56	39.6	1.55	39.94	7,987.20
61	CSCO	42.0	200	20.93	4,186.00	0.51	41.0	0.98	21.42	4,284.00
62	GE	24.3	200	29.01	5,802.00	1.40	20.7	0.85	34.02	6,804.00
63	HD	32.6	200	37.07	7,414.00	1.65	22.5	0.69	53.79	10,758.00
64	HDI	23.8	200	47.41	9,482.00	2.38	19.9	0.84	56.64	11,328.80
65	INTC	24.1	200	32.95	6,590.00	0.69	47.8	1.98	16.63	3,325.80
66	JNJ	25.4	200	50.33	10,066.00	2.56	19.7	0.77	65.02	13,004.80
67	MRK	23.8	200	44.25	8,850.00	3.16	14.0	0.59	75.21	15,041.60
68	MSFT	31.2	200	26.14	5,228.00	1.02	25.6	0.82	31.82	6,364.80
69	ORCL	31.2	200	11.97	2,394.00	0.45	26.6	0.85	14.04	2,808.00
70	PEP	23.3	200	47.82	9,564.00	2.17	22.0	0.95	50.56	10,112.20
71	PFE	29.8	200	31.60	6,320.00	1.17	27.0	0.91	34.87	6,973.20
72	WAG	30.6	200	34.82	6,964.00	1.12	31.1	1.02	34.27	6,854.40
73	WMT	27.3	200	58.95	11,790.00	1.93	30.5	1.12	52.69	10,537.80
74					114,298.00	-5.9%	below the rational value			121,513.00

Figure 4-28. A recent look at the rational value of several stocks

To create named ranges [Hack #9] in your Excel file, select the cells you want to add to a named range and choose Insert Name → Define. Type the name for the range in the Names In Workbook box and click Add.

Name and define the ranges in Table 4-11 if you use *.ssg* files for data. If you use a different data source, substitute these cell ranges with the cell ranges for the same data in your data source.

Table 4-11. Named ranges for calculating rational values

Named range	Cell range
HighPrices	$A$1:$A$10
LowPrices	$A$11:$A$20
EPS	$A$71:$A$80
PE	$A$92
HVR	$D$1

To calculate HVR, type the formula in Example 4-51 in the HVR cell, and then create an array formula by pressing Shift-Ctrl-Enter.

Example 4-51. Formula for calculating the HVR

```
HVR = PE / (AVERAGE(MEDIAN(IF(HighPrices<>0,HighPrices/EPS)),
    MEDIAN(IF(LowPrices<>0,LowPrices/EPS))))
```

The IF function evaluates empty cells as zero. However, the formula in Example 4-51 won't generate a divide by zero error for companies with less than 10 years of data. The third argument for the IF function is missing as well as the comma preceding the third argument. This means that when a value in the HighPrices or LowPrices named range equals zero, the IF function returns False, which in turn triggers the MEDIAN function to ignore that data point because it's text. If you were to include the comma in the IF function, the formula would generate a divide by zero error.

> An array formula permits arrays to be manipulated mathematically by other arrays. When you type an array formula in a worksheet cell, Excel places brackets ({}) around the formula, which appear in the formula bar when you select the cell.

To display the value for HVR in a cell in the worksheet, type **=HVR** in the cell. Because named ranges apply to an entire workbook, you can type **=HVR** in any cell in any worksheet within the Excel workbook. This formula returns the HVR of the company using as many years of P/E ratio history as are available.

—Ellis Traub

HACK #37   Are You Walking on the Wild Side?

Make sure that the investment return your portfolio is earning sufficient compensation for the risks you take.

In investing, risk and return walk hand in hand—the more risk you accept, the more return you should earn. Some investors are so afraid of losing money that they play it safe, purchasing certificates of deposit or hiding money under the mattress. Unfortunately, no investment is without risk. Even if you hide money in your mattress, it can burn in a fire with the rest of your belongings! At the other end of the spectrum, you might be willing to take big risks to grab big gains. In this case, the key is to accept risks only when the payoff justifies the potential losses. By understanding the risks you take and balancing those risks with your investment return, you can reach your financial goals without unnecessary jolts to your system.

Understanding Risk

Risk comes in many forms, and each type of investment carries its own unique combination of risks. For some investments, risk decreases the longer you own them. For others, the opposite is true. For example, over short periods of time, stocks carry a lot of risk. 1931 turned in the largest one-year loss in stocks (the market index of large-cap stocks in this example)—over 43 percent. Even over a few 10-year periods, market indexes have lost principal. However, when you evaluate stock market indexes over

20-year periods, they have *never* lost money. Conversely, with an FDIC-insured savings account, you won't lose any of the money you save. However, inflation decreases the buying power of your money, so that you are guaranteed to have *less* buying power when you keep your money in savings for long periods of time. The dollar amount might be the same, but the value of your savings is less in terms of what you can buy with them.

To get a handle on the types of risks you face and how to tame them, let's review. *Market risk* is the chance that you will lose money on a bad investment. However, the level of market risk depends on how you invest and how long you hold your investments. If you count on a stock tip from a taxi driver, your risk might be high no matter how long you hold your investment. However, if you choose your investments wisely, invest in a diversified portfolio [Hack #74], and hold for the long term, your market risk is barely noticeable.

For a one-year period, the return on the large-cap stock market index is a roller-coaster ride from a one-year high of 54 percent in 1933 to a heart-stopping low of 43.3 percent in 1931. However, for the past 75 years, a hypothetical investment in the large-cap stock market index including reinvested dividends has averaged a compound annual return of about 11 percent.

> Holding-period risk is the risk that you might have to sell an investment prematurely—at a time when its value is depressed.

Economic risk is the danger you face when the entire economy tanks. Fortunately, recessions don't occur that often and don't last that long (although it feels like forever at the time). Interest rates going up, war breaking out, and financial problems occurring in another part of the world all affect the stock market. In the late 1990s, dot-com stocks and initial public offerings (IPOs) were darlings, but when the economy went into hibernation, those investments along with other overvalued stocks dropped like rocks.

When things get tough, investors return to the basics: earnings. Regardless of how steamy the story on a hot prospect, the stock price will still drop if the company doesn't have earnings and steady earnings growth to support its price. The bottom line is to avoid economic risk. Don't speculate. Invest.

Inflation risk is a hidden time bomb. Unlike market risk and economic risk, inflation risk compounds over time. The danger of inflation risk is that cautious people put their money in safe investments for years, only to find that their savings end up worth less than what they started with.

Inflation risk is the loss of purchasing power. Just think of the last time you said something like "I remember when a loaf of bread was only (25 cents, 1 dollar, 2 dollars, fill in your price)." For example, at the end of 30 years of three percent inflation, 1 dollar is worth only about 40 cents. If inflation is 3 percent, and your savings account pays 2 percent interest, you are losing just over 1 percent of your money to inflation each year.

Bond investors [Hack #80] are faced with *interest-rate risk,* which is the chance that your investment loses value because its fixed rate of return doesn't change when interest rates rise. The bond value falls because its rate of return is not as attractive as the going market interest rate. For short-term investments such as CDs, *reinvestment risk* is the risk that rates will be lower when your investment matures.

> If you want to learn more about risk and its effect on your investments, take the "Understanding Risk" course at *http:// www.riskgrades.com/retail/clients/RetailCourse/index.cgi.* You must register (no charge) at the site to access its educational materials.

Retirees face one additional risk: outliving their assets. When you plan for retirement [Hack #96], you make assumptions about how long you will live and how much money you will need. Although you can adjust your spending to compensate for lower investment returns, it's too late to make changes when you live longer than you anticipated. You can mitigate this risk in several ways. Using a ripe old age in your retirement plan can help you build up enough assets to last. Consider purchasing long-term care insurance when you retire to cover the high costs of assisted living and nursing homes. A reverse mortgage on your home can provide expenses for living. The bottom line: if you don't plan in some way for a long life, your choices could be unappealing.

Risk Measures

Modern portfolio theory is an approach to investing that evaluates the market as a whole, and evaluates investments based statistically on their short-term volatility and long-term returns. In this philosophy, volatility equals risk. The goal of modern portfolio theory's statistical calculations is to identify your acceptable level of risk and the portfolio that provides the greatest return for that level of risk. Fundamental investors calculate risks a little differently. They analyze each company's fundamentals to find companies whose stock price is likely to increase due to company growth, quality, strength, and an attractive stock price. They manage risk by diversifying their portfolios [Hack #74] and by buying stocks when their potential return exceeds potential losses by a wide enough margin. However, you can use the statistical risk measures spawned by modern portfolio theory to evaluate risk inherent in the individual investments in your portfolio. You can also evaluate the potential investments you're studying to take into account risk along with fundamental criteria.

> MoneyChimp.com provides a good introduction to modern portfolio theory at *http://www.moneychimp.com/articles/risk/ riskintro.htm.*

Standard deviation is one way to measure an investment's volatility and does so by figuring out how far any given year's return might be from the average return. In statistics, the average is known as the *mean*. To assess your risk tolerance given a standard deviation value (32 percent for example), simply ask yourself, "Would I be comfortable if this stock dropped 32 percent in one year?" If the answer is no, the stock is too risky for you. Move on.

The formula for standard deviation is shown in Example 4-52.

Example 4-52. The formula for calculating standard deviation of data

```
Standard deviation = Σ(X - mean)² / N
```

This formula contains the following elements:

X

   Represents each datum being evaluated (in this case, the annual returns)

mean

   Represents the average of all the data

N

   Represents the number of data points

> In Excel, the STDEV function calculates the standard deviation of a set of values.

The *Sharpe Ratio* [Hack #65] measures reward to risk. For the Sharpe Ratio, reward is measured by the amount of return an investment provides in excess of the return of a risk-free investment (cash). For example, if an investment returns 4 percent and saving money in a savings account returns .75 percent, the reward is 3.25 percent. The risk is measured by the standard deviation of the investment's returns. The result of this ratio is the amount of excess return an investment generates per unit of risk.

The formula for the Sharpe Ratio is shown in Example 4-53.

Example 4-53. The formula for the Sharpe Ratio

```
S(i) = (ri - Rf) / StdDev(i)
```

This formula contains the following elements:

i

Represents the investment you are evaluating

ri

Represents the average annual return for investment i

Rf

Represents the best available return for a risk-free security such as cash or a 90-day U.S. Treasury bill

StdDev(i)

Represents the standard deviation of ri

If two investments have the same return, the one with the higher Sharpe Ratio provides its return with less volatility.

> To learn more about the Sharpe Ratio, visit *http://www.moneychimp.com/articles/risk/sharpe_ratio.htm*.

Beta measures how much an investment changes compared to changes in the overall market. By definition, the beta of a benchmark, such as an index, is 1.0. An investment with a beta of 1.25 performs 25 percent better than its benchmark index in up markets and 25 percent worse in down markets, all other factors remaining constant.

A low beta doesn't necessarily mean that an investment isn't volatile. It simply means the investment's volatility is low in relation to the volatility of its benchmark index. For example, a beta of 0.70 indicates that an investment performs 30 percent worse than the index in up markets and 30 percent better in down markets.

> Beta isn't a perfect measure. Because it rates investments based on their past performance, the beta for an investment doesn't reflect changes to risk, such as when a utility gets involved in the merchant energy business. In addition, beta is a better measure of risk for short holding periods, when price fluctuations add risk. However, for long-term investors, short-term price fluctuations are meaningless. For example, Warren Buffett doesn't care for beta as a measure, because he considers the volatility of the market as an opportunity to invest in attractive companies.

Alpha represents the difference between an investment's actual and expected returns, given the level of risk identified by its beta value. A positive alpha value indicates that an investment has performed better than you would expect based on its beta. A negative alpha value means that an investment has performed worse than beta predicts. The formula for alpha is shown in Example 4-54.

Example 4-54. The formula for calculating alpha

```
Alpha = Excess return - ((Beta x (Benchmark return - Treasury return))
```

This formula contains the following elements:

Excess return
> Represents the excess return that the investment provides above the treasury return

Benchmark return
> Represents the total return of the investment's corresponding benchmark index

Treasury return
> Represents the return on a three-month Treasury bill

In pure statistics, R-Squared [Hack #35] measures how closely a set of data maps to a straight line. However, in investing, R-Squared can represent several things. If you use R-Squared to evaluate a company's sales or earnings, it tells you how predictable the company's performance has been. For mutual funds, R-Squared is often calculated by comparing a fund's performance to the benchmark index performance. In this case, R-Squared represents the percentage of the fund's performance that is explained by the performance of its benchmark index.

An R-Squared equal to 1 means the data and the straight line are a total match. For stock earnings, this means that you can predict the company's future earnings with reasonable confidence. For a mutual fund, an R-Squared of 1 (sometimes normalized to 100) means that the fund completely follows the index [Hack #68].

An Online Tool for Checking Risk Versus Return

All these risk values can be helpful, but on the Web, they're not often presented for stocks. Don't fret. The RiskGrades.com web site (*http://www.riskgrades.com*) provides tools that make it easy to see whether you're balancing risk and return.

The RiskGrade developed by the Risk Metrics Group measures volatility and is similar to standard deviation and the Sharpe Ratio in that respect. However, it differs in several ways. First, it weights historical data so the measure places more emphasis on current conditions. It is also normalized so that a RiskGrade value of 100 represents the typical risk inherent in the global equity market. In addition, the RiskGrade takes into account *currency risk*, which is the risk that currency exchange rates affect an investment's value. For example, if you use U.S. dollars to purchase a European stock, the RiskGrade incorporates both the risk in the stock itself and the currency risk between dollars and euros.

Several RiskGrade tools help you evaluate potential investments or those already in your portfolio. However, all of these tools help you identify whether the risks you take are appropriate for your risk tolerance and for the returns that your investments provide.

Evaluating individual investments. If you want a RiskGrade for only one investment, choose Get a RiskGrade from the menu bar. Select the market in which the investment trades, such as US Equity, type the ticker symbol in the box, and click Go. The ticker and RiskGrade for the company appear in the Get a RiskGrade dialog box. If your tolerance for risk is average, look for RiskGrades below 80. If a RiskGrade is above 100, which indicates risk greater than that of the global equity market, check the investment's return for above-average performance.

To view a chart of the change in risk over time, illustrated in Figure 4-29, type a ticker in the Get a RiskGrade dialog box and click RiskChart. You can select periods from three months to one year or specify the date range you want to evaluate. You can also compare a company's risk to a benchmark index or to other companies. To add other companies to the chart, type additional ticker symbols in the Symbols box separated by commas. To add benchmarks, type the ticker for the benchmark in the "Add benchmarks to chart" box at the bottom of the page and click Add.

You can use the RiskChart in several ways. You can determine whether an existing investment or one that you are considering has a RiskGrade within your risk tolerance. For example, if you are risk averse, look for RiskGrades below 50 and also consider investments whose risk tends to stay low over time. You can also use a RiskChart showing several companies to choose companies with acceptable risk for further study.

Evaluating your portfolio. To use the portfolio risk analysis tools, you must first enter your portfolio. RiskGrades.com portfolios can contain stocks, mutual funds and trusts, bonds, equity options, and cash. If your portfolio is extensive, you can upload a file to build your portfolio. However, if you own only a few investments, it's easier to type in the ticker and number of shares. You can create multiple portfolios, for instance if you want to evaluate the

Are You Walking on the Wild Side?

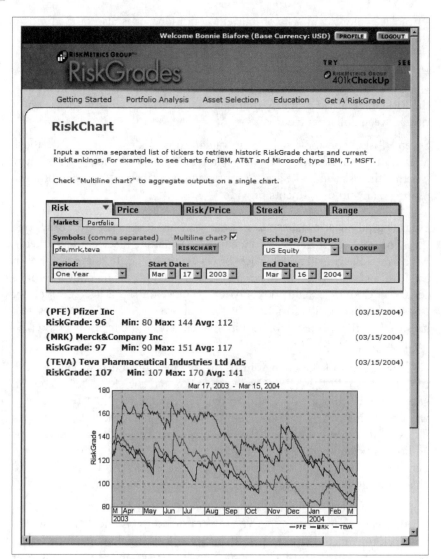

Figure 4-29. Use a RiskChart to compare risks for competitors over time

risk levels of funds earmarked for different purposes, such as retirement and college tuition. To create a portfolio, choose Portfolio Analysis → My Portfolio from the RiskGrades.com menu bar and then click Create New Portfolio.

The portfolio table displays the risk statistics for the investments in a portfolio, as shown in Figure 4-30. As you become more familiar with the Risk-Grade measures, you can modify the fields that appear in the portfolio table to include the ones you want. However, you can use the default fields in the portfolio table to analyze your risks:

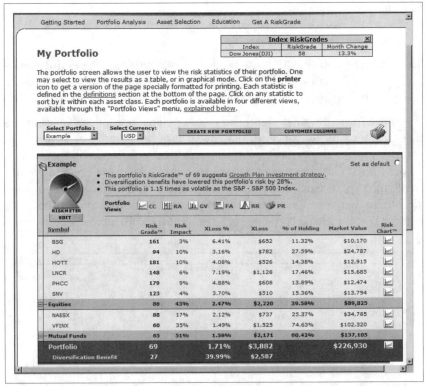

Figure 4-30. Review risk measures for individual stocks and an entire portfolio in the RiskGrades.com portfolio table

RiskGrade

Check the RiskGrade value for each investment to see if it is within your risk tolerance. Depending on your risk tolerance, you might want all your investments to carry low RiskGrades. However, you might also accept higher risk for some investments if the risk and return for your total portfolio risk meets your risk tolerance needs.

RiskImpact

This measure shows how much risk an investment contributes to a portfolio. RiskImpact uses both the RiskGrade and the percentage that an investment represents in a portfolio. If one investment's RiskImpact is too high, you can reduce the size of the holding or replace it with a less risky investment.

XLoss and XLoss %

These measures show the potential loss an investment might contribute to your portfolio. Make sure that you can accept a dollar or percentage loss of this size for the investment. If not, look for a less risky investment.

RiskChart

You can access the RiskChart for any investment by clicking its Risk-Chart icon in the portfolio table.

The RiskGrade, XLoss, XLoss %, and other measures for the entire portfolio appear at the bottom of the portfolio table. In addition, you can see the benefit in risk reduction provided by the diversification of your portfolio.

If you like to sleep well at night, you want to own a portfolio of investments that matches your tolerance for risk. But what's the point of owning a risky investment if it doesn't produce sufficient return to make its risk worthwhile? RiskGrades.com makes risk versus return easy to see on the Risk versus Return chart. Click the icon in the portfolio table for the RA portfolio view to display a chart such as the one in Figure 4-31. Investments above the straight line in the chart provide sufficient return for their level of risk.

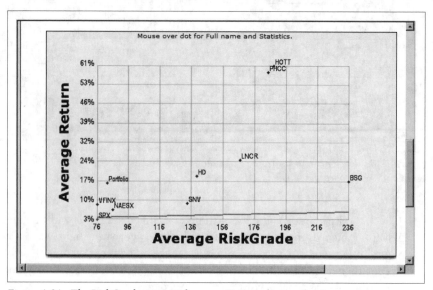

Figure 4-31. The RiskGrades.com Risk versus Return chart makes it easy to spot companies too risky for their return

However, you can also use the chart to spot investments that don't carry their weight compared to other companies in your portfolio. Ideally, you should receive a higher return as you accept higher risk. This means that points in the graph should increase on the Y-axis as they move further to the right on the X-axis. In Figure 4-31, most of the holdings do just this. However, Bisys Group (BSG) is at the right edge of the chart with a RiskGrade of 236, and its return is less than Home Depot's, which carries a RiskGrade of 139.

RiskGrades.com also enables you to evaluate the effect of buying and selling on your portfolio before you make your trades. Choose Portfolio Analysis → Portfolio Simulation → What If? Then you can sell investments in the portfolio, add shares to existing investment, or add shares of new investments. Click Run Analysis to view your new RiskGrade, diversification benefit, and other measures.

Another view of risk. The Reuters Investor web site (*http://www.investor.reuters.com*) tests companies six ways, looking for signs that investors aren't as keen on the stock as they once were. These tests don't use standard statistical risk measures, and a failing grade might not be anything to worry about. For example, a company fails the Estimate Revisions test if only one analyst downgrades the stock, regardless of how many analysts have held the course. However, several failing results can flag that you should check up on your stock. To check the status of the risk alerts for a company, open the Reuters Investor stock page for the company and click Risk Alerts in the navigation bar. The six risk alert tests are as follows:

The Analyst Recommendation Test
> Fails a company if the average analyst rating (1.0 indicating a strong buy and 5.0 indicating a strong sell) has increased in the past four weeks

The Estimate Revisions Test
> Fails a company if at least one analyst in the past week reduced the EPS estimates for the current or next fiscal year

The Shorted Shares Test
> Fails a company if short selling has increased during the past week

The Institutional Selling Test
> Fails a company if institutions such as mutual funds sold more shares in the company than they bought in the most recent reporting period

The Price Deterioration Test
> Fails a company whose shares have performed at least 35 percent worse than the price performance of the industry average

The Price Momentum Test
> Looks at price performance over the past four weeks compared to price performance in the nine weeks prior to that

Use Ready-Made Fundamental Analysis Applications

Although short-term traders have dozens of technical analysis software programs from which to choose, long-term investors have only a few fundamental analysis applications that help evaluate stock fundamentals.

Fundamental analysis evaluates the underlying performance of companies to find stocks that should do well over the long term. By investing in growing companies that are managed well, compare favorably to the competition, and are selling at a reasonable price, fundamental investors make money as stock price grows along with company earnings. Fundamental analysis programs churn through numbers from company financial statements to present historical performance. Then, it's up to you to evaluate company history and forecast how the company will do in the future. Some software applications use your estimates and judgment to calculate future prices and potential return. Here's a review of the contenders.

NAIC Software

The National Association of Investors Corp. (NAIC) is a nonprofit investment education organization that teaches a long-term approach to investing in stocks. Their primary analysis tool, the Stock Selection Guide (SSG), was developed in the 1950s but still works well today. Of course, for decades the SSG was purely a pencil and paper tool, but that all changed in the 1980s as personal computers became popular.

Today, NAIC offers four separate fundamental analysis programs for Windows: NAIC Classic, Investor's Toolkit, NAIC Stock Analyst, and Take Stock. Although the programs share a common approach to stock analysis using the SSG, each offers features and functions geared to investors at different levels of experience. These programs are not black boxes. They depend on input from the user to reach a conclusion about a stock's suitability as an investment.

No matter which NAIC program you use, the software helps you evaluate a company's past revenue and EPS growth and the quality of management through pre-tax profit margins and return on equity. After you add your EPS projections for the next five years, you can examine the stock's past P/E ratio trends and assess the range of P/E ratios at which the company might sell in five years. Multiply these future P/E ratios and your EPS projections to calculate a range of five-year projected prices. By comparing these future high and low prices to the current price, you can determine a good buy price as well as the potential total return if you buy the stock at the current price and the potential downside if the company doesn't perform to your expectations.

Each of the programs integrates NAIC's Online Premium Services (OPS) data [Hacks #15 and #20]. OPS includes more than 400 data fields—nearly all the data necessary for completing a stock study using the software, including up to ten years of annual data and five years of monthly prices and quarterly results. Using the software programs, you can easily download data as long as you're connected to the Internet, making it one of the easiest ways to collect data for fundamental analysis. In addition, you can use data files from the American Association of Individual Investors [Hacks #15 and #20].

NAIC Classic. NAIC Classic is primarily a teaching tool. The program features the Stock Wiz, an animated figure who guides you step-by-step through a stock study. After you've mastered the techniques used in the program, you can change from Beginner to Experienced mode and bypass the Wiz's escort. NAIC Classic Plus adds portfolio management tools; the Plus module is available as an add-on to the original software, or you can purchase the enhanced version all at once.

Take Stock. NAIC Take Stock is another tool that teaches beginners how to analyze stocks. The program guides investors through the steps of investment analysis. A beginner can tackle one concept at a time until he is comfortable with the entire process.

Investor's Toolkit. Investor's Toolkit, NAIC's most widely used program, also uses the Stock Selection Guide as the backbone of its stock analysis. Toolkit incorporates several more features than Classic. For example, additional graphs plot a company's past pre-tax profits and P/E ratios, as illustrated in Figure 4-32, and the Judgment Audit function points out potential problems in your analysis. Investor's Toolkit Pro includes portfolio management features, such as the Stock Comparison Guide, the Portfolio Management Guide, the Portfolio Evaluation and Review Technique charts and graphs, and portfolio reports. As with NAIC Classic Plus, the Pro version is available as an upgrade, or you can purchase the complete edition right away.

The program ships with a directory of stock research sites already configured in the software so that you can find more information at Yahoo! Finance or Quicken with just one click as you study a stock. You can add your own favorite sites to the list, as well.

NAIC Stock Analyst. NAIC Stock Analyst adds even more advanced features to those included in NAIC Classic and Investor's Toolkit. The program includes analytical functions, such as a review of historical debt-to-equity ratios. The balance sheet report, shown in Figure 4-33, takes a look at changes in receivables, inventory, cash, assets, and liabilities, and flags

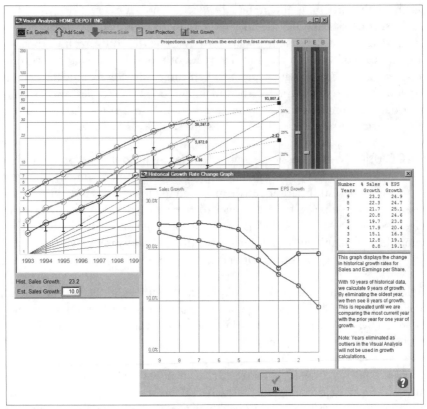

Figure 4-32. Investor's Toolkit shows company growth in a variety of ways

va234lues that might be problematic. You can also enter historical annual data and plot graphs for three additional elements of your choice, which is particularly useful when examining financial stocks **[Hack #44]**, REITs **[Hack #43]**, or other industries that report financial results in a slightly different format.

Downloadable demo versions of all NAIC programs, as well as purchase information, are available at *http://www.better-investing.org*. In the left navigation bar, click NAIC Store and then click NAIC Software. An Adobe Acrobat file comparing the three programs is also available at the developer's web site, ICLUBcentral (*http://www.iclub.com/downloads/compare.pdf*). In addition to the differences in the functions available in each program, the user interfaces are also quite different. The best way to choose is to evaluate each program and then decide which software best fits your way of working. Prices for the three programs range from $49 to $149, depending on the version you select.

Value Line Investment Analyzer. Although the Value Line Investment Survey is known primarily for its printed advisory service, the company also offers the

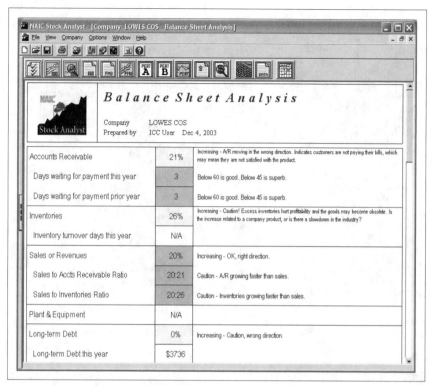

Figure 4-33. NAIC Stock Analyst features a balance sheet report that lets you dig deeper into a company's fundamentals

Value Line Investment Analyzer, as shown in Figure 4-34, which provides an electronic version of data and analysis for Windows for all 1,700 stocks covered by the standard version of the Value Line Investment Survey. With this software, users can screen and sort stocks and industry groups, as well as access all the text for Value Line analyst reports and recommendations. An optional Small and Mid-Cap edition adds another 1,800 companies, albeit in less detail.

The Investment Analyzer provides 350 search fields for each stock, 60 charting and graphing variables, and 10 years of historical financial data. The portfolio management module enables you to create and track stock portfolios and update prices via the Internet. If you use any technical indicators in your stock analysis, the software can also create 60 different technical indicators and 20 different charts.

One drawback to Value Line's product is its cost; it ranges from $595 to $995 for a yearly subscription, which includes regular online data updates. A three-month trial is available at *http://www.valueline.com*.

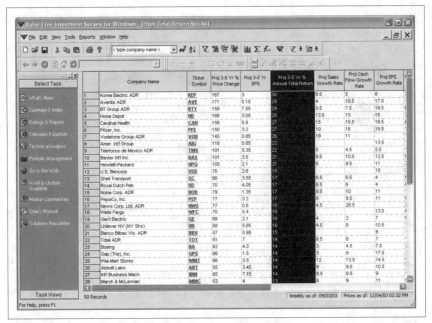

Figure 4-34. The Value Line Investment Analyzer is a warehouse of data with a variety of analysis checkpoints

Expert Investor. If you believe that successful investing is largely based on knowing the right questions to ask, then Expert Investor might be worth a look. This low-cost ($25) Windows application looks at qualitative and quantitative factors to determine a fair value for a stock. The program starts by prompting you to enter up to 18 years of historical financial data for a company. Based on the growth of earnings or equity, it ascertains a fair value for the stock and suggests whether the stock is a weak or strong candidate for investment. Then, it prompts you to consider the company's products and brand value, along with your level of understanding of the business, as demonstrated in Figure 4-35. It calculates several financial ratios and makes a final assessment of the company's potential. You can download a demo or buy a copy of Expert Investor at *http://www.fullertonsoftware.com*.

See Also

- AAII's Stock Investor Pro for Windows (*http://www.aaii.com*) is primarily a screening tool and data service with monthly updates provided on CD-ROM, but it also incorporates analytical functions.

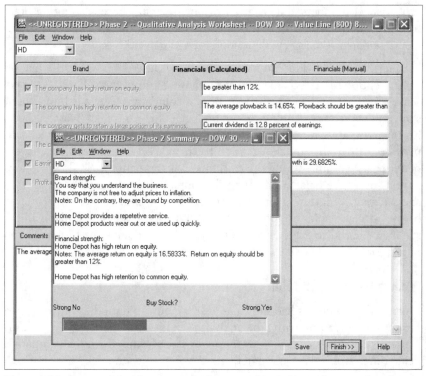

Figure 4-35. You won't be blown away by fancy graphics in Expert Investor, but the principles on which it's based are sound

- SharePricer (*http://www.sharepricer.com*) is another low-cost fundamental stock analysis program. Although it is developed in Finland, it is compatible with U.S. stocks and can retrieve data from Yahoo! Finance.

—Douglas Gerlach

HACK #39 Spot Hanky Panky with Cash Flow Analysis

Although it's no secret that some companies have cooked their books, you can spot signs of questionable bookkeeping before the results or subpoenas are served.

Company books are never cooked evenly—at least *some* of the numbers are real. It's more like they've been microwaved for a few minutes on high rather than baked at 325 degrees until done to perfection. Perhaps the most egregious example of this is Enron, whose saga, along with its master chefs Lay, Skilling, and Fastow, has been beaten to death in the financial press. For all the coverage, hard analysis of the numbers has been hard to find. By putting financial statements under the microscope, you have a chance to spot suspect numbers and cash out of investments whose accounting practices are questionable. Analyzing Enron's and WorldCom's financial statements can help you learn what to look for—and avoid.

Earnings are the obvious number to cook, because that's what the market pays attention to. A good place to start hunting for numbers that don't make sense is the balance sheet: a statement of a company's assets, liabilities, and shareholders' equity. The tenacious financial chef can make balance sheets lie, but companies rarely fudge their balance sheets because Wall Street simply doesn't pay that much attention to them. For that reason, you have a better chance of uncovering the truth about a company's cash flow by comparing successive balance sheets to determine where the money came from and where it went during a particular period. The cash flow analysis offered by the Spredgar analysis application [Hack #42] is not your standard cash flow statement found in 10-K and 10-Q filings, but it points out problems you might not catch otherwise.

Enron's Financial End Run

Most Wall Street firms had Enron as a strong buy up until the company filed for bankruptcy. Apparently, the analysts weren't doing much analyzing during this period. Instead, they were mostly cheerleading—on the company's behalf, their firm's, and, ultimately, their own.

> During the bull market, analysts seemed to be everywhere. Analysts pumping stocks brought to their brokerage firms lucrative investment banking deals, which in turn fattened the analysts' paychecks with bonuses calculated mostly by the amount of investment banking business they generated. Now, fewer analysts than ever cover stocks, because stock analysts have recently become part of brokerage cost centers rather than profit centers.

Enron's balance sheet smelled a bit overcooked as far back as 1997. Looking at the comparison of Enron's EPS to the cash flow that the company generated, shown in Figure 4-36, earnings were positive 15 out of 16 quarters, but cash flow was in the black only three times during the same period. Remember from the introduction to Chapter 3 that net income from the bottom of the income statement appears at the top of the statement of cash flows. So, where did the earnings go?

Let's take a closer look at the September 1997 quarter, in which earnings per share were a positive 17 cents a share, whereas free cash flow was a whopping negative $7.82. The cash flow statement generated by Spredgar in

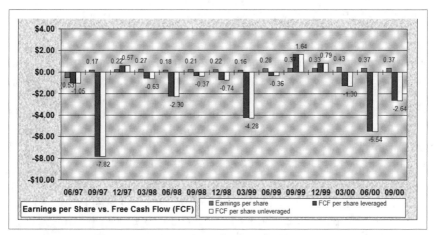

Figure 4-36. The Spredgar application's comparison of EPS and the free cash flow it generates

Figure 4-37 shows a company that required $5.9 billion (cell L134) in net investment activity and $6.2 billion (cell N134) in net financing activity to generate only $134 million in net income (cell D133)! Its return on equity (ROE) during the period was a meager 2.7 percent—using bogus numbers!

	Account	Net changes	Sources	Uses	Operating	Investing	Financing	
			Funds			**Activities**		
116	Cash	(17)	17					
117	Securities	-			-			
118	Receivables	969		969	(969)			
119	Inventory	77		77	(77)			
120	Other current assets	(87)	87		87			
121	Property, plant, and equipment	1,937		1,937		(1,937)		
122	Long-term assets/investments	3,956		3,956		(3,956)		
124	Current Liabilities	345	345		345			
125	Bonds	2,394	2,394				2,394	
126	Other long-term liabilities	2,378	2,378				2,378	
127	Preferred mandatory	-					-	
128	Preferred	-					-	
129	Common	3,729	3,729				3,729	
130	Other shareholder's equity	(2,255)		2,255			(2,255)	
132	Depreciation	110	110		110			
133	Net income	134	134		134			
134	Totals		9,194	9,194	(370)	(5,893)	6,246	(17)
137	Multiply all amounts by $1,000,000 (except per share amounts)				Operating CF + Investing CF + Financing CF = Δ Cash			

Figure 4-37. The Spredgar cash flow statement shows numbers that don't bode well for Enron

Judging from this figure, a significant amount of stock and bonds have been issued. But what are these stocks and bonds actually financing? Given the almost $6 billion flowing to investments, they are finding investments of some kind. Although the authorities are still sorting through the financial wreckage, we now know about the notorious *special purpose entities* (SPEs), which hid Enron's debt. Enron would transfer an asset (often of dubious value) and its associated debt to a subsidiary. The parent company would receive a note payable in return, which would show up as an "investment" on Enron's balance sheet. GAAP rules permitted the debt to stay off Enron's balance sheet as long as outsiders (in this case, usually Enron top management) had at least a three percent ownership of the SPE.

We also know that Enron stock was transferred to these SPEs, which also created a note payable to the parent. It might have been possible for the SPEs to sell off some of that stock, thus generating phony income back to the parent and possibly some for the outside investors. As long as the stock price stayed up, the financial house of cards was more or less intact. When the *Wall Street Journal* scrutinized the SPEs in late 2001, a falling stock price hastened Enron's demise.

WorldCom's Approach to Cooking the Books

WorldCom spun a similar tale to Enron in terms of fudging the financials. In WorldCom's case, it was a ploy of capitalizing some costs instead of recording them properly as expenses, which (surprise!) resulted in higher reported earnings.

How so? It stems from how capitalization and depreciation affect a company's earnings. When a company spends a big wad of money to purchase equipment or other things that it will use over a long period of time, the big wad of money doesn't show up as an expense on the income statement. If it did, earnings would take a huge hit in the year of the purchase, and then would look particularly good for all the remaining years when the equipment helps the company make money with no expenses to match. Depreciation is an accounting mechanism that, in effect, spreads the cost of a capitalized purchase over the useful life of the asset. The purchase cost appears as a use of cash on the cash flow statement; the value of the asset shows up on the balance sheet; and each year of the equipment's useful life, a depreciation expense appears on the income statement. Let's look at a simple example. If a company has revenues of $100,000 and expenses of $50,000, its net income is $50,000. However, if the company plays games and transforms the $50,000 in expenses into capitalized expenditures, the straight-line depreciation assuming no salvage value would be one-fifth of the $50,000 for five years. This ploy increases the net income to $90,000 for the year.

As we did with Enron, let's compare WorldCom's EPS to free cash flow. Figure 4-38 shows a Spredgar comparison from September 1998 through September 2000. Except for two periods, free cash flow is negative—and often dramatically less than reported positive earnings.

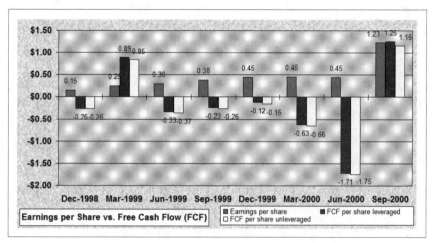

Figure 4-38. WorldCom's EPS looks much better than the cash flow it generates

How is this possible? Let's take a look at Spredgar's net balance sheet cash flow for the quarter ending December 1998, shown in Figure 4-39. World-Com's expenses most likely show up in the Property, plant, and equipment (PP&E) line item (cell D93). During this period PP&E was more than *five times* reported net income! This number doesn't represent long-term assets and investments, which are listed on the next line. From eight quarters starting in October 1998, PP&E ranged from 80 to 400 percent of net income. Stuffing expenses into this area enabled WorldCom to report net income as positive, while the correct categorization of expenses resulted in a loss.

Because of WorldCom's capitalization games, depreciation (cell D104) is higher than net income for the period. If you're capitalizing expenses, you must depreciate and amortize them, which results in high depreciation and amortization expenses. This is not likely to happen to a legitimate business, because it implies purchases of assets that don't produce sufficient income. However, for the next seven quarters, WorldCom's depreciation and amortization ran between 30 and 100 percent of net income

Because these evasive tricks do appear from time to time, you can compare financial measures to industry averages [Hacks #23 and #34] to highlight numbers that appear out of whack. For example, WorldCom's return on equity averaged 3.6 percent during this period compared to AT&T's ROE of over 13 percent. Asset turnover [Hack #31] compares even worse, with WorldCom's at .1 and AT&T's at .7 (seven times higher).

A	B	C D	E F	H I	J K	L M	N O	P
85		Net	Funds			Activities		
86	Account	changes	Sources	Uses	Operating	Investing	Financing	
88	Cash	766		766				
89	Securities	-						
90	Receivables	6,123		6,123	(6,123)			
91	Inventory	-						
92	Other current assets	(4,910)	4,910		4,910			
93	Property, plant, and equipment	2,597		2,597		(2,597)		
94	Long-term assets/investments	137		137		(137)		
96	Current Liabilities	1,886	1,886		1,886			
97	Bonds	51	51				51	
98	Other long-term liabilities	1,399	1,399				1,399	
99	Preferred mandatory	48	48				48	
100	Preferred	-					-	
101	Common	-					-	
102	Other shareholder's equity	298	298				298	
104	Depreciation	590	590		590			
105	Net income	441	441		441			
106	Totals		9,623	9,623	1,704	(2,734)	1,796	766
109	Multiply all amounts by $1,000,000 (except per share amounts)		Operating CF	+ Investing CF	+ Financing CF	= Δ Cash		

Figure 4-39. WorldCom's cash flow shows results not often seen in legitimate businesses

By using tools such as Spredgar, you can scrutinize numbers to find good explanations or perhaps bad business practices. If the numbers don't give you the answers you're looking for, call investor relations and ask them to explain. And, if those answers aren't much help, perhaps it's time to find another company.

—Gordon Gerwig

HACK #40 Use Online Analysis Tools

Target strong contenders and weed out also-rans with a quick fundamental analysis of any stock using these web tools.

There are hundreds of criteria you can consider when you invest in stocks, and the vast amount of information that's available on the Web makes researching a stock an overwhelming effort. Fortunately, there are some tools that can help you perform an instant analysis to see whether a stock might fit your portfolio. While none of these tools substitutes for your own in-depth research, they can spark new ideas and point out potential hazards as you consider investing in a new company.

Research Wizards

A couple of web sites serve to focus your attention on the most important factors to consider before you invest. These research wizards take a step-by-step approach to fundamental analysis, presenting questions for you to answer as well as providing the relevant data you need to make a decision.

Quicken.com's Stock Evaluator (*http://www.quicken.com/investments/ seceval*) is one free tool, shown in Figure 4-40. From a stock page, click Stock Evaluator under Analysis in the left margin. The evaluator steps through a fairly thorough analysis across six areas, including growth trends, financial health, management performance, and market multiples. The Stock Evaluator also helps with industry comparisons and the calculation of a stock's intrinsic value. In each section, data and graphs along with plain-English explanations help you to determine whether the stock meets or falls short of generally accepted guidelines.

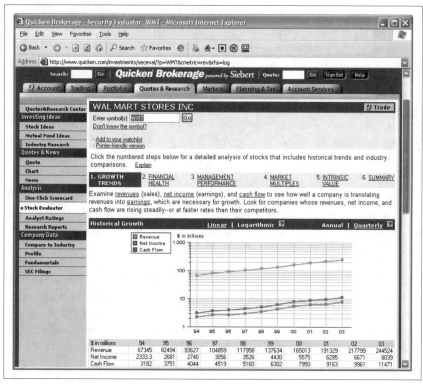

Figure 4-40. The Quicken.com Stock Evaluator assists in research shape and helps your analysis

The MSN Money Stock Research Wizard (*http://money.msn.com/investor/ research/wizards/SRW.asp*) takes a slightly more Socratic approach to research, presenting key questions that investors should ponder before investing in a stock. For instance, in order to understand the company's fundamentals, the wizard asks questions such as "How much does the company sell and earn?" and "How is the company's financial health?" For each question, the wizard suggests answers with data, charts, and industry comparisons.

The main drawback of both of these tools is that they don't dig very deeply. For example, MSN Money's Stock Evaluator suggests future price targets based on the current P/E ratio of a stock and on one- and two-year earnings estimates. Although this provides some guidance about the stock's potential, it ignores the fact that P/E ratios fluctuate in conjunction with price and EPS. If the current P/E ratio is high, then the price targets established by the tool are over-optimistic.

Still, these wizards can certainly help you shape your approach to long-term investing as well as suggest important areas that you might have missed in your own research.

DividendDiscountModel.com

Like discounted cash flow analysis, the *dividend discount model* (DDM) is a technique grounded in academic principles. DDM calculates the *present* value of the *future* dividends investors anticipate that a company will pay, as well as the expected rate of return implied by the current yield and projected growth of dividends. With this information, you can determine if a stock is over- or undervalued.

DividendDiscountModel.com (*http://www.dividenddiscountmodel.com*) is a free site that provides the necessary data and then performs the calculations to analyze stocks using this technique. Of course, the model only works on stocks that pay significant dividends, such as utilities and real estate investment trusts (REITs). You don't have to accept the tool's default values, either—you can tweak figures such as projected EPS growth rates to fit your own projections. For example, if you disagree with the 6.98 percent projected EPS growth rate for Kimco Realty in Figure 4-41, you can click the projected growth rate value in the table, type the growth rate you want in the window that opens, and click Done to view the analysis with your projections.

In Figure 4-41, Kimco Realty's expected return is 12.06 percent based on future EPS growth of 6.98 percent. This return is higher than the S&P 500's average of 11 percent.

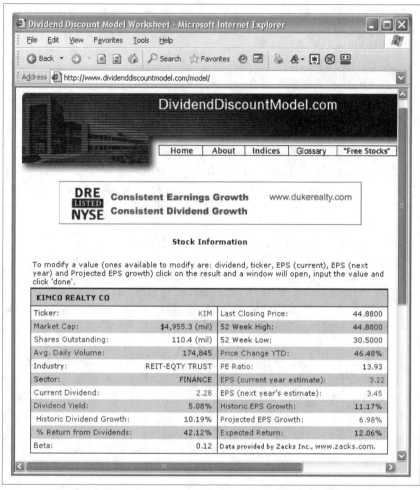

Figure 4-41. DividendDiscountModel.com quickly calculates the expected return of dividend-paying stocks

If you're scouting for ideas, DividendDiscountModel.com maintains a list of *free stocks*, too. These are companies that are expected to pay enough in dividends over the next ten years to pay back their initial stock price.

Quicken One-Click Scorecards

Back in grade school, receiving your report card was either a time of trepidation or celebration, depending on your studiousness and how well you got along with classmates. Another of Quicken.com's tools, the One-Click Scorecard (*http://www.quicken.com/investments/strategies*), takes a similar approach and checks whether companies pass or fail specific criteria.

Instead of taking a generic approach to fundamental analysis as the Quicken.com Stock Evaluator does, One-Click Scorecards are available for four different methodologies:

The Motley Fool's Foolish 8 Strategy
> Aimed at identifying small-cap companies using an eight-point checklist. Use this approach if you're looking for upstart small-cap companies for the aggressive portion of your portfolio.

The Warren Buffett Way
> Based on Robert Hagstrom's book of the same name, this scorecard deconstructs the investment approach of one of the all-time great investors and evaluates companies as Buffett does. Use this approach if you prefer to balance growth and value when choosing companies in which to invest.

NAIC's Established Growth Strategy
> Loosely based on the long-term approach created by the National Association of Investors Corporation (NAIC), this scorecard looks for solid growth stocks that are likely to double in value in five years. Use this approach to find companies that are likely to grow steadily over the long term.

Geraldine Weiss's Blue-Chip Value Strategy
> Searches out high-quality, high-yielding income stocks selling at attractive prices. Use this approach if you want to invest in solid large-cap stocks that pay above-average dividends and that are also undervalued.

For each approach, you'll find a concise explanation of the techniques used to qualify candidates as well as passed or failed grades for a series of specific questions.

> Investment methodologies are difficult to condense into simple checklists of questions. In addition, raw data often doesn't convey a true portrait of company performance. For this reason, you shouldn't rely on these One-Click Scorecards to do your homework for you. However, you can use them to learn more about these methodologies and then evaluate stocks thoroughly on your own.

One of Warren Buffett's favorite stocks is Coca-Cola. In fact, Buffett's Berkshire Hathaway is the largest shareholder of Coca-Cola stock. Hagstrom's "Warren Buffett Way" strategy can help you see the key considerations that Buffett uses in evaluating companies and what Buffett likes so much about Coca-Cola. Stocks are analyzed based on the following questions devised from the master investor's value strategy:

Has the company performed well consistently?

Has the company avoided excess debt?

Can managers convert sales to profits?

Are managers handling shareholders' money rationally?

Has management actually increased shareholder value?

Has the company consistently increased owner earnings?

Is the stock selling at a 25 percent discount to intrinsic value?

The One-Click Scorecard illustrates each answer with charts and data as well as a text description of the reasons that the company passed or failed each checkpoint, as shown in Figure 4-42. A summary provides a quick visual determination of the company's strengths and weaknesses.

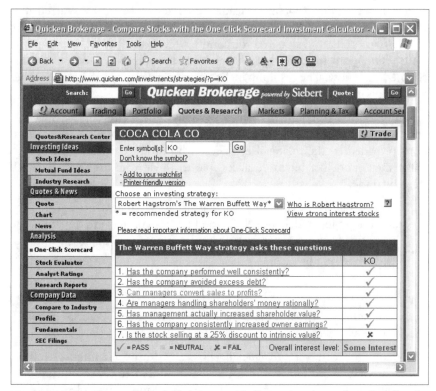

Figure 4-42. Quicken.com's One-Click Scorecard offers an instant stock analysis based on any of four different methodologies

You can use these tools in two ways. First, you can visit the Scorecard and find a list of *strong interest stocks* for each strategy. Like any screening tool, though, the stocks that are highly rated aren't necessarily appropriate for your portfolio. You must research to delve deeper into the specifics of each company.

The second way is to use the Scorecard as a starting point when researching a new stock idea. Enter the ticker symbol to see whether one of the methodologies finds the stock attractive at the current price.

Some stocks will fly through the Scorecard with a passing grade, but you might eliminate them based on recent bad news or other criteria that make the stock less attractive. And finally, some stocks might fail one or more criteria, but you might find them acceptable after further research shows that the company's problems are short-lived or not significant.

ValuePro.net

One textbook approach to fundamental analysis is known as the *discounted cash flow* technique. Popular in academic circles and used by Warren Buffet, DCF analysis calculates the intrinsic value of a stock based on future cash flows and an estimated discount rate. ValuePro.net (*http://www. valuepro.net*) is a free site that allows you to analyze any stock using discounted cash flow. The resulting intrinsic value gives you a sense of whether the stock is a good buy at its current price.

You'll find that discounted cash flow analysis is fairly complex. If this approach to investing interests you, check out the tutorials and explanations provided by the financial engineers who produce the site. These aids make their models a bit more accessible to those who aren't mathematicians by trade.

Once you've analyzed a company, you can see the cash flow streams that the program used in its model, as well. If you like this approach to investing, the site also sells a software program that hooks into its web database and provides more detailed analyses.

See Also

For more online research tools available primarily on a subscription basis, check out these services:

- ValuEngine.com (*http://www.valuengine.com*) uses quantitative analysis techniques based largely on earnings growth. A free valuation summary is available on any company, while a subscription provides access to more detailed analyses.

- StockWorm.com (*http://www.stockworm.com*) mixes technical and fundamental analysis techniques, highlighted by innovative visual displays. Its fundamental approach places much weight on industry comparisons. Monthly subscriptions are available at several levels.

—*Douglas Gerlach*

Find the Best Free Excel Tools for Fundamental Analysis

HACK #41

If you don't want to coerce too many brain cells into building an analysis spreadsheet, you can find a few Excel tools for free.

Spreadsheets are great tools for analyzing stocks, but building your own [Hack #45] takes some time—particularly when you're still trying to learn what financial measures mean and how financial ratios reflect performance. The Web offers plenty of free tools as the results from any online search will indicate, but finding tools that are worth something is another matter entirely. However, you can count on someone who volunteers his time teaching investing to offer an outstanding, free web site with both tools and education.

Bob Adams, a director on the national NAIC Computer Group Advisory Board as well as the Puget Sound chapter, has a web site (*http://bobadams. homestead.com/bobsite.html*) that offers several spreadsheets for analyzing the fundamental measures of companies, not to mention other spreadsheets for portfolio management [Hack #76]. What makes these analysis tools the best is that they include comments that explain what measures and ratios represent, and identify desirable values or red flags for each. The web site is intended to provide access to files for people who attend Mr. Adams's investment classes. However, anyone who wants to learn how to analyze stocks can download any of the files. Here are some of the analysis tools you can use:

MS Excel Spreadsheet

Click the Excel button in the Analyzing the Annual Report section of the web page to download an Excel spreadsheet suitable for analyzing manufacturing companies. The spreadsheet contains macros for downloading most of the data you need from NAIC Online Premium Services data files [Hack #20]. However, for a completely free analysis, you can enter values manually.

The web site also includes a version of the manufacturing spreadsheet for MS Works.

Annual Report Instructions

If the small books that companies publish and call their annual reports seem daunting, learn what's important and how to interpret it by clicking the Instructions button in the Analyzing the Annual Report section of the web page.

Enron Analysis

For another view of spotting Enron troubles **[Hack #39]** before they hit the news wires, click the Enron button.

Analyze Bank Stocks

Click the Bank Analysis button to download an Excel spreadsheet suitable for analyzing banks as investments **[Hack #44]**.

> Because bank analysis uses some data that you won't find for other types of companies, click the Bank Data button to download an Adobe Acrobat *.pdf* file guide to bank financial statements.

Analyzing Ratios

Whether you use the analysis spreadsheet for manufacturing companies or banks, the financial ratios you want to evaluate appear on the left, as shown in Figure 4-43. Most of the cells that contain ratio values display the red triangle that indicates an Excel comment. If you want to find out what a ratio indicates or the values you want to see, position the mouse pointer over the triangle to display its comment. For example, the comment for the Inventories Change measure is "If increasing, is the increase related to a company product, or is there a slowdown in the industry." Ratio cells also include highlighting **[Hack #8]** that indicates whether the value is good, bad, or warrants further research.

Additional hints appear to the right of most ratio cells indicating whether the value in the cell is good or bad. These hints use Excel IF functions **[Hack #12]** along with formulas to display different hints depending on the value in the cell. Home Depot's inventories change is –2 percent. The hint indicates that decreasing inventories are what you want to see.

For some measures, you must evaluate a result in comparison to another result and this spreadsheet includes hints for that as well. For example, Home Depot's cost of sales has increased 11 percent. The spreadsheet hint asks why the value is increasing. However, another hint informs you that sales are increasing faster than the cost of sales. If a retail company such as Home Depot increases its sales that means it's selling more products, which in turn means it must pay more for the inventory it puts on its shelves.

The spreadsheet for analyzing bank stocks includes cells at the bottom of the data column for types of loans and the percentage they represent in the bank's loan portfolio. Each type of loan carries a different level of risk, and the spreadsheet uses these values to calculate a loan risk ratio.

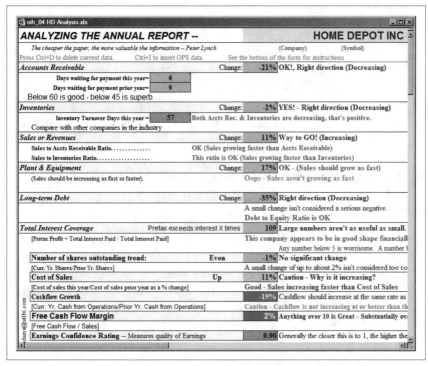

Figure 4-43. *Learn what to look for in ratios with Bob Adams' Excel spreadsheet*

When you click cells other than those for data in the spreadsheet, you'll notice that the data cells are the only ones you can edit. The rest of the spreadsheet cells are protected, so you can't inadvertently edit their formulas. However, if you want to examine the formulas in the spreadsheet cells, choose Tools → Options, select the View tab and check the Formulas checkbox under the Windows options heading.

Data Requirements

These Excel spreadsheets contain macros that import data from an NAIC .ssg *data file* [Hack #20], which you can download when you subscribe to NAIC's Online Premium Services. However, you can also enter data from annual reports manually. In fact, a few data items aren't available from Online Premium Services. When you see three question marks (???) in a cell, you must find that value in the financial statements in a company's annual report or 10 K filing.

See Also

- JaxWorks *(http://www.jaxworks.com/download.htm)*, the "Small Business Spreadsheet Factory," has a free spreadsheet that compares a company with the average values for its industry. Click the Financial Comparison Analysis link to download it.

- You can download a spreadsheet that performs a *technamental* stock analysis, as defined by Ellis Traub, at Yahoo! Finance *(http://finance. groups.yahoo.com/group/TSSW_Excel)*.

HACK #42 Find the Best Excel Tools for Fundamental Analysis for a Fee

If you're willing to spend money to make money, some stock analysis spreadsheets for a fee offer comprehensive analysis features that are worth the price.

If you don't want to build your own spreadsheet, a few spreadsheet tools can help you evaluate company fundamentals, while relieving you of only a small amount of cash. None of the products is perfect. However, each one offers some intriguing views of fundamental measures that might augment your current analysis.

Spredgar (http://www.spredgar.com)

Spredgar is an Excel add-in that combines SEC filing data and ratio analysis in one product. It collects data for more than 8,000 companies from SEC filings and updates the downloadable data available on the Spredgar web site once a week. The spreadsheet calculates 70 financial ratios, and displays them in tables as well as graphs. By collating data for companies within a SIC code, Spredgar can compare a company's ratios to the averages for the industry. Spredgar calculates free cash flow from company balance sheets [Hack #39] to track down the real sources and uses of company cash. The spreadsheet also calculates the sustainable growth rate, which indicates how quickly a company can grow from funds generated by the business and not by borrowing money. With several periods of financial data, the spreadsheet can show trends in values. However, it doesn't provide any advice or instruction on how to evaluate the numbers and trends you see.

Spredgar is priced as a subscription from $25 for one week up to $450 for an entire year. If you study and update stocks once a quarter, you can limit your costs by subscribing to Spredgar for four one-week periods.

ValueSheet (http://www.valuesheet.com)

You have to find data to feed a ValueSheet spreadsheet, but the information a ValueSheet provides might be worth the effort. This tool includes instructions for understanding and evaluating financial measures and ratios, how to use each worksheet, and what to look for in different industries. It uses Excel conditional formatting [Hack #8] to highlight company performance. In addition to graphs of growth, ValueSheet calculates numerous ratios including free cash flow. You can specify weightings for ratios to score companies based on the criteria you care about. The Comparison worksheet shows scores for multiple companies side by side. ValueSheet is available for a one-time charge of $39.95.

Valuesoft (http://www.sherlockinvesting.com)

This Excel add-in from Sherlock Investing is touted by its creators as offering analysis based on an accurate implementation of Warren Buffett's brand of analysis. The product includes a manual explaining its approach. The product is available for a one-time charge of $75. However, you can return it for any reason within 90 days to receive a complete refund of the purchase price.

Analyze Real Estate Investment Trusts

Want a stake in real estate without the headaches of hands-on property management? Invest in real estate investment trusts (REITs).

For a portfolio stuffed with stocks and bonds, *real estate investment trusts* (REITs) are a nearly perfect diversification tool. REITs invest in different types of real estate, in which the earnings of the REIT often have more to do with rental and occupancy rates than the interest rates that affect stocks and bonds. Financial planners recommend investing up to 10 percent of your portfolio in REITs as part of a disciplined asset allocation strategy [Hack #74]. By buying shares in a REIT, you can invest in real estate without forking over a bundle of cash—and without the low liquidity because of the time it takes to sell real estate that you own directly. Although analyzing REITs requires a few more financial measures, you can easily expand your studies to include REITs in your portfolio.

What Is a REIT?

Originally created in 1960 by an act of Congress, REITs enable individual investors to easily participate in the commercial real estate market. In structure, REITs are pooled asset vehicles similar to mutual funds, but they invest in properties rather than stocks and bonds. REITs are required by tax law to distribute 90 percent of their taxable income to shareholders. Although the generous dividends that result are a boon for dividend-hungry investors, REITs also offer the potential for stock price appreciation.

> The Tax Relief Act of 2003 eliminated the double taxation of dividends and reduced taxes on long-term capital gains. However, because of the way REITs operate, their dividends aren't taxed twice, so you still have to pay taxes on the dividends you receive from them. For that reason, tax advisers recommend that investors hold REITs in tax-deferred accounts such as IRAs or 401(k)s.

Publicly held REITs trade on the major stock exchanges and some belong to major stock indexes, such as the S&P 500 index. Although some REITs invest in all types of property all over the country, others specialize by type of property, region of the country, or both. Types of property typically owned by REITs include shopping malls, strip malls, apartment buildings, office buildings, resorts, hotels, storage facilities, industrial complexes, health-related facilities, and residential real estate. REITs come in three flavors:

Equity REITs
> Own and operate income-producing properties.

Mortgate REITs
> Lend money directly to real estate owners or purchase real estate loans. They also invest in mortgage-backed securities.

Hybrid REITs
> Combine the features of equity and mortgage REITs.

Real estate is a highly *cyclical* industry, going through cycles of boom and bust. At the top of the cycle, demand for real estate is high and supplies are lean, so that rental rates and real estate sale prices climb, pulling REIT profits up as well. Then, developers rush in and construct more buildings to satisfy the demand, which eventually results in an oversupply. Sale prices fall, and property managers must cut rental rates in order to lease space, which results in fewer profits for REITs. When rents fall, there's less incentive to build, which eventually brings the commercial real estate market full circle.

Diversification in real estate is just as important as in other areas of investing. Geographic location, interest rates, disposable income, and business staffing levels all affect REITs to some extent. For example, equity REITs are less affected by swings in interest rates than mortgage REITs. In addition, the cycles for different sectors of the REIT market peak and hit bottom at different times.

REIT Analysis: Something Old, Something New

Similar to the evaluation of traditional growth stocks, good REITs produce consistent growth in sales and earnings, despite the cyclical nature of the real estate market. However, REITs do differ from other types of companies in the way they operate, so you must analyze a few additional financial measures not found in manufacturing or service companies.

The National Association of Real Estate Investment Trusts (NAREIT) recommends that investors look for REITs that employ their cash flow effectively by reinvesting money in new opportunities. REITs can increase earnings by raising rents and lease rates as building occupancy increases. However, like any other business, REITs must set competitive rates to maintain building occupancy, and also balance the costs and benefits of property maintenance and improvements. Many REITS grow by acquiring new properties or developing new buildings. In 2001, Congress passed the REIT Modernization Act, which enables REITs to create subsidiaries to provide cutting-edge services to their tenants, such as wiring buildings for broadband Internet service. For REITs that construct buildings, avoid those that have trouble completing projects on time and within budget. Construction delays and budget overruns can both make deep cuts into profits.

 Look for the status of ongoing development activities in REIT annual reports and 10-K and 10-Q filings.

One major difference between analyzing REITs and other types of companies is the handling of depreciation of assets. Because other types of companies often own assets comprised of equipment, which lose value over time, depreciation attempts to show the reduction in usefulness and value over time. However, REITs own large quantities of real estate assets, which typically increase in value over time. Therefore, earnings per share, which is reduced by depreciation and amortization, is not a good measure of REIT performance. Instead, analysts typically use the following measures to evaluate REIT performance, also shown in the income statement in Figure 4-44.

Funds from operations (FFO)
  Also called *income from continuing operations*, FFO excludes property depreciation and gains or losses from sales of property.

 If you use FFO in place of EPS, be sure to use the price/FFO ratio (P/FFO ratio) in place of the P/E ratio.

CONSOLIDATED STATEMENTS OF INCOME
For the years ended December 31, 2002, 2001 and 2000

	2002
(in thousands, except per share data)	
Revenue	
Real estate rental revenue	$152,929
Other	680
	153,609
Expenses	
Utilities	7,987
Real estate taxes	11,186
Repairs and maintenance	6,121
Property administration	4,069
Property management	4,655
Operating services and supplies	5,718
Common area maintenance	2,152
Other real estate expenses	2,017
Interest expense	27,849
Depreciation and amortization	29,200
General and administrative expenses	4,575
	105,529
Income from continuing operations	48,080
Discontinued operations:	
Income (loss) from operations of property disposed	(82)
Gain on disposal	3,838
Income before gain on sale of real estate	51,836
Gain on sale of real estate	—
Net Income	$ 51,836
Income from continuing operations per share—basic	$ 1.23
Income from continuing operations per share—diluted	$ 1.22
Net income per share—basic	$ 1.33
Net income per share—diluted	$ 1.32

Figure 4-44. The income statement for the Washington REIT includes additional categories of income and expense

Adjusted funds from operations (AFFO)

Some analysts further refine FFO by using adjusted funds from operations (AFFO), which measures the cash flow generated by a REIT's operations. According to NAREIT, AFFO is calculated by straight-lining rents and subtracting the normalized recurring expenditures (such as installing new carpeting) that REITs usually capitalize and amortize. Straight-lining rents represents the use of the average of a tenant's rent payments over the lifetime of a lease and is required by generally accepted accounting principles (GAAP).

Earnings per share (EPS)

You can use EPS if it is adjusted to reflect earnings from continuing operations, which exclude revenue gains from extraordinary and special items.

Operating net income per share

To further muddy the waters, some REIT analysts focus on operating net income per share as a better reflection of the scope of a REIT's operations and its worth.

> Because REITs purchase real estate, you'll see higher levels of debt than for other types of companies. Because of this, compare a REIT's debt level to the average for the industry or to debt ratios for competitors.

Screening for REITS

If you're interested in finding a profitable REIT in which to invest, start by screening [Hack #4] the more than 150 publicly traded REITs with Yahoo! Finance's basic screen (*http://screen.yahoo.com/stocks.html*). In the category section, select Real Estate Operations (Services). To further refine your search, you can define minimums and maximums for profit margins, PEG ratios, and analysts' estimates for future growth.

Obtaining REIT Data

Unlike the measures you use to study other types of stocks, the measures for analyzing REITs require some digging. Value Line (*http://www.valueline. com*) provides annual data for FFO but doesn't provide quarterly FFO results. In addition, Value Line doesn't provide REIT revenue numbers. EdgarScan   [Hack #18]   (*http://edgarscan.pwcglobal.com/servlets/edgarscan*) doesn't provide FFO or AFFO numbers, but does provide operating net income. You can divide operating net income by the total shares outstanding to calculate the operating net income per share.

Many REITs include FFO and AFFO data in their quarterly reports, annual reports, and SEC filings, which you can access from their web sites. NAREIT provides links to the web pages for member REITs (*http://www.nareit.com/ aboutreits/linkstext.cfm*). If a REIT doesn't provide FFO in its income statement, calculate FFO using the equation shown in Example 4-55.

Example 4-55. Calculate FFO using other numbers from a REIT income statement

```
FFO = Income before gain on sale of real estate + Depreciation + Amortization
```

If you're not interested in analyzing individual REITs, but still want to take advantage of this type of investment, consider REIT mutual funds. You can choose from actively managed REIT funds, closed-end REIT funds, or REIT index funds. Morningstar is a good place to start (*http://www.morningstar.com*).

See Also

- The National Association of Real Estate Investment Trusts (NAREIT) web site (*http://www.nareit.com*) is full of helpful information, including FAQs about REITs, a 16-page *.pdf* file "Investor's Guide to REITs," detailed information about REIT accounting, and an extensive glossary of REIT investing terms.

—*Amy Crane*

HACK #44 Bank on Banks

Although you've probably used banking products and services such as checking accounts, savings accounts, and loans, do you know how banks make money and how to translate that into investment opportunity?

The money business doesn't work quite like other businesses. Unlike other companies that sell products or services, banks buy and sell money. A dollar is a dollar, so how do banks make a profit? By charging a higher interest rate for the money they loan out than they pay for the money that comes in as deposits and by charging fees for the money-related services they offer. Because of this difference in business model, banks use a few financial measures you won't see for other companies. However, taking the extra steps to study banks is worth your while—financial stocks can grow quite well and are a great way to diversify your portfolio.

Banks come in several flavors, each with its own unique blend of pros and cons:

Money-center banks

These banks borrow from and lend to governments, large corporations, and other banks. They offer no consumer banking functions. Money-center banks can deliver more consistent earnings than other types of banks due to their large bases of operations. However, their sheer size can limit how quickly they grow. They are also vulnerable to losses from big corporate and international loans.

Investment banks

> These are commercial banks that specialize in lending money to corporations for investment activities, such as initial public offerings and leveraged buyouts. Investment banks are also vulnerable to losses from corporate and international loans.

Regional banks

> Regional banks confine their operations to one part of the country and typically lend to mid- and small-sized businesses. These banks offer consumer banking services. Regional banks are popular with investors, because they offer higher growth rates than other types of banks and are sometimes acquired by money-center banks. Regional banks looking to expand often acquire smaller savings banks and savings and loans.

Savings banks

> These community banks focus on lending to consumers and small businesses. Smaller banks usually have steady growth rates, although these can vary widely by region and individual bank.

Savings and loans

> Also known as thrifts or S&Ls, these institutions are owned either by shareholders or customers. Savings and loans offer both consumer and commercial banking services and were originally chartered to supply funds for building, buying, and remodeling homes.

> Banks and S&Ls are chartered either by the federal government or state governments, and are regulated by the Federal Deposit Insurance Corporation (FDIC), the Comptroller of the Currency, or state regulators. Bank examiners visit institutions every year to ensure that they use sound operating procedures and have sufficient operating capital. Despite this regulation, banks and S&Ls aren't immune to failure. More than 1,000 S&Ls failed during the late 1980s and early 1990s because of mismanagement and outright fraud, combined with a poor economy, lax regulations, and intense competition in the banking industry.

Revenue Measures for Banks

A bank *buys* your money when it accepts your deposit, and pays you interest for the use of your cash. A bank *sells* money when it loans out money from its deposits. A person or corporation that borrows money pays the bank interest and fees for the use of the money, and pledges to repay the money over a specific period of time. The bank's profit on its money business, *net interest income*, comes from the difference between the interest that the bank earns on its loans and investments and the interest it pays on deposit, checking, and certificate of deposit accounts, or funds it borrows from other sources. As the spread between these two types of interest rates—known as the *net interest margin*—increases, so do the bank's profits.

Net interest margin is extremely interest-rate sensitive. When the Federal Reserve lowers interest rates, banks charge lower rates on loans and also pay lower rates on deposits. No impact to profits there. However, when interest rates are very low for a sustained period of time—as they were from 2000 to 2004—banks get squeezed because they have to pay some interest, however small, on their deposit accounts, while their interest rates on loans continue to dwindle. Competition also precludes banks from pushing their interest rate spreads too wide. Banks that depend on net interest margin can grow only by increasing the amount of money they loan, which carries its own set of risks as described in the next section.

Fortunately, banks can earn money from other sources besides buying and selling money: credit card fees and interest on credit cards they issue, safety deposit box fees, checking account fees, mortgage origination and servicing fees, and income from brokerage services. Collectively, these sources of revenue are known as *non-interest income*. Non-interest income can make banks more attractive as investments, because it is consistent and not sensitive to changes in interest rates. In addition, by developing additional products and services with commensurate fees, banks can grow their earnings without increasing their deposits or loan base. Many years ago, only a tiny percentage of a bank's income came from non-interest sources. Now, analysts favor banks with a diversified base of non-interest income over those that derive most of their income from traditional banking activities.

You can check a bank's proportion of net interest income to non-interest income to the sources of bank income. Calculate a ratio for interest income by dividing the net interest income value by the total revenue, as shown in Example 4-58. To see if a bank is moving toward more non-interest income, you can calculate this ratio for the past few years and look for a downward trend.

One additional component to bank income is the *tax equivalent adjustment*. Because some bank assets are held in tax-exempt securities, this adjustment increases the tax-exempt portion of interest income to the equivalent value in fully taxable interest income.

Examples 4-56, 4-57, and 4-58 provide a synopsis of the revenue measures for banks.

Example 4-56. Formula for bank revenue

```
Revenue = Net Interest Income + Tax Equiv. Adjustment + Non Interest Income -
Loan Loss Provision
```

Example 4-57. Formula for net interest margin

```
Net Interest Margin = Interest Charged on Loans - Interest Paid on Deposits
```

Example 4-58. Formula for revenue ratio

```
Interest/Non Interest Ratio = Interest Income / Revenue
```

Look for steadily increasing revenue just as you would for other types of companies. If you want to invest in a bank that isn't as sensitive to interest rates, look for lower numbers in the interest/non-interest ratio. Net interest margin values are typically quite small; three to five percent isn't uncommon. However, because very small changes in net interest margin result in huge changes in profits, look for banks that deliver above-industry-average margins. In addition, calculate the bank's net interest margin for the past several years to watch for downward trends that lead to lower profits and eventually lower stock price.

The Lowdown on Loan Loss

It's inevitable that some of the loans that banks make will go bad. If a bank is too strict in its lending criteria, it might not have as many bad loans, but it also won't be able to loan as much money out. Conversely, if a bank is too liberal when evaluating its borrowers, profits might boom initially but crash when too many borrowers can't repay their loans. To make money with loans, banks must be careful, but not overly restrictive, in choosing their borrowers. Banks that carefully track late payments and stay on top of delinquent loans stand the best chance of getting their borrowers back on track and keeping their loans in the black.

The following measures help evaluate the impact of bad loans:

Loan loss provision
> This is the amount of money that banks are required to set aside to cover potential loan losses. In a bank's income statement, the loan loss provision is deducted from net interest income in much the same way as sales returns and allowances are deducted from gross sales in a manufacturing company.

Loan loss reserve
> If any money in the loan loss provision account hasn't been used to cover bad loans by the end of a quarter, it transfers to the loan loss reserve account on the bank's balance sheet. If a bank uses more money

than was reserved in the loan loss provision, the deficit is taken out of the loan loss reserve account.

Loan loss provision ratio

This ratio compares the loan loss provision to the bank's total loan base. It is useful for comparing loan loss provisions between competing banks or over several years for the same bank.

Loan loss reserve ratio

This ratio compares the loan loss reserve to a bank's total loans. It is useful for comparing loan loss reserves between competing banks or over several years for the same bank.

Non-performing assets ratio

Non-performing assets are loans in which the interest is past due by 90 days or more, that are not being paid on schedule, or that are being paid at a reduced rate. To calculate the ratio, divide non-performing assets by total loans.

All three ratios are useful in assessing loan loss trends and actual loss experience. In setting a loan loss provision, a bank walks a fine line. When the loan loss provision ratio is too low, a bank might have to take a charge against earnings to bolster the provision. Conversely, when a bank sets aside too much money for loan losses, it removes some of its assets from income-producing activities, which cuts into profits. Banks usually set the provision and reserves based on their past experience and the current economic climate. Bank regulators can also require a bank to set aside additional amounts if they believe it is overexposed to potential loss. Although it's good to see downward trends in the loan loss provision ratio or loan loss reserve ratio, these ratios might increase when the economy falters or a big client goes belly-up. When the non-performing assets ratio trends downward over time, the bank is doing a good job of keeping its bad loan exposure under control.

Banks usually recover at least some of the balance of defaulted loans, even in huge bankruptcies such as Enron or WorldCom. The red flag in loan losses is a bank that keeps taking charges against earnings to shore up continually deteriorating loan loss provisions.

Evaluating Bank Profitability

Banks don't make a lot of money on individual transactions, but they work with such a large volume of money that a little bit of profit on each transaction adds up fast. Because banks carry so much debt, return on equity (ROE) [Hack #32] isn't a good measure of profitability. The best measure of bank

234profitability and quality of management is return on assets (ROA), which measures how much money a bank makes on each dollar of assets. Compare a bank's ROA [Hack #34] from year to year, as well as to industry average values or the values for specific competitors. Ideally, ROA should increase steadily or at least hold steady over a number of years. Don't expect big increases, because the numbers aren't that large to begin with. Quicken.com notes that the average ROA for the banking industry is 1.02 percent. Analysts consider banks that consistently deliver an ROA at or slightly above 2 percent as extremely well managed and highly profitable.

Dividends are another gauge of a bank's health and profitability. Bank directors walk a fine line between the desire to provide shareholders with a healthy dividend and the need to retain enough profit to grow the bank's various businesses.

Flavors of Data

Data providers report bank data in different ways [Hack #15], just as they do for other types of companies. Most data providers break out net interest income and non-interest income. Value Line doesn't provide the tax equivalent adjustment or net interest margin. However, S&P data, obtained directly from S&P or through NAIC's Online Premium Services, does. S&P calculates bank revenue by adding gross interest income and non-interest income. Unfortunately, gross interest income is more sensitive to interest rates than net interest income because it includes interest expense. You can obtain all the components of bank income by using bank quarterly and annual income statements [Hack #19]. Because of the differences in reporting methods, don't mix and match data sources for your bank analyses.

If you want to invest in financial companies without getting up to speed on these additional measures, consider mutual funds that invest in financial services stocks. You won't find a pure-play bank fund, but the Financials Funds category at Morningstar's web site (*http://www.morningstar.com*) provides several options.. Funds that invest in one sector can be volatile, so be sure to diversify your portfolio [Hack #74].

—Amy Crane and Bonnie Biafore

HACK #45 Steps to Building a Financial Analysis Template

A checklist of steps to perform and questions to ask can produce more consistent stock studies as well as better investment results.

As you gain investment experience, you'll find that you concentrate on different items in your stock studies, sometimes adding measures, sometimes removing them, and usually improving your ability to judge whether a company's performance is good or bad. No matter how good or bad your memory is, a checklist or set of guidelines for your unique approach to analysis will increase the consistency of your stock studies. By evaluating each company in the same way, you can compare companies with confidence and choose the best contender more often than before. In addition, constructing a template for your analysis forces you to think about what you do, which might prompt steps you've forgotten or highlight errors in your ways. Your template can be a simple reminder list or a sophisticated collection of tools. Either way, increased investment returns will compensate you for your time.

Asking Questions and Documenting Decisions

A stock study is an evaluation of a company as an investment. For the best results, your stock studies should analyze a company, its competitors, and the industry to which they belong to find the best investment for your portfolio. Ultimately, it should convince you that you are investing your money in the best possible way. With this definition of a stock study, two things might occur to you:

- A stock study represents more than numbers—qualitative aspects of a company can affect your decisions.
- Not every stock study will result in a decision to buy. You might evaluate a company or an industry and find nothing that interests you. Or, you might realize that you should sell a stock that you own and that you must perform additional studies to find a new investment. Is this common sense? Of course. However, it's a good idea to include a question at the end of every study to document the action items you've identified.

The results of a qualitative analysis are often text rather than numbers. However, after you evaluate the qualitative aspects of a company, you can rank the results to compare them to competitors. Text documents and spreadsheets both work as templates for qualitative analysis. Depending on your preference, you can include both qualitative and quantitative results in a spreadsheet, or you can use a text document for the qualitative analysis and a spreadsheet for financial ratios.

If you've already knocked out most of the also-rans by screening stocks, starting with a qualitative analysis of the remaining companies might make the most sense.

Qualitative steps. If you haven't developed your own approach to studying stocks, here are some ideas for items to evaluate:

Business summary

Describe the company's business. What does the company do to make money? Does it focus on one product or does it diversify into several industries? Is it regional, national, or global in scope?

The Business section of a Value Line stock page is a great example of a business summary. The Outlook section is a concise version of business outlook. When you create your own studies, you aren't constrained to a portion of a page, so you can document business outlook in as much detail as you want.

Business outlook

Describe positive and negative influences on the company's business, such as acquisitions, divestitures, cost control, cost increases, management changes, successful or dismal product strategies, the economy, currency exchange rates, and competition.

Business strategy

Determine how the business grows: from acquisitions, increased market share, higher volume, higher profit margins, building stores, developing new products, or other approaches. For example, Oracle applied their productivity products to their own business to cut costs and increase earnings.

SWOT analysis is a business management technique for evaluating strengths, weaknesses, opportunities, and threats, hence the acronym. It provides a framework for analyzing a company's current situation. SWOT analysis begins with an inward look at the company's strengths and weaknesses, such as its product lines, management, human resources, or infrastructure. An outward look considers the opportunities and the threats present in the environment in which the company operates. For example, demographics might change consumer demand for the company's products and services. Competitors or technological changes can affect products and prices.

When you evaluate SWOT, consider how the company has performed in the past. Good management can sometimes turn threats into opportunities and weaknesses into strengths.

Quantitative steps. Many of the hacks in this chapter discuss the purpose of financial measures and identify what to look for and what to avoid. You can use these hacks to develop your own list of quantitative items or start with one of the ready-made tools [Hacks #38, #41, and #42]. If you use a ready-made tool, it's still a good idea to create a checklist of the quantitative items you want to evaluate. You can remind yourself to research and explain unusual performance patterns or values significantly different from the industry average. In addition, you can grade the company in question on each item to see whether you want to buy it or to compare it to its competitors [Hack #71]. Here are some items you might want to include:

Growth rates
Evaluate historical growth for consistency and compare to the growth of direct competitors. Research unusual growth events, such as losses, major dips, or changing trends.

Ratios
Evaluate financial measures and ratios for the company, and compare measures to the industry average and to competitors. Research above or below average performance, or positive or negative trends in the values.

Valuation
If a company's growth rates and financial ratios look good, you can take the next step of evaluating its historical P/E ratios, PEG ratio, relative value, and other valuation measures to see if purchasing at the current stock price provides you with sufficient return on your investment.

Action items. Documenting your decision and deciding what you want to do next are important steps in your analysis. Whether you include cells in a spreadsheet to grade a company's measures or just come to a decision in your head, write down what you plan to do. For example, you might answer the following questions to conclude your stock study and prepare for your next step:

- Does the company grow quickly and consistently enough to warrant consideration?

- Do its business strategy and current environment bode well for continued or better performance in the future?

- Do the company financial measures look good compared to its industry and competitors and are the ratio trends desirable?
- Is the company at a price that provides enough total return to meet your investment objectives?
- Would purchasing the company improve your portfolio allocation and diversification?
- If you plan to buy the stock, are you going to buy at the current price, place a limit order, or watch the stock for a drop in price?
- If you own the stock and plan to hold onto it, are there any items you should watch carefully?
- If you plan to sell the stock, document your reasons. For example, if you are selling because of portfolio diversification or because the stock is extraordinarily overpriced, you might keep it on a watch list for repurchase in the future. If the company's fundamentals have deteriorated or its business outlook is grim, you might scratch it permanently off your list.

Using a Checklist

If you often forget to include attachments with emails, you can use Word or Excel templates so you don't overwrite your standard checklist by mistake. By creating new documents or spreadsheets from template files, you must save the document with a new name. If you store your templates in a special template folder, it's easy to access them when you create a new file.

To save a checklist as a template, choose File → Save As in Word or Excel. Select the folder in which you want to save the template. If you are saving a Word document as a template, select Document Template (*.dot) in the File of Type box. To save an Excel template, select Template (*.xlt) in the File of Type box. Click Save.

To access your templates quickly, you can specify the folder that contains your templates for all Office applications by following these steps:

1. Choose Start → Programs → Microsoft Office Tools → Microsoft Office Shortcut Bar.
2. Right-click the title area of the Office Shortcut Bar and then choose Customize.
3. Select the Settings tab.
4. To specify the location of all Office templates, select User Templates in the Item list and click Modify to specify the folder path.
5. Click OK.

To use a template, choose File → New in Word or Excel. In the New Document taskbar in Word or the New Workbook taskbar in Excel, choose General Templates under the New from Template heading. In the Templates dialog box, select the template you want to use, and then click OK to create a new file based on that template.

Clicking the New icon in the Standard toolbar creates a new blank file and does not provide a method for selecting a template.

Technical Analysis
Hacks 46-53

In the stock market, *technical analysis*, known affectionately as TA, represents the study of the behavior of price and, in many cases, trading volume of stocks or other investments. This approach contrasts with fundamental analysis, which is described in Chapter 4, in which investors for the most part ignore price and instead determine the fair or intrinsic value of a share of stock by evaluating the company's basic financial metrics. Technicians, also known as technical analysts, believe that price movement reflects all that is important to know about a stock or tradable investment. Ignoring the fundamental factors that may have fueled a rise or decline in price or might do so in the future, technicians concentrate on changes in supply and demand as reflected in price movement, often using volume to test and verify the genuineness of a move, and make all trading or investing decisions on such price movements and volume flow.

To technical analysts, stock prices tend to follow trends and, like a physical object in motion, exhibit a tendency to continue moving in an established direction. Technicians attempt to exploit these tendencies to make money trading investments. Of course, trends do stop, change direction, or drift sideways (what is called a trendless market), but technicians can see and often anticipate such changes through signals that appear in technical charts or are generated by technical analysis tools.

Because trends can change, the most important key to technical success is sound money and trade management. Technicians must proactively set protective stops that remove them from a trade before or shortly after a trend change signal is generated or whenever a trade suddenly goes against them. Traders use protective stops to get them out of a losing trade with at most a small loss while letting their winning trades run.

Fundamental analysts scoff at the idea that someone can profitably practice technical analysis over time. However, technicians have been doing just that for over 100 years. The debate over which form of analysis is best has raged for that entire period.

A Short History of Technical Analysis

In its formative stages, technical analysis was particularly well suited for money managers and investors who did not want to rely on brokers, or become victims of trading pools and back room price manipulations. In those early days, the requisite company financial measures for a fundamental analysis approach were hard to obtain: the financial trade press was in its infancy; daily newspaper coverage was mainly price and, in some cases, volume; the SEC didn't exist; company financial statements weren't readily available; no minute-by-minute Wall Street coverage on television; no calculators; no computers; and definitely no Internet with its flood of free or cheap financial information.

Technical analysis was particularly suitable for these early market environments, because the only information available was exactly what technical analysis wanted. After regulators tamed Wall Street and financial statements were regularly required of publicly traded companies by the then-fledgling SEC, financial information became easier to acquire and technical analysis stepped back into the wings to await calculators, computers, and the Internet. However, technical analysis is the weapon of choice for investors who trade market and sector indices, commodities, and derivatives, where fundamental measurements are unavailable or inapplicable.

More so of late, many investors rely on technical analysis to trade stocks because they feel fundamental measurements are unreliable. It's true that financial results of publicly traded companies are susceptible to aggressive accounting practices and, unfortunately in some all-too-well known cases, outright fraud. Technicians would rather not rely on questionable or fictional financial metrics. Instead, they use price and volume, which is almost impossible to manipulate.

Technical analysis has survived and even thrived under the glare of public scrutiny. Pension plans, mutual fund managers, and hedge fund managers use technical analysis in their day-to-day investment decisions. Major brokerage firms employ high-ranking technicians to develop investment recommendations based primarily on technical analysis and publicize these services to their clients. Many money managers and investors use a hybrid approach: they select companies to study based on fundamental analysis, but trade or invest in them based on technical analysis. As a result, technical analysis has entered the mainstream of investment management. Through constant refinement and incorporation of new technology, technical analysis now improves the investment results of millions of practitioners.

Computers and Technical Analysis

The computational demands of technical analysis restricted its adoption and growth until the mid-1960s. Dow Theory and rudimentary charting techniques began in the 1890s, but the availability of reasonably priced calculators and computers, and easy access to price and volume data propelled technical analysis into prominence just a few decades ago.

The ability to calculate and plot basic indicators, such as moving averages, fueled interest in technical analysis. Then, personal computers and standalone software packages that digested data culled from the financial pages of newspapers made it available to a broad audience. The now-ubiquitous Internet and high-speed connections have made the dissemination of online financial information, charting, screening, and new technical analysis techniques speedy, efficient, and practical.

Methods and systems can now be easily backtested, and either proven effective or discredited in just a few hours. Ease of global communication has helped spread knowledge and adoption of U.S. and non-U.S. derived techniques, such as candlestick charting. Technicians around the world collaborate enthusiastically to refine existing approaches and indicators, and to create new indicators and trading systems.

So, what are the most popular tools in the technical analysis toolbox? How do technicians evaluate technical indicators to determine when to buy, sell, or hold? This chapter introduces the most popular technical analysis tools. For example, you'll learn the basics of technical charting, how to spot trends and trend lines, and how to understand the importance of channels, support, resistance, moving averages, oscillators, indicators, and cycles. For the aspiring technician, this chapter contains references to numerous books and web sites to continue your education.

Technical Charts

There are four basic types of charts used to track tradable stocks and other investments: line charts, bar charts, candlestick charts, and point and figure charts. Graphs are appealing because they often present a clear picture of the trading state and equilibrium of a tradable item, such as a stock, index, or even a mutual fund. Charts have been used to trade commodities long before U.S. markets came into existence—Japanese rice dealers in the 1700s employed candlestick charts to set prices and trade their wares.

All four chart types share a few characteristics, in addition to having their own unique features. Most technical analysis chart users favor one type of chart and usually stick with their charting weapon of choice. Other practitioners employ several types of charts, and a few people use all of them. As a beginner, it's best to absorb all you can about one type of chart before branching out to another.

Although printed chart books are available, technicians can use a software charting package [Hack #53], such as MetaStock from Equis International, to create charts on their desktop or laptop computers. However, these applications require data, usually daily updates, to create charts of interest. Generally, the more stocks, indexes, funds, or other investments covered and the more data fields provided, the greater the cost of the data.

Charting web sites have their own data source automatically updated daily, usually at no extra cost for delayed data. However, charts based on real-time data are the life blood of short-term and day traders, and these do cost more. Other important financial capabilities, such as streaming real-time quotes and access to direct trading platforms or electronic communication networks (ECNs), also typically come with a fee.

The Importance of Money Management

In technical analysis, money management means balancing risk and return [Hack #37]: determining how much risk you're willing to accept, and managing the trade positions you undertake to control your risk and protect your profits. Because technical and fundamental analysis both evaluate past performance to try to forecast the future, the success of technical trades and fundamental investments are by no means guaranteed. Traders and investors who are successful over the long term know that going for broke is usually a self-fulfilling prophecy, so they share a common characteristic of disciplined actions to protect themselves from trades and investments that turn sour.

Spectacular wins can clearly turn a small portfolio into a fortune. The danger is that disasters don't have to be nearly as spectacular to wipe out the gains. For example, if your portfolio drops by 20 percent, you might think you need only a 20 percent return to get back on track. Not so. Consider a portfolio of $100,000. If it drops 20 percent to $80,000, you need 25 percent ($20,000) to get back on track. By the same calculations, you need a 100 percent gain to recover from a 50 percent loss. Unfortunately, 50 percent losses seem much easier to come by than investments that provide 100 percent gains. So, protecting your portfolio from losses is a key to success.

Fortunately, protecting your portfolio with money management isn't complicated. It requires a small amount of common sense and a large dose of discipline—so it's not necessarily easy. Here are a few guidelines that traders use to keep their overall gains in the black:

- The technical traders have a saying: "Plan your trade, and then trade your plan." This means that you must choose a system or approach for evaluating the success of failure of a trade. If the trade goes against you—meaning it violates the criteria you use for success—admit you made a mistake, get out of the trade, and don't look back. This is harder than it might sound, but savvy traders know that discipline is the key.

- Take an honest look at your tolerance for losing money. After you identify the level of risk you're willing to accept, implement the following steps with that risk level in mind.

- Risk only a small percentage of your money on a trade. The best traders limit their risk typically to a set percentage of the trade value. Limit the risk you take to an acceptable percentage of your total portfolio, such as two to five percent. This means that you add a stop to your trade to limit the amount you might lose to the predetermined percentage of your portfolio.

- When you determine the level of risk you plan to take on a trade, create an actual stop in the market to take you out of the trade if it goes against you. Otherwise, you're liable to give the trade a second chance, or you might miss the warning signal.

- Manage your risk so that your overall ratio of return to risk is at least 3-to-1.

- When you win, consider locking in at least a portion of your profits by selling some of the trade position and moving the money into another trade.

- If you end up with several bad trades, stop trading, take a breather, recharge your mental batteries, and reevaluate your approach. The market doesn't make mistakes, only traders do.

See Also

- *Technical Analysis From A to Z* by Steven A. Achelis (Probus) is an introduction and reference source for technical analysis and is suited for beginners.

- *The Technical Analysis Course, Revised Edition* by Thomas A. Myers (McGraw-Hill) is a good survey of technical analysis for beginner to intermediate students.

- *Technical Analysis of the Financial Markets: A Comprehensive Guide to Trading Methods and Applications* by John J. Murphy (Prentice Hall) is a comprehensive work for technical analysis practitioners. I highly recommend it! A copy belongs in every technical analysis library along with its optional companion, *Study Guide for Technical Analysis of the Financial Markets*, also published by Prentice Hall.

- Investopedia (*http://www.investopedia.com*) is a free investing-education web site that offers both technical and fundamental analysis information. Geared more toward beginner to intermediate investors, it includes a good glossary and timely articles on technical analysis.

Use Line and Bar Charts

HACK #46 Line charts and bar charts help you focus on price changes.

Line and bar charts are often used to represent *price action* (price changes during individual periods as well as over multiple periods in the timeframe you're evaluating) over daily, weekly, monthly, or custom time periods. Line charts are the ultimate in simplicity, graphing daily closing prices and nothing more. Line charts are the only option for analyzing investments that have only a closing price, such as mutual funds. Bar charts display a fair amount of price action while remaining easy on the eyes, but they can show opening, closing, high, and low prices. By using simple line and bar charts, you can narrow in on basic trends. Technical analysis web sites and standalone software applications make it easy to create these charts regardless of the combination of options you choose.

Line Charts

Line charts are made up of simple lines that typically connect closing prices over a predetermined period. Many technical analysts consider closing prices to be the most important price metric and see no need to clutter the line chart with other price information. Analysts who favor line charts find them easier to interpret because they ignore intraday price fluctuations and focus on the end-of-day status of the running battle between the bulls and the bears. For technical analysts who draw their own charts from daily newspaper data or for those who follow mutual funds, which only publish closing prices, line charts are the only game in town.

On a line chart, the vertical axis represents price and is usually linear, meaning that each vertical subdivision represents the same number of dollars. However, some technical analysts prefer a logarithmic scale, in which each vertical subdivision represents the same percentage change. As shown in the logarithmic line chart in Figure 5-1, the change from $10 to $20, a 100 percent increase, is equal to the distance on the axis for the change from $15 to $30, also a 100 percent increase. Logarithmic scale makes it easier to see the rate of price change, because constant growth appears as a straight line. The horizontal axis represents time on line charts. Daily charts slice the horizontal axis into the trading days for the period depicted by the chart. Similarly, weekly and monthly charts show the closing prices for each week or month, respectively.

Figure 5-1. A logarithmic line chart from StockCharts.com uses the same distance on the vertical axis to represent equal changes in percentage

Price action over short, intermediate, and long periods can reveal totally different scenarios. Analysts often study price action using different timeframes, looking for consistency in the action over each timeframe. For example, if a monthly chart fails to confirm an apparent trend change in a daily chart, short-term patterns or price actions aren't as likely to follow the predicted trend change.

Chart books are fixed in format and focus on daily charts. An analyst using chart books can't switch between time-frames as charting software or web-based tools can.

To create a line chart on the StockCharts.com web site, follow these steps:

1. Navigate to *http://www.stockcharts.com*.

2. At the very top of the web page, make sure that the Style box displays SharpChart. Type the ticker for the stock you want to graph in the Symbol box and click Go.

You can also select SharpCharts in the navigation bar on the left side of the web page.

3. Under the Price Plot Attributes heading, select Line (NAV) from the Style drop-down list.

4. Toggle between a linear line chart and a logarithmic line chart by selecting the Log or Linear option.

5. If you want to display a specific duration, select the timeframe you want from the Duration drop-down list.

6. Click Update Chart.

By default, StockCharts.com plots two moving averages on the chart and includes additional boxes for two indicators beneath the chart. To remove these, select –None– in the drop-down lists under the Price Overlays and Indicator Windows headings.

Bar Charts

Bar charts are the most popular type of chart in use today. They graph price against time using linear or logarithmic scales, just as line charts do. However, in a bar chart, a vertical bar represents each time segment instead of a single point. Each daily, weekly, or monthly bar shows the open, close, low, and high price for the trading period it represents. Bar charts can even show intraday trading down to the minute. Although day traders make extensive use of such charts, more information crowding into a chart can mask the details of what's happening. Short-term traders typically stick to short-term charts. Intermediate traders, on the other hand, usually review charts of different time periods looking for confirmations of signals in each period they review.

As shown in Figure 5-2, the top of the bar represents the high for the period, whereas the bottom of that same bar represents the low for the period. The opening price is shown by a tick mark facing to the left of the bar. The closing price tick mark faces to the right. No lines connect high, low, closing, or opening prices between adjacent bars on a bar chart. Technical analysts use techniques, such as pattern recognition, trend lines, and support and resistance levels, to forecast future prices from overall patterns formed by the adjacent and equally spaced bars.

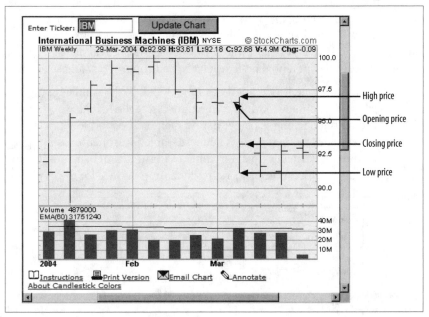

Figure 5-2. Bars and tick marks show high, low, opening, and closing prices on a bar chart from StockCharts.com

To create a bar chart on the StockCharts.com web site, follow the steps listed for a line chart. In Step 3, under the Price Plot Attributes heading, select OHLC Bars from the Style drop-down list to show opening, closing, high, and low prices. To display only high, low, and closing prices, select HLC Bars.

—Saul Seinberg

Light the Way with Candlestick Charts

#47   Price patterns are easier to spot when you graph price movement with candlestick charts.

Japanese rice growers and merchants used candlestick charts to track and trade rice contracts as far back as the 1600s. The Japanese financial markets adopted and refined them, and then imported them to the U.S. as they have many other products. Candlestick charts have become the default representation for many Internet charting sites. Although candlesticks show the same data found in bar charts, albeit in a different way, candlesticks convey price action with no more than a quick glance. Using candlesticks effectively takes time and study. However, the rewards can be significant; candlestick charts can show trends, flag potential price reversals, and confirm buy and sell signs.

A candlestick bar earned its name because it looks like a candle, complete with a wick at the top and bottom, which are also called shadows. Candlestick bars show the opening, closing, period high, and period low prices in a way that accentuates price action. When a tradable investment closes higher for the day, the candlestick is open or white, as illustrated in Figure 5-3. Conversely, closed or black candlesticks represent a drop in price for the day.

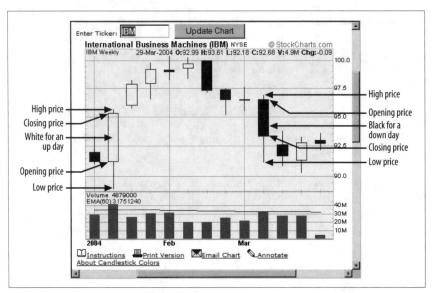

Figure 5-3. Candlesticks make price action more apparent (from StockCharts.com)

As shown in Figure 5-3, the top of an *up* candle body represents the closing price for the period represented by the candlestick. Its bottom represents the opening price. If the high price exceeded the closing price, an upper wick or shadow extends from the closing price to the high for the period. A wick below the candlestick shows the low price for the period.

Because a down period means that the closing price is lower than the opening price, the top of a *down* candle body represents the opening price while its bottom depicts the closing price for the period. As with an up candlestick, an upper wick indicates the high price for the candle period and a lower wick shows the low.

The colored candle bodies make it easy to see whether price action for the period was up or down. In addition, the length of the candle body is a good visual indicator of trader sentiment. Long bodies show a strong opinion, bearish when the candle is black and bullish when the candle is white. The presence and length of wicks shows whether there was significant action outside the range of the opening and closing prices. The colored bars also emphasize the evolution of price action across adjacent periods. For example, the upward trend on the left side of Figure 5-3 is obvious because the chart is so white, whereas the downward trend stands out with multiple black candlesticks.

To create a candlestick chart on the StockCharts.com web site, follow these steps:

1. Navigate to *http://www.stockcharts.com*.

2. At the very top of the web page, make sure that the Style box displays SharpChart. Type the ticker for the stock you want to graph in the Symbol box and click Go.

> You can also select SharpCharts in the navigation bar on the left side of the web page.

3. Under the Price Plot Attributes heading, select Candlesticks from the Style drop-down list.

4. Toggle between a linear line chart and a logarithmic line chart by selecting the Log or Linear option.

5. If you want to display a specific duration, select the timeframe you want from the Duration drop-down list.

6. Click Update Chart.

Although candlesticks are typically shown as black or white depending on price movements, candlestick charts at Stock-Charts.com might display candlesticks in white, black, and red. To learn more about the color rules, click the About Candlestick Colors link below the chart.

See Also

- *The Candlestick Course* by Steve Nison (Wiley & Sons)
- *Japanese Candlestick Charting Techniques* by Steve Nison (Prentice Hall) is the leading work on candlesticks. Its author, a leading candlestick charting expert, is credited with introducing candlestick techniques to U.S. and other western market technical analysts.
- StockCharts.com does more than provide charts for your technical analysis. Learn about all aspects of technical analysis at *http://stockcharts.com/education/Overview/techAnalysis1.html*.

—*Saul Seinberg*

HACK #48   Point and Figure Charts

Resistance, support, and the direction of price action are easy to identify in point and figure charts once you learn to interpret them.

Growing from Charles Dow's theories about supply and demand, *point and figure* (P&F) charts are easy to create and maintain even without a computer. In fact, P&F charts fell from favor when handheld calculators and home computers made other types of charts easier to produce. However, some P&F chart features have attracted renewed interest, particularly from intermediate-term traders. Although their appearance might be startling at first, P&F charts provide advantages over other charts, such as emphasizing the direction of price action, and making resistance and support levels easier to identify.

Although P&F charts have been applied to short-term trading, they are most appropriate for intermediate-term trading because their construction by definition removes short-term price fluctuations from the picture. Investors who use P&F charts can quickly determine the meaning of price activity and formulate trading decisions with a single glance. In a P&F chart, a stock or other tradable item shows either a buy or a sell signal—there is no middle ground. The P&F chart user can review many charts without reaching information overload or worrying about ambiguous chart patterns or price activity.

P&F charts work a bit differently from bar charts and candlestick charts. First, the X-axis doesn't represent a fixed length of time. Time, from a price action perspective, is of minimal importance in a P&F chart. Years and months are shown only as reference points on the chart. The numbers 1 through 9 for January through September and A through C for October through December, respectively, appear in a cell right in the P&F chart to denote that the month began while that price activity occurred, as demonstrated in Figure 5-4.

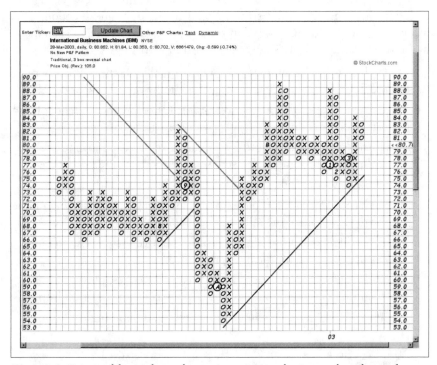

Figure 5-4. Point and figure charts show price activity and price trends with no reference to volume and minimal connection to time

P&F charts feature alternating columns of Xs, indicating demand through steadily rising prices, and columns of Os, indicating supply through falling prices. The vertical axis of a P&F chart shows prices. Each price subdivision represents the same price movement as in other types of charts. However, the zones vary depending on the price of the stock you're evaluating:

$0 to $5 per share
    Each vertical box equals $.25 in price change

$5.5 to $20 per share
    Each vertical box equals $.50 in price change

$20 to $100 per share
Each vertical box equals $1 in price change

$102 and above
Each vertical box equals $2 in price change

In a P&F chart, the price (which represents either high or low prices, not opening or closing prices) is either on the way up or on the way down. You won't find Xs and Os mixed in the same column. To filter out the noise of short-term price changes, a P&F chart doesn't acknowledge a change in direction until the price moves three boxes in the opposite direction. This means the price has to jump or fall three boxes in a day before you can move into the next column. Here's how the algorithm works:

1. If the chart is in a column of Os (prices are falling), check the low price for the day. Do one of the following, depending on the low price:

   a. If the low price dropped lower, insert Os below the current column of Os down to the cell for the low price for the day.

   b. If the low price increased by at least three boxes, move to the next column to the right, and insert Xs in the cells for the price increase.

   c. If the low price didn't move lower or reverse, do nothing.

2. If the chart is in a column of Xs (prices are rising), check the high price for the day. Do one of the following, depending on the high price:

   a. If the high price rose higher, insert Xs above the current column of Xs up to the cell for the high price for the day.

   b. If the high price decreased by at least three boxes, move to the next column to the right, and insert Os in the cells for the price drop.

   c. If the high price didn't increase or reverse, do nothing.

 StockCharts.com P&F charts automatically display trend lines. Blue diagonal lines indicate upward trends, whereas red diagonal lines indicate downward trends.

Volume [Hack #50], which is almost always used to confirm and validate price movements and forecasts in line, bar, and candlestick charts, is not shown at all in P&F charts. Many technical analysts that work with P&F charts do not feel that volume is necessary. However, you can verify P&F chart predictions by displaying volume on a P&F chart with a few clicks on a charting web site.

 To learn how to interpret signals in P&F charts, refer to "Look for Patterns in Technical Charts" [Hack #49].

To create a P&F chart on the StockCharts.com web site, follow these steps:

1. Navigate to *http://www.stockcharts.com*.

2. At the very top of the web page, select P&F Chart in the Style box. Type the ticker for the stock you want to graph in the Symbol box, and click Go.

 You can also select P&F Charts in the navigation bar on the left side of the web page.

3. Under the Chart Attributes heading, select Daily or Weekly from the Periods drop-down list.

4. If you want to change the number of boxes required for a reversal, type a number in the Reversal box under the Chart Scale heading.

5. To display trend lines on the chart, select Trend Lines in one of the drop-down lists under the Chart Overlays heading. You can also display other indicators by choosing them from the other two drop-down lists.

6. Click Update Chart.

See Also

- *Charting Made Easy* by John J. Murphy (Marketplace Books) is an introduction to charting that covers the basics in Murphy's easy-to-read style.

- *Technical Charting for Profits* by Mark L. Larson (Wiley & Sons) is a good beginner to intermediate book with quizzes and a CD-ROM video that illustrates some basic chart patterns and their use.

- *Point and Figure Charting: The Essential Application for Forecasting and Tracking Market Prices* by Thomas J. Dorsey (Wiley & Sons) is the bible for point and figure charts. It is comprehensive, yet easy to read—a reference for beginner to advanced P&F chartists.

- StockCharts.com (*http://www.stockcharts.com*) is a comprehensive web site that provides charts of all types, including candlesticks and point and figure charts, along with excellent educational material for an overview of technical analysis. The site provides free and fee based capabilities, with greater functionality and convenience as you ascend the pay scale.

- BigCharts.com (*http://www.bigcharts.com*) is another good charting web site, which offers a wide range of chart indicators, including candlesticks, at no charge. However, it lacks point and figure charts.

- Dorsey Wright (*http://www.dorseywright.com*) is a fee-based site for point and figure devotees that is reasonably priced and includes a lot of P&F capability based on individual, index, and portfolio criteria. The Dorsey Wright web site works for the beginner (free P&F education with quizzes) to the advanced P&F chartist.

—*Saul Seinberg*

HACK #49 Look for Patterns in Technical Charts

Studying price charts for patterns helps you identify future price movements that you can translate into profits.

Over time, people who studied charts noticed that when prices generated specific patterns, the price action that followed was usually the same. Through the first half of the previous century, technical analysts studied and analyzed charts to increase their knowledge of chart patterns and the price actions that those patterns predict. Although some analysts have used computers to develop sophisticated, complex indicators that they claim replace the need for studying chart patterns, some tried-and-true chart patterns remain unchallenged. By learning to recognize these patterns and what they prophesize, you can identify potential price changes and prepare to take appropriate action, whether it be a purchase to achieve a profit or a sale to protect your portfolio.

Chart patterns are divided into two main groups: continuation or consolidation patterns that suggest that an existing trend will pause or continue, and reversal patterns that suggest that the trend will go the other way. Pattern analysis can be complicated because some patterns act as either continuation or reversal patterns depending on what happened in earlier price action as well as current volume and other indicators.

The Art of Charts

Chart reading is not a science, despite what many chart readers say. Skill in chart reading and pattern recognition comes with practice and analysis of many, many charts. In addition, pattern recognition is open to interpretation, and even computer programs sometimes disagree on whether a particular pattern is present in a chart. Because a chart pattern is one indicator, technical analysts make it a habit to verify what a pattern suggests by using at least one other independent indicator or tool.

Recognizing Reversal Patterns

Trend reversals occur when prices hold at levels of resistance or support [Hack #52]. The most popular reversal patterns are called head and shoulders, double tops, triple tops, double bottoms, and triple bottoms.

Head and shoulders patterns. The head and shoulders reversal pattern can appear either as a top head and shoulders pattern (someone standing up) or a bottom head and shoulders pattern (someone hanging upside down). As shown in Figure 5-5, a top head and shoulders pattern consists of a left shoulder, a head, and a right shoulder. Although the left shoulder in this pattern forms at the end of what is usually a vigorous advance in price, it isn't apparent or confirmed until after the head and the right shoulder are formed. The left shoulder forms when the price drops after the run-up to the left shoulder high. A rally and subsequent drop form the head. One more advance in price (to a lower level than the top of the head) is followed by another price decline to form the right shoulder.

The final component of a head and shoulders reversal pattern is a neckline, which is drawn horizontally from the bottom of the left shoulder past the head and the right shoulder. The price dropping below the neckline at the end of the right shoulder confirms the upcoming trend reversal, in this case a decline. Once the neckline is broken, the neckline price level serves as resistance [Hack #52] to any increase in price.

A bottom head and shoulders reversal pattern also has two shoulders with a head in between but, in this case, the shoulders and head are upside down. This reversal pattern indicates a trend reversal that will lead to an increase in price.

In real life, most head and shoulders patterns aren't symmetrical or perfectly formed. Don't expect to see shoulders of equal height or width or equal spacing from the head. Symmetry doesn't add anything to a head and shoulders pattern. However, one important rule for a head and shoulders pattern is that the neckline of a top head and shoulders reversal pattern must be lower than the top of the pattern's right shoulder. The neckline for a bottom head and shoulders pattern must be higher than the bottom of the pattern's right shoulder.

Volume confirmation is important for head and shoulders reversal patterns. To confirm a top head and shoulders pattern, volume should be heavier during the rally that defines the left shoulder and head with less volume on the rally that defines the right shoulder. Look for volume to dry up during the declines that complete the left shoulder and head, with accelerating volume as the price drops off the right shoulder.

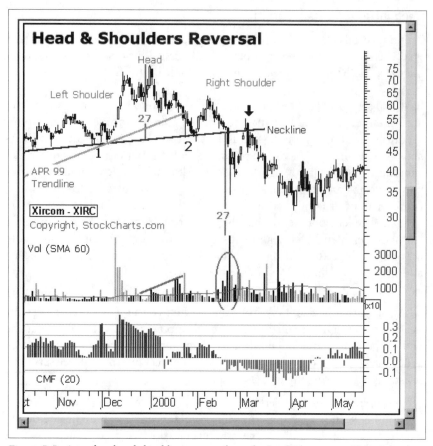

Figure 5-5. A top head and shoulders pattern from the StockCharts.com Chart School

Double top and bottom reversal patterns. A double top reversal pattern, shown in Figure 5-6, consists of two distinct tops that form the letter M, particularly on a line chart. When completed, a double top marks a change from bullish (increasing prices) to bearish (decreasing prices). The two tops don't have to be equal in height. The valley between the two tops should be distinct, not shallow, and the two tops should be far enough apart in time, usually at least a month, so that it's clear they don't represent a consolidation, described in the next section.

Patience is important with a double top reversal pattern: wait for the formation to be completed with the second top clearly formed. In addition, the support for the uptrend must be broken, which means that price after the second top must drop below the lowest price in the valley between the peaks, preferably on increasing volume.

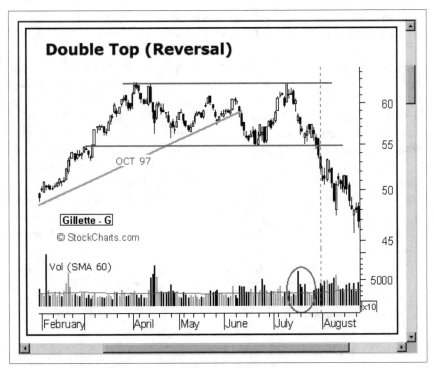

Figure 5-6. A double top pattern from the StockCharts.com Chart School

A double bottom reversal pattern has two distinct bottoms, which together resemble the letter W. It marks a change from bearish to bullish when completed.

Recognizing Continuation and Consolidation Patterns

Continuation and consolidation patterns indicate that an existing trend will pause, continue, or do both. Popular continuation or consolidation patterns are flags, pennants, and (our new friend) the head and shoulders pattern.

Head and shoulders continuation patterns. Head and shoulders patterns can indicate reversal or continuation depending on the volume behavior that accompanies the pattern. In its role as a continuation pattern, the head and shoulders pattern is reversed from the direction of the chart trend in which it appears. A top head and shoulders pattern that appears in an overall downtrend indicates the downtrend will continue. A bottom head and shoulders pattern in an overall uptrend indicates that the uptrend will continue. You can differentiate head and shoulders continuation and reversal patterns by volume behavior. When volume decreases on the rally that defines the left shoulder and head of a top pattern and on the drop that defines the right shoulder, the pattern indicates that the uptrend will continue.

Flags and pennants. Flag and pennant patterns represent consolidation and appear when price action moves sideways. Flag continuation patterns resemble real flags, a series of bars contained between parallel lines, as shown in Figure 5-7. They are short-term continuation patterns that identify a price consolidation or pause before the previous price action resumes. A significant volume change usually precedes the appearance of a flag, and then volume dries up as the flag pattern forms. After the flag is complete, volume dramatically expands, and prices break out of the flag pattern in the direction of the previous trend. Flags usually appear midway through an overall trend and indicate that prices should continue in the same direction for about the same magnitude of increase or decrease that occurred before the consolidation.

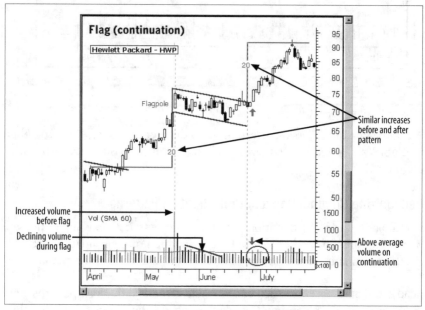

Figure 5-7. A flag pattern from the StockCharts.com Chart School

A pennant pattern, shown in Figure 5-8, is formed by converging bars rather than parallel bars, and also represents consolidation and continuation. Volume and price action in a pennant pattern is similar to that of a flag pattern, the only real difference being in their appearance.

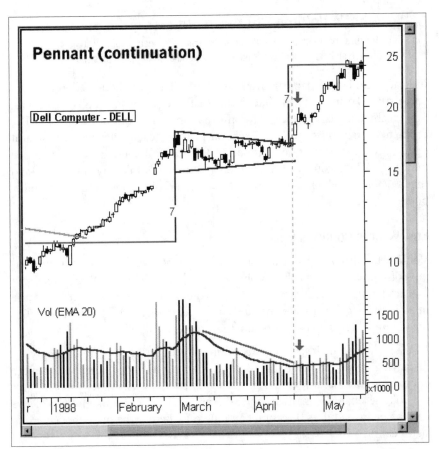

Figure 5-8. *An example of a pennant pattern from the StockCharts.com Chart School*

See Also

- *Encyclopedia of Chart Patterns* by Thomas N. Bulkowski (Wiley Trading Advantage) is a comprehensive reference for chart patterns, their meaning, and trading usage, and belongs in every chartist's library.

- *Technical Analysis From A to Z* by Steven A. Achelis (Probus) is an introduction and reference source for technical analysis that is suited to beginners.

- *Technical Analysis of Stock Trends* by Robert Edwards and John Magee (St. Lucie Press) is a book that includes excellent material on charting and chart patterns, and is still being used and updated more than 50 years after its original publication.

—Saul Seinberg

HACK
#50

What's Volume Got to Do with It?

Because most charts and indicators rely solely on price, trading volume can provide an independent confirmation or contradiction to the signals you see.

Indicators and chart patterns aren't infallible. Their predictions don't always come true. To increase the likelihood that you're getting the right signals, most technical analysts look for confirmation before executing a trade. The problem is that most indicators rely on price, so each price-based indicator operates on the same price data and often confirms any other price-based indicator. What you need is an indicator that doesn't rely on price—and that's *volume*, which represents the number of shares traded during a period.

How Volume Confirms Price

Volume has become the standard for testing the validity and trustworthiness of a price-based signal. "Volume precedes price" is the Wall Street saying, and indeed it often does. When volume increases, the trend of the market or a stock usually continues in the same direction. However, declining volume often signals an upcoming trend reversal.

Many technical analysts evaluate volume from period to period simply by displaying volume bars below a line, bar, or candlestick chart, and visually comparing how volume tracks price movements. For example, you can look for volume changes as price increases or decreases. The magnitude of the volume change and its direction can tell you whether the price movement is significant:

Price goes up and volume increases well above its average
> The stock is being accumulated. For example, in Figure 5-9, the price increased in early 2004 when volume was above average, and a trend of accumulation followed.

Price goes up but volume decreases
> The stock is about to peak and drop to a more reasonable price level.

Price heads south and volume is above average
> Significant selling or distribution is occurring.

Price drops and volume is below average
> The stock is about to level off or rise to a more reasonable level.

Charting software programs and online charting tools use different colors for volume bars for the days on which the price closes up and for the days when the price closes down. In most cases, green indicates an up day, and red indicates down. In Figure 5-9, StockCharts.com uses black for up days

Figure 5-9. Any chart from StockCharts.com can include volume below the price chart

and red for down. To help you identify whether volume is significant, most charting tools display a moving average line for volume, illustrated in Figure 5-9. StockCharts.com uses a 60-day exponential moving average [Hack #51] to show whether volume change in a day or other period is above, below, or at its current average.

> By default, StockCharts.com overlays volume within a price chart. However, if prices dip to lower bands in the price chart, price and volume both become difficult to read. To make charts easy to read, select Separate on the Volume drop-down list to display volume in a separate indicator window below the price chart, as in Figure 5-9.

On-Balance Volume

Another technique for evaluating volume is called On-Balance Volume (OBV), an indicator made popular by Joe Granville almost 30 years ago. OBV is a cumulative volume total that adds volume to the total when the price closes higher and subtracts volume when the price closes lower. Most analysts don't consider OBV useful for predictions on its own, but a divergence between OBV and price action during a period can signal a trend change. For example, OBV and price moving in opposite directions or one indicator staying put while the other moves in either direction can signal a change in price trend, which can forewarn a trader. Conversely, OBV and price moving in the same direction typically signals a continuation of the current trend.

> Reliance on OBV has ebbed over the years, although many still use it as a confirming indicator. Advancing-declining issues and money flow indicators [Hack #51] have largely replaced OBV as predictive indicators.

To calculate OBV, first see whether the price for the stock or other investment you're studying closed higher or lower for the period. If the price closed higher, add the volume for the period to the running total for past periods. If the price closed lower, subtract the volume for the period from the running total. Although it's important to understand how to derive OBV, you don't have to calculate it yourself. To display OBV on a chart on the StockCharts.com web site, follow these steps:

1. At the very top of the web page, select SharpCharts in the Style box. Type the ticker for the stock you want to graph in the Symbol box, and click Go.

2. Under the Indicator Windows heading, select On Balance Volume from one of the drop-down lists for indicators. Select Above or Below from the first set of drop-down lists to specify whether the On Balance Volume indicator appears above or below the main chart.

3. Specify any other changes that you want for the chart.

4. Click Update Chart.

—Saul Seinberg

HACK #51   How to Use Indicators and Oscillators
Indicators and oscillators are mathematical constructions based on price and volume that predict price movements.

Indicators and oscillators are additional technical tools that you can use to predict future price movements. Some indicators predict where the overall market is headed, while others prognosticate the direction of individual stocks or other investments. In general, technical analysts don't trust signals from a single indicator; they prefer to obtain confirmation from several. However, because many indicators are based on price and tend to agree with other price indicators, traders prefer volume-based indicators for confirmation of price-based signals. This hack reviews some of the more popular indicators and oscillators used in technical analysis.

An Introduction to Indicators

Many indicators, such as moving averages or the Relative Strength Index, evaluate the price and volume for an individual stock or other investment to predict the movement of price in the future. In addition to investment indicators, market indicators provide insight into the entire market. Unless you've been living with a family of wolves for the past few decades, you're probably familiar with some monetary market indicators: the inflation rate and interest rates, such as the Fed rate. Because monetary policy affects the appeal of different investments, monetary indicators can indicate what different types of investments might do as a whole. For example, when interest rates go up, stocks become less appealing, as the return investors receive from bonds increases.

Technical analysts also consider sentiment and momentum indicators. Sentiment indicators convey investor expectations—what investors expect of prices in the market. For example, the ratio of bullish to bearish investment advisors might predict the optimism or pessimism that investors exhibit in the near future (if you accept the assumption that most investors listen to investment advisors).

Momentum indicators return to the evaluation of price and volume, but take into account price and volume of entire markets. By looking at price trends in conjunction with the level of volume, momentum indicators indicate the direction of the market and how strongly investors feel about that direction. For example, the advancing-declining issues indicator represents the difference between the number of stocks listed on the New York Stock Exchange that increase in price and the number of stocks that decrease in price. The New York Stock Exchange represents approximately 2,800 companies. Strong up days might deliver an advancing-declining issues value of more than 1000, meaning that 1,800 companies or more increased compared to 1,000 or less that decreased. Seriously pessimistic days might show an advancing-declining issues indicator of less than −1000.

Oscillators are a type of indicator that vary or oscillate between high and low values, sometimes normalized to fluctuate between 0 and 100, or between two values on either side of a zero line.

The *Arms Index*, often called the *TRIN Index*, is an overall market indicator, created by Dick Arms in the late 1960s, that combines volume with advancing and declining issues. This indicator shows the relationship between the number of advancing and declining stocks compared to the volume of each. The formula for this indicator is shown in Example 5-1.

Example 5-1. The formula for calculating the TRIN Index

```
TRIN Index = ((Advancing issues/Declining issues)/(Advancing volume/Declining
volume))
```

The TRIN Index identifies *overbought* (prices that are too high and might decline) and *oversold* (prices that are too low and might increase) conditions in the market. Analysts typically use the TRIN Index to evaluate short-term market potential. The TRIN Index moves in the opposite direction to the market; a rising TRIN Index is bearish, whereas a falling TRIN Index is bullish. Some charting tools, such as StockCharts.com, show an inverted representation of the TRIN Index (shown in Figure 5-10), so it moves in the same direction as other indicators and makes it easier to understand what it is indicating. In Figure 5-10, the inverted TRIN Index appears in the middle band. The decline in the inverted TRIN precedes a decline in the NYSE Composite.

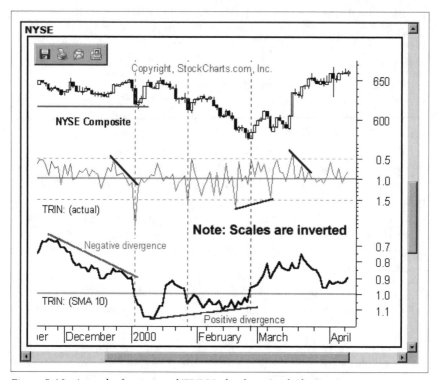

Figure 5-10. A graph of an inverted TRIN Index from StockCharts.com

Another volume indicator, *money flow*, a cousin of OBV **[Hack #50]**, tracks the flow of money into and out of a stock or other investment. Money talks, so a flow of money into an investment is a positive sign, whereas a flow out of an investment doesn't bode well for future prices. For example, if the price increases, money flow is positive. If the price decreases, money flow is negative. As in On-Balance Volume, money flow is the cumulative total of the money flow for each period you're studying.

Moving Averages

Moving averages are some of the most popular technical analysis tools around. Acting as indicators as well as serving as support and resistance levels [Hack #52], moving averages smooth out short-term price or volume fluctuations to present a clearer picture of trends.

A moving average starts off by calculating the average of the values for a number of periods. The moving part comes from the fact that each calculation uses the values from the most recent set of periods. For example, the value of a ten-day moving average on any given day is the average of the values from the previous ten days. When you move forward a day, you add in the current day and drop off the tenth day from the previous day's moving average calculation. The spreadsheet in Figure 5-11 demonstrates the calculation of a moving average and highlights the benefits of using moving averages.

> This example uses a ten-month moving average instead of a moving average based on days so that the price changes over the months better illustrate the effect of a moving average.

The first moving average calculation in cell C11 is the average of the prices in cells B2 through B11, prices for October through July. The next average in cell C12 is the average of the prices in cells B3 through B12, representing prices for the months November through August. The remaining cells continue to drop off the oldest month while adding the newest month.

As you can see in the chart in Figure 5-11, the prices zig-zag, while the moving average smooths out the short-term perturbations and shows the overall trend of the prices, which is up.

Moving averages come in several flavors:

Simple
> The simple moving average is nothing more than an arithmetic mean that is recalculated each time you advance one period. The simple moving average adds the prices for a number of periods and divides by that number of periods, as demonstrated in Figure 5-11. One complaint about a simple moving average is that it assigns equal weight to each period instead of emphasizing more recent price activity.

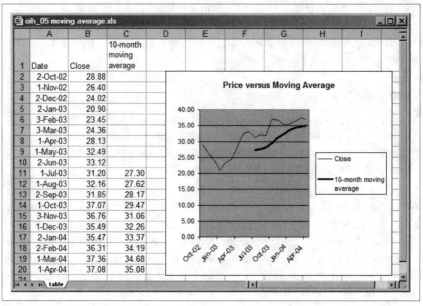

Figure 5-11. *An example of the calculation of a moving average and a chart of price versus the moving average*

Weighted

The weighted moving average places more emphasis on more recent activity by multiplying each price value by a weight: the oldest period is multiplied by 1, the next oldest by 2, and so on. To calculate the weighted average, you must divide the total value by the sum of the weights. For example, for a ten-day moving average, the weights range from 1 for the oldest day to 10 for the most recent day. Divide the total value of the weighted prices by the sum of the weights, which is 55 for weight values from 1 to 10.

Exponential

An exponential moving average also emphasizes more recent activity. However, an exponential moving average continues to incorporate older data, but places much less weight on it. For example, a five-day exponential moving average might represent more than 20 days of prices, with the most recent 5 days receiving the most weight and days 6 through 20 receiving less and less.

As an indicator, a moving average is often compared to the price of a stock or other investment. The price line crossing and rising above the moving average is a buy signal, whereas the price dropping below the moving average is a sell signal. Other signals are generated when you compare moving averages of different lengths. For example, in Figure 5-12, the 10-day moving average line and the price line both drop below the 50-day moving average on March 9. In this example, the sell signal came true as the price dropped from 96.5 to 91.

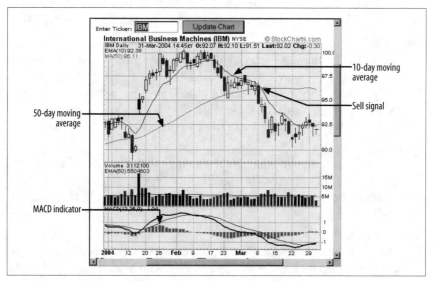

Figure 5-12. A shorter-term moving average crossing a longer-term moving average generates a buy or sell signal, as demonstrated by a chart in StockCharts.com

Moving averages are lagging indicators, which means they tell you what has happened after the fact. Because of this, it's important to choose carefully the duration of the moving averages you use. For example, a 200-day moving average is slow to change, because it takes significant changes in current prices to impact the previous 200 days of data. Therefore, the 200-day moving average is also slow to give you a signal, and you might miss trading opportunities as a result. On the other hand, a 5-day moving average might whipsaw back and forth, which results in more buy and sell signals. Too many signals are also undesirable, because you'll be buried in commissions if you trade on each signal. Typically, moving averages between 10 days and 50 days provide indications of changes in trends without going overboard.

To display a moving average on a StockCharts.com chart, choose either Simple Moving Average or Exponential Moving Average from one of the Price Overlays drop-down lists. Type the number of periods you want to use in the average, such as **10** or **50**.

Moving Average Convergence/Divergence (MACD) is another popular indicator based on moving averages. It shows the relationship between a 26-day and 12-day exponential moving average. MACD is often shown as a histogram, illustrated in the bottom box of Figure 5-12, in which the action of this indicator is easier to see. Technical analysts use MACD in several ways:

Crossovers
> The MACD generates a sell or buy signal when it falls below or above its signal line (represented by the MACD of one in Figure 5-12), respectively. Some analysts consider the MACD moving below or above zero as sell or buy signals. For example, in Figure 5-12, MACD dropped below zero on February 9, just prior to a major sell-off in the stock.

Overbought/oversold
> MACD increases when the 12-day moving average grows faster than the 26-day moving average. This acceleration in price increase might indicate that the price is getting too high and might return to more realistic levels.

Divergences
> The MACD heading in a different direction than the price can also predict price movements. For example, the MACD heading lower while the price stays the same indicates that prices might drop further.

The *Relative Strength Index* (RSI) is an oscillator that evaluates the internal strength of a stock or other investment. RSI ranges between 0 and 100. Many analysts look for divergence between RSI and the underlying price: if the price reaches a new high but the RSI does not, that divergence indicates that the price is about to reverse and start heading back down. RSI values above 70 indicate an overbought condition, while values below 30 suggest that the stock is oversold.

See Also

- *A New Strategy of Daily Stock Market Timing for Maximum Profit* by Joseph E. Granville (Simon & Shuster) is a classic work that sets the stage for the study and use of volume in technical analysis.

- *The Arms Index (TRIN): An Introduction to Volume for Analysis of Stock and Bond Markets* by Richard W. Arms, Jr. (Irwin Professional Pub) is another classic on the use of volume that deserves a place in a well-rounded technical analysis library.

- *Trading on Volume: The Key to Identifying and Profiting From Stock Price Reversals* by Donald Cassidy (McGraw-Hill) is a survey of volume indicators and considerations, such as the predictive effect of surges and confirmation.

Support and Resistance

Knowing how to recognize and profit from levels of support and resistance can improve your trading success.

In trading, supply and demand is easy to spot. As the price of a stock or other investment drops, it reaches a price at which enough traders and investors are willing to buy, and its price stops falling and even starts to head back up as the buying starts. Conversely, as the price of a stock or investment increases, it reaches a price at which no trader or investor is willing to buy, and the excess supply of stock causes the price to stop increasing and head back down. By learning to identify levels of support and resistance and by understanding the implications when those levels are broken, you can improve the results of both your technical trading and your fundamental analysis investing.

An old saying in technical analysis circles is "Stocks don't have memory, but people do." People's memories, not to mention psychology, generate levels of support and resistance. For example, many people who buy and sell stocks can't stomach losing money on an investment. Although it would be better to sell a losing trade and invest the proceeds in a more profitable endeavor, these people hang on to their stock until it reaches their original purchase price and only then do they sell. That original purchase price is one form of resistance. Similarly, a company might have a well-known *buy* price, whether it's based on the dividend the company pays, a previous low, or the company's inherent value. When the stock price drops to that buy price, everyone jumps in and buys, and the price goes back up. Figure 5-13 shows obvious examples of both support and resistance.

> Although you can't configure charts at StockCharts.com to show levels of support and resistance, you can set up price alerts **[Hack #24]** to notify you when a support or resistance level is reached.

Moving averages **[Hack #51]** can also act as levels of support and resistance. Many traders consider the price moving below the moving average as a sell sign. Any change in opinion is a psychological barrier, so prices often have difficulty moving below a widely acknowledged sell sign, such as the price-moving average crossover. Therefore, when the price is higher than the moving average, the value of the moving average becomes a support level. For example, in Figure 5-12, IBM's price dropped in the middle of February. However, as the price approached the 50-day moving average, it started to level out. For two weeks the price hovered just above the 50-day moving average, which provided strong support against a further drop in price.

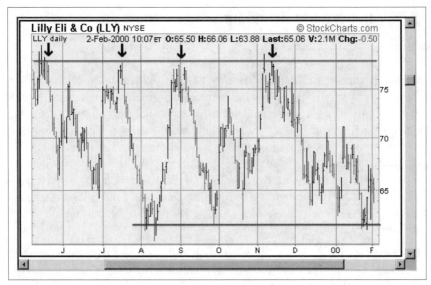

Figure 5-13. Examples of support and resistance in a StockCharts.com Chart School bar chart

However, on March 8 the price dropped below the moving average. As soon as the sell signal triggered and the support level was broken, traders acted on the sell signal and the price continued to drop rather rapidly. Similarly, a moving average represents resistance when the price is below the moving average. The price crossing higher than the moving average is a buy sign, which is a psychological barrier to further increases. However, if that resistance level is breached and the price rises above the buy sign, the price often increases rapidly.

When the price breaks through a level of support or resistance, it often continues its trend. However, as soon as the price breaks through a level of resistance, it becomes difficult for the price to drop back below that level. What is the difficulty in dropping below a particular price called? Support. Therefore, the price that just before was a level of resistance has magically turned into a level of support! If you think about it, a trader isn't much different from a dog that has run through its electric fence. With this image in mind, it's easy to understand why these role reversals are quite common. In addition, prices trading near a level for a long time indicates that the level is a strong one. However, the stronger the level is, the higher the chance of that level reversing roles. That is, if the price breaks through a strong level of resistance, it is more likely that the price will turn into a strong level of support.

The Best Tools for Technical Analysis

Technical analysis tools range from online tools that display charts and indicators to software applications that offer technical screening and trading strategies.

Because technical analysis tools come in a variety of shapes, sizes, and price tags, you should take the time to identify the features you want before you begin shopping. These days you can choose from numerous web sites if you want to create charts, view technical indicators, and screen investments based on technical measures. However, to obtain a robust set of technical indicators or to use or create a trading system that identifies buy and sell signals, you'll want a technical analysis software package. With technical analysis web sites, the data comes with the site. When you purchase a technical analysis software application, you must consider your source and the cost of data. Some applications act as self-contained systems that include the software and data you need to perform your analyses. Other applications use data from third-party data providers, although each application and even versions of the same application might support different data feeds. Here's a shopping guide to help you sort out your choices.

Online Trading Tools

With online tools, you won't spend as much for technical analysis features. Many web sites offer several types of charts and a dozen or more technical indicators at no charge. In most cases, you can obtain end-of-day data or even delayed intraday data at no charge as well. However, if you want real-time data, you'll have to part with some cash. In addition, some of these sites offer educational material to help you learn more about technical analysis as you work:

StockCharts.com (http://www.stockcharts.com)
> StockCharts.com offers excellent charting capabilities in addition to great educational material for technical analysis. For no charge, you can create line, bar, candlestick, and point and figure charts for daily or weekly periods up to six months in the past. Point and figure charts automatically display pattern alerts, which are not only useful for trading, but great if you are learning. In addition, you can choose from several dozen indicators, display up to four indicators per chart, and modify indicator parameters. Predefined technical screens using end-of-day data are also free. For $19.95 a month, you can display up to 100 indicators, create charts using intraday or real-time data, obtain data beyond six months in the past, and create customized technical screens.

BigCharts (http://www.bigcharts.com)

> BigCharts is a free online charting service owned by CBS MarketWatch. With a database of over 50,000 securities, BigCharts provides three levels of charting functionality. Quickcharts are basic charts that require only a ticker symbol and a timeframe. Interactive charts provide features such as intraday and custom timeframes, overlays of popular indicators, and display options for different price data and different types of charts, such as bar charts and candlestick charts. Java charts offer a few more features including trend lines.

ClearStation (http://www.clearstation.com)

> ClearStation is another free online charting service, and is owned by E*Trade. Its interactive charting tool enables you to specify timeframes, indicator overlays, moving averages, and as many as five different stocks or indexes on the same chart for comparison.

Wall Street City (http://www.wallstreetcity.com)

> Wall Street City offers free charting using as many as 12 indicators and data that goes back several decades. For $9.95 a month, you can use Power ProSearch, which is one of the best online technical screening tools.

Standalone Software Applications

Technical analysis programs range from simple charting programs to applications that incorporate trading systems to flag buys and sell signals when the trading rules are triggered. Trading rules might be a value for one indicator or a set of criteria for several indicators in concert, a breakout system or a return to support or resistance levels. In addition, some of these programs enable you to run historical data through trading systems to calculate the performance and return it would have delivered, which is known as backtesting.

MetaStock (http://www.equis.com)

> Equis International offers two versions of its popular MetaStock technical analysis software: End of Day and Professional. Both of these programs are comprehensive yet relatively easy to use. MetaStock Professional provides real-time capabilities, whereas End of Day works with end-of-day data as its name implies. Both programs provide nine styles of charts and offer more than 120 technical indicators in addition to the capability to build custom indicators, which is quite similar to developing formulas in Excel. You can use built-in technical screens or build your own. MetaStock includes 35 trading systems, with more being added with each release of software. You can backtest and optimize trading systems, and create your own systems. MetaStock 9.0 End

of Day is $499. However, you can purchase MetaStock with a subscription to Reuters Data Link Professional Data Package for $599 a year. A monthly subscription is $59. MetaStock Professional 9.0 is $1,695.

> MetaStock offers educational tools, called expert advisors, that explain what a technical indicator on a stock or tradable item is telling you. Expert advisors also plot buy and sell signals on the charts you view. MetaStock Professional includes alerts based on expert advisors that you can receive via your pager, email, or cell phone.

TC2000 (http://www.tc2000.com)

TC2000.com provides easy-to-use charting and technical analysis for free! Well, the software is free. The Worden data feed that nourishes the TC2000 software is $29.75 a month. However, as a data subscriber, you receive CDs with historical data back to 1984. TC2000 includes dozens of indicators, tips on trading from Don and Peter Worden, screening features including both built-in and customizable screens, and even fundamental data to measure your technical analysis signals against.

TradeStation (http://www.tradestation.com)

TradeStation costs $795 a month for the program and data, and it's not compatible with any third-party data. Now that you've regained consciousness, it turns out that there's a way to get the program and data for free. If you're a serious trader, which means you have at least $30,000 and place at least 20 trades a month, you can get TradeStation for free when you open a brokerage account with TradeStation Securities. With TradeStation software and an account with TradeStation Securities, you can place trades directly through TradeStation. In addition, TradeStation includes trading system features, backtesting, access to streaming real-time data, alerts, and, of course, a full complement of nine types of charts and more than 130 indicators.

CHAPTER SIX

Executing Trades
Hacks 54-58

When it's time to buy and sell investments, you can complete your transactions on the Web in most cases. Submitting your orders electronically offers a lot of advantages. You can place trades any time you want, day or night, regardless of whether the markets are open. If you want to check something before completing a transaction, you can stop in the middle without tying up a broker on the telephone. In most cases, orders are executed almost immediately. Even better, you usually pay a lower commission for taking the do-it-yourself route.

Submitting your orders electronically does have some disadvantages, though. Stock trades come in many shapes and forms [Hack #54] and not all brokerage firms offer every type of trade [Hack #89] as an online option. If you invest in bonds [Hack #58], your choices are downright limited. However, all these limitations will continue to disappear as online trading becomes the method of choice and brokerages update their services to keep clients happy.

Because online trades are automated, they present special challenges unseen in interactions with humans. If you've got a fast trigger finger, a few extra mouse clicks could execute duplicate orders in your brokerage account—and you will have to execute additional trades to recover from those duplicates because most brokerages don't provide a mechanism for undoing erroneous orders. When a web site's response is slow, be very careful when placing online trades—wait until your browser has definitely stopped spinning or responds with an error message that says that the request wasn't completed. Conversely, there are times when a broker's site jams up, particularly when market volume skyrockets, and trades don't get through no matter how patient you are. The best solution for this is prevention. Before you create an account with an online broker [Hack #88], find out how dependable its web site is under heavy load and what your options are if its web site is down. Queuing up trades when the markets are closed can generate other surprises, such as opening prices significantly different from the previous day's close.

If you're not sure whether your buy or sell request actually went through, review your open and completed orders before hitting that buy/sell button again.

Online trading has spawned unheard-of features and services in old-style investment circles. For a start, low-cost broker commissions are orders of magnitude less than full-service broker fees. With commissions like these, the benefits of diversification and dollar-cost averaging are available to investors with the most modest of portfolios. Some web sites have even initiated build-your-own mutual funds.

HACK #54 Pick the Right Type of Trade

Brokerage firms offer different types of trades or orders that you can use to limit the risk of buying and owning stocks.

Sometimes it seems as if everything about investing has to be as complex as possible. The act of buying and selling shares has its own set of rules and terms. You don't have to be an expert in every type of trade available, but you can increase your success and avoid nasty surprises by taking advantage of specialized trade types.

Let's start with the basics. If you want to buy or sell a stock, but don't care about how much you'll pay or receive for the shares, use a *market order*, which means that your brokerage firm fills your order as soon as possible at the best available price at that time. The advantage of market orders is that you're practically guaranteed that your order will be filled, usually within seconds. Market orders go to the front of the line in the marketplace, taking precedence over any other type of trade placed at the same time.

In general, the longer you intend to own a stock, the more appropriate it is to use a market order to buy it. A long-term investor who intends to hold a stock for five or ten years doesn't need to worry about getting the absolute best price on every trade. The difference of a few pennies or even dollars today isn't likely to make any appreciable difference in total return in five years.

The disadvantage of market orders is that the best available price might be significantly worse than you expected, particularly in a fast-moving or volatile market. Stock prices can change dramatically in a matter of moments, so your order to buy or sell a stock *at the market* (as the pros say) might execute at a price that's substantially higher or lower than the last price quote you saw before you placed the order.

At most brokerage firms, you won't be able to change or cancel a market order that you place while the market is open. In most cases, the order will be filled before you can click to check the status of the order on your brokerage's web site. When you place a market order after the market closes, your brokerage fills it as soon as the market opens on the next trading day.

> Because trading continues after the market closes for the day, the price of a stock can change significantly before the market opens the next day. However, market orders still buy or sell stocks at the going price when they're filled.

The other popular type of trade is the *limit order*, which is shown in Figure 6-1. When you place a limit order, you set the minimum price that you'll accept when selling shares or the maximum amount that you'll pay to buy shares. The advantage of a limit order is that it protects you from buying too high or selling too low when a stock's price rises or falls rapidly. However, there is a drawback in placing a limit order: there might not be any shareholders in the market willing to accept your terms and, if so, your order remains unfilled. For short-term traders, a few cents' difference can make or break the profits they earn, so limit orders are the standard for short-term trading.

Some online brokerage firms tack a surcharge onto limit orders, which you should take into consideration if you're on the fence about which type of trade to use. The benefits of a limit order might not be worth paying a higher commission for any but the most volatile stocks.

Suppose you don't want to pay more than $25 a share for Intel. In checking the stock's current price, you see that the quote is at a $27 *bid* (the best price at which other investors are willing to buy shares) and $27.25 *ask* (the best price at which other shareholders have offered to sell shares). A limit order at $25 executes only if the price drops to $25 or lower.

Limit orders are useful in several situations, as long as you understand and accept the risks that they entail:

- When a stock's price is volatile, you can use a limit order to make sure you don't pay more than you think a stock is worth.
- To take advantage of daily changes in price or short-term trends, you can specify a limit order to buy below the current price or a limit order to sell above the current price. The order executes if the price reaches the limits you set and you earn a few extra dollars. However, the order could go unfilled if no one meets your limit price. In this situation, the order is filled as soon as your limit price is met. However, there's no guarantee that the price won't continue to rise or fall after you've bought or sold.

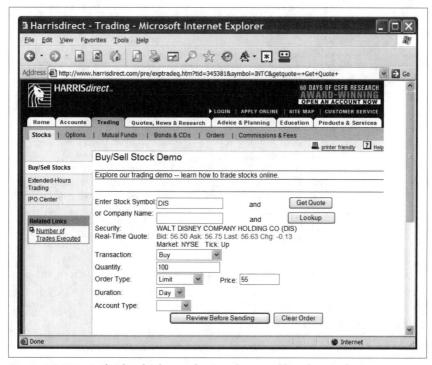

Figure 6-1. A typical online brokerage firm's order screen for a limit order

- To handle sudden unexpected changes in price, you can use limit orders to buy a stock when it drops suddenly in price or to sell on an unexpected spike. However, it's risky to buy or sell a stock automatically in response to a sudden price change without investigating the reason for the change. The price might have dropped because of business-breaking news, or the price might have increased because of new, long-term opportunities.

Some investors maintain sell limit orders on all of their stocks to sell shares automatically if the price falls or rises to a certain level. This can be counterproductive if limit prices are set too close to the current price. Stock prices are typically quite volatile—it's not uncommon for a stock to rise or fall 10 or 20 percent for no apparent rational reason and then quickly bounce back. If you sell shares because of a limit order, you have nothing to show for the effort except a tax liability and extra commissions that you must pay to your broker. If you plan to use limit orders in this way, first check historical price charts to see how much a stock's price varies over a day, week, or month. Then, set your limit outside the stock's typical fluctuation range. For example, if a $30 stock often drops to $25, set a sell limit below $25.

Setting your limit outside the stock's typical fluctuation range is definitely not a set-and-forget technique. As a stock's price steadily increases, you should increase the sell limit price to match. This keeps the percentage that you might lose from increasing.

Brokerages might also offer you the choice to *sell short* or *buy to cover*. These trade types are related to *short selling*, the brave attempt to make a profit from a belief that a stock is going to drop in price. When you sell short, you borrow the shares from your brokerage and immediately sell them. To succeed, you must be able to buy back the shares (buy to cover) at a lower price in the future and return the borrowed shares to your brokerage. Aside from those professional psychics who can accurately predict the future price of stocks, short selling is extremely risky. There are a lot of special rules about short selling, and not all stocks are available for shorting.

If you want even more control over the prices of your trades, you might consider using *stop* or *stop-limit orders*, if your brokerage offers them. By setting sell stop orders, you can protect your profits or prevent further losses by selling before a stock price drops further.

When you place a stop order (sometimes known as a *stop-loss order*), you designate a *stop price*. Your order executes at the market price only when the stock hits your stop price (to be technically accurate, when a round lot of 100 shares trades at or better than your stop price). Because a stop order turns into a market order after the stop price is triggered, there's no guarantee that your order will be filled at a price that's better than the stop price—but it will be filled. If your order for Intel is filled at $25, you might place a stop-loss order to sell shares if the price falls to $20 to protect you from a rapid drop in the stock's price, helping you to bail out before your losses grow too large. If Intel's stock falls to $21, nothing happens. But if the company announces bad news after the close of the market on Friday, and then opens at $17 on Monday, your stop-loss order is triggered and your shares are sold—at much less than $20.

To avoid executing a stop order when the price has fallen beyond your stop price, you can employ a stop-limit order, which is like a stop order but becomes a limit order either at the stop price or at a separately designated stop-limit price. This added level of control on the prices you pay means that your stop-limit order might not be filled even if the stop price is reached. Suppose you use a stop-limit order on your Intel shares, with a stop at $20 and a limit price of $19. When the shares open at $17, the stop is triggered, but unless (or until) the price rises to $19, your shares aren't sold.

There's a bit more nomenclature that you're likely find on your brokerage firm's order screen. For instance, your firm might include a checkbox specifying *all or none* (AON). Sometimes, a brokerage can't find buyers or sellers for all of the shares in a trade. By checking the AON box on the order, you instruct your brokerage to forget the order if it can't fill it all at once. You can use this option to make sure that you execute only one trade when you buy or sell a large number of shares or shares in thinly traded stocks. Otherwise, you might end up holding a small number of shares after your order has been partially filled. The AON option also prevents your brokerage from placing multiple trades to fill your complete order, which would result in the payment of multiple commissions.

With limit orders, your brokerage might give you an option to specify how long it should try to fill the order. The two timeframes most frequently used are *day orders* and orders that are *good 'til cancelled* (GTC). A day order is cancelled if it can't be filled before the next market close. Use a day order if your interest in a stock is driven by short-term events or analysis. For instance, if a stock announces bad news after the close of the market, you might place a day order to buy the stock in the next trading day only if it drops to what you reckon to be a bargain-basement price. In theory, GTC orders remain open until they are filled or cancelled by the customer. In practice, many firms automatically terminate GTC orders after 30 or 90 days, so check with your brokerage firm.

GTC orders work well if you have an acceptable price at which you're willing to sell the shares that you own. Place a limit order to sell at that price, and the rest is automatic. If the stock doesn't reach your sell price before the order expires, simply place another order.

Because GTC orders can remain in place for such a long period, make sure that you cancel them when you're no longer interested in making that transaction. If a stock's price changes and triggers your limit order, you might find yourself the owner of a stock that you had forgotten about. Worse, if you don't have enough cash in your account to cover the buy, the trade could trigger a margin call on your account or your brokerage could require you to deposit additional funds into your account—for a stock you didn't want to buy in the first place. Online brokerage firms provide an order status screen that lists all active and past trades in your account, making it easy to keep tabs on these orders.

Occasionally, brokerage firms offer a *fill or kill* option on limit orders. If your trade can't be executed immediately at your limit price (either in full or in part, depending on whether you selected AON), then your order is cancelled. Short-term and day traders use fill or kill orders so that pending orders don't stack up in their accounts and possibly execute while the trader's attention is focused elsewhere.

Finally, a brokerage might offer a *do not reduce* (DNR) option on limit orders. This only affects stocks that pay dividends. When a company pays a dividend, its share price is adjusted immediately by the amount of the dividend. If your limit price isn't reduced when dividends are paid, you might end up paying a pre-dividend price for a post-dividend priced stock. However, your limit price is reduced automatically by the amount of the cash dividend unless you check the DNR box when you place an order. DNR applies only to stocks that pay cash dividends (not stock dividends), but it's usually not something you have to worry about.

If you use sell limit prices to protect profit positions in your stocks, you might want to choose DNR when placing those orders. Otherwise, your sell prices are reduced as dividends are paid, leading to unintended sales in your account.

Every brokerage has its own rules about placing trades, so check with your firm for further information on the types of trades that it supports.

—*Douglas Gerlach*

HACK #55 Execute After-Hours Trades

News can affect the stocks in your portfolio, even when the markets are closed. Some brokerage firms offer after-hours trading that enables you to buy and sell stocks, and possibly avert disaster—as long as you understand the risks.

In the U.S., the stock markets and exchanges (New York Stock Exchange, American Stock Exchange, and Nasdaq) are open from 9:30 a.m. to 4:00 p.m. eastern standard time. What happens when a company announces bad news after the close of the market? Must you wait until the market opens the next business day to sell your shares? Not necessarily—if you're willing to venture into *after-hours trading* and accept the risks that this type of trading incurs.

Since the late 1990s, individual investors have had access to tools and networks that enable them to trade stocks in the hours before and after the market is open. These trading systems, known as *Electronic Communications Networks* (ECNs), have long been used by institutional investors to buy and sell stocks amongst themselves without using the services (and costs) of a broker.

Today, most major online brokerages offer extended hours trading through arrangements with one of the two leading ECNs, Archipelago or INET (formed by the merger of Island and Instinet). Ameritrade, E*TRADE, Fidelity, Harrisdirect, Schwab, and TD Waterhouse, to name a few, offer trading both before and after the markets close, although each has different hours of operations, opening as early as 7:30 a.m. and closing as late as 8:00 p.m. eastern standard time.

> You can obtain price quotes for stocks that trade in after-hours markets **[Hack #16]** at many research sites, including Yahoo! Finance (*http://finance.yahoo.com*). After you obtain a price quote, look for the After Hours link above the quote information.

Placing an Extended Hours Trade

To place an after-hours trade, log in to your brokerage firm's web site, surf to the trading section, and look for a link to extended hours trading, which is almost always separate from the order screen for regular trading. For example, at TD Waterhouse, you select the Extended Hours tab on the Trading page to place extended hours trades. Otherwise, you specify your order as you would any other, as shown in Figure 6-2.

At most firms, you'll be restricted only to limit orders (no market or stop orders) and won't have the option to specify GTC or AON. Some firms are beginning to offer market orders, and they might even allow pre-open market orders to carry over into the regular trading session if unfilled before the market opens.

Drawbacks of Extended Hours Trading

Before you jump into after-hours trading, there are some drawbacks to consider carefully. First, after-hours trading is often a jungle. ECNs function by *crossing* trades—matching buyers to sellers—and therefore lack the liquidity controls that help maintain an orderly market during regular hours. On stock exchanges, a *specialist* (either human or computer) is assigned to every stock, acting as a traffic cop to keep the flow of buys and sells moving smoothly. If there is a temporary shortage of buyers or sellers in a stock, its specialist will jump in and trade from its own account, assuring liquidity and a certain amount of price stability throughout the day. On Nasdaq, *market makers* serve a similar role. Without these specialists, a shortage of sellers can dramatically increase the price of a stock, whereas a shortage of buyers can decrease the price.

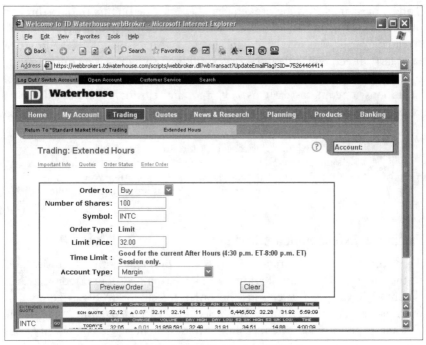

Figure 6-2. TD Waterhouse is one firm that offers extended hours trading

No specialists or market makers serve the same role on ECNs. As a result, the spreads—the difference between a stock's ask and bid—can be quite large. Prices can widely fluctuate from minute to minute. In addition, smaller company stocks often won't have any activity at all. The prices might bear no resemblance whatsoever to the closing price of the stock or to the next day's opening—the stock might fall in price in after-hours markets due to panic selling and then recover when the market opens in the morning.

By picking your stock price carefully for your orders and remaining rational about your stocks, you can take advantage of opportunities in after-hours sessions without getting trounced.

See Also

- *Understanding After Hours Trades* from the Securities and Exchange Commission, *http://www.sec.gov/investor/pubs/afterhours.htm*
- Archipelago ECN, *http://www.archipelago.com*
- INET ECN, *http://www.island.com*

—Douglas Gerlach

Sell Fractional Shares

HACK #56

Selling fractional shares isn't obvious when you place online orders. You must know how different brokerages handle fractional shares so you don't end up paying a big commission to dump a piddling investment.

Many online brokerage firms, such as TD Waterhouse, Charles Schwab, E*TRADE, Harrisdirect, and Muriel Siebert, offer dividend reinvestment services. With these programs, all dividends paid on stocks you own are reinvested automatically into new shares. However, these dividend reinvestments almost always include some fractional shares. You must place your sell orders correctly to make sure that you sell all your shares including the fractional ones.

Generally, brokerages that offer dividend reinvestment plans reinvest dividends with no commissions or fees. Over time, the reinvestment of these dividends can help you add significantly to the stocks that you own and help you keep the dividends you receive invested in stock. Reinvesting even a small amount of dividends instead of spending the money can enhance your returns over time. According to Ibbotson Associates, large company stocks returned an average of 10.2 percent per year from 1925 to 2002, with all dividends reinvested in additional shares along the way. Without that dividend reinvestment, the return averaged just 5.7 percent a year during the same timeframe. By taking advantage of dividend reinvestment services, you obtain the benefits of reinvested dividends without paying commissions to do so.

Some firms, such as TD Waterhouse, enable clients to sign up for automatic dividend reinvestment for all stocks they own or to designate reinvestment for some stocks but not for others. In most cases, if you don't select the option to have dividends reinvested when you first buy shares of the stock, then you must make a special request later by completing a form or speaking with the brokerage's customer service representatives.

When it's time to sell a position, any fractional shares you own might need to be handled differently from whole shares. Fractional shares can't be sold in the open market as whole shares can, so brokerages must liquidate those partial shares themselves on behalf of their customers. Some firms make it easy to sell fractional shares—on the screen showing your stock holding, just clicking a link to trade the stock pre-populates the order screen with the number of whole and fractional shares that you own. Some brokers don't explicitly show the fractional shares; instead, they place a trade to sell the fractional shares when you specify a trade that sells all your whole shares.

At other firms, selling is a bit more complicated. E*TRADE, for example, requires you to submit a separate request to liquidate fractional shares within five days of selling the rest of the stock. If you submit this request, the firm will give you the original price for the whole shares sold.

> In most cases, the trade for your fractional shares is separate from the sale of your whole shares, so you might see two separate trades before all your shares are sold. In addition, some brokers wait until they have enough fractional shares to sell whole shares, so your fractional shares might remain in your account for several days.

—Douglas Gerlach

HACK #57   Build Your Own Mutual Funds

A few online brokerage services help you build a diversified portfolio of stocks that serves as a personalized mutual fund to reach your financial goals.

Building a diversified portfolio from scratch can take time and money. Academic research suggests that a properly diversified portfolio should include 15 to 20 stocks of varying sizes from disparate industries. Even if you have $10,000 to start with, that equates to less than $500 in each of those 20 stocks. Particularly with full-cost brokers, you could spend 10 percent or more just on broker's commissions, which almost guarantees that you won't keep up with the market. If you're set on investing in individual stocks but want to diversify without the expense, you can take advantage of folio services offered by some online brokerages.

Brokerages that offer folio investing enable you to buy and sell stocks for an annual or monthly subscription fee or at a comparatively low cost per trade. Fees range from $4 or less per individual stock trade to $200 a year for up to 2,400 trades. Investigate each company's pricing schedules to see which one offers the best deal for the number of trades you typically make. These brokers often change their pricing to keep up with their competition, so it might be better to go with the service you like the most—its price could drop before you know it. The following brokerages offer folilo investing:

> FolioFN.com (*http://www.foliofn.com*)
> Fidelity Brokerage (*http://www.fidelity.com*)
> ShareBuilder.com (*http://www.sharebuilder.com*)
> BuyandHold.com (*http://www.buyandhold.com*)
> MyStockFund.com (*http://www.mystockfund.com*)

You can group stocks as you please. You might create different baskets for your investment goals, such as a college fund or a new home, or for different industries, such as biotechnology or utilities. With these services, you can create portfolios of as many as 50 different stocks and allocate the amount you invest in each one either by dollar amount or percentage of your total contribution. Every time you deposit new money into the account, you automatically buy every stock in the folio in your pre-designated amounts. If you sign up for a regular monthly transfer from your bank account, your funds will be invested with no additional effort on your part. Even deep discount brokers can't compete with this approach. If you buy shares in 15 stocks at $7 a trade, you spend $105 in commissions. You would have to invest $10,000 at a time to make the commissions a reasonable percentage of your investment.

Some firms offer pre-selected folios of stocks in a particular industry or other category. At FolioFN.com, you can start with a prepared basket, and then edit it to remove or add stocks. For example, if you already own a large position in a stock included in one of FolioFN's folios, you can remove it from that basket.

Another advantage of the firms that offer folio investing is their focus on *dollar-based investing*. By letting you purchase fractional shares of stock instead of whole shares, they put all of your dollars to work right away.

Typically, these low-cost brokerage services operate by buying shares only during preset trading windows during the day, grouping all customer orders into batches that are executed all at once. As such, you can't control the limit prices on trades from your account, so this approach is more suitable for long-term investing. If you're looking to invest in a particularly volatile stock and don't want to risk the price changing dramatically from the time you place your order, these services also offer real-time trades at a higher cost, usually around $15 per transaction.

FolioFN.com and Fidelity also have the capability to rebalance your portfolio automatically when needed. You can either sell shares either to generate the least or the most capital gains, or sell shares of both winners and losers to create a neutral tax liability. This can come in handy at year-end tax planning time.

—Douglas Gerlach

Buy Bonds Online

#58   Online trading for bonds isn't in the same league as online stock trading, but a few brokerage firms offer true electronic bond trading.

When a corporation or government borrows money, it issues bonds [Hack #80], which are nothing more than promissory notes. The organization that issues bonds pays interest to the people who loan them money—the investors who purchase the bonds. After a period of time, the organization pays the money it borrowed back to the bondholders. Many investors purchase bonds to receive a steady stream of income. However, bonds can also provide capital gains when interest rates fall. Sad to say, online bond trading hasn't kept pace with its electronic stock trading counterpart. Many online brokers act as if they offer online bond trading, but the service might be no more than a glorified messenger service, in which the online trade forwards the order information to a human broker who fills the order the old-fashioned way. Other brokers provide online research but resort to phone calls for orders. However, a few brokers are starting to offer automated bond trading for individual investors. The services are fairly limited and fees can be high, so review your options carefully before you become an online bond trading pioneer.

Although many brokerage companies are beefing up their electronic bond trading systems, the beneficiaries of these enhancements are often professional traders. However, plans are in the works to build electronic trading networks similar to those available for stocks that enable the automatic cross-matching and execution of anonymous buy and sell orders. These systems that cater to professional investors are becoming the infrastructure for electronic bond trading services aimed at individuals. For example, E*TRADE (*http://www.etrade.com*) now offers an online bond trading center for individuals based on software and bond data provided by BondDesk.com (*http://www.bonddesk.com*).

In the world of electronic bond trading, the steps are similar to those for stocks. Specify the following items:

- Whether you want to buy or sell a bond.
- The bond CUSIP, which is its unique identifier. You can search for bonds using E*TRADE Bond Finder feature.
- The number of bonds you want to trade.
- The price or yield at which you want to place the order. You can also place a market order to accept the going price or yield.

You can preview the order before you submit it or review your open orders. You receive an electronic alert when the order executes.

Keep an Eye on Online Bond Trading Fees

Commissions and fees for buying bonds that have already been issued can be so high that they remove any potential for your investment. In many cases, you're better off buying new bond issues. Although investors can purchase one bond at a time online, the fees for small trades can be so exorbitant and the yields so pitiful that they just aren't worth it. Most brokerages embed their commissions in the price of bonds. Because there's no easy way to find out what a broker paid for a bond, you can't determine the markup that the broker is charging. In addition, many brokerages vary their commissions based on the size of your order but don't advertise that fact. The only way to reveal whether a brokerage varies its commission is to enter a few prototype bond trades using the same bonds (without executing them, of course) to see how the price changes. However, $50 is a typical minimum markup—whether you buy one bond or several.

> To make matters worse, some online brokers add service fees to small purchases. For example, E*TRADE charges a $40 fee when you buy fewer than 20 Treasury bonds, or fewer than 10 municipal, corporate, or agency bonds.

In addition to costly and hidden fees, different brokerages offer different bonds, so it's almost impossible to comparison shop. The best way to get a reasonable deal is to buy new-issue bonds. The TreasuryDirect online program (*http://www.treasurydirect.gov*) sells new-issue government bonds with no commissions, and you can sign up to receive emails alerting you to upcoming auctions.

See Also

For research, tools, and other information that can help you purchase the bonds you want, try some of the following web sites:

- BondsOnline (*http://www.bondsonline.com*) offers educational materials, news, research, ratings, bond price quotes for 12,000 bonds, and a bond search tool [Hack #2].
- Investing in Bonds.com (*http://www.investinginbonds.com*) is run by the Bond Market Association and provides educational material, bond prices for 1,000 bonds, and a bond search tool [Hack #2].
- The Bureau of the Public Debt Online web site (*http://www.publicdebt.treas.gov*) is run by a unit of the Treasury Department and provides information about Treasury securities and U.S. Savings Bonds. It also hosts the Treasury Direct program described in this hack.

CHAPTER SEVEN

Investing in Mutual Funds
Hacks 59-72

The first U.S. mutual fund, a common stock fund, was founded in 1924. 1940 saw mutual fund assets reach $500 million and the enactment of the Investment Company Act, which defined the framework for the regulation of the mutual fund industry. It took another 45 years for mutual fund assets to reach $500 billion. However, both the proliferation of 401(k) retirement programs and the increasingly diverse selection of financial assets available through mutual funds helped the mutual fund industry come of age in the 1990s. By mid-2003, after almost four years of poor market performance, mutual fund assets stood at almost $7 trillion.

Some investors put their investment dollars in mutual funds because that's what their 401(k) retirement plans offer. But many more investors have invested willingly in mutual funds to obtain diversification and professional management—more easily and at lower cost than investing in individual stocks and bonds. In addition, as the pace of life has increased, plenty of people have grown fond of mutual funds as the no-muss, no-fuss investment. With professional management, many investors think that mutual funds provide good investment returns without any effort on the part of the mutual fund shareholders.

Perhaps things got a bit out of hand in the 1990s. A long bull market and steadily decreasing interest rates made just about every investment—stocks, bonds, mutual funds, real estate—look good. Potential investors looked no further than recent sky-high returns and rushed to buy shares, fund prospectus unread, salivating at the prospect of more market-beating returns. In fact, many gladly paid several percentage points worth of expenses and fees, thinking that years of extraordinary investment returns were worth the cost. Of course, the inevitable and long-overdue bear market hit, and the highest flyers (mutual funds and stocks alike) hit the ground the hardest. Mutual fund shareholders started to question the sanity of paying two percent or more in expenses to mutual funds that lost more money every year.

A few years later, just as the market was dragging itself out of its bear cave, the mutual fund scandal broke. As it turns out, some of those professional managers weren't acting so professionally. Mutual funds have a fiduciary responsibility to protect the financial interests of their shareholders. However, some mutual fund managers and executives were allowing and even participating in activities that made them money at the expense of their shareholders.

All this excitement has some investors questioning whether they should trust mutual funds with their money. With other scandals, including Enron and WorldCom, you might wonder if there's any investment you can trust. In the end, all this excitement could be the kick everyone needed to get their mutual fund and overall investment act in gear. Maybe now, investors will diligently research mutual funds (not to mention individual stocks and bonds) to make the best investment with their money. Perhaps the mutual fund scandal has made the SEC see that additional regulations are needed, and has also helped fund shareholders appreciate tried and true mutual funds that understand the meaning of fiduciary responsibility.

Mutual Funds Are Here to Stay

Excitement aside, mutual funds are more blessing than burden to investors. A mutual fund pools money from investors to purchase stocks, bonds, or other types of investments. Each share in a mutual fund represents a piece of ownership in every investment the fund holds as well as the income that those investments generate. By offering diversification with even the smallest share purchase, mutual funds help investors reduce their risk by allocating their investment dollars among multiple sectors and industries, companies of different sizes, and different types of investments. When fund management is truly professional, mutual funds offer the benefits of investing to people who don't yet know how to pick good stocks and bonds, or to those who know how but don't have the time.

 As a mutual fund shareholder, you give up some control—it's difficult to find out the investments that make up a fund's portfolio at any given time. You can't choose the securities that a fund manager buys or sells, or when those trades take place.

Mutual funds charge shareholders fees and expenses for performing their investment activities. That's not necessarily a disadvantage—fund management does work for you and you pay them to do it. However, you'll learn in this chapter that some funds are overly enthusiastic about assigning expenses to shareholders. Regardless how reasonable or outlandish, fees and expenses reduce the returns that shareholders receive. In addition, taxes are an issue for mutual fund shares held in taxable accounts. Funds that buy and sell create gains on which you must pay tax, which further reduces returns.

It's Your Money

Doing your homework before buying is the key to successful investing with mutual funds. Mutual funds don't require as much research as individual stocks before you purchase or while managing your portfolio, but they do require some. First, you should choose mutual funds whose philosophy and performance match your goals and risk tolerance, so start by researching a fund's philosophy, potential performance, and risks. Second, make sure that a fund is dependable and trustworthy to act as your fiduciary. You wouldn't hand your investment dollars over to a stranger who walked up to you and proclaimed he was the best financial manager in the world—at least not without a serious background check.

Put any mutual fund you're considering under the microscope before you buy. In particular, read the fund prospectus before you buy. Were you listening just now? *Read the fund prospectus before you buy.* Mutual funds must give you a prospectus when you buy shares, but by then it's too late. With most mutual funds providing links to download their prospectuses online, you have no excuse. The SEC requires that mutual funds include specific information in their prospectuses and use a standard format to present key data so that you can compare funds more easily. Although prospectuses aren't the lightest reading in the world, they include just about everything you need to know about a fund:

- Its investment goals
- Its strategies for achieving its goals
- The risks associated with investing in the fund
- The fees and expenses it charges
- Its past performance
- Its managers and advisers
- How to purchase and redeem shares

Index Funds, Anyone?

So you want instant diversification, basic asset allocation, low costs, less chance of management shenanigans, and you're content to achieve the long-term average returns in the stock market? You can have all this by purchasing shares in index mutual funds. These funds don't try to beat the market—they try to match it or at least a part of it by buying all the companies represented in an index. For example, if you want to split your money 50/50 between large and small companies, you can put half your cash in an S&P 500 Composite Stock Price Index Fund for the large-cap stocks and the other half in a fund that follows the Russell 2000 index for small-cap stocks.

Index funds typically charge very low expenses, because the funds don't have to research or trade very much. The fund manager follows only the securities (stocks or bonds) that comprise the index and trades only when the composition of the index changes, or to fulfill purchases or sales of fund shares.

Index funds are as close to *what you see is what you get* as you can reach in the financial world. Index funds are easier to research, but they still aren't automatic investments. Because index funds must primarily purchase the securities in an index, you can identify an index fund's objectives and strategies by the index it follows. The fund risks are the same ones you encounter investing directly in the securities in the index. However, some index funds take extra steps to keep their returns above the index, so you still should read the prospectus to see if there are any extra strategic twists that you don't like.

Why Don't My Funds Perform #59 as Well as Others?

Learn how mutual fund expenses cut into the money you make on your fund investments.

It can be downright disheartening. You check annual returns for some of your mutual funds, and notice that they never seem to perform as well as other funds or their corresponding stock market indexes. Even worse, a fund might trail most of the other funds in the same category. Some funds are simply dogs, but, in a lot of cases, below-par returns result from excessive fund expenses. You can improve your results by understanding how mutual fund expenses drag down returns, and trading in your high-cost funds for similar funds with lower expenses and correspondingly better results—see and "The Best Mutual Fund Screens for Free" [Hack #66] and "The Best Mutual Fund Screens for a Fee" [Hack #67].

It costs money to run a mutual fund, so don't be surprised that you, as a fund shareholder, pay a portion of those costs every year. Fund expenses directly impact your investment returns because they're deducted from your investment in a fund. They literally take money right out of your pocket. To make matters worse, you pay even more if you use a financial advisor or broker to purchase fund shares. Expenses are easy to forget because funds show them as a percentage of your investment. You rarely see the actual dollar costs you pay every year for the privilege of investing in a mutual fund.

The commissions that funds pay to brokers for trades [Hack #61] take a further bite out of results—one to two percent a year. Unfortunately, fund companies don't deduct brokerage commissions when they calculate the fund performance figures that they publish, even though they deduct them from your fund assets. The net of that—the returns you receive from your fund investment—will be even lower than the published performance figures.

The Good, the Bad, and the Ugly: How Expenses Impact Returns

Most fund expenses are subtracted from fund returns, so high expenses hurt returns. The returns for funds with similar portfolios and investment philosophy can vary significantly simply due to a difference in expenses. To get an idea of how much fund expenses impact performance, compare a mutual fund's performance to the performance of its peer group or to a corresponding benchmark index. For example, every fund in Table 7-1 achieves the same nine percent return as the index, but expenses gnaw away at the returns you receive.

Table 7-1. Mutual fund expenses reduce investment returns

Fund	Expense ratio	Front-end load	Effective annual return	Value after ten years for $10,000 investment	Ten-year expense costs
Index	0%	0%	9.00%	$23,673.64	None
Fund A	.5%	0%	8.46%	$22,516.23	$806.79
Fund B	.5%	5.75%	7.81%	$21,221.55	$1,335.40
Fund C	1.0%	0%	7.91%	$21,410.01	$1,572.31

A one percent increase in fund expenses doesn't guarantee a better-performing fund, nor does it reduce your investment risk, but it does cost you over $1,500 dollars over ten years. On the other hand, Fund B with the hefty front-end load in Table 7-1 surrenders .65 percent of annual return because of the money paid up front in commission. Some extraordinary fund managers produce such strong results that they overcome the drag of the higher fees they charge for their expertise. Managers with higher expenses have to perform better just to stay even with their low-cost cousins. The problem is that very few managers do that over long periods of time.

Expense ratios range from as low as 0.18 percent of invested assets to as high as 3 percent, depending on the type of fund, the frugality of the fund family, and individual fund characteristics. Use the following guidelines to quickly gauge a fund's expense ratio:

- Domestic stock and bond funds generally carry lower expense ratios than foreign stock and bond funds, because it's cheaper to research and buy U.S. stock and bonds.
- Look for large-cap stock and bond funds with expense ratios at or below 1 percent.
- Look for small-cap, mid-cap, and foreign funds with expense ratios at or below 1.5 percent.

Mutual funds pass operating costs, such as administrative expenses, fund management expenses, marketing and distribution fees, and brokerage commissions, to their shareholders. However, only the administrative expenses, management costs and marketing, and distribution fees are incorporated into a fund's published expense ratio. Marketing fees are identified separately and the costs of brokerage commissions are typically hard to find [Hack #61]. You can't avoid paying operating costs, but you can look for funds with the lowest percentages:

Administrative costs
> Include back-office expenses, such as customer service, bookkeeping, audit of fund accounts, and the processing of fund share purchase and redemption orders.

Fund portfolio management costs
> Cover the salaries of fund managers and analysts, the research and services they need, and the costs of running a trading desk (minus the brokerage commissions).

Marketing and distribution expenses
> These expenses are incurred by all funds, but not all funds charge a separate fee (known as the 12b-1 fee) to cover them. If the 12b-1 fee is more than 0.25 percent, funds have to publish it separately from the expense ratio. Do you really want to pay a fund company to find new investors so that it can earn more fees?

Brokerage commissions
> The actual costs that a fund company pays a brokerage firm to buy and sell securities. These costs will reduce your return below the published fund return.

Sales charges or loads are the fees that investors pay when they purchase fund shares through a broker or financial planner. Loads are the price of obtaining so-called financial advice, which is a far more expensive education than reading this book. These charges cut into your investment above and beyond regular fund expenses, so they increase the pain. Make sure they're worth it! There are three types of sales loads:

Front-end load

Also known as Class A shares. Investors pay a cut out of their initial investment, reducing the amount of money they have to invest. Brokers and advisers receive that percentage as a sales commission. If you're going to invest for the long term and really want to buy shares in a load fund, studies show that paying a front-end load is the least expensive of all of the sales charges.

Back-end loads

Also known as Class B shares. You pay a deferred load when you sell fund shares. The actual percentage you pay depends on how long you own fund shares, because back-end loads usually follow a sliding scale that zeros out at some point, usually between five and seven years. After the load zeros out, these funds usually convert to Class A shares, which carry a lower expense ratio.

Level loads

Also known as Class C shares. You pay no front-end or back-end load, but pay an ongoing 12b-1 fee that can be as high as one percent a year to pay the broker's or advisor's ongoing commission. For long-term investors, level loads hurt the most because they recur as long as you own fund shares.

If you've found a load fund with a terrific track record, you might decide to bite the bullet and pay the load. Just remember, you're paying for past performance, which is no guarantee of future results. If a fund falters after you pay a front-end load, there's nothing you can do about it. However, you don't have to tolerate high annual fund expenses for a fund that doesn't do better than its competition. Sell it and buy shares in a good low-cost fund that invests in the same types of investments.

When you type a mutual fund ticker symbol into the Quote box at *http://www.morningstar.com*, you can see the basic expense information for the fund in the Key Stats section, as in Figure 7-1. If the value for Expense Ratio % seems reasonable and you see the word None under Front Load % and Deferred Load %, chances are the fund is frugal about spending your hard-earned money for its expenses. The Vanguard Group is known for low expenses, such as the 0.18 percent expense ratio for their Vanguard 500 Index Fund, shown in Figure 7-1. Over 10 years, you pay about $230 in expenses for this fund to match the return of the S&P 500 index.

Because fees and expenses cut directly into the mutual fund returns that you receive, it's a good idea to thoroughly research a fund's fees and expenses before you buy. The Morningstar Snapshot page is good, but it doesn't tell the whole story. For example, the Avatar Advantage Equity Allocation fund

Figure 7-1. The Snapshot page at Morningstar.com is your first step to finding expense information

is a Large Blend stock fund similar in style to the Vanguard 500 Index Fund. Its 1.52 percent expense ratio and 4.5 percent front load appear pricey on the Snapshot page. However, if you click the Fees & Expenses tab, you can see that the fund also charges a redemption fee of 1 percent and 12b-1 fees of 0.25 percent, shown in Figure 7-2. This fund charges you approximately $2,161 per $10,000 invested over 10 years to underperform the S&P 500 index by several percentage points per year.

See Also

- For a thorough education in the benefits of low-cost mutual funds, read *Bogle on Mutual Funds* by John Bogle (Dell).

—Amy Crane and Bonnie Biafore

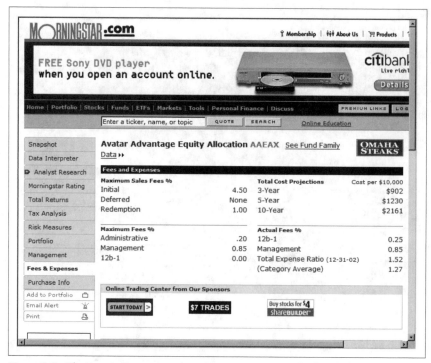

Figure 7-2. *The Fees & Expenses page at Morningstar.com tells the whole expense and sales load story*

Calculate the Damage
#60 of Mutual Fund Expenses

HACK

Calculate the hard cash you pay to own a fund to determine whether its expenses are worth the price.

Mutual funds with high expenses can put a serious hurt on your investment returns [Hack #59]. But how do you determine just how bad the damage is? Some web sites include estimated annual fees and compare a fund's costs to the average for the fund category, but that's just the beginning. The bottom line is how much more money would you have, if you didn't have to pay those darned fees? If you're trying to decide between several funds with similar investment philosophies, comparing your ending balance after several years, taking into account fund return and expenses, can help. You can use built-in Excel functions to calculate the potential cost of ownership and your bottom line return.

To calculate the true cost of mutual fund expenses, you need only a few items of data, shown in highlighted cells at the top of the spreadsheet in

Figure 7-3. You must enter the value of your initial investment and the number of years you expect to own the fund. Whether you're trying to decide which fund to buy or looking to replace a fund you already own, enter the number of dollars that you're ready to invest as the initial investment (cell B2 in the example) to obtain the most accurate picture of costs and their effect. If your mutual funds are for retirement, you might hold them for decades. If you invest in funds to pay for your kids' college education, your timeframe might be five to ten years.

The expected annualized return in cell B4 is how much you expect the fund value to increase on average for each year that you own the fund. A higher annual return makes your investment grow, which in turn increases your fund costs. What number should you use? It depends on how conservative you are. Because very few funds beat the market over the long term, you can use a long-term average return for a comparable index, such as the ten-year return for the Russell Mid-cap index for a fund that invests in mid-cap stocks. However, if you think a fund will beat the market, because it has for a long time or you just have an inkling, you can use the fund's long-term annual return, such as the ten-year return or, even better, its annualized return since its inception, which is from the first day the fund existed. The best place to find these numbers is at the fund web site, which typically includes annual returns for the fund for one year, three years, five years, ten years, and since inception, if that's longer than ten years. Web sites often show returns for comparable indexes or fund categories for similar time periods.

You can type in the values for the four types of mutual fund expenses in cells B7 through B10 or capture fund expenses automatically [Hack #14]. The expenses fall into three categories: annual expenses, up-front expenses, and expenses you pay when you sell. If a fund charges a fee with a name you don't recognize, find out when you pay the fee. If it's an annual expense, add it to the expense ratio. If you pay it up front or when you sell, add it to the front-end sales load number or the deferred sales load percentage, respectively.

Calculating Mutual Fund Costs and Return

Now, let's see how these expenses affect investment return by walking through the calculations for Intermediate Values and Results in the spreadsheet in Figure 7-3.

Front-end sales loads are painful because they take money out of your investment before you even buy any shares. At least they're easy to calculate, as shown in Examples 7-1 and 7-2.

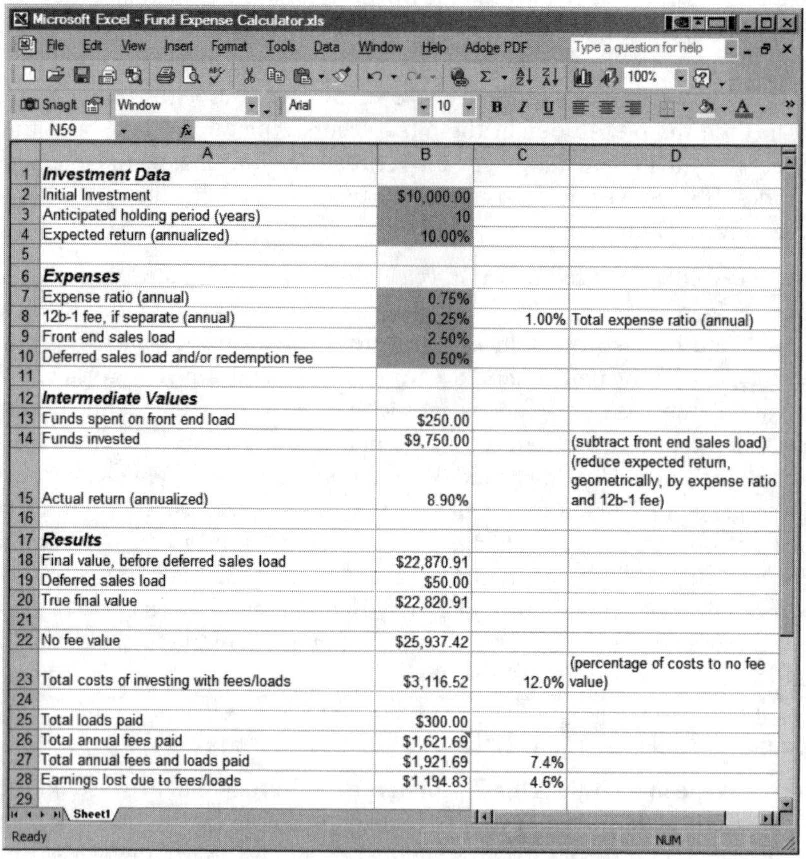

	A	B	C	D
1	***Investment Data***			
2	Initial Investment	$10,000.00		
3	Anticipated holding period (years)	10		
4	Expected return (annualized)	10.00%		
5				
6	***Expenses***			
7	Expense ratio (annual)	0.75%		
8	12b-1 fee, if separate (annual)	0.25%	1.00%	Total expense ratio (annual)
9	Front end sales load	2.50%		
10	Deferred sales load and/or redemption fee	0.50%		
11				
12	***Intermediate Values***			
13	Funds spent on front end load	$250.00		
14	Funds invested	$9,750.00		(subtract front end sales load)
15	Actual return (annualized)	8.90%		(reduce expected return, geometrically, by expense ratio and 12b-1 fee)
16				
17	***Results***			
18	Final value, before deferred sales load	$22,870.91		
19	Deferred sales load	$50.00		
20	True final value	$22,820.91		
21				
22	No fee value	$25,937.42		
23	Total costs of investing with fees/loads	$3,116.52	12.0%	(percentage of costs to no fee value)
24				
25	Total loads paid	$300.00		
26	Total annual fees paid	$1,621.69		
27	Total annual fees and loads paid	$1,921.69	7.4%	
28	Earnings lost due to fees/loads	$1,194.83	4.6%	
29				

Figure 7-3. Build a spreadsheet that calculates mutual fund expenses and shows their effect on your investment

Example 7-1. Formula for funds spent on front-end load

```
Funds Spent On Front End Load (B13) = Initial Investment (B2)* Front End
Sales Load (B9)
```

Example 7-2. Formula for funds invested

```
Funds Invested (B14) = Initial Investment (B2) - Funds Spent On Front End
Load (B13)
```

The actual return (annualized) in cell B15 is the return that you receive after subtracting the annual expenses you pay. It's not as simple as subtracting the total expense ratio from the expected annualized return, and here's why: at the end of the first year, your investment increases by the expected annualized return (1 + expected return) but is then reduced by the expense ratio

(1 – total expense ratio). Example 7-3 shows the formula for your investment value at the end of the year.

Example 7-3. Formula for investment value at end of year

```
InvestEnd = InvestBegin * (1 + Expected Return) * (1 - Total Expense Ratio)
```

The actual return is the percentage increase over your investment at the beginning of the year, as shown in Example 7-4.

Example 7-4. Formula for actual return achieved

```
Actual Return (decimal) = (InvestEnd / InvestBegin) - 1
```

By substituting the formula in Example 7-3 into the actual return equation in Example 7-4 and dusting off your algebra skills, you will end up with the formula for actual return in Example 7-5.

Example 7-5. Actual return calculated from the expected return and total expense ratio

```
Actual Return (B15) = (1 + Expected Return (B4)) * (1 - Total Expense Ratio
(C8)) - 1
Actual Return = (1 + .1) * (1 - .01) - 1 = .089 or 8.9%
```

To calculate your investment value at the end of the holding period but before you pay any deferred fees or loads, multiply your funds invested by (1 + actual return) for every year you own the fund, which is the equivalent of the Excel formula in Example 7-6.

Example 7-6. Formula for final investment value before paying deferred sales loads

```
Final Value Before (B18) = Funds Invested (B14) * POWER((1 + Actual Return
(B15)),Holding Period (B3))
```

> In Excel, the ^ operator performs the same calculation as the POWER function, but uses the format (1 + Actual Return)^Holding Period.

You must subtract any deferred sales load or redemption fees to obtain the true final value of your investment. The deferred sales load depends on whether your fund increased or decreased in value. If the fund increased, you pay the deferred sales load percentage on your initial investment. If the fund decreased, the deferred sales load is based on the final investment value. You can use the Excel MIN function to multiply the deferred sales load percentage by the smaller of the two numbers, as shown in Example 7-7.

Example 7-7. Formula for true final value of investment

```
Deferred Sales Load (B19) = Deferred Sales Load (B10)
    * MIN(Initial Investment,Final Value Before Deferred Sales Load)

True Final Value (B20) = Final Value Before Deferred Sales Load (B18)
    - Deferred Sales Load (B19)
```

Finally, to determine the true cost of mutual fund fees, compare the true final value you receive from a fund to the money you would have if you invested your entire initial investment and achieved the expected annual return. You calculate the investment value with no fees subtracted (cell B22) like the final value before subtracting the deferred sales load in Example 7-7, except that you use the expected return instead of the actual return, as shown in Examples 7-8 and 7-9.

Example 7-8. Formula for investment without paying any fees

```
No Fee Value (B22) = Initial Investment (B2) * POWER((1 + Expected Return
    (B4)),Holding Period (B3))
```

Example 7-9. Formula for total costs for investing in a fund

```
Total Costs (B23) = No Fee Value (B22) - True Final Value (B20)
```

> If you check the example in Figure 7-3, you'll notice that a 2.5 percent front-end load, a 0.5 percent deferred load, and an annual expense ratio of 1 percent leads to total mutual fund costs equal to 12 percent of the investment value you would receive if you paid no fees.

You can also calculate the loads and fees you must pay. The loads paid are straightforward because they occur only once—you add up the front-end load and deferred sales loads. The annual fees are a little different, because the fund company applies the expense ratio percentage to the value of your investment at the end of every year.

You must consider the increase in value from a mutual fund's return before you deduct the expenses, so the formulas for calculating your annual and total fees are shown in Examples 7-10 and 7-11. To simplify the calculations, this example assumes that the fund increases by the same amount each year.

Using a Geometric Series to Calculate Regular Deductions or Contributions

Although the investment value changes each year, you calculate expenses by multiplying the balance by the total expense ratio. Each year, you multiply the previous balance by the total expense ratio (er), which means that you can apply a geometric series to the problem. A geometric series calculates the results of adding up powers of numbers, such as:

```
Geometric Series = 1 + z + z² + z³ + ... + zⁿ
```

However, you can transform this calculator nightmare into a formula, which might not be any easier to read but is easier to calculate when you make Excel do it for you.

Suppose you want to calculate a geometric series for n years, starting with an investment P, using an annual growth rate r, deducting a percentage for expenses er each year. By simplifying the annual multiplier $(1 + r)*(1 - er)$ to the geometric series term z, the basic formula for annual fees paid is:

```
Fees(n) = P * (1 + r) * (er) * (zⁿ - 1)/(z - 1)
```

You can learn more about the math behind a geometric series at *http://www. moneychimp.com/articles/finworks/fmgeom.htm*.

Example 7-10. Formula for annual fees paid

```
Annual Fees Paid (B26) = Funds Invested (B14) * (1 + Expected Return (B4))
    * TotalExpenseRatio (C8)
    * ((1 + ActualAnnualReturn (B15))^Holding Period (B3)-1)
    / ActualAnnualReturn
```

Example 7-11. Formula for total fees and sales loads

```
Total Fees and Loads (B27) = Load Paid (B25) + Annual Fees Paid (B26)
```

There's one last cost of mutual funds that you won't ever see in mutual fund cost estimates: the earnings you lose due to fees and loads. When you pay fees and loads, that's money that you could have invested to make more money. The only way to see this hidden cost is to calculate it in Excel using the formula in Example 7-11 or the SEC Online Calculator.

—*Bonnie Biafore and Amy Crane, with finer points of mathematics provided by Jim Thomas*

Using the SEC Online Mutual Fund Cost Calculator

If you don't want to build a spreadsheet to calculate mutual fund costs, you can use the SEC's Online Cost Calculator at *http://edgar.sec.gov/investor/tools/mfcc/mfcc-int.htm*. If you plan to evaluate several mutual funds, the data entry is tedious but very easy. Click the Run the JavaScript SEC Cost Calculator link. You can read the SEC's introduction to the effect of mutual fund expenses or go directly to the calculations by clicking the "Click here to skip the introduction" link. Type or select one value on each page of the calculator and press Enter to progress to the next page. The calculator requires the number of years you plan to own the fund, your initial investment in dollars, the type of fund, the average annual return, the name of the fund to identify the results when you print them, the sales charge, the deferred sales charge, whether the fund converts to one class of share to another, and the total annual operating expenses.

Analyze the Hidden Costs of Fund Turnover

When fund managers jump in and out of stock or bonds in search of quick profits, the fund companies pick your pocket for the cost for all those transactions.

Mutual fund managers who enthusiastically swap investments cost you money both in brokerage commissions and taxes on capital gains. John Bogle, the mutual fund investing guru, views such managers as no more than short-term speculators, who raise your fund costs an estimated 2 to 3 percent of your fund assets annually through higher brokerage commissions and market impact costs. A recent Standard & Poor study validated Bogle's suspicions, proving that low-turnover funds outperform their higher-turnover cousins. If you're investing in a taxable account, taxes take another bite out of your profits when mutual funds distribute capital gains, interest, and dividends. A look at a fund's turnover rate can tell you whether a fund manager trades frequently, or buys and holds for the long term. Fund companies calculate annual turnover rates by dividing a fund's total investment buys and sells by average monthly assets. In addition, tax-adjusted returns represent the return you earn with a fund if you have to pay taxes on distributions, such as when you hold funds in a taxable account. Before you buy a mutual fund, particularly in a taxable account, use turnover rates and tax-adjusted returns to determine whether it's appropriate.

The average stock fund has a turnover rate of close to 100 percent a year, which means a manager sells the equivalent of the entire asset value of the mutual fund each year. Higher turnover is not unheard of, with some aggressive growth funds sporting turnover rates in excess of 200 percent.

When new fund managers take over funds, they generally clean house, selling their predecessor's holdings and stocking up on their favorites. With the average manager remaining at a fund a little less than five years, there is plenty of potential for high turnover. Before you buy a mutual fund, make sure that the manager who produced the past returns is still steering. If a new manager with an unproven track record takes over, it might be time to find another fund.

Bond funds carry higher turnover rates than stock funds for a number of reasons. For example, bonds mature and must be replaced. In addition, as the outlook for interest rates changes, fund managers might buy bonds with shorter or longer duration to manage risk. Average bond fund turnover comes in at around 150 percent, but some bond funds trade in excess of 300 percent a year. Given that bonds return less than stocks over the long term and are also subject to taxes on interest, losing 2 to 3 percent to turnover really hurts.

Turnover rates at index funds are generally low, because index funds have to replace stocks only when their benchmark indexes change or to satisfy purchases and redemptions. Tax-managed funds are becoming more popular as investors recognize the importance of after-tax returns. Managers of tax-managed funds employ investment strategies designed to minimize fund investors' tax liabilities.

The Direct Costs of Turnover

Brokerage costs are a slippery aspect of turnover. Although brokerage costs are deducted from fund assets, they aren't published in any report or prospectus. Funds typically hire a number of different brokerages and aren't obligated to consider cost when directing trades to a particular brokerage firm. To muddy the waters, brokerages court fund companies by offering them research services in exchange for brokerage commission business, known as *soft dollar transactions*. By exchanging services whose costs would normally appear in the expense ratio for commissions, which don't show up in the expense ratio, these soft dollar transactions make fund costs appear lower without actually reducing the fees that funds pay.

Market impact costs are even tougher to grasp than the slippery slope of fund brokerage commissions. When fund managers sell large blocks of stocks, the market pays attention, and the price drops before the fund can sell all its shares, reducing the total amount the fund receives for its stock. When funds buy large blocks, prices can rise quickly, and fund management ends up paying more for some of the shares. These less-than-ideal transaction results are known as market impact costs.

Managers specializing in small or foreign companies face even higher commissions and market impact costs than those investing in large domestic companies, because small companies trade less frequently, which magnifies market impact. On foreign exchanges, commissions are higher than in the U.S. and trading volume in small companies might be extremely light, affecting buy and sell prices significantly.

Together, brokerage commissions and market impact costs can deduct 2 to 3 percent a year from returns, depending on the type of fund. Total return numbers are the telltale indicator, because they reflect all the expenses you pay even if they don't appear in the expense ratio. The less a manager trades, the smaller the hit on fund returns. In all domestic fund style categories—growth, blend, and value—lower turnover funds beat their high-turnover cousins during the past three- and five-year periods.

Studies have found that turnover rates as low as 20 percent a year can impact fund taxes significantly. For investors holding mutual fund shares in taxable accounts, taxes matter [Hack #62]. As carved out in the new tax law, the gulf between short- and long-term gains is painfully deep. Short-term gains—those paid on investments held by a fund for less than a year—are taxed at ordinary income rates, which can be as high as 35 percent, whereas long-term gains are taxed more delicately at 15 percent.

The effect of turnover and taxes on long-term results is obvious in the fund comparison shown in Table 7-2. The two funds in the table boast low expense ratios, invest in stocks in the S&P 500 index, and have managers who have been at the helm for more than five years, but their trading patterns lead to quite different results, particularly after taxes. Although the returns include the bear market from 1999 through 2003, the effects of brokerage costs, market impact, and taxes are clear. The Vanguard Tax-Managed fund didn't perform as well as PIMCO Stock Plus before taxes, having lost 1.56 percent compared to the PIMCO fund's 0.71 percent loss. However, after taking into account taxes paid, the tax-managed fund produced almost 1.5 percent more return than the PIMCO fund.

Table 7-2. Turnover and taxes can cost investors precious percentage points of return

Fund name	One-year turnover in percent	Five-year average turnover in percent	Five-year pre-tax return in percent	Five-year after-tax return in percent	Percent lost to taxes
Vanguard Tax-Managed Growth	9	5.4	−1.56	−2.03	.47
PIMCO Stock Plus	455	185.6	−.71	−3.57	2.86

Some aspects of fund turnover are outside a manager's control. Managers must invest new money fairly quickly and cash out investors who sell shares on the same day. Although most funds keep some cash on hand, managers might be caught off guard by a tide of redemptions, forcing the sale of stock or bonds, increasing turnover, and decreasing returns for the investors who stay put. Fund turnover is one risk that investors in individual stocks can avoid, because they can decide how often to trade and whether to take a taxable gain or loss.

Neutralizing Turnover

Both in buying funds and managing their investment portfolios, savvy investors do well to emulate the nation's best-known buy-and-hold investor, Warren Buffett. He holds shares in companies for decades and decries the whirling dervish turnover behavior of fund managers.

You can find fund turnover for the most recent year at Morningstar (*http://www.morningstar.com*) and Yahoo! Finance (*http://finance.yahoo.com*). If you want to use a longer history of turnover, check the web site for the fund company. You can also obtain five-year average turnover when you subscribe to NAIC's mutual fund services [Hack #67] at *http://www.better-investing.org/funds*. Use the following turnover checklist before purchasing fund shares:

- Look for stock funds with average annual turnover rates of 20 percent or less.
- Look for bond funds with average turnover less than 100 percent.
- Consider index funds. Both stock and bond index funds boast much lower turnover rates than funds run by active portfolio managers.
- Purchase tax-managed funds for investments in your taxable accounts.

See Also

- The NAIC Mutual Fund Education and Resource Center (*http://www.better-investing.org/funds*) offers five-year average turnover rates for more than 14,000 funds. Subscriptions run $60 a year for non-members, $35 for members. In addition to the turnover data, you receive fundamental fund analysis tools that help you find, compare, and track quality stock, bond, asset allocation, money market, international, and exchange traded funds.
- For more information on sneaky fund expenses, read *Common Sense on Mutual Funds: New Imperatives for the Intelligent Investor* by John Bogle (John Wiley & Sons).

—Amy Crane and Bonnie Biafore

HACK #62 The Taxman Cometh for Your Fund Returns

Although taxes can chew through your mutual fund returns when you invest in a taxable account, the new tax law of 2003 can trim your tax bill.

The 2003 tax law is Washington's gift to the long-term investor, offering substantial cuts in the tax rates on both capital gains and dividends. For investors using taxable accounts, buying and holding makes more sense than ever before. Because distributions of capital gains and dividends are taxable in these accounts, you must pay taxes on all of your distributions, whether you receive them in cash or reinvest them in fund shares. Paying taxes on distributions can cost you 2 to 3 percentage points of return each year. To make matters worse, when you reinvest mutual fund distributions, you must come up with cash from somewhere else to pay the taxes on those distributions on April 15. However, if you buy shares in tax-efficient funds to begin with, and then choose the shares you sell wisely, you can minimize your pain at tax time.

Uncle Sam is watching you and your fund company, and come April 15 he wants his cut. As a fund investor, you should evaluate the tax ramifications of the following mutual fund actions:

- Selling shares of a fund that has increased in value.
- Receiving interest from bond, money market, and REIT funds, distributed monthly to fund investors and taxed as ordinary income.
- Receiving capital gains from any fund, including municipal bond funds.
- Writing checks from any type of fund account other than a money market account, which triggers a sale of shares and is potentially taxable.
- Exchanging (selling) shares in one fund family for another in the same family. If the exchange is in a taxable account, you'll owe taxes on any gains.

The 2003 tax law cuts corporate dividend and long-term capital gain rates to 15 percent through 2008. If the law isn't renewed before 2008, these rates go back to their pre-2003 levels. Fund managers and investors who hold stocks and bonds for a year or longer shelter more of their own profits as a result of the new law. Likewise, fund managers and investors favoring dividend-paying stocks also benefit. The new law punishes short-term traders—managers or investors who hold stock, funds, or other assets for less than a year—with high tax rates.

Over time, the tax-savvy long-term investor's returns will far outpace those of the short-term trader, as invested principal grows and compounds. There's a big gulf between tax-aware managers who hear investors' pain over high tax bills and the happy-go-lucky manager who reaches for high returns at all costs. The two funds in Table 7-3 have similar objectives. Both outperform market benchmarks during the long term, are managed by long-term managers, and charge low expenses. Although their pre-tax annual returns are fairly close, the after-tax return of the tax-inefficient fund is only 68 percent of the tax-efficient fund return, and produces almost $11,000 less on a $10,000 investment over 10 years.

Table 7-3. Taxes can take a huge bite out of mutual fund returns

Fund	Ten-year pre-tax return in percent	Ten-year after-tax return in percent	Percentage lost to taxes	Dollar difference investing $10,000 for ten years
Muhlenkamp Fund	12.88	12.52	.34	$32,531
Gabelli Equity Income	11.12	8.54	2.58	$22,693

While stock investors cheered the 2003 tax cuts, investors in bonds and real estate investment trusts (REITs) weren't so happy. Whether you invest in bonds and REITs directly or through mutual funds, you are taxed at ordinary income rates on their income.

Municipal bond funds offer investors a haven from high tax rates. These bond funds make sense for investors who live in high-tax states and hit federal tax brackets of at least 27 percent. InvestinginBonds.com (*http://www. investinginbonds.com/cgi-bin/calculator.pl*) offers a simple calculator that helps you figure out whether you're better off investing in taxable or tax-free bonds or bond funds. When you compare taxable and tax-free funds, remember to pick funds with similar durations and credit quality. Duration [Hack #64] measures a fund's sensitivity to interest rate changes, whereas credit quality assesses the financial stability of the companies issuing the bonds in the funds' portfolios.

Before you buy shares in any kind of mutual fund for a taxable account, look under the hood for hints on management tax strategies and potential tax issues. Morningstar.com provides pre-tax and tax-adjusted returns as well as other tax statistics when you select the Tax Analysis tab on a Snapshot report web page:

Pre-tax return
Total return including reinvested capital gains and income prior to paying taxes.

Tax-adjusted return

Total return with all capital gains and income distributions taxed at the maximum federal rate at time of distribution and the after-tax portion reinvested in the fund. If you invest in taxable accounts, use this measure to evaluate which fund provides the better return taking your tax bill into account.

Tax cost ratio

The percentage reduction in annualized return resulting from income taxes. Look for numbers under 1 percent for taxable accounts.

Potential capital gains exposure

The percentage of a fund's total assets that would be subject to capital gains taxation if it were to liquidate. This measure indicates how likely the fund is to distribute capital gains in the future. A negative potential capital gains exposure means that fund carries capital losses it can use to offset future gains. A positive number indicates the potential for capital gains distributions in the future.

Morningstar Snapshot reports include other measures you can use to evaluate tax efficiency:

Turnover rate

Shown on the Snapshot page, this is the percentage of a fund's net assets sold in a year. Look for lower numbers for taxable accounts.

Morningstar rank

Shown on the Morningstar Rating page, this is the rank within the fund category, which is calculated based on tax-adjusted returns for funds with similar investment strategies.

Tax Avoidance Strategies

All is not lost. There are plenty of ways you can minimize your mutual fund tax bill:

- Hold tax-inefficient mutual funds in 401(k) and IRA accounts when possible.

- Contribute the maximum to 401(k) and IRA plans before investing in taxable accounts. Although capital gains rates are low now, that won't last forever. Deferring taxes over a long period of time juices your returns, adding to the powerful effect of compounding.

- Invest in tax-managed funds in taxable accounts. Most large fund families offer several tax-managed funds with different investment options.

- Don't make purchases in tax-inefficient funds late in the year. Funds must distribute their capital gains, dividends, and interest before

December 31, so the shares you purchase in November or December are like buying the distribution and paying taxes on gains that you didn't earn.

> It's also a good idea to check a fund's distribution dates before buying and selling at other times. Don't buy a fund right before a quarterly distribution or sell immediately after one.

• Check your potential gains in a fund before exchanging it for another fund in the same fund family. Such an exchange is a sale for IRS purposes and could trigger capital gains. If your capital gains are large and you need the money, set aside 20 percent of your profits to pay taxes on the capital gains.

• Use losses to offset capital gains. If you own shares in a poorly performing fund, sell it to offset gains in other parts of your portfolio. Even if you don't have gains, dump that dog and use up to $3,000 in losses to offset ordinary income. You can carry forward losses of more than $3,000 to future years.

The IRS allows four different methods for figuring gains or losses on sales or exchanges of fund shares. Before you sell, you should choose a method because your results can vary significantly, as shown in Figure 7-4. For example, selling 100 shares of the Vanguard 500 Index Fund purchased between 1999 and the end of 2003, your tax bill can vary from zero to $427.11. If you use a personal finance tool, such as Quicken or Microsoft Money, you can export your mutual fund transactions into a spreadsheet. Using that data, you can calculate the tax bills for each of the methods and choose the one that meets your needs.

> After you select a method for an investment, you must use that same method for every sale of that investment.

Average cost per share method

Most mutual fund companies use this method when calculating your gain or loss. Average cost divides the total amount invested by the total number of shares. You calculate your gain by subtracting the average cost per share from the price at which you sold. Record-keeping is easy, so this is the preferred method if taxes aren't a big issue for you.

The Taxman Cometh for Your Fund Returns

Left window — oih_07 mutual Fund Tax calc.xls:1

Purchase Date	Transacti	Price	Shares	Cost Basis	Cumulative Shares	Cumulative Cost
3/26/1999	ReinvLg	117.69	0.03	3.06	0.03	3.06
6/25/1999	ReinvDiv	121.50	0.00	2.74	0.03	5.80
9/20/1999	BuyX	123.73	4.12	509.53	4.15	515.33
9/24/1999	ReinvDiv	119.13	0.02	2.74	4.17	518.07
12/6/1999	BuyX	131.83	5.72	754.22	9.89	1272.29
12/23/1999	ReinvDiv	133.33	0.05	6.00	9.94	1278.29
12/23/1999	ReinvSh	138.33	0.01	0.83	9.94	1279.12
12/23/1999	ReinvLg	134.55	0.08	10.36	10.02	1289.48
2/22/2000	Buy	124.70	21.37	2664.20	31.38	3953.68
3/24/2000	ReinvDiv	139.69	0.06	8.94	31.45	3962.62
4/11/2000	BuyX	138.29	2.45	339.37	33.90	4301.99
6/23/2000	ReinvDiv	133.03	0.08	10.11	33.98	4312.10
7/13/2000	BuyX	138.05	6.88	949.38	40.85	5261.48
9/22/2000	ReinvDiv	133.58	0.11	14.56	40.96	5276.04
12/22/2000	ReinvDiv	120.77	0.14	17.27	41.11	5293.31
1/2/2001	Buy	118.44	2.53	300.00	43.64	5593.31
3/16/2001	ReinvDiv	105.92	0.13	13.77	43.77	5607.08
3/27/2001	Buy	109.09	3.14	342.00	46.90	5949.08
6/22/2001	ReinvDiv	112.96	0.13	14.12	47.03	5963.20
6/25/2001	Buy	112.47	2.45	275.00	49.47	6238.20
9/21/2001	ReinvDiv	89.28	0.19	17.32	49.67	6255.52
12/28/2001	ReinvDiv	107.10	0.20	21.42	49.87	6276.94
2/14/2002	Buy	103.14	4.77	491.89	54.64	6768.83
8/15/2002	Buy	85.96	18.61	1600.00	73.25	8368.83
9/27/2002	ReinvDiv	75.66	0.05	4.01	73.30	8372.84
12/9/2002	Buy	82.61	36.44	3010.51	109.75	11383.35
12/27/2002	ReinvDiv	80.94	0.19	15.54	109.94	11398.89
2/3/2003	Buy	79.44	29.29	2326.51	139.22	13725.40
3/7/2003	Buy	76.72	48.88	3750.00	188.10	17475.40
3/28/2003	ReinvDiv	79.69	0.71	56.90	188.82	17532.30
4/10/2003	Buy	80.51	12.42	1000.01	201.24	18532.31
5/8/2003	Buy	85.08	11.75	1000.03	212.99	19532.34
6/9/2003	Buy	90.37	11.07	1000.03	224.06	20532.37
6/20/2003	ReinvDiv	91.94	0.74	67.67	224.79	20600.04
7/11/2003	Buy	92.26	10.84	1000.01	235.63	21600.05
8/7/2003	Buy	90.12	11.10	999.97	246.73	22600.02
9/8/2003	Buy	95.59	10.46	999.97	257.19	23599.99
9/26/2003	ReinvDiv	92.08	1.01	93.09	258.20	23693.08
10/10/2003	Buy	95.95	10.42	999.99	268.62	24693.07
					Total Shares	Total Cost

Right window — oih_07 mutual Fund Tax calc.xls:2

Current Price: 95.76

Average Cost Per Share Method

Avg Cost	Date Acquired	Gain on selling 100 shares	Tax paid on gain
91.92	3/26/1999	383.50	57.53

Double Category Method

Avg LT Cost	Avg ST Cost	Gain on selling 100 LT shares	Tax paid on LT gain	Gain on selling 100 ST shares	Tax paid on ST gain
114.22	83.56	-1846.23	0.00	1220.32	427.11

First In First Out Method

Cost of First 100 purchased shares	Gain on selling 100 shares	Tax paid on gain
9177.88	398.12	59.72

Specific Shares (lowest price shares purchased)

Cost lowest priced shares	Gain on selling 100 shares	Tax paid on gain
9465.00	111.00	16.65

Figure 7-4. Each method of calculating gains produces a different tax bill

Double category method

A similar approach to average cost per share method, except that short-term and long-term purchases are separated. Average long-term cost is the total amount invested in shares held more than one year divided by the number of shares held for more than one year. Average short-term cost is calculated in the same way using number of shares and dollars in shares held less than one year.

> With the long decline in share prices over the period in this example, the double category method results in a significant loss selling long-term shares, but the largest gain selling short-term shares.

First in first out method

An inventory method in which the first shares bought are the first sold. Because shares held the longest often have the lowest cost basis, this method can lead to the largest capital gains. The IRS assumes you use this method if you don't specify one on your tax return.

Specific shares

You can choose the shares you want to sell to produce the tax results you want, such as the smallest capital gains. The record-keeping burden for this method is painful but can lead to significant reductions in the taxes you pay.

—Amy Crane and Bonnie Biafore

HACK #63 Evaluate Short-Term and Long-Term Returns

Examine mutual fund long-term returns and risk characteristics to avoid getting burned by funds on a momentary hot streak.

For fund companies, attracting investors is as easy as shooting fish in a barrel. They just advertise recent short-term returns for their best-performing fund and watch fund investors fall for the oldest trick in the mutual fund book. Buying based on short-term performance is a loser's game, as you buy one fund at the top, and sell it when it falls in order to buy the next hot fund. It's no wonder so many are soured on investing. But don't be fooled—buying based on short-term performance isn't investing, it's gambling. And like the addict who keeps running back to the lottery ticket window, mutual fund gamblers won't have much to show for all their efforts. In fact, a recently released Morningstar study shows that short-term mutual fund performance doesn't predict future results. Many funds that top category averages in one short period are likely to trail going forward. Even good three-year and five-year average annual returns are not enough. For true winners, look to longer-term returns—average annual returns for 10, 15, and 20 years. By calculating rolling returns, you can smooth out the volatility of yearly returns and see growth trends more clearly.

Long-term returns are worthwhile only for predicting future performance when the same manager has directed a fund the entire time. With fund manager tenure averaging less than five years, funds with long-term managers aren't easy to find, but you can dig them up by screening for them **[Hack #66]**.

Fund companies advertise their highest returns, not necessarily the ones that help you choose the best fund for your objectives. Unfortunately, there are several variations on fund return. Before you pay attention to a fund's top-notch returns, know what you're looking at and how to interpret it:

Total return

A fund's percentage gain or loss from income and capital returns, minus expenses. Total return figures are usually not adjusted for loads or sales charges unless indicated as such.

Load-adjusted return

> A mutual fund's percentage return reduced to reflect any load or sales charge. Because loads cut into your total return, use this type of return to evaluate any load fund you're interested in.

Tax-adjusted return

> A percentage return reduced to reflect the payment of taxes on fund distributions. If you hold a fund in a taxable account, use this type of return to evaluate its performance.

Average annual return

> The annual return calculated by averaging a fund's percentage returns over a period of time, such as thee years, five years, or ten years. Using averages smooths out the ups and downs of year-to-year returns, so you can see trends.

Cumulative return

> An investment's return over several years. Do not compare cumulative return for one fund to the annual return of another fund.

Rolling returns

> Returns calculated for a multi-year period ending with a particular year. Takes the concept of average annual return one step further by examining the trends in longer-term returns. For example, you can calculate the average return for the previous five years for each of the past ten years.

> Many fund investors wonder why their individual returns don't match published returns. Published returns are standardized and include assumptions about dividend and capital gains reinvestment. Contributing to a fund at different times or not reinvesting dividends and capital gains produces different results. You can use Excel to calculate returns for different lengths of time [Hack #81].

As you can see in Table 7-4, annual returns make it hard to determine whether the Vanguard 500 Index Fund (VFINX) or Franklin Growth A fund (FKGRX) is more dependable. Both are large-blend funds with long-time managers, but VFINX wins in some years, FKGRX in others.

Table 7-4. Annual total returns in percent for two similar funds

Fund	1995	1996	1997	1998	1999	2000	2001	2002
VFINX	37.45	22.88	33.19	28.62	21.07	−9.06	−12.02	−22.15
FKGRX	38.4	16.68	18.6	18.52	12.19	7.53	−9.47	−24.24

Table 7-5 shows average annual total returns for 3-year, 5-year, 10-year, and 15-year periods. These averages are more revealing than yearly returns, showing that Franklin Growth comes out ahead in more recent periods, whereas Vanguard is superior over longer periods.

 You can use 15-year comparisons for these funds because they use similar investing philosophies and have long-term managers.

Table 7-5. Average annual total returns for different timeframes

Fund	3-year return	5-year return	10-year return	15-year return
VFINX	−11.26%	−1.63%	9.97%	11.29%
FKGRX	−9.05%	−18%	8.68%	9.23%

Rolling returns, shown in Figure 7-5, reveal the superiority of the Vanguard 500 Index Fund, whose five-year rolling returns beat Franklin Growth's for the last six years. Known as *time series analysis*, this method of presenting data removes some of the distortion that comes with yearly and average annual returns. You can also use rolling returns to gauge a fund's consistency. Many fund investors can't stomach wild swings in fund performance. By combining rolling returns with other risk measurements, you can find superior funds with more consistent performance.

To calculate rolling returns, you chain the returns from shorter periods to obtain the average return for a longer period. To understand the formula, let's start with something simple—the cumulative return for five years of constant return. Multiply the initial investment by (1 + return) for each year, as in Example 7-12.

Example 7-12. Formula for cumulative return for constant annual return

    Cumulative return for five years of constant return = (1 + return)⁵

The geometric average return for a constant annual return is (1 + return), which is the fifth root of the cumulative return (raising the cumulative return to the power of 1/5). The cumulative return for five years of actual returns is shown in Example 7-13.

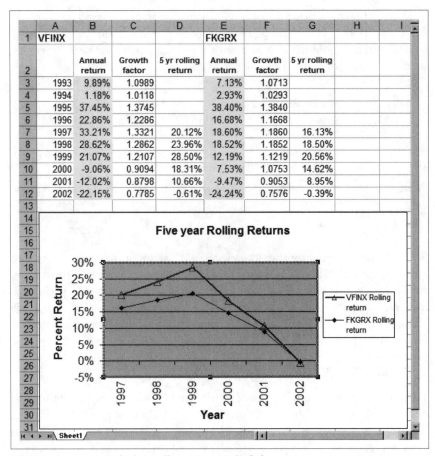

	A	B	C	D	E	F	G	H	I
1	VFINX				FKGRX				
2		Annual return	Growth factor	5 yr rolling return	Annual return	Growth factor	5 yr rolling return		
3	1993	9.89%	1.0989		7.13%	1.0713			
4	1994	1.18%	1.0118		2.93%	1.0293			
5	1995	37.45%	1.3745		38.40%	1.3840			
6	1996	22.86%	1.2286		16.68%	1.1668			
7	1997	33.21%	1.3321	20.12%	18.60%	1.1860	16.13%		
8	1998	28.62%	1.2862	23.96%	18.52%	1.1852	18.50%		
9	1999	21.07%	1.2107	28.50%	12.19%	1.1219	20.56%		
10	2000	-9.06%	0.9094	18.31%	7.53%	1.0753	14.62%		
11	2001	-12.02%	0.8798	10.66%	-9.47%	0.9053	8.95%		
12	2002	-22.15%	0.7785	-0.61%	-24.24%	0.7576	-0.39%		

Figure 7-5. You can calculate rolling returns to look for consistency over time

Example 7-13. Formula for cumulative return for actual annual returns

```
Cumulative return of five years of actual returns =
    (1+return1 (B3))*(1+return2 (B4))*(1+return3 (B5))
    *(1+return4 (B6))*(1+return5 (B7))
```

The rolling return for those five years is the geometric average for the five years—the fifth root of the cumulative return—as shown in Example 7-14.

Example 7-14. Formula for rolling return

```
Rolling return =
((1+return1)*(1+return2)*(1+return3)*(1+return4)*(1+return5))^(1/5) - 1
```

> Subtract 1 from the return so the rolling return reflects only the increase in value not the original investment.

If you download ten years of annual mutual fund returns [Hack #14], you can calculate six years' worth of five-year rolling returns. You can't calculate rolling returns for every year, because you need the oldest five years for the first rolling return alone. Figure 7-5 shows the calculations for rolling averages for three-year and five-year periods. Column B contains the annual returns for the Vanguard 500 Index Fund for the past ten years. To simplify the formula, the cells in column C contain (1 + return) for the annual return in column B. The rolling return formula uses the Excel PRODUCT function to multiply a range of cells, as shown in Example 7-15.

Example 7-15. Using the PRODUCT function to calculate rolling returns

```
5-year rolling return (D7) = PRODUCT(C3:C7)^(1/5) - 1
```

> Each rolling return uses the cells one row lower in the spreadsheet.
>
> Some fund companies provide more years of data than Yahoo! Finance, and longer-term rolling returns are even more useful. Check your fund company's web site for more years of data [Hack #14].

Hacking the Hack

If you love statistics, you'll feel right at home assessing fund risk. Most fund sites, including Morningstar (*http://www.morningstar.com*) and Yahoo! Finance (*http://finance.yahoo.com*) provide standard risk measurements [Hack #37], such as R-Squared, standard deviation, beta, and alpha, which work the same for stocks and funds. You can use these risk measures to evaluate whether a fund is likely to continue its past performance or ricochet in another direction.

The Sharpe Ratio measures risk-adjusted performance specifically in mutual funds. It indicates the amount of return earned per unit of risk and is one of William Sharpe's contributions to modern portfolio theory. Much of current mutual fund analysis is based on these theories, which earned Sharpe and two collaborators a Nobel Prize in 1990. The higher the Sharpe Ratio, the more return you earn for each unit of risk you accept. For example, the Vanguard 500 Index Fund has a Sharpe Ratio of –.64, whereas the Franklin fund has a Sharpe Ratio of –.51. Although the Vanguard 500 Index Fund has earned higher returns over time, it does so by taking on a bit more risk than the Franklin fund. For more on the nuts and bolts of the Sharpe Ratio and an online Sharpe Ratio calculator, go to InvestinginBonds.com (*http://www.investinginbonds.com/cgi-bin/calculator.pl*).

> If you want funds with portfolios and performance close to market indexes, look for R-Squared and beta values close to 1. If you're more interested in less volatility from year to year, look for lower standard deviation values. For an assessment of risk in and of itself, use the Sharpe Ratio. Alpha represents the percentage of return the manager of an actively managed fund achieves over the market return.

See Also

- *The Intelligent Asset Allocator* by William Bernstein (McGraw Hill)
- *A Random Walk Down Wall Street* by Burton G. Malkiel (W.W. Norton & Company)

—*Amy Crane*

HACK #64 Manage Interest Rate Risk with Bond Fund Duration

Use bond fund duration to find out whether your bond fund investments could tank if interest rates rise.

When you buy a bond, you receive ongoing interest rate payments based on the interest rate set when the bond was issued. That rate might be great or lousy compared to current market interest rates, but at least it's guaranteed as long as you hold onto the bond. Bond prices are another story. They move in the opposite direction of interest rates, rising when interest rates fall, falling when interest rates rise. Bond investors made out like bandits in the 1990s when they sold their bonds after interest rates fell for several years in a row. However, bond funds don't work like bonds. Bond managers don't hold onto bonds, so you don't get a guaranteed return as you do if you hold a bond until it matures. Bond fund values and the returns you receive change along with interest rates. You can find out how much you stand to lose or gain from interest rate changes by checking the duration of your bond fund—and switch to a lower risk investment if the potential drop is too big.

Bonds Versus Bond Funds

Bond funds are made up of bonds [Hacks #2 and #80], but they're riskier and you could get into big trouble if you don't understand the risks. Bonds are debt issued by governments and corporations, who promise to pay ongoing interest to bondholders and then return the bondholders' original investments when the bonds mature. The interest rates that bonds pay depend on several things, including market interest rates when the bonds are issued and the financial shape of the issuers.

Traded on the market, the prices of bonds already issued go up or down based on supply and demand as well as current interest rates. Bond traders buy and sell bonds as they make bets on the direction that interest rates are headed. In the bond market, when interest rates fall, the prices of existing bonds rise, because those bonds offer higher interest rates than new ones. When interest rates rise, the value of existing bonds falls, because the higher interest rates of new bonds are more attractive. The bond price adjusts so that the yield you earn on a bond based on its current price matches the interest rates in the market.

If you're an individual investor and buy a bond to hold to maturity, fluctuating bond price isn't an issue unless you sell. Even if interest rates go through the roof, you'll receive the same interest payments and get your money back when your bond matures, as long as you hold your bond and the issuer doesn't go broke.

This is not so for bond fund investors. Although owners of individual bonds can decide whether to sit tight or sell, bond fund investors can't pick up the phone and tell their fund manager when to trade. Interest rates affect bond fund investors much more than those who buy individual bonds, because bond fund values are directly and immediately affected by the change in price of the underlying bonds.

Using Duration to Evaluate Risk

Because bond funds hold many bonds with different maturity dates, there is no one date at which all the bonds in a fund mature. Instead, bonds mature and fund managers buy new bonds to replace them. Fund managers also trade bonds in and out of fund portfolios. Because bond fund portfolios constantly change, bond funds have what is known as an *average effective duration*, which is the average duration in years of all the bonds in the fund. It represents the theoretical length of time until the entire portfolio matures.

So, how can you determine whether your bond fund will get hammered when interest rates rise? Refer to the bond fund duration. A fund's average effective duration tells you exactly how a bond fund will respond to rising or falling interest rates. A fund's average effective duration takes into account bond maturity as well as the timing and flow of interest rate payments from bonds in the fund portfolio.

Companies that track mutual funds divide bonds and bond funds into categories based on maturity and duration. As you would expect, shorter-term bond funds have shorter average effective durations than intermediate or long-term bond funds. Table 7-6 shows how Morningstar and Standard & Poor's (S&P) classify bond funds by duration.

Table 7-6. Bond fund duration classifications

Data provider	Short-term	Intermediate-term	Long-term
Morningstar	< 3.5 years	3.5 to 6 years	> 6 years
Standard & Poor's	< 3 years	3 to 7 years	> 7 years

The shorter a fund's duration, the less it is affected by increases in interest rates, as illustrated in Table 7-7.

Table 7-7. Effect of a one percent interest rate increase on bond funds of different durations

Average effective duration	Percentage change in fund value	Value of a $10,000 investment
2 years	–2 %	$9,800
4.5 years	–4.5 %	$9,550
7 years	–7 %	$9,300

For every one percent change in interest rates, a bond fund's value moves in the opposite direction by a percentage equal to its average effective duration, as calculated in Example 7-16.

Example 7-16. Formula for percent change in fund value from interest rate change

```
% Change in Fund Value = - % Interest Rate Change x Average Effective
Duration
```

It's hard enough to swallow the losses inflicted by even a one percent increase in interest rates. Think about how much money you could lose if interest rates went from the four percent of late 2003 to the double-digit rates in the 1980s. Fortunately, you can limit your losses by sticking with short-term or intermediate-term bond funds when interest rates are rising. Buy longer-term bond funds when you expect interest rates to head down for a while.

Where to Find Duration Information Online

Fund companies compute and provide average effective duration values to fund data-trackers, so it makes sense to get duration information directly from your fund company. Visit the fund family's web site or call its customer service toll-free number for current duration information. Depending on the fund company, duration information is available on a monthly, bimonthly, quarterly, or semi-annual basis. Because fund managers replace maturing bonds with newer ones bearing current interest rates, you must keep tabs on the frequent changes in a fund's average effective duration.

If you want duration information for several funds, go to Morningstar (*http://www.morningstar.com*). Type your fund's ticker symbol or name in the Quote box under the toolbar, and click Quote. In the Morningstar mutual fund Snapshot report, Average Effective Duration is the first measure in the Portfolio Analysis section, as shown in Figure 7-6.

—Amy Crane

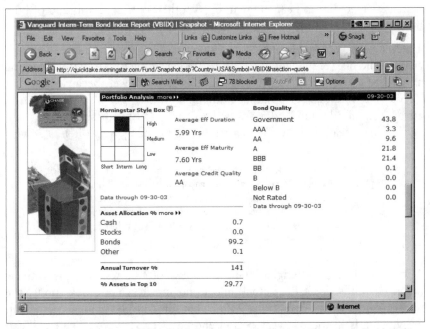

Figure 7-6. Use the average effective duration value from Morningstar.com to identify interest rate risk for bond funds

Evaluate Mutual Funds

#65 Check key fund measures to find funds that are likely to outperform the
competition.

Let's face it: most funds don't beat the market. With more mutual funds
available than individual stocks, how can you know which ones are the best?
You must hone in on the factors that lead to outstanding performance, such
as management tenure, low expenses, past performance, and low portfolio
turnover.

The Index Advantage

There are two major types of mutual funds: index funds and actively managed funds. Index funds mirror the investments represented by market
indexes, some tracking broad segments, such as the total stock market,
while others focus on more narrow niches, such as small-cap growth companies. Actively managed funds, on the other hand, hire hotshot portfolio
managers who aim to beat the market with their own special brand of buying low and selling high.

The indexing advantage rests on two pillars: low costs and market efficiency. The task of managing an index fund is simpler than that of building
a market-beating portfolio, so index fund costs are lower. Because costs cut
directly into a fund's performance numbers, lower-cost funds carry a built-in
advantage. In addition, index funds don't trade as much as actively managed funds, because the stocks in an index don't change very often.

> Efficient market theory holds that the total return of the
> stock market equals the return of all investors. Therefore, if
> some investors outperform the market, others must under-
> perform it. And because the overall market return doesn't
> include costs, all investors as a whole must underperform the
> market due to those costs.

A study published by Vanguard Group in July 2003 shows that most actively
managed funds don't beat stock and bond indexes. For stock funds, the
mid-cap growth indexes beat 92 percent of actively managed mid-cap
growth funds in the five-year period ending Dec. 31, 2002. The small-cap
value index for the same period beat only 44 percent of actively managed
funds. For bond funds, the results were stark, with indexes beating actively
managed funds by more than 80 percent in almost every bond category.

If you like the idea of using index funds, try the following low-maintenance
portfolio:

- For stocks, pick a low-cost index fund that tracks a total stock market index, such as the Wilshire 5000 or the Russell 3000.
- For bonds, choose either an intermediate or short-term bond index fund that tracks investment-grade bonds.
- Diversify further with a smaller percentage of your portfolio in an index fund that tracks all foreign markets or those in the developed world, based on the Morgan Stanley Europe, Asia, and Far East (EAFE) index.

Some actively managed funds do outperform index funds, but no crystal ball can show which ones will come up roses in the future. It's easier to find market-beating funds by evaluating a few key measures. But don't forget that even the best actively managed fund carries no guarantees. Your savvy manager might lose the magic touch or even quit. A greedy fund shop could also hike costs to the point where even the best manager can't eke out an index-beating return.

Management, Cost, and Turnover

Although many people race to check a fund's past performance, there are other measures that can make or break a mutual fund's suitability as an investment.

Management isn't a lifetime job. Fund managers come and go, with some fund companies moving managers from fund to fund like players in a game of musical chairs. However, many funds with top-notch track records have managers that stick around.

A fund manager controls the investments that makeup a fund's portfolio; she directly controls the return the fund achieves. When investigating funds, look for a manager who's been in charge for at least three to five years (longer is even better). It doesn't do any good to buy a fund based on the performance that another fund manager produced. In addition, judge a manager based on her published track record, not on fund ads or market hype.

 A manager might be new to a fund, but still have a long-term winning record at other funds.

Costs are an important component of future fund performance [Hack #59]. To figure out how much mutual fund expenses cost, read "Calculate the Damage of Mutual Fund Expenses" [Hack #60]. In general, try to limit the annual expense ratio to no more than one percent and avoid funds with sales loads.

Turnover is a rough measurement of how often the fund manager buys and sells holdings in a mutual fund's portfolio [Hack #61]. Fund managers who frequently flip stocks and bonds in search of quick profit also rack up high trading costs. Those trading costs come directly from your fund profits, because fund shareholders are the ones who pay brokerage commissions. Large funds that own millions of shares can cost you even more. If a fund manager dumps a lot of shares in a stock at one time, the price of that stock can tumble, reducing the sell price for that stock and the value the fund receives for its shares. If a manager makes a big purchase, the price increases before the purchase is complete, ultimately costing the fund more for the new shares.

Turnover often increases sharply when a new manager takes over, as she generally remakes the fund's portfolio. When examining turnover rates, consider averaging rates for the past three to five years. Look for stock funds with an average annual turnover rate of 50 percent or less, and bond funds with an average annual turnover rate of 100 percent or less.

Past Performance

Past performance is no guarantee of future results, but if all other important variables are equal, funds are likely to continue producing similar results. Compare a fund's average total annual return figures for three, five, and ten years to comparable market indexes. Give more weight to longer-term performance than shorter-term numbers. You can find year-over-year performance, long-term total return, and the growth of $10,000 invested compared to an index in the Total Returns section of a Morningstar mutual fund report.

However, recent events can distort total return figures—even average annual total return for ten years [Hack #63]. Just as the long bull market of the 1990s made past performance look far better than you would have expected, the bear market of 2000 through 2002 made past performance look worse.

Return and risk go hand in hand. Investments likely to reap higher returns usually carry more risk of loss. Before you buy a fund with hot past performance, think about your tolerance for gut-wrenching drops in fund value. A fund that rockets up 80 percent in one year during a bull market can easily drop that much or more in a bear market year.

Tools for Evaluating Mutual Funds

The National Association of Investors Corporation (NAIC) offers fund analysis tools for a small subscription fee (*http://www.better-investing.org/funds*). In addition to data for over 14,000 mutual funds (yes, there are more mutual

Assessing Mutual Fund Risk

You can assess risk using ratings developed by fund data trackers. For example, Morningstar (*http://www.morningstar.com*), a widely followed fund analyst firm, offers a star-based rating system that includes risk-adjusted performance. It compares funds in the same category and assesses risk-based performance for three, five, and ten years. The funds in the top 10 percent of their peer group receive five stars; the funds in the bottom 10 percent receive one star, with the rest of the funds somewhere in between. Ranking funds can be a good place to start, but it's better to assess risk on your own by looking at how a fund performs in bear markets.

funds than individual stocks), you can evaluate and compare mutual funds before you buy or exchange. Subscriptions are $35 a year for NAIC members and $60 a year for nonmembers.

The site includes:

- A screening tool [Hack #67]
- Standard & Poor's Mutual Fund Reports in PDF and HTML format
- An online tool for evaluating a mutual fund
- An online tool to compare similar funds and decide which one best suits your needs [Hack #72]
- An online tool to check on a fund to see whether it still meets your objectives

If you would rather save your pennies and don't mind a little Excel elbow grease, you can build your own spreadsheet to evaluate and compare mutual funds. Read "Download Mutual Fund Data" [Hack #14] and "Comparison-Shop for Mutual Funds" [Hack #71].

—Amy Crane and Bonnie Biafore

HACK #66 The Best Mutual Fund Screens for Free

With over 14,000 funds to choose from, you can use help finding the ones that meet your needs.

Looking for a good fund is like sifting through grains of sand on the beach. Not only are there thousands of them, each with its own objectives, costs, and track record, but fund companies and financial advisors also compete

The Best Mutual Fund Screens for Free

against each other, touting favored funds in print, on the Web, and on TV. Fortunately, free screening tools on the Web help dig you out of this sand pit and find funds for the long term.

Sifting Through Fund Criteria

Screening tools offer a bewildering variety of criteria, ranging from the important to the inane. When using a screen to find funds, focus on key criteria, ignoring the others altogether. For example, if you're looking for funds for long-term growth, use measures such as three-, five-, and ten-year total return, manager tenure, turnover, loads, and costs. If you're trying to choose funds for your 401(k) plan, use a screening tool that includes a filter for fund family so you can evaluate only the fund families available in your 401(k) plan.

 Avoid screening for short-term or year-to-date performance, as these melt away as fast as last winter's snow.

Most personal finance and financial sites offer screening tools. The two best screening tools feature industrial-strength capabilities that help you hone in on important variables. These tools use slightly different values for key criteria, so Table 7-8 provides criteria you can use to screen for mutual funds appropriate for long-term growth.

Table 7-8. Criteria for long-term growth fund screens for the two best mutual fund screening tools

Criteria	Morningstar	Yahoo! Finance
Category/objective (type of fund and investment style)	4 main categories, 62 subcategories	4 main categories, 49 subcategories; both are lumped together
Manager tenure	Greater than or equal to category average and one, two, three, five, or ten years	Longer than one, three, five, or ten years
Performance	Input values or select greater than or equal to category average	Numerous options for various timeframesfrom up 100 percent to down 50 percent
Turnover	Less than or equal to 150, 100, 75, or 25 percent	Minimum/maximum values from 5 to 500 percent
Loads	Load/no load option	Load/no load option or load less than 2, 4, or 6 percent
Expense ratio	Less than or equal to category average, 2, 1.5, 1, or 0.5 percent	Any or less than 0.3, 0.5, 0.7, 1, or 2 percent

The best free screens provide options for all the essential criteria. Most personal finance sites enable you to enter criteria to fit your needs. Many also provide predefined screens built by fund analysts. Screening tools draw on data from different fund providers, such as Morningstar, Standard & Poor's, Value Line, and Lipper. However, fund companies provide data to these providers, so data is virtually identical from one provider to another.

Morningstar (http://screen.morningstar.com/FundSelector. html?fsection=ToolScreener)

The best-known fund site on the Web offers a clear, crisp screening tool that includes all the important variables, as shown in Figure 7-7. For return criteria, you can input criteria or screen for results against the S&P 500 index or category averages. If you're new to screening, select from five predefined starter screens designed by Morningstar analysts: long-term winners, sold small-growth funds, standout foreign stock funds, conservative bond funds, or little funds with big returns. Click on the little yellow lightbulb next to each criterion, and a new window pops up with a short explanation.

- Best feature: on the Results page, choose from four different views. Sort results by clicking on a column heading. With a click, get feedback from Morningstar's Test in a Portfolio feature to see how the funds that your screen retrieved complement your existing portfolio.

- Worst feature: the site offers so much content—and the home page is redesigned so frequently—that finding the screening tool takes work. Click Tools on the toolbar at the top of the page.

Yahoo! Finance (http://screen.yahoo.com/funds.html)

Yahoo! Finance provides a well-organized screening tool built around five overall criteria: overview, ratings, performance results, and purchasing/fees. Like the Morningstar tool, you can screen for Morningstar ratings, return ratings, and risk ratings. The Yahoo! Finance screen has one advantage over Morningstar: it enables you to pick minimum and maximum criteria in these areas. Specialized criteria allow you to screen for fund asset size and median market capitalization, so you can avoid bloated funds and select funds investing in large, medium, or small companies.

- Best feature: screening criteria provided for the major fund families.

- Worst feature: some of the performance criteria are downright baffling. Wouldn't we all love to invest in a fund with a five-year annualized return of more than 100 percent? The problem is that no such funds exist!

—*Amy Crane*

Figure 7-7. The Morningstar fund screen includes several views for comparing fund measures

The Best Mutual Fund Screens for a Fee

Although free screens get the basic job done, turbo-charged mutual fund screens can improve your results and earn their subscription fee.

Mutual fund investors are stingy, if the number of mutual fund screens for a fee is any indication. Compared to stock screens that cost money, the pickings are pitiful for fund investors willing to pay for extra bells and whistles. That's probably because the best free fund screens on the Web are good enough for most investors. But what you're missing when you opt for a free mutual fund screen is not only enhanced screening capabilities, but extra goodies such as in-depth, independent analyst research at Morningstar or cool data-visualization fund analysis tools at SmartMoney. If you put these additional tools to use making better mutual fund choices, the fees involved are a pittance compared to the money you can earn with improved returns.

What You Pay For

When you pay a fee, you want a site that helps you figure out what kind of fund you need, sorts through all of the options, and makes it easy to regularly check on your portfolio. With some sites, you can access current financial news, investment information and analysis for funds, stocks and bonds, as well as portfolio tracking tools. Table 7-9 differentiates the tools that come with a price offered by three top web sites.

If you're a fund investor trying to get your portfolio on track or just checking on it now and then, consider subscribing to one of these services for a month or two instead of a whole year.

Table 7-9. Tools from Morningstar, SmartMoney, or NAIC can improve your results from your mutual fund investments

Features	Morningstar	SmartMoney	NAIC
Screening capabilities	Ten built-in screens	Six built-in screens	Basic screening
	Do-it-yourself screen with 54 criteria for 5 fund categories	Do-it-yourself screen with 53 criteria for 8 major categories	Offers a full list of fund families
Fund data and reports	Over 14,000 funds; 2,000 have analyst commentary	6,000 funds	Over 14,000 funds
			NAIC customized reports
Tools	Similar fund analyzer	Fund map data visualization	Fund comparison tool
	Portfolio X-ray		Fund performance trend tool

Table 7-9. *Tools from Morningstar, SmartMoney, or NAIC can improve your results from your mutual fund investments (continued)*

Features	Morningstar	SmartMoney	NAIC
Current commentary	Thorough; top-notch coverage of fund scandal	Focuses on results of Smart Money screens plus magazine articles	Articles from *Better Investing* magazine
Education	Extensive; covering funds, portfolio management, stocks, and bonds	Wide-ranging; covering investing, retirement, debt management, and more	Focuses on basics of investing in mutual funds
Data Source	Morningstar	Lipper and Morningstar	Standard & Poor's

Morningstar (http://www.morningstar.com)

Although Morningstar is the most expensive option, it's the best value for the money. With the Morningstar Premium Fund Screener, you can specify precise screening criteria to find exactly what you want. When screening for funds, you can save your screens for future reference or customize Morningstar's built-in screens, as shown in Figure 7-8. In addition, you can read what analysts have to say about 2,000 funds as well as current fund industry topics, such as the mutual fund scandal of 2003. As a bonus, subscribers get full access to Morningstar's stock analysis. Analysts cover 1,000 stocks, rating them with a discounted cash flow analysis system. The site is also packed full of education, tools, and message boards. For example, you can put your portfolio through its paces using subscriber-only tools, such as the risk analyzer, which measures the level of risk in your holdings, and the trade analyzer, which helps you calculate the tax consequences of buying and selling. You can use the Portfolio X-Ray [Hack #77] to see whether your portfolio meets your objectives. You can create multiple portfolios, such as retirement, short-term savings, and saving for college. The Portfolio X-Ray evaluates the stocks held in your accounts and within your mutual funds to show your portfolio allocation by type of investment, Morningstar style box, stock sector, stock type, and world region. It also shows stock statistics such as P/E ratio, return on equity, projected earnings growth and yield for your entire portfolio.

- Best feature: screening tool is easy to use and offers variables to satisfy the most compulsive researcher. Screen results are well organized with crisp presentation of data. Offers other effective tools.

Figure 7-8. You can choose from 54 mutual fund screening criteria with Morningstar's Premium Fund Screener

- Worst feature: busyness of the home page makes it hard to find what you need. The site has so much information that it's overwhelming for the new investor.
- Price: $12.95 a month; $115 a year; $199 for two years.

SmartMoney (http://www.smartmoney.com)

The SmartMoney fund screener offers numerous criteria plus customized screens built around *Lipper Leaders*, which are funds that meet standards set by Lipper fund analysts. The fund map tool presents information and a separate screen through data-visualization technology. It categorizes the fund universe by fund objective and company size. Funds with positive performance show up in green; those with negative performance in red. Click on a part of the map, and a fund's name pops up as well as a link to more information. Use it to find funds with specific objectives or to look for replacements for a fund that you currently own but want to sell. Like Morningstar, SmartMoney offers lots of information and tools for fund investors, but it's more like a stock site with some fund information and tools.

- Best feature: weekly features built around topical fund screens. For example, Bond Funds Built For Rising Interest Rates explains how rising interest rates hurt bond fund investors and offers a screen that you can view or download.

- Worst feature: tools are very slow to load, even with a high-speed connection.

- Price: $5.95 a month; $59.95 a year.

NAIC Mutual Fund Education & Resource Center (http://www.better-invest-ing.org/funds)

The only non-profit option of the bunch, NAIC offers unique tools that go right to the heart of fund analysis. The fund comparison tool lays out key fund criteria side by side and incorporates a ranking system that helps you figure out which fund is best. Keep an eye on trends in an individual fund through the trend report, which provides historical data and lets you filter the data by month, quarter, or semiannually. Help buttons next to each part of the tools explain fund criteria and S&P data. The screen, like much of the site, is functional but doesn't have a lot of bells and whistles. The University provides a sound basic education in mutual fund investing fundamentals.

- Best feature: fund analysis tools.

- Worst feature: no daily update of fund net asset values, so you have to go offsite to get the current NAV of your fund.

- Price: $35 a year for members; $60 a year for nonmembers; no monthly option available.

—Amy Crane

HACK #68 Beware of the Closet Index Fund

Some actively managed mutual funds have portfolios that read like stock index funds, but their fees are higher.

Low-cost index funds are a genuine boon. Tracking broad or narrow sectors of the market, they are the perfect buy-and-hold investment for busy investors. What isn't such a good deal are mutual funds that charge actively managed fund prices for index fund investments. These funds range from big names with well-known managers to smaller, more obscure funds. Their portfolios are nearly identical to that of an index fund. Why pay more for less return—when a plain vanilla, low-cost index fund can do the job just as well? You can identify and avoid these closet index funds by inspecting their portfolios under a microscope.

The popular image of fund managers as swashbuckling risk-takers simply doesn't jive with reality. Institutional investors in charge of gigantic pension funds buy mutual funds that track sections of the market. Managers who stray from that safe niche could lose their asset management contracts and the fees that go with them. With corporate bean counters and institutional investors breathing down their necks, most fund managers can't afford to fall too far behind the averages, resulting in big fund complexes and obsessed managers who are trying to beat their peers and track the indexes. Taking the risks required to beat the index by a wide margin might not pay off, so most managers don't take them.

For those few managers who do take risks—many of whom are employed by smaller fund shops—their success in beating the market sows the seeds of their own downfall. It doesn't take long for investors obsessed with short-term returns to jump on the bandwagon and buy shares in successful funds. As assets grow, fund managers find it more and more difficult to craft a market-beating portfolio. Fund firms looking out for their investors often close such funds to new investments to preserve the manager's style and independence, but many fund firms won't take a step that crimps their own profits.

Owning closet index funds costs you big-time. The least expensive index funds charge less than 0.25 percent of your assets in ongoing expenses and carry no loads. Buy into a closet index fund that charges the average expense ratio for an actively managed fund, and you might pay 1 percent or even more. The Vanguard 500 Index Fund, the nation's largest mutual fund, tracks the S&P 500 index and charges 0.18 percent of assets, which is far better than the 1.4 percent for the average, actively managed, large-blend fund. Translated into dollars and cents, a $10,000 investment in the Vanguard 500 Index Fund costs $18 a year, whereas a similar investment in an actively managed fund costs $140 per year—more than seven times more. Hold that fund for even five years, and you'll pay at least $610 more than the fees for the index fund. Because costs directly reduce your bottom-line returns, you're not earning as much as you could. Add a front, back, or level load onto that higher expense ratio, and you'll dig yourself into an even deeper hole.

Some investors collect funds like other people collect antiques. When you collect four or more funds in the same investment style, you're setting yourself up for index-like returns. In fact, you're turning your own portfolio into a closet index fund and paying additional fund expenses to do so. Only buy a new fund if it is substantially different from the funds you already own.

Using Data to Spot an Index-Hugger

Spotting an index-hugging fund manager is a snap. Pull data off the Internet [Hack #14] from Morningstar, Yahoo! Finance, or any other fund site, and throw it into a spreadsheet [Hack #71]. You can find a fund's benchmark index either in fund reports or in Morningstar data. When you compare your target fund to an index fund that tracks that particular index, focus on the following prioritized points to spot signs of index investing.

> Make sure the data is from the same date so that you're comparing apples to apples.

R-Squared [Hack #35]

A fund with an R-Squared of 90 or higher is a strong candidate for closet index fund status. The lower the R-Squared, the lower the correlation between the fund's performance and that of the benchmark index.

Beta [Hack #37]

A fund with a beta of 1.0 has performance volatility on par with the index. The more the beta value differs from 1.0, the less likely the fund mirrors the index.

Sector weightings

Fund data providers classify sectors differently, but a fund with sector weightings close to the index is likely an index-hugger.

Average annual total returns [Hack #65] *for three, five, and ten years*

Few funds beat indexes over the long term. Closet index funds might have performance close to the three- or five-year performance of an index fund, but are likely to fall away by ten years because of the drag of their higher expenses. Managers with a more independent mindset are less likely to closely track index performance. For funds that charge a sales load, compare the load-adjusted returns to the index returns.

> You won't necessarily spot a closet index fund by its tax-adjusted average annual returns. However, closet index funds might not be as tax-conscious as the index funds they emulate, so check the tax-adjusted returns to make sure you aren't getting stung by lower returns and higher taxes. Similarly, you should evaluate the costs you'll pay for the index fund and its copycat. There's no point investing in a closet index fund and paying for the privilege.

Average P/E ratios [Hack #27]

Values within a point of the index are suspicious.

Average EPS [Hack #26]

Figures within a percentage point of the index are suspicious.

Holdings

You can compare either the top ten holdings or the entire portfolio to see how many companies are the same for the fund and its corresponding index, and look for similarities in the largest holdings.

Company size by market-cap [Hack #74]

As with sector weightings, a portfolio close to the index in terms of market cap is suspicious.

Country weightings for world or foreign funds

Indexes followed by foreign and world stock fund managers are strict in terms of the country weightings. Funds that don't go out of bounds are candidates for closet indexhood, while those that venture outside their limits are likely run by more independent-minded managers.

The spreadsheet in Figure 7-9 compares the Vanguard 500 Index Fund, Mairs & Powers Growth fund, and GE U.S. Equity A fund. Mairs & Powers clearly goes its own way, whereas GE U.S. Equity A closely follows the index. Although the expense ratios of GE U.S. Equity and Mairs & Powers Growth are similar, Mairs & Powers's results blow the socks off the index, while GE U.S. Equity outperforms the index by a smidgeon over ten years.

When you run these funds through the SEC Cost Calculator (*http://www. sec.gov/investor/tools/mfcc/get-started.htm*), the results for a $10,000 investment held for ten years show what a difference management and expenses make, as illustrated in Table 7-10.

Table 7-10. A true index fund often beats the pants off a copycat actively managed fund

Mutual fund	Ending investment value
Vanguard 500 Index Fund	$26,801.31
Mairs & Powers Growth Fund	$43,843.75
GE U.S. Equity Fund	$23,674.26

A quick scan of the language in a fund report also provides clues to a fund's strategy. Look for words like *sector-neutral* and *disciplined*, which are tip-offs to a closet index fund. Consider whether a fund's strategy is likely to produce index-beating results. Hundreds of funds invest in large growth companies, but how many funds invest that much differently than a low-cost S&P 500 Index Fund?

—*Amy Crane*

	A	B	C	D
		Vanguard 500 Index Fund	GE U.S. Equity A:	Mairs & Powers Growth
2	R-Squared	100	97	66
3	Beta	1	0.89	0.62
4	**Sector Weightings:**			
5	**Info**	23%	21%	3%
6	Software	5%	5%	0%
7	Hardware	11%	7%	2%
8	Media	4%	5%	0%
9	Telecom	3%	4%	1%
10	**Service**	47%	52%	56%
11	Health	14%	18%	21%
12	Consumer	9%	5%	8%
13	Business	4%	7%	11%
14	Financial	21%	23%	17%
15	**Manufacturing**	29%	27%	41%
16	Goods	9%	7%	15%
17	**Industrial Materials**	11%	10%	25%
18	Energy	6%	9%	0%
19	Utilities	3%	2%	0%
20	**Average Annual Returns:**			
21	3-years	-6%	-4%	8%
22	5-years	-1%	1%	11%
23	10-years	11%	11%	17%
24	**Tax-Adjusted Annual Returns**			
25	3-years	-6%	7%	7%
26	5-years	-1%	-1%	10%
27	10-years	10%	8%	16%
28	**Price/Earnings**	18	18	18
29	**Long-term Earnings**	0	0	0
30	**Company size by market cap**			
31	Giant	51%	51%	31%
32	Large	37%	42%	23%
33	Mid	12%	7%	34%
34	Small	0%	1%	8%
35	Micro	0%	0%	4%
36	**Expenses**			
37	Expense Ratio	0.18%	0.87%	0.78%
38	Loads	0%	Front-end 5.75%	0%

Figure 7-9. By comparing mutual fund measures to an index fund, you can spot actively managed funds that mirror the index

Spot Mutual Funds That Don't Play Fair

HACK #69

Some fund companies have betrayed your trust. Before you bail out of mutual funds completely, get a handle on what's happening, who did what to whom, and what you can do about it.

It's a scandal fit for the tabloids—a crusading district attorney uncovers financial shenanigans, while a clueless regulator looks the other way. But this time, the scandal hit close to home if you're one of the 91 million Americans who hold shares in U.S. mutual funds. Fund companies violated the law and broke their own rules. What's worse is that some CEOs and fund managers—the very people that you count on to protect your interests—blatantly betrayed you by enriching themselves at your expense. As of early 2004, New York Attorney General Eliot Spitzer and the federal Securities and Exchange Commission (SEC) implicated 11 firms in the budding scandal. Investigations were expanding into other firms. Many fund companies that have so far escaped scrutiny have launched internal probes to find out if any foxes are guarding their hen houses. Already wearied by a string of corporate scandals, such as Enron and WorldCom, investors are wondering if they can trust anyone. By understanding the underlying issues, you can identify mutual funds you can trust.

During the last four months of 2003, regulators uncovered two types of mutual fund wrongdoing: *late trading* and *market timing*. The first is flat-out illegal, and the second violates the internal rules of many fund companies. Late trading means that fund companies allow hedge funds or other investors to place orders for mutual funds past the regular 4 p.m. deadline. Funds begin to calculate the net asset value of their portfolios at 4 p.m. based on closing prices for stocks and bonds, and are supposed to defer filling any share buy or sell orders until the start of trading the next business day. By trading late, investors can act on late-breaking news and make money at the expense of other shareholders. Here's a hypothetical example: Mutual Fund ABC owns a lot of shares of Company XYZ, which announces a big jump in earnings after the market closes at 4 p.m. A hedge fund manager buys shares of Fund ABC at 4:30 at a net asset value based on Company XYZ's closing price. Company XYZ's price goes up in response to its higher earnings, which in turn increases the net asset value of fund ABC, at which point the hedge fund manager sells the shares in fund ABC.

Market timing means that individual investors, hedge funds, or institutional investors buy and sell shares of a fund during a short period of time. Such transactions are against the stated rules of many fund companies and, in addition, raise the costs for all investors in a fund to cover the increased brokerage commissions. Regulators uncovered a number of cases where mutual funds allowed hedge funds to market time funds in exchange for investing money with the fund company. Because fund profits are based on the amount of overall assets under management and fund shareholders cover the costs of brokerage commissions, fund companies benefit from such an arrangement. One particularly egregious example of market timing occurred where company executives allowed market timing over the repeated objections of fund managers, who felt it was hurting fund performance. In other cases, fund managers and CEOs actually used market timing in their own funds, enriching themselves at the expense of investors whose assets they were supposed to protect.

Not content with busting the fund industry over late trading and market timing, regulators are pursuing fund companies and brokerages regarding distribution practices. The sleazy underside of fund company–brokerage relationships includes the following practices that are now under regulatory scrutiny:

- Brokerage firms that take payments from fund companies to sell those funds over others. Brokerages get cash that enhances their bottom line, while individual brokers might be rewarded with vacations for meeting sales targets.

- Fund companies that give commission business to brokerages in exchange for marketing their funds or providing research and other services. Known as soft-dollar arrangements, these practices aren't illegal, but regulators might force fund companies to publish the details of these arrangements.

- Brokers who fail to inform clients of cheaper options for purchasing funds or who don't give breaks on commissions for large investments. Thousands of misinformed investors have paid higher commissions than necessary, resulting in higher profits for brokers and financial advisors.

- Mutual funds that charge marketing and distribution fees known as 12b-1 fees. Initially intended to help funds gain assets in the late 1970s, these fees get shareholders to pay for brokers' compensation and fund advertising. Such fees increase your costs and decrease your returns.

The SEC, the New York State Attorney General's Office, and regulators at the National Association of Securities Dealers (NASD) were actively investigating a number of fund companies and brokerage firms in early 2004 on these distribution issues. Morgan Stanley settled SEC and NASD charges, but faces shareholder lawsuits and must pay $50 million to affected investors.

Staying Current

Regulators settled several cases by the end of 2003, including one where Alliance Funds not only agreed to reform fund practices, but also agreed to pay restitution to investors and cut fees by 20 percent for a five-year period. To keep up to date on the latest developments, check out these sites:

- Morningstar (*http://www.morningstar.com/fii/fundindustryinvestigation. html*) offers ongoing coverage, commentary, and updates on each fund firm under fire.

- CBS MarketWatch (*http://www.cbs.marketwatch.com/pf/fund*) provides a special report that keeps tabs on the most recent news and commentary.

- The SEC web site (*http://www.sec.gov*) includes speeches and statements by SEC officials and employees at *http://www.sec.gov/news/ speech.shtml*; press releases regarding the filing and settling of charges against fund companies, brokerages, and individuals at *http://www.sec. gov/news/press.shtml*; Congressional testimony from SEC Chairman William Donaldson and SEC employees at *http://www.sec.gov/news/ testimony.shtml*. This web site also provides audio webcasts of recent SEC meetings and live webcasts at *http://www.sec.gov/news/ openmeetings.shtml*.

- As attorney general of New York, Eliot Spitzer has a web site at *http:// www.oag.state.ny.us* with his speeches and testimony on the site's home page. Press releases, which identify the companies that have been charged and that have settled, live at *http://www.oag.state.ny.us/press/ agpress03.html*.

- For subscribers, the Wall Street Journal Online has thorough coverage of the scandal and ongoing developments at *http://www.online.wsj.com/ 0,,2_1050,00.html*.

News junkies who just can't get enough can search Google for more news by using the keywords `mutual+fund+scandal`, `market+timing+scandal`, or `late+trading+scandal`.

What You Can Do

If you're not sure whether any of your funds are implicated in the scandal, check the previously mentioned web sites. In most cases, only some funds within a mutual fund family are involved. What if your fund family hasn't been implicated? How can you be sure that nothing funny is going on?

Late trading is clearly against SEC rules established in the 1930s to curb stock and fund trading abuses uncovered after the crash of 1929. Unfortunately, there is no way to be 100 percent sure in terms of market timing and late trading. Many of the funds involved had rules against market timing and blithely ignored them. Still, it is worthwhile to go to your fund company's web site, and download the fund prospectus where such rules are enshrined. Rules are all well and good, but are even better when backed up with some teeth. Many fund companies impose penalties on market timers in the form of short-term redemption fees. These fees hurt market timers where they live, and because they are less likely to profit from market timing activities in funds with stiff redemption fees, they are more likely to go elsewhere. Current SEC rules limit redemption fees to 2 percent.

After you've scanned the prospectus, look at your fund company's web site for some type of statement from the CEO or chairman; most firms have issued one. If you own a fund that is implicated in the scandal, the tone of that statement can tell you a lot. You want to see clear steps outlined to stop any wrongdoing, including termination of any employees involved; promises of restitution to shareholders; and some expression of contrition. It's important that any fund company involved outline a detailed plan for preventing future abuses. If your fund company is involved, look for reforms that include:

- Hiring a chief compliance officer or ombudsman who will monitor compliance with company and SEC rules, and who will report directly to the board of directors.
- Adding or increasing short-term redemption fees to curb market timing.
- Explicitly banning market timing in fund prospectuses and company rules.
- Requiring that top fund officials or the board of directors must approve all new business relationships.
- Ending all soft-dollar deals with brokerage firms.
- Disclosing fund portfolios publicly on a monthly or bimonthly basis.
- Requiring that the chairman of the board be chosen from the independent directors.
- Instituting internal policies to monitor frequent trading by fund managers and other employees.
- Hiring an independent investigator to uncover any remaining issues.

Beyond prospectuses and statements, look at your fund's board of directors. The fund industry is ripe with insider relationships and cozy arrangements. It is common practice for fund managers and executives to sit on fund boards, leading to potential conflicts of interest. It's much harder for a fund board to set a fair management fee when some of its members profit directly from that fee. Look for funds with a majority of independent directors—those that have no ties to the fund company. Directors are named in the fund's annual report, which should also state whether directors are independent. The SEC is considering proposals to strengthen the role of independent directors on fund boards.

The stickiest question is whether you should sell shares in funds involved in these scandals. Morningstar shocked the fund community early on by recommending that investors sell shares in Janus and other implicated fund families. Take your own circumstances into account before deciding whether to sell. If you hold such a fund, determine whether you'd owe any taxes [Hack #62] upon sale of fund shares. If your fund is in a retirement account, find out if a better alternative is available. Tax considerations aside, consider whether you want to trust your money with people who were obligated to protect it, but didn't.

Whether you're personally involved or just teed off, don't be shy: express your opinions to your representatives and your regulators. You can find your representative and senators at *http//www.congress.org*. Congress has held hearings and several bills have been introduced to strengthen mutual fund regulation. The SEC has an online complaint form and phone numbers at *http://www.sec.gov/complaint.shtml*. The SEC is working on beefing up fund regulation: proposed rules, final rules, and commentary on rules can be found on its web site. To reach New York Attorney General Spitzer, go to *http://www.oag.state.ny.us/contact.html*. Spitzer initiated the investigation, and has pushed stringent settlements down the throats of reluctant fund companies and the SEC. If your fund company is involved, write to the CEO with your thoughts about how the company has responded to any issues. Fund companies are eager to retain their customers, so they should pay attention to what you have to say. Go to your fund company's web site and look for email and snail mail addresses under the Contact Us link.

—*Amy Crane*

HACK #70 Know When to Fold 'Em

Buying funds is easy—selling them when the time's right is the tricky part.

It's an uncomfortable feeling, opening the statement of a fund that you really don't want to own any more. For many fund investors, lack of time, lack of knowledge, and possibly lack of guts conspire against selling even the worst mutual fund dog. Too many investors cut the tie at the wrong time, whereas others turn to new funds for their investing thrills, leaving the old ones collecting dust and poor returns. Don't ignore your mutual funds. It's easy to review them and decide what to do.

When Funds Go Bad

Sometimes, you need to sell to protect your portfolio from a mutual fund that is heading for a dive. Funds usually give off warning signs before things go south. If you're paying attention, you can decide what to do before a warning sign becomes a real problem:

Departing manager
> With actively managed funds, a fund manager is the rock on which the success of a fund rests. Look at a new manager's record to see whether he has produced results similar to the previous manager, and, if not, consider another fund.

Proposed fund merger
> When a fund company sends you a proposal to merge your fund into another fund, check out the new fund to make sure you want to invest in it.

Changing investment philosophy
> When a mutual fund no longer invests a majority of its funds in the type of investments it represents, such as a small-cap fund that invests primarily in mid-cap stocks, look for a fund that fits your objectives.

Significant increases in assets
> If your fund is really successful, investors tend flock to its resulting in a big increase in fund assets. As assets increase, the fund company might make more money through fund expenses, but the fund managers might have to compromise the investing style that led to such great gains in the first place. Successful small- and mid-cap stocks funds are especially vulnerable to asset bloat. Mutual funds that close to new accounts help protect fund performance and existing shareholders.

Increasing or new fees
> Increases in fees or addition of new fees cost you money and cut into your fund's returns.

An increasing turnover rate
> A sustained rise in the turnover rate can impair fund tax efficiency and lead to higher tax bills and brokerage costs.

Turmoil
> Fund family turmoil, merger, acquisition, or other loss of focus can distract managers from their investing duties and result in lower returns.

Before ditching your fund shares, find out what's going on. Your manager might be leaving, but if a long-time assistant manager is taking over, it's probably OK. If fund fees were very low to start with, a small increase might not matter. On the other hand, a proposed merger could put you into a mediocre mid-cap value fund when you were invested in a pretty decent large-cap blend fund. In that case, you can justify selling your shares and looking for a new fund. Just as there are events that legitimately prod you into selling your fund, the following are nonevents that lead some investors to sell when they shouldn't:

- A bad quarter of fund performance doesn't make a fund a dog—the whole market could be off or just the sector that your fund occupies. Give a fund two or three quarters to prove itself before giving it the heave-ho.

- Your broker calls, touting the latest sector fund, and you don't have any cash. At all costs, don't get into the habit of trading an old fund in for the latest hot model.

- A mutual fund rating service downgrades your fund from five- to four- or three star territory. Find out why, and think about whether it's a legitimate reason to sell.

- Abrupt movements in fund price, including steep declines or sharp increases in fund net asset value, are no reason to sell in and of themselves. Keep a long-term perspective and remember that markets are fairly volatile on a day-to-day basis.

When to Sell

If warning signs are turning into frantically waving red flags, by all means, sell. If you haven't seen any warning signs, don't relax just yet. There are plenty of other reasons that you might want to sell your fund shares, including:

Portfolio balance
> You might find that one fund occupies too large a space in your portfolio. You might want to sell part of your shares, and reinvest those shares elsewhere to bring everything back into sync [Hack #74].

Fund overlap
> If you own too many funds of the same type, your returns tend to gravitate to the return of a market index, and there are easier and cheaper ways to invest in indexes. Keep the best fund of a given type and sell the rest, reinvesting the proceeds back into the better funds.

Changing goals
> When your goals change, it's time to reevaluate your portfolio. For example, if you've been saving for college and your only child earns a full ride to Harvard, you can deploy most of your college savings elsewhere (reserving a bit for uncovered and unexpected higher education expenses).

I need the money
> This is a perfectly good reason to sell.

Don't invest any money that you expect to need during the next five years.

Investment stress

Volatility is a fairly easy issue to deal with during the day. Intellectually, you know that fund prices rise and fall and funds with more potential for gain are more risky in the short term. But a 35 percent loss that you might be able to accept at three o' clock in the afternoon can seem a lot different at three o' clock in the morning. If fund volatility is driving you crazy, look for funds with more consistent performance.

Poor long-term performance

If your fund has underperformed its peers or its benchmark index for a couple of years, it's time to pull the plug.

Overvaluation

Because actively managed funds rarely trounce the market over long periods of time, a fund on a tremendous tear is often a sell candidate. For example, Munder NetNet Fund (yes, that's its real name) increased 97.92 percent in 1998 and 175.65 percent in 1999. However, the fund lost 90 percent of its net asset value during the bear market before it staged a rebound in 2003. A huge run-up in fund net asset value can be a sign of major overvaluation in the stock market at large or in the sector you're invested in.

Taxes

If you've got capital gains from selling one investment, it might make sense to generate some capital losses [Hack #62] by cutting a mutual fund dog loose. Married taxpayers filing jointly can also deduct up to $3,000 of capital losses against ordinary income. By all means, seriously consider replacing any tax-inefficient funds that you own in a taxable account with funds where the manager takes tax issues seriously.

In fact, before you actually sell your fund shares, take a couple of minutes to run your planned scenario through a couple of useful web calculators. If you're not clear on whether your fund investment made money, check out the "What is my return if I sell now?" calculator at *http://partners. financenter.com/kiplinger/calculate/us-eng/fund01.fcs*. This calculator shows your pre-tax and taxable return and your overall profit from owning the fund, as illustrated in Figure 7-10. To get a quick-and-dirty glimpse of your potential tax liability, use the "Should I sell my fund now and invest the money elsewhere" calculator at *http://partners.financenter.com/financenter/ calculate/us-eng/fund02.fcs*.

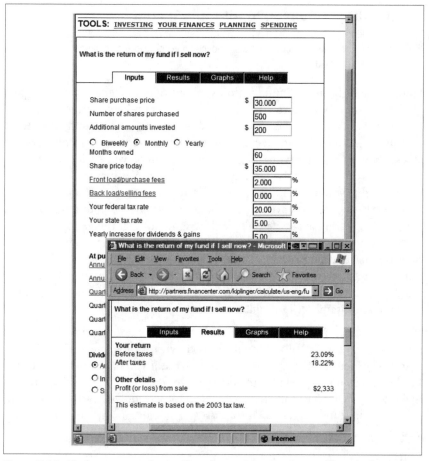

Figure 7-10. Find your return from selling a mutual fund with an online calculator

Keep in mind that you don't have to watch your funds every day. Don't let them drift indefinitely in limbo either. A mutual fund check-up once or twice a year fits the bill for most investors. At that time, check for any potential warning signs or red flags. Many investors keep tabs on their portfolios by entering their fund information in either a money management software program such as Quicken or MSN Money; others use online tools [Hack #73] available at sites such as Morningstar (*http://www.morningstar.com*) or Yahoo! Finance (*http://finance.yahoo.com*). NAIC (*http://www.better-investing.org*) offers the Mutual Fund Trend Report, where you can track many fund variables over time. Data is downloaded automatically into this and other fund evaluation tools.

—Amy Crane

Comparison-Shop for Mutual Funds

Picking the best mutual fund for your investment goals can not only increase your investment returns, but also reduce your portfolio maintenance efforts down the road.

Finding the right mutual fund isn't just about the numbers. True, a big part of choosing the best mutual fund is comparing numbers between contenders. However, some answers are found only by reading the fund prospectus and judging for yourself. Because mutual funds represent a collection of stocks, bonds, or other types of securities, the criteria you evaluate are much different than those for the underlying individual investments. Therefore, to do this right, you'll need a mutual fund checklist, so you compare mutual funds fairly and don't leave out anything important. The mutual fund data you need is readily available online, although you might have to tap several web sites to find everything you want [Hack #14]. In addition, some web sites offer online fund comparison tools that make it easier to make a decision, but each of these tools has small drawbacks [Hack #72]. Fortunately, it's easy to build your own checklist and comparison spreadsheet to evaluate qualitative and quantitative criteria alike.

With more mutual funds on the market than there are individual stocks to buy, weeding the list of potential funds down to a manageable number is your first order of business. On the other hand, if you have only one mutual fund in mind, it's a good idea to add a few competitors to the list before you make your final decision. The easiest way to pare down your choices is to use a mutual fund screen [Hacks #66 and #67]. You can cut the field quite a bit with a few criteria, as follows:

Category

When you're looking for a fund to fit part of your portfolio allocation plan [Hack #74], choose a category, such as large growth, small value, or international.

Manager tenure

Screen for funds whose manager has been in charge for more than five years [Hack #65]. Later, you can place greater weight on the funds whose managers have been around even longer.

Minimum initial investment

When you have only a small fixed amount to contribute, use that value as the minimum initial investment.

Front load

Screen for funds with no loads. If you are interested in buying a load fund, definitely screen for no-load funds to see whether the load fund is really worth the extra expense.

Total expense ratio

Unless you're a glutton for punishment, screen for funds whose expense ratios [Hack #59] are below the average for the category of fund. Later, you can reward funds with attractively low expenses.

The Mutual Fund Checklist

Some criteria can boot a fund out of the running fast, so you can save yourself time by evaluating criteria in the right order. Table 7-11 lists the essential mutual fund evaluation criteria in prioritized order.

Table 7-11. Appraise the suitability of a mutual fund with these criteria

Criteria	Purpose	How to evaluate
Consistent philosophy	Make sure that the fund invests in the segment of the market that you want, such as large growth or international. The SEC requires funds with names that suggest a focus on a particular type of investment to invest at least 80 percent of their assets in those investments, but that other 20 percent might be too aggressive or tame for your liking.	Read the prospectus to find the investment objective and fund strategy. Make sure that measures such as the portfolio composition, sector percentages, company size percentages, growth rates, average portfolio P/E ratio, and tax-adjusted returns back up the prospectus.
Trustworthiness	Assure yourself that the mutual fund will act responsibly with your money.	Read the prospectus for rules and penalties for market timing and other bad behaviors that can cost you money. Check for independent directors on the board and, at the very least, an independent chairman of the board. Check the fund web site for steps in the works to prevent problems in the future.
Minimum investments	Make sure the fund will accept the amount of money you have to contribute.	Check both the minimum initial investment and the minimum subsequent investments.
Increase in assets	Check whether a fund that invests in small companies isn't heading toward disappointing returns from having so much money that it has to turn to larger and slower-growing investments.	Read the prospectus for the fund assets and look for language that indicates that the fund will close to new investors if assets reach a specific level.

Table 7-11. Appraise the suitability of a mutual fund with these criteria (continued)

Criteria	Purpose	How to evaluate
Tax issues	If you plan to hold the mutual fund in a taxable account, make sure you won't lose too much of your return to taxes.	Look for below-average turnover and also compare the tax-adjusted returns to a comparable index and to the average for the fund category.
Manager tenure	Make sure that the manager who produced past returns is still in charge.	Look at the management tenure value. When the tenure is short, you can research the fund manager's previous experience at other funds.
Total return	Look for returns that beat the average consistently for the category as well as the return for a comparable index. If a fund doesn't beat the index, an index fund is a cheaper alternative.	Check the annualized total returns for the last ten years. If the fund carries a load, compare the load-adjusted returns to the category and index returns.
Expenses and fees	Fund costs can chew through returns. If the expense ratio and fees are high, make sure the fund produces enough additional return to make the cost worthwhile. But, remember that very few actively managed funds beat the index over long periods of time.	Look at the expense ratio, front and back loads, 12b-1 fee, and redemption fees.
Closet index funds	Make sure that an actively managed fund isn't charging you for returns you can get from a low-cost index fund.	Watch out for a beta equal to 1 or R-Squared greater than 90 percent (.9). Also, compare sector weightings, company size percentages, the average P/E ratio, and average EPS for similarities to the same measures for a comparable index fund.
Number of holdings	The more holdings a fund has, the less volatile it is likely to be. However, large numbers of holdings can also lead to index-like returns.	Check the number of holdings, such as stocks for a stock fund.

Hacking the Hack

You can create an Excel checklist that is as simple or fancy as you want. At the low end of the spectrum, simply build a spreadsheet with each criterion you want to evaluate. As you review a fund's measures, you can add a rating for each criterion and add up the votes to find the winner, much like NAIC's Comparison Guide does, but with the criteria you want to use. On the fancy end, you can build your own spreadsheet to download, summarize, and evaluate mutual fund data.

The spreadsheet shown in Figure 7-11 uses web queries to download data for each fund ticker you enter. Then, the summary page uses Excel reference functions, such as VLOOKUP, to assemble the key fund information on the comparison page. The cells in the rating columns include drop-down lists, so you can rate a fund as 1, 2, or 3 for the measurement. An Excel chart shows the annual returns of each fund for the past ten years. Finally, the rating cells use conditional formatting to show the winner.

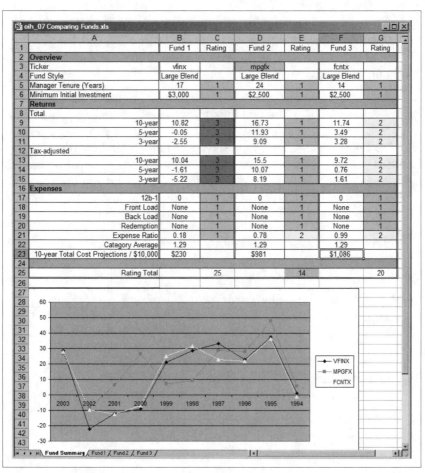

Figure 7-11. Compare all the criteria you want in your own custom comparison spreadsheet

Compare Mutual Funds Online

HACK #72

If you don't have specific criteria you use to compare funds, an online fund comparison tool might meet your needs with far less work.

Several of the most popular financial web sites offer tools that help you compare mutual funds. In addition, many mutual fund companies also provide fund comparison tools to evaluate multiple selections from their fund family or to compare their funds to those of their competitors. Of the tools evaluated here, only one comes with a subscription fee, but its features might be worth the price.

Fund Comparisons for a Fee

NAIC offers mutual fund education, a library of mutual fund investment articles, and a number of mutual fund tools [Hack #67], including mutual fund comparisons, for an annual subscription price of $60 per year ($35 a year for NAIC members). The subscription service includes a database that provides Standard & Poor's data for over 14,000 mutual funds. Comparing mutual funds begins with a Mutual Fund Checklist for each fund you want to compare. The Mutual Fund Checklist presents most of the information you need to know about a fund:

- Investment style
- Minimum purchase
- Total assets
- Portfolio composition by asset type, company size, sector, and top ten holdings
- Five-year sales and EPS growth, and P/E ratio
- Manager tenure
- Annual return for the past ten years including the relative performance to the comparable index
- Average returns for three, five, and ten years
- Tax-adjusted returns for three, five, and ten years
- Turnover rate
- Expense ratio, fees, and loads, with the average expense ratio for fund peers

> In the Cost Considerations section of the checklist, you can click the SEC Cost Calculator link to see the dollar costs of owning the fund [Hack #60].

When the checklist for a fund looks good, click Add to Comparison Guide. After you add up to three funds to the comparison guide, the results line up the essential criteria side by side in columns. You can choose a value from a drop-down list for each criterion to rank the funds. At the bottom of the table, the tool shows how many votes each fund received.

Fund Comparisons for Free

You can find tools that compare mutual funds at no cost on many web sites. Some of the tools available from mutual fund companies are very good. In most cases, you can use them without being a shareholder in the fund's products. For example, the Vanguard Group offers a comparison tool that is almost as good as a homegrown spreadsheet [Hack #71] or NAIC's subscription-based tool.

With Vanguard's tool, you can compare two funds from any fund family that is available through Vanguard's FundAccess program—most, but not all, of the fund families out there. After you select the two fund families and specify the funds to compare, the Compare Funds results show fund information side by side and also include the data for the comparable index in the third column. The comparison includes most of the information that NAIC's Mutual Fund Comparison Guide shows and delves deeper with the following information:

- Minimum initial investments for regular accounts, IRAs, Uniform Gift to Minor accounts, and the minimum additional investment amount
- Dividend reinvestment and eligibility for dollar-cost averaging
- Volatility measures, such as beta and R-Squared
- Portfolio characteristics, such as ROE and foreign holdings

You must click a link to view tax-adjusted returns.

To access the Vanguard tool, go to *http://www.vanguard.com*, click the Personal Investors link, and then select the Research Funds & Stocks tab at the top of the Personal Investors page. In the navigation bar on the left, click Compare Funds.

Morningstar.com's approach to fund comparison is a bit different. In its Fund Compare tool, you can compare the information for numerous funds by the data shown on each Morningstar mutual fund page, such as Snapshot, Performance, and Nuts & Bolts. You can rate the funds by clicking Score These Results. The results include a numerical score and a bar chart, which adjusts as you modify the weightings of the criteria. Although you can place higher or lower weighting on several criteria, the criteria that Morningstar uses are incomplete. For example, criteria for fund returns include only three- and five-year returns. You can change the criteria that the tool uses to rate the funds by clicking Customize Criteria and then adding new criteria to the list or removing existing ones. You can include up to eight different criteria, so choose wisely.

On the Morningstar home page (*http://www.morningstar.com*), click Funds in the toolbar and then click Mutual Fund Compare under the Morningstar Tools heading on the right side of the Funds page. After you add the ticker symbols for each fund you want to compare to the list, click Show Comparison.

Yahoo! Finance offers a fund comparison tool that uses some of your financial situation to evaluate funds for you. However, you can't enter ticker symbols to retrieve fund data—you must type in values, such as growth rate, loads and fees, and annual and quarterly gains. The results show your return before and after taxes, and summarize the fees and taxes you would pay. Yahoo's tool doesn't evaluate many of the criteria that identify strong consistent performers, so you might want to evaluate your funds in another tool and then enter the information for the top two contenders on the Yahoo site.

To access Yahoo's tool, go to *http://biz.yahoo.com/funds* and click Calculators under the Tools heading in the left margin. In the Comparing Different Funds list, click the "Which fund is better?" link.

CHAPTER EIGHT

Managing Your Portfolio
Hacks 73-86

Some people consider investing a hobby. However, most of us don't save and invest for the heck of it. We participate in these activities because we have goals that require money: retirement, college education, a home, a business, and recreation. As we save and invest, we build a portfolio, or two, or three, for our different goals. Portfolio management is the work you do to ensure that your portfolios are sufficient to fund your financial goals.

What Is Portfolio Management?

Portfolio management doesn't mean keeping a vigil over the prices of the stocks in your portfolio and, on spotting some unfavorable signal, calling your broker yelling, "Sell, sell, sell!" (Although there are people who live this way.) On the contrary, managing a portfolio can be a far more tranquil endeavor. Successful portfolio management starts with planning, and flourishes on regular evaluation and disciplined action.

Although every successful investor eventually develops his own approach to portfolio management, the following steps provide a framework for portfolio management:

1. Identify your financial goals: how much money you need and when.
2. Identify your tolerance for risk.
3. Identify the financial strategy you plan to use to achieve your goals: how much you will save and how often; how you will allocate your money between different types of investments.
4. Determine which investment philosophies (fundamental analysis, technical analysis, a bit of both) you will use.
5. Document the investment rules you plan to use: how much you are willing to risk; guidelines for evaluating investments; rules for when you will buy or sell.

6. Initiate your plan by creating accounts if necessary and setting up automatic deposit programs.

7. Set up reminders and alerts to notify you of important events in your holdings, such as when rules are breached and when good buy or sell prices are reached.

8. Evaluate the events that occur to determine whether they warrant action (is a buy really a buy, is a sell really a sell).

9. Regularly (monthly or quarterly) review your individual investments to see if they are meeting your expectations.

10. Regularly (annually) review your overall strategy and adjust it as needed. For example, you might adjust your allocation or reduce the risk you assume as you approach retirement.

Regardless of the approach you use, portfolio management is a balancing act. It's natural to want higher returns—they could turn a modest portfolio into a fortune, reducing the amount of money and length of time you have to save. However, higher risks of losing money typically accompany higher returns and, unfortunately, those risks can chew through hard-earned gains.

Successful fundamental and technical investors alike decide how much risk they are willing to accept. They then manage their individual investments as well as their overall portfolio to obtain the best returns they can without taking on too much risk. Balancing risk and return can be difficult, particularly when greed and fear step in. Greedy investors go for returns regardless of the risk, and when things go against them, they could lose everything. On the other hand, investors who are afraid of losing any money take such a safe route that they risk falling short of their financial goals. Smart investors manage risk to achieve higher returns while still protecting their portfolios from disastrous downturns.

Portfolio management and its risk management counterpart have two components. The first is protection. You work hard to build your portfolio, so you don't want to see it shrink. Fundamental investors protect their portfolios by watching for deterioration in the fundamental measures and business outlook of the companies they own. Technical traders use price stops to close out a trade before it loses too much. Either approach helps to prevent significant declines from jeopardizing portfolios.

The second component is continuous improvement. Look for other investments that are better than the ones you have, whether they be higher quality, lower risk, or higher return and quality for less risk. If you're pressed for time, improving your portfolio can wait. However, many corporations have made continuous improvement a part of their philosophy, because the benefits far outweigh the costs. This holds true for the individual investor: a few hours a month improving your portfolio can result in dramatically better performance.

Tracking Results

By tracking the performance of individual investments you can see whether your investments are doing the jobs you've assigned them. Tracking your overall portfolio shows you whether your portfolio management efforts are working. A well-tuned portfolio is a balance of risk [Hack #74] and return [Hack #83], which also implies the proper doses of quality [Hack #85] and diversification of several types.

As it turns out, you have a choice when it comes to calculating returns, a fact that many mutual funds take advantage of when they tout their winning records. You can learn how to calculate returns for different purposes in "Calculate Investment Return Over Different Time Periods" [Hack #81], "Forecast Future Returns" [Hack #83], "Compare Returns for Alternative Investments" [Hack #84], and "Compare Your Return to a Benchmark" [Hack #82]. However, before you head there, you must understand *internal rate of return*.

If you have previously read other investing books, you may have encountered compound annual growth rate (CAGR) [Hack #26], which also goes by the name *compound annual rate of return*. In finance circles, the technical term is *internal rate of return* (IRR), whose definition in finance textbooks is "apogees of obfuscation" (yes, exactly as helpful as this sentence). Let's try to do better.

Suppose you deposit some money in your portfolio on December 31, 1995. In addition, you contribute the money your aunt gives you for Christmas each year to the portfolio. Your initial deposit and your annual contributions are both examples of *cash flow in*. Withdrawing money from the portfolio, for example to pay for a vacation, would be a *cash flow out*. At some point in time, say December 31, 2004, you decide you want to know the return you have earned based on the portfolio's current value. The internal rate of return is the *compound annual return* you need each year to take your portfolio from the starting value, considering the cash flows in and out, to the ending value. It's the equivalent of the yield that a bank would have to pay on a savings account opened with the same starting value on the same starting date, and receiving your same annual deposits on the same dates, to equal your portfolio's value on December 31, 2004. If it helps, the internal rate of return is the equivalent of the yield (APY) that you earn on a savings account paying a fixed interest rate (APR). The spreadsheet in Figure 8-1 shows an example of cash flows over time and the resulting internal rate of return.

	A	B	C	
	oih_08 returns.xls			_ □ x
	A	B	C	
1	Initial cash flow in	-$50,000	12/31/1995	
2	Annual contribution	-$1,000	12/31/1996	
3	Annual contribution	-$1,000	12/31/1997	
4	Annual contribution	-$2,000	12/31/1998	
5	Annual contribution	-$2,000	12/31/1999	
6	Annual contribution	-$2,000	12/31/2000	
7	Annual contribution	-$3,000	12/31/2001	
8	Annual contribution	-$3,000	12/31/2002	
9	Annual contribution	-$3,000	12/31/2003	
10	Final value	$175,000	12/31/2004	
11				
12	Internal rate of return	12.77%		

Timeframes \ **XIRR** / Init Contrib

Figure 8-1. Internal rate of return calculates an annual return based on a series of cash flows and the dates on which they occur

In Figure 8-1, the final value is a positive number, which represents money flowing into your pocket. The value at the end of the period that you are evaluating is depicted as a cash flow out for the purposes of the IRR calculation—you don't actually have to withdraw that value from your portfolio.

For internal rate of return, the timing of cash flows is important; the earlier that cash flows in or cash flows out, the more it's affected by compounding. For example, an early deposit has more time to compound and grow, thereby increasing the return you earn. However, if you withdraw money from the account early, you have less money to compound for a good part of the time, which reduces your return more than withdrawing money later on.

The portfolio for this discussion could be as simple as a single stock or could be all the stocks, mutual funds, bonds, and cash you have in your retirement portfolio. As you'll learn in this chapter, determining what is a cash flow depends on what you consider a portfolio and the return you are trying to calculate.

Build an Online Portfolio

#73 Before you can use online portfolio tools to track your investments, allocate your assets, or rebalance your portfolio, you must create an online portfolio of your holdings.

To build an online portfolio, gather your most recent investment account statements. Keep this information handy in case you need to obtain specific information in a later step. If you have only a few holdings in your portfolio, it's easy to build an online portfolio by entering the ticker symbols and numbers of shares for your stocks and mutual funds. If you have a larger portfolio and track your holdings in a spreadsheet or a financial application such as Quicken, you can build your online portfolio by uploading your information.

> After you build your portfolio, manage it using tools described in "Evaluate Mutual Funds" **[Hack #65]**, "The Best Mutual Fund Screens for a Fee" **[Hack #67]**, "The Best Portfolio Management Tools for Free" **[Hack #76]**, and "The Best Portfolio Management Tools for a Fee" **[Hack #77]**.

The steps for building a portfolio at Morningstar.com (*http://www.morningstar.com*) are similar to those at most other sites, so we'll use it as an example. You must register on the web site first, but registration is free. Morningstar offers two methods for creating a portfolio. The Quick Portfolio requires only ticker symbols, shares, and basic purchase information, which is adequate for most investors and most purposes. For example, you can watch for stocks to reach target prices, and review portfolio growth and allocation. The Transaction Portfolio, on the other hand, tracks details of buys, sells, splits, dividends, and historic transactions, which provides a more accurate view of your portfolio and returns. You must decide whether it's worth your time to track this level of detail with your online portfolio. If you use a personal finance application such as Quicken or Microsoft Money, it's much easier to download this information from your brokerage accounts and manage your portfolio on your computer.

Follow these steps to create a basic portfolio at *http://www.morningstar.com*:

1. Click Portfolio on the Morningstar.com menu bar.

> To learn about portfolio features, click the View Portfolio Manager Tour link in the Portfolio Manager toolbar.

2. Click the New Portfolio link under the Portfolio Manager heading.

3. Type your portfolio name in the Please Name Your Portfolio box.

4. Select the Quick Portfolio option and click Continue.

5. If you want to receive a daily portfolio email or use alerts, leave the appropriate checkboxes checked.

6. For each holding, enter the ticker symbol. Optionally, you can enter the number of shares, the purchase price, and the commission you paid.

7. Click Save Portfolio. Morningstar displays your portfolio as shown in Figure 8-2.

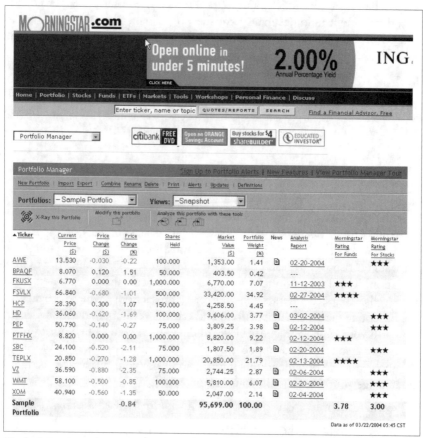

Figure 8-2. A sample portfolio at Morningstar.com

You can create different views of your portfolio data:

- To create a custom view with the columns of information you want to see for your portfolio, select My View 1 or My View 2 in the Views drop-down list. You can choose dozens of fields from several categories and add them to the view.

- Add or delete holdings at any time by clicking Modify this portfolio. You can delete holdings, add new ones, or modify the number of shares and purchase price when you add to your portfolio.

- To delete a portfolio, click Delete on the Portfolio toolbar, select the option for the portfolio you want to delete, and then click Submit.

- If you want to aggregate portfolios, for instance to show all your IRA portfolios as one, click Combine on the Portfolio toolbar. Specify the name for the combined portfolio, check the checkboxes for each portfolio you want to combine, and then click Continue.

- To analyze your portfolio allocation if you have subscribed to Morningstar's premium service, click X-Ray this Portfolio. You can also use other Morningstar tools depending on whether you subscribe to the site's premium service. Without subscribing to the premium service, you can view a portfolio X-Ray by choosing Instant X-Ray from the portfolio tool drop-down list. You must enter the ticker symbols and dollar values for your portfolio each time you want to use Instant X-Ray.

> To create a true watch list to keep an eye on stocks you want to buy if the price hits your target, create a portfolio and specify one share for each stock you want to watch. Instead of the purchase price, enter the price at which you want to buy the stock. When the gain on that stock is negative in the watch list, it means that the current price has fallen below your purchase target.

Morningstar provides several options for importing a portfolio. For example, you can import portfolio information from Quicken, Microsoft Money, as well as from portfolios built at the Quicken.com, Yahoo! Finance, MSN Money, and America Online web sites. To use tools on other web sites, such as the risk analysis features at RiskGrades.com [Hack #37], you must build a portfolio at each site. If you plan to use tools on several web sites, it's worth your time to build a comma-delimited file of your portfolio holdings, so you can upload your portfolio instead of retyping the information each time.

—Martha Sippel

HACK #74 Asset Allocation: Less Risk on the Road to Returns

Allocating your money to different types of investments can reduce your investment risk while still producing gratifying investment returns.

You've no doubt heard the real estate adage, "Location, location, location." In the financial world, asset allocation is to investing what location is to real estate, so the mantra on Wall Street is "Diversify, diversify, diversify." To invest with success, define your investment goals and then use asset allocation to achieve those goals without losing any sleep. Savvy investors don't try to keep pace with market averages or pursue trendy investment sectors. Instead, they assess the level of risk that makes sense for them, choose an asset allocation appropriate for their levels of risk and return, and stick with the plan. By focusing on the big picture, you too can work less and make better investments.

Determining Your Risk Tolerance

Time horizon, investment objectives, investment experience, and your stomach's ability to accept price volatility all influence your tolerance of risk. If you are investing to fund your retirement 30 years from now, you can afford to take more risks because you have more time to recover from temporary setbacks. However, if you want to invest the money you need to pay taxes in three months, you'd better find a safe place, because Uncle Sam won't listen to your excuses.

Beginners are better off with safer investments. Watching the ups and downs of volatile investments might make a neophyte investor second guess his decisions or decide to stop investing altogether—and that is far riskier in the long run. As you grow more confident in your investing abilities, you'll recognize short-term volatility for what it is—temporary noise that you must learn to ignore. In addition, experienced investors can differentiate between short-term volatility and investments that are heading down for the long haul. Some people can sleep at night owning volatile stocks, aggressive mutual funds, and real estate, whereas others would rather know that their principal is safe and their investments are growing at a slow but steady pace.

Although determining your risk tolerance is a little more complicated than most of the online tests indicate, you can identify your basic risk tolerance level with any of the following tools:

- Mutual Fund Investors Center has a basic Investor Personality Profile (*http://www.mfea.com/GettingStarted/LearningTopics/ UnderstandingRisk/TypeOfInvestor.asp*).

- Take Ms.Money.com's Test Your Risk Tolerance quiz (*http://www.msmoney.com/mm/investing/get_started/about_risk/risk_test.htm*).

- A discussion of investment risks and a basic two-question test is available at *http://www.msmoney.com/peoples/GenderNeutral_msmoney/html/step5/determining_your_risk_profile1.asp*. To take the test, click the What's Right for You? link in the navigation bar.

- Frank Armstrong describes risk concepts and uses graphs of different asset classes to show how some types of risk decrease over time (*http://www.fundsinteractive.com/21st/ch2.html*).

- InvestorGuide describes building a portfolio and provides explanations on asset allocation, risk, and diversification (*http://www.investorguide.com/iguinvestportfolio.html*).

Lessons from the Bear Market

During the last bull market, many investors thought that diversification within asset classes limited their potential. They didn't want to sacrifice sky-high returns for lower portfolio risk. However, by chasing those returns, these investors faced serious consequences when the market bubble broke and high-fliers, such as tech stocks, dropped by 80 percent or more.

Maintaining a diversified portfolio is much easier in a bear market when the benefits of diversification and asset allocation are obvious. By remembering what happens in a bear market, you can move money confidently to slower-growing categories when stocks are outpacing other investments and stay on track when your diversified portfolio is trailing soaring small-cap stock returns.

Managing Risk

Accumulating enough money to retire with safe savings, such as passbook accounts or certificates of deposit, is doable, but you probably won't have much fun before or after you retire. As you save and protect your money from market mayhem, inflation insidiously ravages the purchasing power of your nest egg. To retire comfortably, you must risk losing money here and there.

Truth be told, you can't avoid risk no matter how you invest your money. Even saving money in your mattress runs the risk of burning up if your house catches fire. Risk isn't inherently bad. The trick is to manage the risks you take. Don't accept higher risks unless they offer the potential for higher returns. In addition, time and portfolio diversification reduce your overall level of risk without sacrificing much in the way of investment returns.

Volatility is a short-term phenomenon. You can use measures such as beta and standard deviation [Hack #37] to evaluate the short-term risks for the investments in your portfolio. However, over longer periods of time, volatility just about disappears into the average returns. Since 1926, there have been years when large-cap stocks as a whole increased and dropped more than 40 percent in one year. However, on average large-cap stocks have returned almost 12 percent a year since then. Similarly, the price of an individual stock might bounce up and down by 20 percent in a week, while its long-term price trend grows on average at 10 percent a year. As your investment timeframe increases, the margin of safety becomes more important than volatility. Experts consider the increase they expect from an investment, as well as how much they can possibly lose. An investment offers a margin of safety when its upside potential is significantly larger than the downside.

Consider Overall Risk

When your portfolio grows large enough or you're fortunate enough to be way ahead of your game plan, you can expand your diversification into higher-risk asset classes, such as high-yield bonds [Hack #80] and real estate investment trusts [Hack #43]. However, many financial advisors recommend as a general rule of thumb that the *average* investor should allocate no more than 20 percent to alternative investments.

Asset Allocation Saves the Day

Portfolio management includes allocating your assets so their combined returns achieve your primary investment goals in a way that's comfortable for you. Asset allocation represents the distribution of portfolio assets between stocks, bonds, real estate, and cash. It is the first step toward diversifying your portfolio and uses the long-term performance of different types of investments to produce more consistent returns over time.

Asset allocation grows more complex as more investment options become available. However, it generally includes stocks for its long-term higher returns, bonds to reduce your overall risk and provide income, and a cash reserve for emergencies or to take advantage of investment opportunities.

For a rough estimate of asset allocation, many professionals recommend the following: determine the percentage of stocks in your portfolio, and subtract your age from 100. However, this guideline doesn't take into account your marital status, health, income needs, and other critical factors, so it might not be appropriate for your specific situation.

> Your asset allocation isn't cast in stone. When life events occur—marriage, divorce, children (preferably not in that order)—your financial situation changes, and you must reevaluate your asset allocation plan [Hack #75].

To see how asset allocation works, let's examine the effect of different allocations on portfolio risk. For example, people in different phases of their lives might use different levels of risk and return, as shown in Table 8-1.

Table 8-1. Scenarios for low-, medium-, and high-risk portfolios

	Retirement	College	Financial situation
Low risk 5.5 percent to 7.5 percent return	Elderly retired couple unable to tolerate losses in portfolio	Family with children in college	Family with little disposable income
Medium risk 8 to 9 percent return	Retired couple with enough assets to tolerate occasional losses	Family with children three to five years from college	Family that can save and still have money left over
High risk 9.5 percent to 10.5 percent return	Young couple saving for retirement 30 years in the future	Young couple starting a college fund at the birth of a child	Dual-income couple with no children

Online Tools for Asset Allocation

The Quicken personal finance application (starting from $49.95 at *http://www.intuit.com*) describes how asset allocation works and provides excellent examples of model portfolios. To access these tools, run Quicken on your computer and choose Investing → Asset Allocation Guide. Quicken categorizes asset classes as large-cap, small-cap, and international stocks; domestic and global bonds; and cash and money market. It also describes how to update asset classes and what your allocation should be, and provides examples of low-, medium-, and high-risk portfolios, as shown in Figure 8-3. The example portfolios address the time horizon, primary goal, risk tolerance, expected returns, and standard deviation.

If you don't own Quicken, you can obtain similar information online from Quicken.com (*http://www.quicken.com*). Register on the site for free and then click Investing in the Quicken.com menu bar. Click Portfolio on the next menu bar. If you haven't done so already, define your portfolio [Hack #73].

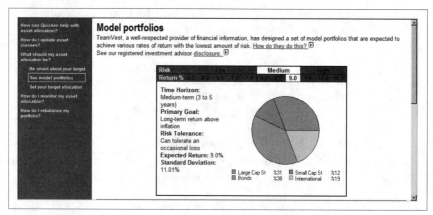

Figure 8-3. Quicken software provides examples of appropriate allocations for the level of risk you're willing to assume

Click the Asset Allocation link under the Portfolio Tools heading to view a pie chart of your portfolio allocation. Click the Model Allocation link to compare your portfolio to a model allocation and view your rate of return, risk level, standard deviation, and the amount you can expect your return to fluctuate from year to year. The Security Diversification link displays the percentage each stock represents in your portfolio and identifies investments that represent more than 10 percent of your portfolio.

SmartMoney's One Asset Allocation System (*http://www.smartmoney.com/ oneasset*) is an excellent tool for determining your ideal asset allocation. Enter your current mix of assets on the left. Use the sliders on the right to define parameters, such as how much money you will spend in the next ten years, how much you plan to leave to your heirs, how much equity you own in your home, and how high you expect inflation to be. You can switch between your current allocation and the ideal allocation. The tool suggests the amounts you should add or subtract in each asset class to reach your target allocation. SmartMoney's One Asset Allocation System also provides different sets of questions for parents and retirees.

Morningstar.com offers free and for a fee asset allocation tools. You can enter ticker symbols and dollar values with the Instant X-Ray tool to view your allocations by asset type, sector, geography, expenses, and style. With Morningstar's premium subscription ($115 per year or $12.95 per month), you can analyze a saved portfolio with the Portfolio X-Ray tool [Hack #77] and use other portfolio tools, such as Asset Allocator, Risk Analyzer, and Clear-Future. Asset Allocator helps you determine which combination of asset classes gives you the best chance of meeting your investment goals. The Portfolio Allocator provides specific ideas to rebalance your assets.

Don't Put All Your Eggs in One Basket

Diversification further modulates risk by blending a variety of investments in a portfolio, so a big drop in one holding doesn't devastate your portfolio performance. Mutual funds provide instant diversification, because they own multiple investments often distributed among large-, mid-, and small-size companies, numerous industries and sectors, and in some cases international stocks, cash, and bonds.

Isn't Your Job Enough?

Don't invest heavily in the stock of the company for which you work. Although you might be tempted to invest a significant portion of your retirement or 401(k) account in company stock, the past few years have demonstrated the dangers. If you end up out of work, you don't need the frustration of losing money in your retirement portfolio as well.

Diversification is an important factor in producing long-term results and helps weather the fluctuations of the market. So, what are your options? Table 8-2 summarizes the types of diversification you can use.

Table 8-2. Asset allocation and diversification reduce risk and provide more consistent returns

Diversification	Result
Asset type	Use a mixture of stocks, bonds, real estate, and cash. If you can't afford real estate of your own, invest in REITs [Hack #43].
Sector and industry	Protects against sectors that fall out of favor or the impact of unfavorable government regulations.
Geography	U.S. and foreign companies sometimes hit peaks and valleys at different times.
Company size	Large companies often grow slowly but more consistently. Small companies might grow quickly but can collapse just as fast.

See Also

- NETirement.com enables you to click the More Risk or Less Risk buttons to see how increasing or decreasing risk affects your asset allocations over 30 years (*http://www.netirement.com/calcs/pnaapie.htm*).

- FirstTrade enables you to select more or less risk to see how you can rebalance your portfolio (*http://www.firstrade.com/public/learning_spl_start_4.html*).

- InvestorGuide.com offers a good overview of portfolio development, asset allocation principles, and risk assessment (*http://www. investorguide.com/iguinvestportfolio.html*).

—*Martha Sippel*

Keep Allocation in Line

HACK
#75

Keeping your asset allocation on target means adjusting how much you own of each holding as investments grow or shrink.

Experts often advise investors to stay in the market for the long haul and warn that changing investments leads to losing ground. However, maintaining your target asset allocation [Hack #74] requires some changes to your investment, because markets experience ups and downs that translate into gains in some areas of your portfolio and losses in others. Realigning your portfolio to its target asset allocation at the beginning of each year mends the effects of assets performing differently. If you build a portfolio [Hack #73] in your personal finance software or at some web sites, you can use software and online tools to figure out the adjustments you need.

How Often Should I Rebalance?

Rebalancing your allocation is like going to the doctor for a physical. If you don't go regularly, your health might be in jeopardy. Likewise, if you don't review your portfolio from time to time, your asset allocation eventually becomes unbalanced, which could mean insufficient returns or unacceptable risk. If you're struggling to find New Year's resolutions, add checking your portfolio to the list. Checking your portfolio once a year is sufficient. Don't make yourself crazy or incur unnecessary commission costs because your allocations are a few percent away from their targets. If your target stock allocation is 50 percent and your portfolio stock percentage is 48 percent, relax. Let it be.

> To keep your asset allocation aligned with your goals, revisit your allocation plan periodically, particularly after significant life events such as the birth of a child or the beginning of retirement. Reassess your objectives and tolerance for risk, and revise your target asset allocation.

Suppose you have $100,000 in your portfolio and you want 60 percent in stocks and 40 percent in bonds. After one year, your stocks increase 10 percent to $66,000 while bonds increase 5 percent to $42,000. Your new allocation is 62 percent stocks and 38 percent bonds—still close to your target.

However, if stocks get to 70 percent, bonds are down to 30 percent, which might be a riskier portfolio than you had in mind. It's time to reallocate.

Here are three philosophies for rebalancing your portfolio:

Calendar rebalancing
Choose a time period (annually or semiannually) and rebalance your portfolio to your target allocation percentages at that time. Rebalancing annually keeps your transaction costs manageable. Most experts recommend evaluating your portfolio once a year.

Targeted rebalancing
Targeted rebalancing means you set a range for your asset classes and rebalance when they fall outside of that range. For example, if you have 60 percent in stocks and set a range of 5 percent, you will rebalance when the stock percentage grows to 65 percent or falls below 55 percent. This method keeps your investment mix in line, but requires more frequent monitoring and might increase transaction costs if the market is volatile.

Tactical rebalancing
Tactical rebalancing takes the market into consideration. For example, you designate stocks as 45 percent to 65 percent of your portfolio. When stocks are cheap, you move your stock percentage closer to 65 percent. If bonds comprise 35 percent to 55 percent of your portfolio, you might buy more bonds when bond prices fall. This method is time-consuming and more risky, but it is another approach.

Rebalancing Strategies

Portfolio rebalancing simply means cutting back on winners and buying more of the investments that didn't keep pace—more commonly called "buy low, sell high." However, you can choose from several approaches to bring your portfolio back into balance.

Match guidelines
When it's time to reallocate, buy and sell investments to bring your allocation back to your target percentages.

Dollar-cost average
Contribute consistent amounts on a regular basis to your portfolio and add your contributions to the assets that are below their target percentage.

Contribute money
For those investors with spare cash lying around, don't sell the high performers, but channel new cash into below-target assets. This approach

reduces transaction costs and taxes you must pay in a taxable account. If you don't have extra money to invest, consider depositing your mutual fund distributions into a money market account and using that cash to rebalance.

Reduced tax consequences

Reallocate in your tax-deferred accounts first, because you won't have to pay taxes on your gains. Sell winning funds before they make their annual distributions and buy funds after their distributions so you don't have to pay taxes on gains and dividends. If you rebalance in January, you have the rest of the year to find offsetting capital losses. For example, you can use a short-term loss in the fourth quarter to offset a long-term gain from the first quarter.

Tools to Help Rebalance Your Portfolio

Both Quicken personal finance software and the Quicken.com web site provide tools to rebalance your portfolio. In Quicken, choose Investing → Asset Allocation Guide, and then click the "How do I rebalance my portfolio?" link in the navigation bar. Quicken compares the percentages you have in each asset class to your target percentages, and tells you how much money you must add or remove to bring the allocation back into balance.

If you save your portfolio at Morningstar.com (*http://www.morningstar. com*), you can find out how much money to add or remove from each investment in your portfolio at no charge. Click Portfolio in the menu bar of the Morningstar home page. If you haven't done so already, create your portfolio [Hack #73]. Choose Portfolio Allocator from the tool drop-down list. After you agree to Morningstar's terms and conditions, you specify your target asset allocations in several ways:

Asset allocation

Specify percentages for cash, U.S. stocks, foreign stocks, bonds, and other.

Equity investment style

Specify percentages for large value, large growth, mid/small value, mid/small growth, and unclassified styles.

Sector allocation

You can choose to allocate by industry, sector, or super-sectors such as Service and Manufacturing.

Bond style

Specify the interest rate risk and credit quality you want.

If there are holdings that you don't want to touch, check their checkboxes so the Portfolio Allocator maintains those holdings and reallocates with the others. Click Results to see what changes you should make, as illustrated in Figure 8-4.

Holding Name	Suggested Mix %	Current Mix %	Increase/Decrease * Holding ($)	Increase/Decrease * Holding (shares)
Verizon Communications	0.00	2.88	-2,796.26	-75.09
PepsiCo	9.15	4.16	4,844.92	89.97
Wal-Mart Stores	3.35	6.04	-2,611.79	-44.57
ExxonMobil	3.68	2.16	1,475.81	35.21
Templeton Growth A	32.49	22.15	10,039.36	466.73
AT&T Wireless Services	8.08	1.40	6,485.78	476.20
SBC Communications	0.00	1.92	-1,864.18	-74.96
Putnam Municipal Income A	14.88	8.92	5,786.71	668.21
Home Depot	0.00	3.78	-3,670.10	-100.06
Health Care Property	3.90	4.35	-436.92	-15.52
Fidelity Select Home Finance	21.48	34.93	-13,058.94	-192.55
Franklin U.S. Government Secs A	3.00	6.89	-3,776.90	-564.56
Sample Portfolio	100.00	99.58		

* Before making changes to your portfolio, click here for important insights on the results.

[Input Goals] Save as a new portfolio

Figure 8-4. The Morningstar Portfolio Allocator tells you how much to add or remove from each of your portfolio holdings

—*Martha Sippel*

HACK #76 The Best Portfolio Management Tools for Free

Prevent unpleasant drops in your portfolio from the poor performance of one investment by analyzing and adjusting your portfolio diversification with free online portfolio management tools.

Online portfolio management tools fall into two categories: those that determine how to allocate your assets and those that analyze your current portfolio to see if it matches your asset allocation goals **[Hack #74]**. The tools that provide recommendations on asset allocation ask you questions about your goals, tolerance for risk, and the length of time until you want to withdraw your money. Some of these recommendation-oriented tools analyze your current portfolio taking into account your time horizons to suggest some allocation guidelines. With an asset allocation goal in hand, you can use other tools to see what your portfolio looks like now, whether your stock and fund holdings overlap, and your chances of achieving your goals. You can also use these tools to figure out how to rebalance your portfolio to get back on track **[Hack #75]**.

The Best Portfolio Management Tools for Free

Table 8-3 lists the best free portfolio management tools available online. Read about the best and worst features of each site and check out the extra features you can use to improve your portfolio performance.

Table 8-3. Evaluating the top portfolio diversification tools

Features	Morningstar	SmartMoney	Motley Fool	FinanCenter
Tools	Portfolio Allocator; Portfolio Manager; Instant X-Ray	Asset Allocator; Portfolio Tracker; Portfolio Map	My Portfolio; Analyzer; Allocator	What kind of investor am I? How should I allocate my current investments? How does my risk tolerance affect my portfolio? Will I reach my investment goals?
Best features	Instant X-Ray analyzes your portfolio by asset allocation, style box diversification, stock sector, stock type, fees and expenses, stock statistics, and top ten holdings.	Easy-to-use worksheet to view your current asset allocation and specify settings to define an ideal allocation. You can import existing portfolios into Portfolio Tracker. Portfolio Map provides graphical displays of diversification.	Analyzer allows you to chart each holding for multiple time periods up to ten years and compare them to four different market benchmarks.	Easy-to-use and extensive help sections explain the intent of each tool.
Worst features	Instant X-Ray requires the input of ticker symbols and dollar values each time you use it. Portfolio Allocator requires you to specify target percentages by sector and industry. Doesn't allow Mac users to import or export portfolios.	Can't integrate your portfolio with the Asset Allocator information or save your ideal allocation.	Doesn't provide tools to help you figure out initial allocations or set allocation targets.	Some questions are strange and wander into speculative-investment territory.

Table 8-3. Evaluating the top portfolio diversification tools (continued)

Features	Morningstar	SmartMoney	Motley Fool	FinanCenter
Extras	Extensive article archives on investing and diversification, and statistics and analysis for thousands of funds.	Numerous tools for all aspects of investment planning and analysis.	Tons of articles and tools on all aspects of personal finance and stock and fund investing.	Numerous calculators and planners that help with overall financial planning and plans specifically for retirement and college.

Morningstar (http://www.morningstar.com/tools)

Talk about knowing what you own—Morningstar's Instant X-Ray slices and dices your portfolio, serving up useful views of the types of assets you own and how they are deployed, as shown in Figure 8-5. (To access the Instant X-Ray, choose Instant X-Ray from the portfolio tools drop-down list. If you choose the X-Ray this Portfolio link on the Portfolio menu bar, the Premium membership page appears, because X-raying a saved portfolio is a premium feature.) Many investors don't have a clue how much they pay to own mutual funds, so Morningstar's Fees & Expenses section reports how much you're paying and compares your costs to category averages, so you can decide whether to find lower-cost funds. Use Stock Intersection to see whether any of your funds hold positions in individual stocks you own. The Portfolio Allocator tool [Hack #75] can suggest how to rebalance your portfolio, but you must first specify target allocations by type of asset, investment style, and company size, and allocation by sectors or industries—which are more decisions than most people want to make.

SmartMoney (http://www.smartmoney.com/tools)

SmartMoney's One Asset Allocation System helps you determine your ideal asset allocation. Enter your current dollar amounts for investments in cash, bonds, small caps, large caps, and international stocks on the left. Use the sliders on the right to define parameters, such as your years to retirement, the money you want to leave to heirs, the equity in your home, your tolerance for volatility, and your view of the economic outlook. You can view a pie chart of your current allocation and select Ideal Allocation to see what SmartMoney recommends. SmartMoney suggests amounts you should add and subtract in each asset class to reallocate your assets to a more appropriate allocation model. You can also use special versions of the One Asset Allocation System if you are a parent or retired.

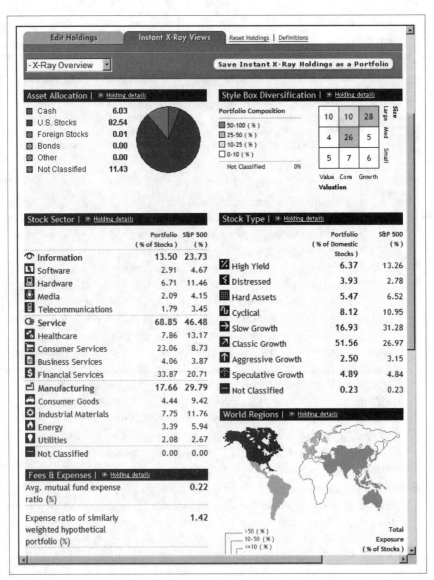

Figure 8-5. Morningstar's X-Ray Overview shows portfolio diversification from every angle

The Motley Fool (http://www.fool.com)

After you create a portfolio on the Motley Fool web site, access your portfolio by clicking My Portfolio in the top toolbar. Click Analyzer in the Portfolio toolbar to view price histories for individual holdings with index comparisons for periods from three months to five years. Click Allocation to see pie charts of your portfolio by ticker symbol, sector, or asset class. Although short-term price changes aren't something to focus on [Hack #79], you can see whether you gained or lost money the day before.

FinanCenter (http://www.financenter.com/products/planners)

The only site on the list that doesn't work with a stored portfolio, FinanCenter nonetheless offers worthwhile tools that help you assemble the nuts and bolts of portfolio diversification and asset allocation. If you're a newbie to the world of asset allocation, start with the "What kind of investor am I?" tool to figure out your risk profile. From there, you can move into "How should I allocate my current portfolio?" to see where you are and get suggestions of what to do. It's best to have at least a rough idea of where your money is now so that you can obtain meaningful results. The most valuable tool is "Will I reach my investment goals?," which tells you whether you have a chance of reaching a particular retirement, college savings, or overall goal, based on your current situation.

Standard & Poor's (http://fc.standardandpoors.com/htdocs/corp_v2/calculators_edups.html)

The Standard & Poor's Financial Communications tools warrant a brief mention. Two asset allocation calculators list questions that you answer easily by selecting options.

Entering your portfolio at a new web site can be a major pain when you're getting started with portfolio diversification tools. In addition, you must keep your portfolio up to date to obtain meaningful feedback. Spend some time determining which site you want to use before you enter portfolio information, or you'll end up with portfolios scattered all over the Web. If you want to analyze your portfolio taking into account all your transactions, including dividends paid, choose a web site that enables you to import portfolios, such as Morningstar or SmartMoney.

HACK #77 The Best Portfolio Management Tools for a Fee

Free tools cover the basics, but you can conduct an in-depth examination of your portfolio with these for-fee portfolio management tools.

What starts out as a reasonably well-diversified portfolio can become a mish-mash of mutual funds, stocks, and bonds that won't help you meet your goals. Although free management tools offer tremendous features [Hack #76], more sophisticated tools can offer more detail to help you decide what to do.

For many investors, digging up details doesn't mean parting with additional cash. Many fund companies and brokerages provide strong portfolio management tools for their clients. The fees are included already in the expense ratios, brokerage commissions, and other fees you're currently paying. Table 8-4 profiles the tools available at three of the largest and most popular fund companies and brokers: Vanguard (*http://www.vanguard.com*), Fidelity (*http://www.fidelity.com*), and Charles Schwab (*http://www.schwab.com*). It's particularly convenient to work with portfolio management tools when your broker or fund company provides your portfolio information online.

Many sites enable you to enter or import data from other accounts, so you can use one site's analysis tools for your entire portfolio, even if your funds are with a fund company and your stocks with a broker. If you use a broker or fund company other than the ones in this hack, check its web site for portfolio management tools.

Table 8-4. Portfolio allocation tools from top brokerages and fund companies

Features	Vanguard	Fidelity	Charles Schwab
Types of tools	Asset allocation and goal setting; analysis of fees, taxes and management risk; portfolio analysis.	Goal setting and portfolio review; retirement and college planning.	Goal setting, retirement, and college planning tools.
Unique tools	The Risk/Return Allocator shows how the asset classes in which you're invested have performed over a 40-year period.	Retirement Income Planner helps you match assets and investments to your post-retirement income needs.	Goal planning helps you figure out how much you need to invest on an ongoing basis to meet your goals.
Fee add-ons	Offers financial planning and ongoing asset management services; some tools are free to clients with assets in excess of $100,000.	Ongoing advice and portfolio management fees range from 0.25 to 1.1 percent plus fund fees.	Portfolio review for $350; portfolio consultation for $650–$900; creation of personal financial plan for about $3,000; ongoing advice and portfolio management for .75 percent of assets plus fund fees.

If your broker doesn't offer management tools or you want more features, look to personal finance sites, such as Morningstar, MSN Money, and Motley Fool. You have to pay, but each site offers extras and goodies that might be worth the price, as outlined in Table 8-5. Look for free trials—Morningstar usually offers a free two-week trial for premium membership and the Motley Fool occasionally offers free 30-day trials.

Table 8-5. Portfolio management tools that come with a price

Features	Morningstar	MSN Money	The Motley Fool
Tools	X-Ray; Asset Allocator; Risk Analyzer; ClearFuture; Most Similar Funds.	Portfolio Manager	The Motley Fool Advisor
Best feature	Risk Analyzer shows how your portfolio would perform in a bear market.	Can import data from financial institutions so that you don't have to input your portfolio.	Advice is personalized. You can play with different scenarios to see how they affect your savings and investment goals.
Worst feature	Doesn't allow Mac users to import or export portfolios.	Must buy all of MSN Premium's features to get the financial features; broadband access not available in some areas.	Planning tool misses some key issues like asking for your current college savings balance and doesn't account for employer contributions to retirement plans.

Morningstar (http://www.morningstar.com/Cover/Tools.html)

Cost: $12.95 a month; $115 a year; $199 for two years

Subscribers get more in-depth asset allocation information than free members. X-ray a saved portfolio with X-Ray this Portfolio. Use Asset Allocator to see the probability of reaching your goals. Risk Analyzer shows how much each holding in your portfolio might gain or lose in a bear market and whether adding to that holding would increase or decrease risk. ClearFuture is an online retirement and 401(k) planning tool that helps you set realistic goals and define a plan to reach them. Morningstar has a lot of other goodies for premium members, including premium stock and fund screeners, a fund cost analyzer, trade cost analyzer, investment analysts' commentary on 1,000 stocks, more than 3,000 funds plus additional stock and fund data, articles, and commentary.

MSN Money (http://money.msn.com/home.asp)

Cost: $9.95 a month

MSN Money helps you determine an appropriate asset allocation and plan for college, retirement, and other long-term goals. Portfolio Manager gives you an in-depth look at your asset allocation and portfolio. You can interface with subscriber-only online tools to find new investment ideas and improve your portfolio. Track your current investments and stay up to date with investing news and commentary. Subscribers get numerous noninvesting extras, including a firewall, MSN parental controls, bill payer, project planner, and budget tracker.

The Motley Fool Advisor (http://www.fool.com/ma)
   Cost: $199 a year

   Once you enter your goals and financial information, the Motley Fool
   Advisor creates a complete financial plan with personalized asset allocation based on your goals and current financial situation. It also suggests
   rebalancing and fund selection, and generates a report that tells you
   whether you can meet your goals. After you input more detailed data,
   you get an in-depth report that suggests ways you can save more money
   and reallocate your assets to meet your short- and long-term goals. You
   can update your information as it changes. In addition, the plan offers
   phone consultations with live planners and access to the Fool's semi-
   nars on various financial and investing topics.

Personal Finance Software and the Web

Web add-ons for Quicken and Microsoft Money make these software packages great deals. With Quicken, you can upload your Quicken account data
to the Quicken web site (*http://www.quicken.com*) and download data from
your financial service providers. If you enter portfolio transactions on the
Web, you can download them into Quicken on your computer later. You can
also pay bills online and update the prices in your portfolios from the Web.
Microsoft Money offers the same features.

Portfolio Record Keeper, offered by Quantix Software (*http://www.
quantixsoftware.com*), is designed exclusively for tracking your investments.
It offers in-depth asset allocation reports for your stock, bond, and fund portfolios, and enables you to classify your assets by detailed investment objective
categories. You can download stock, bond, and fund prices to update your
portfolio, and create links to your favorite investment and personal finance
web sites.

HACK #78 Portfolio Management with Excel

A spreadsheet is a great aid for deciding what steps you need to take to
manage your portfolio.

Spreadsheets come in handy for all sorts of investment activities, but it can
take time to build all the features you want and make them work properly. If
you're looking for a spreadsheet to help manage your portfolio or just looking for ideas, Jim Thomas (read about him in the Contributors section) has a
spreadsheet you might like. In addition to slicing and dicing a portfolio of
stocks from every direction, several worksheets include checklists of questions to ask and steps to take depending on how you answer the questions.

Download this portfolio management spreadsheet at *http://www.bivio.com/ irw/files/Public%20Files/ToolKit4/TK4Portfolio.xls*. The spreadsheet is designed to use fundamental analysis results stored in an Investors' Toolkit database [Hack #38]. However, you can open the spreadsheet and review the results for a sample portfolio without the Investors' Toolkit software loaded on your computer.

> If you use Investors' Toolkit and want to use this spreadsheet to evaluate your portfolio, click Locate Toolkit Database on the Diversification worksheet, and specify the path and filename for the database you want to use in the Locate a Toolkit 4 Database dialog box. When the portfolios in your database appear in the Toolkit Portfolio Name list, select the portfolio you want.

Here are some of the portfolio management features in this tool:

Diversification worksheet
> This worksheet shows portfolio diversification by company size and by sector. It also shows the projected diversification five years in the future if the companies in the portfolio grow as you expect them to. The worksheet lists each of the stocks in the portfolio along with a quality rank, a projected return (called RPAR for Projected Annual Return), and your estimate of future sales growth. The Projected Portfolio 5 Yr Compound Price Appreciation is the annual compound growth rate for the entire portfolio, which is a great way to see if your overall portfolio meets your growth objectives.

Charts worksheet
> For visually oriented investors, the Charts worksheet contains pie charts of diversification by company size, sector, current value of stocks, and five-year future value for stocks.

PERT Defense worksheet
> PERT stands for Portfolio Evaluation and Review Technique. The PERT Defense worksheet shows current growth rates for sales, EPS, and pre-tax profit, and your estimated future growth rates for sales and EPS. If the current growth rates are less than your estimated rates, the stock might not deliver the performance you want. The worksheet calls attention to these values by highlighting the below-expectation growth rates in pink, as shown in Figure 8-6 in "Flag Fundamental Sell Signals" [Hack #86].

> If many of the growth rates for many of the stocks are pink,
> look for overall economic or market issues. When short-term
> issues drag the entire market down, it's better to wait it out
> or buy more if prices are low.

PERT-A

This worksheet displays values for trailing 12-month sales, pre-tax profit, and EPS growth, and graphs those values in charts as shown in Figure 8-6. By graphing growth rate in the Y-axis and time in the X-axis, trends in growth rates are easy to spot. For example, sales, EPS, and pre-tax profit growth rates have all been falling for the past 12 quarters.

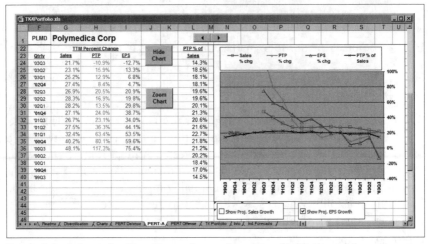

Figure 8-6. A chart of trailing 12-month growth rates can highlight growth trends

PERT Offense worksheet

Improving your portfolio means looking for stocks with higher quality and higher returns, or those that aren't delivering the performance you want. This worksheet highlights good and bad values. For example, growth rates that are below your minimum acceptable growth rate are highlighted in yellow, represented with gray shading in Figure 8-7. Stocks whose risk ratios are excessively high or low are highlighted in pink. Relative values that are too high or too low are highlighted in yellow. Stock prices are highlighted in green if the price provides an acceptable total return and the risk level is below your maximum. If you want to revise the highlighting criteria to match your guidelines, simply change the value in the Highlight If table at the top of the worksheet.

—Portfolio management spreadsheet developed by Jim Thomas

TK4Portfolio.xls												_ □ x
	B	C	D	E	F	G	H	I	J	K	L	
1	Toolkit Portfolio Name		Portfolio Management Workshop									
2	BB Owned											
3	Financial											
4	Healthcare			HIGHLIGHT IF ...				BUY REQUIREMENTS				
5	Sample / StockStudyHandbook		below	14.9%	5%	80		14.9%	min. 5yr Total Return			
6			or above		50%	150		25%	max. Risk Ratio			
7												
8												
9				Z	Y	R		Q	AB	W X	V	
10	Shares	Name	Ticker	5yr Total Return	Risk Ratio	Future Relative Value	Buy Below	Current Price	Hi Price	PEG	Proj. EPS Growth Rate	
11	700.0	Lincare Holdings	LNCR	34.0%	2%	62.7	$55.3	$31.25	$135.0	0.63	20.0%	
12	750.0	SYNOVUS FINANCIAL CP	SNV	20.6%	26%	83.8	$24.9	$25.14	$57.5	1.32	13.0%	
13	600.0	LOWES COS	LOW	17.8%	20%	108.0	$61.6	$57.10	$128.1	1.20	18.0%	
14	400.0	SUNGARD DATA SYSTEMS	SDS	16.6%	29%	102.7	$26.0	$27.78	$59.9	1.31	16.0%	
15	500.0	HOME DEPOT INC	HD	9.3%	51%	125.7	$24.0	$32.74	$49.4	2.05	9.2%	
16		Overall Portfolio:		21.4%	18%	96.2						

Readme / Diversification / Charts / PERT Defense / PERT-A / **PERT Offense** / TK Portfolio / Info

Figure 8-7. Highlighted cells indicate high risk, low quality, or prices that are too high or too low

Take the Sting Out of Portfolio Management

HACK #79

Buying stocks can be fun, but managing your portfolio can seem like drudgery unless you automate recurring tasks.

Contrary to what many think, managing a portfolio is neither tracking the performance of your holdings nor selling stocks whose prices have declined, languished, or increased to some target price. Tracking performance is merely measuring how well or poorly you *have* managed your portfolio. Selling stocks based on price performance alone is actually mismanaging your portfolio. The notion of managing your portfolio can seem daunting, especially because many people think that portfolio management means staying on top of the market at all times and religiously watching the price performance of your stocks. As a long-term fundamental investor, however, managing your portfolio is the proactive art of playing defense—protecting your portfolio from harm—as well as playing offense to enhance your portfolio's performance. Surprisingly enough, with a bit of organization and the help of your computer, the task is much less demanding than you might think, requiring only a few minutes of work several times a year. This hack shows you how to accomplish your essential portfolio management tasks in a minimum amount of time.

Playing Defense

The long-term fundamental investor looks for growth of sales, profits, and earnings per share, because a company's ability to grow its earnings eventually increases its stock price and, in turn, the value of an investment in the stock. It stands to reason, therefore, that the primary chore in defensive portfolio management is to watch for deterioration in the growth of sales, profits, and earnings, so that a significant decline doesn't jeopardize the investment.

Watching growth does not mean watching a stock's price. Over the long term, stock price should follow the growth of earnings; but in the short term, minute-to-minute, hour-to-hour, day-to-day, it can fluctuate as much as 50 percent above and below its average price. Stock price might languish because the stock is out of favor for reasons other than the health of its fundamentals but, in these situations, the price bounces back eventually to reflect those all-important earnings.

What's more, the price of a stock is a reflection of what other people think the stock is worth, but they are often wrong! Refrain from throwing away good-quality companies just because others lose faith in them or overreact to short-term situations.

Now that you're liberated from worrying about daily prices, you can focus on stock fundamentals and enjoy relatively carefree portfolio maintenance— you only need to monitor the growth of sales, profits, and earnings, which companies report only four times each year. You don't have to play defense every day, week, or month. Your work is already reduced, because you can be completely conscientious simply by checking each stock quarterly!

A typical portfolio for a long-term investor contains between 10 and 25 stocks. Of these, about two thirds end their fiscal year on the last day of the calendar year. This means that the bulk of your defense is played in four months of the year—March, April, July, and October. Retailers end their fiscal years typically at the end of January so that they can include the holiday activity in their annual reports. For these companies, you play defense in April, May, August, and November. You might have a few companies that report earnings in the other months of the year, but you will likely have those months off.

Because the SEC gives companies extra time to report their fourth quarter and annual data, your defensive tasks are not evenly distributed throughout the year.

The trick to taking the pain out of playing defense is to organize the companies you own by their fiscal year end dates and schedule your defensive work so you don't worry about it until it's time. You can use Excel to create a portfolio database containing the names, ticker symbols, and fiscal year end dates for each of the stocks in your portfolio, as shown in Figure 8-8. In Excel, it's easy to calculate the quarterly reporting dates for each company from the fiscal year end date and flag the next date that you should check a company's fundamentals. To simplify even more, you can use Excel functions to evaluate the upcoming reporting dates for all the companies you own and tell you the next day you have a portfolio management task.

oih_08 portfolio mgt.xls							
	A	B	C	D	E	F	G	H

	A	B	C	D	E	F	G	H
1	**Earnings Reporting Schedule**							
2				As of:	2/18/04		Next Date	3/29/04
3								
4	Company	Ticker	FYE	1st Qtr.	2nd Qtr.	3rd Qtr.	4th Qtr.	Next Rep
5	Aflac	AFL	12/30/02	5/14/03	8/14/03	11/14/03	3/29/04	03/29/04
6	Amgen	AMGN	12/31/02	5/15/03	8/14/03	11/14/03	3/30/04	03/30/04
7	Cisco	CSCO	1/1/03	5/16/03	8/15/03	11/15/03	3/31/04	03/31/04
8	General Electric	GE	12/31/02	5/15/03	8/14/03	11/14/03	3/30/04	03/30/04
9	Harley Davidson	HDI	12/31/02	5/15/03	8/14/03	11/14/03	3/30/04	03/30/04
10	Home Depot	HD	2/2/03	6/16/03	9/16/03	12/17/03	5/2/04	05/02/04
11	Intel	INTC	12/31/02	5/15/03	8/14/03	11/14/03	3/30/04	03/30/04
12	Johnson & Johnson	JNJ	12/31/02	5/15/03	8/14/03	11/14/03	3/30/04	03/30/04
13	Merck	MRK	12/31/02	5/15/03	8/14/03	11/14/03	3/30/04	03/30/04
14	Microsoft	MSFT	6/30/03	11/14/03	2/13/04	5/14/04	9/28/04	05/14/04
15	Oracle	ORCL	5/31/03	10/15/03	1/14/04	4/14/04	8/29/04	04/14/04
16	Pepsico, Inc.	PEP	12/31/02	5/15/03	8/14/03	11/14/03	3/30/04	03/30/04
17	Pfizer	PFE	12/31/02	5/15/03	8/14/03	11/14/03	3/30/04	03/30/04
18	Walgreen's	WAG	8/31/03	1/14/04	4/14/04	7/15/04	11/29/04	04/14/04
19	Wal-Mart	WMT	1/31/03	6/14/03	9/14/03	12/15/03	4/30/04	04/30/04

Sheet1 \ Sheet2 / Sheet3 /

Figure 8-8. Flag the next date you should check the fundamentals for each stock you own

The only information you must provide is the company name in column A; the ticker symbol in column B; and the date on which the company's *last* full fiscal year ended in column C. Format the cells for the year end date as *m/d/yy*. For the ultimate in easy updates, you can specify the ticker symbol and then use Excel web queries to download the company name and fiscal year end [Hack #7].

Companies must report financial results to the SEC within 45 days of the end of each quarter except the fourth quarter, for which the SEC generously allows them 90 days to report full year performance. To calculate the quarterly reporting dates based on the fiscal year end date, use Excel's EDATE function, which returns a date a number of months after the date you specify.

EDATE belongs to the Analysis Toolpak add-in. If EDATE isn't available on your computer, choose Tools → Add-Ins. Check the Analysis ToolPak checkbox, and then click OK.

To calculate each quarterly reporting date, you add three more months to the end of the fiscal year. For example, you add three months to the fiscal year end date for the first quarter, six months for the second quarter, nine months for the third quarter, and twelve months for the fourth quarter. In addition, for the first three quarters of the year, you add 45 to the EDATE result, because most companies submit their quarterly reports on the SEC deadline date. For the fourth quarter, you add 90 to reflect the additional days that the SEC allows for reporting annual data. Fill in the columns for the four quarters, as shown in Example 8-1.

Example 8-1. Use EDATE to calculate quarterly reporting dates

```
1st Qtr (D5) = EDATE(C5,3)+45
2nd Qtr (E5) = EDATE(C5,6)+45
3rd Qtr (F5) = EDATE(C5,9)+45
4th Qtr (G5) = EDATE(C5,12)+90
```

In Example 8-1, C5 is the cell that contains the fiscal year end for the company. You can select the formulas in columns D through H in the row for the first company and copy them to as many rows as you need. Because Excel uses relative cell references, the formulas in each row refer to the fiscal year end cell in that row.

To calculate the next quarterly reporting date for a company, use a combination of Excel functions. The formula in Example 8-2 returns the earliest quarterly reporting date after today by using a combination of Excel functions in an array formula that evaluates each quarterly reporting date for a company.

Example 8-2. The Excel formula for finding the earliest reporting date after today

```
Next Reporting Date = {MIN(IF(NOW( )<D5:G5,D5:G5))}
```

The formula in Example 8-2 is an array formula (indicated by the brackets at each end), which you create by pressing Shift-Ctrl-Enter after you finish typing the formula in the Excel formula bar. By defining the Next Reporting Date formula as an array formula, Excel applies the functions iteratively for each cell in the formula array. The formula in Example 8-2 is the equivalent of performing each of the calculations in Example 8-3.

Example 8-3. An array formula iterates through the cells in a formula array

```
IF(NOW( )<D5,D5)
IF(NOW( )<E5,E5)
IF(NOW( )<F5,F5)
IF(NOW( )<G5,G5)
```

Here's how the overall formula works. Before you can find reporting dates in the future, you need today's date for comparison, which Excel returns from the NOW function. The NOW function doesn't require any arguments—just include empty parentheses. By omitting the third argument to the IF function in Example 8-2, the IF clause returns False when a reporting date is earlier than the current date. The MIN function ignores non-numeric values including False, and therefore evaluates only future reporting dates for the company and returns the earliest one.

You can apply conditional formatting [Hack #8] to help you quickly locate upcoming reporting dates. For example, by following these steps, you can italicize and shade the dates that have already passed:

1. Select the reporting date cells (D5:G5 in this example).

2. Choose Format → Conditional Formatting.

3. For the first condition, select Cell Value in the first drop-down list, "Is less than" for the condition test in the second drop-down list, and then type =NOW( ) for the comparison value in the third field.

4. Click Format and set the font format to Italic.

5. Select the Patterns tab and select the lightest shade of gray to shade all the cells with reporting dates that have passed.

The final step for a company entry is to add hyperlinks in the cells containing the ticker symbol and name to simplify access to the information that you use for portfolio management on your favorite investing web site. One of the best sites for this purpose is the Reuters Investor web site (*http://www. investor.reuters.com*), which provides the latest quarterly income statement. Another good source for earnings reports is *http://TheStreet.ccbn.com*. Regardless of the web site you choose, the mechanics of adding a hyperlink to a cell are the same. To add a hyperlink to a cell, follow these steps, replacing the URL for the Reuters site in the steps with the web site you choose.

 To use the Reuters Investor web site, register as a member, which is free of charge.

1. In your browser, navigate to the web site you want to use, such as *http:// www.investor.reuters.com*. Type the ticker symbol for the company in the Stock Quotes box, and click Go. Click Financial Statements in the navigation bar on the left to view five quarters of quarterly income statements for the company.

2. Select the URL that appears in the Address box in your browser, and press Ctrl-C to copy that address to the Clipboard. For example, using

AFL as the ticker and the Reuters web site, the URL is *http://www. investor.reuters.com/IS.aspx?ticker=AFL&target=_stocks_financialinfo_ statements_incomestatement_quarterly.*

3. Back in your spreadsheet, right-click the cell with the company ticker symbol and choose Hyperlink from the shortcut menu. If the URL doesn't appear automatically in the Insert Hyperlink dialog box, click the Address box in the dialog box and press Ctrl-V to paste the URL from the Clipboard. Click OK to create the hyperlink.

4. To follow the hyperlink in the cell, simply click the cell.

> When a cell contains a hyperlink and you want to select the cell instead of following the hyperlink, click and hold the mouse button down until the pointer changes to a plus sign.

5. To add another hyperlink for a company, repeat Steps 1 through 4 using a different cell in the spreadsheet.

> When the URL conforms to a fixed format, you can define the URL using the Excel HYPERLINK function and reference the cell that contains the ticker symbol within the formula.

To add additional rows to the spreadsheet to track more companies, select the cells in columns A through H, A5:H5 in the example. A small black square appears at the lower right corner of the selection, as illustrated in Figure 8-9. The pointer changes to a plus sign when you position the pointer over this copy handle. Drag the copy handle down as many rows as you have new companies to add. If you use the Hyperlink function with a ticker symbol cell reference, copy the formula to the other cells. If you use Insert Hyperlink to create a hyperlink, follow these steps to modify cells to show another company:

1. Type the name of the new company, its ticker symbol, and its fiscal year end date in the cells in columns A, B, and C, respectively.

2. Right-click the cell in a new row that contains a hyperlink and choose Edit Hyperlink from the shortcut menu.

3. In the Address box, locate the ticker symbol of the previous company embedded in the address (AFL in this example), and change it to the ticker symbol for the new company, as shown in Figure 8-9.

Finally, you can add today's date as a reference and include a calculation that reminds you of the date for your next defensive portfolio task. To show today's date, type =NOW( ) in cell D2. To add the next defensive action date, type the formula in Example 8-4 in cell H2 in this example.

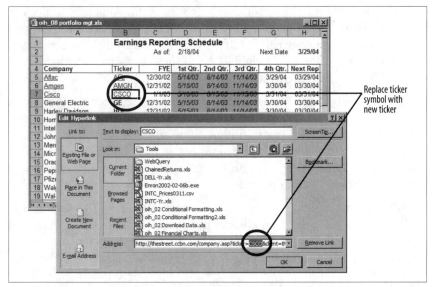

Figure 8-9. Edit a hyperlink to use the new company ticker symbol

Example 8-4. Excel formula to report next portfolio management date

```
Next date = MIN(H5:H50)
```

Now, you can open this spreadsheet once a week or once a month, and review the dates in column H to see if you have portfolio management actions to perform. You can also add these dates to your calendar. To see all the companies that you should evaluate on the same date, sort the spreadsheet by the next reporting dates in column H by following these steps:

1. Drag across the row headers to select the row that contains your column headings and all the company rows, rows 4 through 19 in the example.

2. Choose Date → Sort.

3. In the Sort dialog box, select the Header Row option and then, in the Sort By drop-down list, select Next Rep or the label you use for the column that contains the next reporting date for companies.

4. If necessary, select the Ascending option, and then click OK.

Playing Offense to Increase Returns and Reduce Risk

Offensive strategy is considerably different from defense. It's far less urgent and the consequences of neglecting it less dire. Offensive portfolio management doesn't require a schedule. In fact, you can perform it at any time. Unlike defensive strategy, which evaluates fundamentals, not price, offensive strategy considers the price, but only if it's too high. Although you're not likely to lose money on good quality stocks whose prices are too high, you won't make much money either. Offensive strategy identifies the companies you own whose prices have been bid up so high that your potential return doesn't meet your requirements.

The easiest way to spot overvalued companies is to look for companies whose rational values [Hack #36] are substantially below their current values. When investors currently place far more value on a company than it is really worth, the potential for additional return is small. In addition, the added risk of the price and P/E ratio declining to the company's rational value makes the stock a candidate to sell.

When you find significantly overvalued companies in your portfolio and decide to sell, you can use the hacks in Chapter 1 to screen for potential replacements, and then apply the hacks in Chapter 4 to find a company of equal or better quality, but with a greater potential for return.

HACK #80   Use Bonds in a Portfolio

Bonds are a great way to reduce risk and provide income—as long as you use them correctly.

Almost any investment plan can benefit from bonds, but many investors don't understand them, thinking they're boring income investments, and therefore shun this important class of assets. Some income investors view bonds as the ultimate in safety, which they aren't, and therefore accept risks they aren't even aware of. By learning what you should do with bonds in your portfolio, you can reduce your overall portfolio risk, earn current income, and obtain capital gains.

Understanding Bonds

We all know that when someone lends money to someone else, that transaction is called a loan, and the amount lent is called the *principal*. The lender charges interest on the amount of the loan. Over time, the borrower pays back the principal and the interest. If you understand this, you at least know what a bond is, because it's nothing more than a loan to a borrower, who happens to be a corporation or government entity.

When you buy a bond, you lend the borrower money for a specific duration, known as the *maturity* of the bond. The borrower pays you interest (the *coupon rate*) on the borrowed money until the bond matures (reaches the end of its duration), at which point the borrower also pays back the principal. Pretty easy, huh?

Some investors think of bonds as certificates of deposit (CDs) that pay higher interest rates. However, bonds pay higher interest rates because they carry more risk than CDs. Most of the time, bondholders receive their interest payments and their principal without mishap. Sometimes, the company or the government runs into trouble and defaults on the bond, which means you lose most if not all of your investment.

Interest rate risk is also a consideration. The value of bonds fluctuates in inverse proportion to market interest rates. As market interest rates increase, the value of an already-issued bond at a set interest rate drops, because the new market rates are more attractive. Conversely, if market interest rates drop, an existing bond at a higher rate is more attractive so its price increases. If you have to sell a bond before maturity, you might receive less than you paid for the bond if interest rates have increased.

You can take advantage of falling interest rates to earn capital gains with bonds. More about this in the later section, "Putting Bonds to Work."

Bonds Versus Bond Funds

Sure, bond funds are made up of bonds, but they don't work in the same way. Bondholders of individual bonds can hold onto their bonds if it's a bad time to sell. However, bond funds buy and sell as fund investors purchase or redeem their fund shares or when bonds mature. Interest rates play a much larger role in the returns that bond fund investors receive than in the returns of those who buy individual bonds. Table 8-6 summarizes the reasons you might choose bonds or bond funds.

Table 8-6. The benefits of bonds and bond funds

Bonds	Bond funds
Buy bonds and hold to maturity so you won't lose money.	Invest small amounts of money and set up regular contribution schedules.
Commissions to buy new-issue bonds are lower than mutual fund expenses.	Reinvest dividends into the fund.
Buy bonds that mature when you want to withdraw your money.	If your timeframe isn't fixed, you can access your money with less risk than selling a bond before its maturity date.
	Make a profit on bond prices when rates fall.
	Funds diversify bond investments, which is important for lower-quality, higher-yield bonds.

Putting Bonds to Work

Bonds might be right for you if you answer yes to any of the following questions:

Do you want to reduce the overall risk of your portfolio? Although bond prices sometimes drop at the same time that stocks do, their declines are usually less traumatic. In addition, if you hold a bond to maturity, you receive the coupon rate for the bond. By purchasing top-quality bonds such as Treasury bonds or AAA-rated corporate or municipal bonds and holding them to maturity, you won't lose money.

Do you want to protect money you've saved for a goal in the next few years? Bonds don't provide as high a return as stocks over long time-frames. However, when a savings goal looms, you want to keep your savings safe without sacrificing your purchasing power to inflation. Purchase bonds that mature when you'll need the money.

Do you want steady income to live on? Most bonds pay interest on a regular schedule, so you can obtain income by investing in bonds. However, the lower returns that bonds pay compared to stocks over the long term means that you probably can't afford an entire portfolio of bonds. Instead, combine bond income with mutual fund distributions and, if necessary, small withdrawals of your portfolio principal to pay the bills.

> Although longer-term bonds pay the highest interest rates, short-term and intermediate-term bonds are better for an income-producing ladder **[Hack #100]**. Intermediate-term bonds often pay rates quite close to those of long-term bonds, but your risk of a loss if you have to sell before maturity is much lower.

Are interest rates high and do you want to earn capital gains from your bonds? Falling interest rates are the flip side of interest rate risk. Because bond prices increase when interest rates fall, you can buy bonds when market interest rates are higher than average and sell the bonds for more than you paid for them when rates fall. Investing in bonds for capital gains is far riskier than buying bonds to hold until maturity. Don't consider investments such as these as part of the bond percentage in your asset allocation plan.

HACK #81   Calculate Investment Return Over Different Time Periods

By calculating the compound annual return you earned over different lengths of time, you can determine your portfolio performance.

If you own mutual funds, you're probably familiar with returns calculated for different periods. Mutual funds typically publish their returns [Hack #63] for the most recent one-year, three-year, five-year, and ten-year compound annual returns, and will publish their compound annual return since the inception of the fund if it has existed for longer than ten years. For mutual funds, the long-term returns are more important, because funds can run hot and cold in shorter periods. Individual investors and investment clubs can also use compound annual return calculations to see how they're doing. However, you must understand internal rate of return calculations to evaluate your performance in a meaningful way.

Using Internal Rate of Return to Calculate Performance

For mutual funds or your portfolio, long-term performance is usually more revealing than short-term returns. Long-term results can indicate how well an investment or portfolio performs through good times and bad. Although long-term performance still does not guarantee future results, you can forecast similar returns for the future with more confidence. On the other hand, short-term performance can be misleading, and the distortion increases as the timeframe shortens.

The compound annual returns you want to calculate are also known as the internal rate of return, which is described in the introduction to this chapter. It takes some time to adjust to internal rate of return, so if you haven't read the introduction, now's the time to do so. The calculation of internal rate of return takes into account any cash that you contribute to or withdraw from a portfolio, and when those cash flows occur. The first step is to determine what is a cash flow for this type of calculation.

Suppose you have a portfolio that you seeded with $10,000 five years ago, and you have conscientiously deposited your birthday money every year since. In this scenario, your first *cash flow in* is the $10,000 that you deposited. The annual birthday deposits are also cash flows in. If you withdrew any money from the account, each withdrawal would be a *cash flow out*.

Now, how about the stock dividends that you receive and reinvest in more shares of stock? Reinvested dividends are not cash flows for an internal rate of return calculation, because the money for the reinvested dividends doesn't come out of your wallet. Reinvested dividends are just like the interest a savings account pays. The interest you receive and the subsequent compounding on that interest increases the yield on your savings account.

The following identify other investment events and whether those events generate portfolio cash flows:

Unreinvested dividends in a portfolio
> If you deposit unreinvested dividends into the money market fund associated with your portfolio's brokerage account, the money doesn't leave your portfolio, so it isn't a cash flow. However, if you withdraw the dividends you receive, that withdrawal is a cash flow for the purposes of the portfolio IRR calculation.

Unreinvested dividends for a single stock
> If you don't reinvest the dividends for a single stock, the money leaves that investment and becomes a cash flow for the IRR calculation for that stock.

Switching investments in a portfolio
> For the IRR for a portfolio, changing the investments you use doesn't generate cash flows, because the money remains in the portfolio. Selling an investment and keeping the proceeds in the portfolio money market also does not generate a cash flow for a portfolio.

The spreadsheet in Figure 8-10 shows three internal rate of return calculations for a five-year-old portfolio. Column A lists cash flow dates, including the initial date, the birthday deposit dates, and one date at the end of each year for the calculation of the return. Because the Excel XIRR function works with an array of cells such as B2 through B4, the cash flows for each period that you want to evaluate appear in their own columns.

For the first year (2000), column B shows three cash flows in, which are negative numbers. Cell B2 represents the opening balance for the account. Cell B3 is the birthday deposit. Cell B4 is the value of the account at the end of the first year. The cash flows in are negative because they represent cash coming out of your wallet and into the portfolio. The ending value must be a positive number (for a cash flow out) for the IRR calculation to work, although the money isn't actually coming out of your portfolio.

Cell G4 shows the IRR for 2000. The IRR calculation produces a 47 percent annual compound return. That's fantastic! However, closer inspection says otherwise. Because the initial contribution occurred in June of 2000, this return represents an annual return based on a portfolio in existence for only six months. The portfolio did increase in that six months by almost $3,000, but the IRR calculation extrapolates the return to a full year. In effect, it calculates the return as if you received a similar increase during an additional six-month period.

Column C includes the cash flows for years 2000 and 2001, which cover the first 18 months for the portfolio. As you can see in Figure 8-10, the IRR for the first 18 months is dramatically lower than that of the first 6 months (25 percent compared to 47 percent), even though the portfolio increased by a similar amount. Finally, column D includes all the cash flows from the initial deposit to the most recent balance.

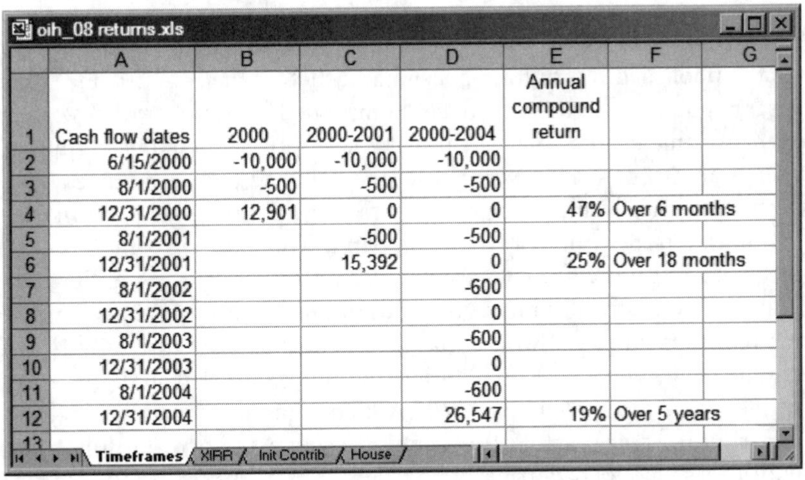

	A	B	C	D	E	F	G
					Annual compound return		
1	Cash flow dates	2000	2000-2001	2000-2004			
2	6/15/2000	-10,000	-10,000	-10,000			
3	8/1/2000	-500	-500	-500			
4	12/31/2000	12,901	0	0	47%	Over 6 months	
5	8/1/2001		-500	-500			
6	12/31/2001		15,392	0	25%	Over 18 months	
7	8/1/2002			-600			
8	12/31/2002			0			
9	8/1/2003			-600			
10	12/31/2003			0			
11	8/1/2004			-600			
12	12/31/2004			26,547	19%	Over 5 years	
13							

Timeframes / XIRR / Init Contrib / House /

Figure 8-10. IRR calculated for different timeframes

The Excel functions for calculating IRR for different timeframes are shown in Example 8-5. The XIRR function accepts two parameters: the first parameter is a range of cells that contain the cash flows and the second parameter is a range of cells for the dates on which those cash flows occurred. For example, the cash flows for the first six months are in column B, so the first parameter for the one-year XIRR is B2:B4. The dates for those cash flows are in column A, so the second parameter is the range A2:A4.

Example 8-5. The Excel functions for IRR

```
IRR over 6 months (cell E4) = XIRR(B2:B4,A$2:A$4)
IRR over 18 months (cell E6) = XIRR(C2:C6,A$2:A$6)
IRR over 5 years(cell E12) = XIRR(D2:D12,A$2:A$12)
```

Calculating the internal rate of return for a series of cash flows requires an iterative approach. In effect, you must try different answers until you get the correct one, which happens to be the interest rate that sets the present worth of all the cash flows to zero. You really don't need to understand what that means. However, by default, XIRR uses 10 percent as its guess. If XIRR can't find an answer that is accurate to 0.000001 percent after 100 iterations, it displays #NUM! in the formula cell. When this occurs, enter a different interest rate guess.

The spreadsheet in Figure 8-10 shows that the compound annual return for a short period of time can be misleading. Longer-term results that cover the ups and downs of the business cycle are more indicative of your performance.

Compare Your Return to a Benchmark

HACK #82 Portfolio cash flows must be identical to compare the returns for your portfolio to a benchmark.

Many investors think that they can compare the return for their portfolios with the published return for a benchmark, such as the S&P 500 index over the same period of time, and conclude that the larger return represents the better investment performance. In many cases, this approximate approach provides an acceptable answer. However, published returns assume a single investment typically at the beginning of the time period. If you contribute to or withdraw from your portfolio, comparing your return to the published benchmark return might not mean as much as you might think. For example, if you were contributing regularly during a recent slump in the market, your return might look worse than the benchmark's return, until prices recover. Then, your investing during the low periods would make your return outpace the benchmark. In short, to obtain meaningful results from a comparison of two portfolios, you must evaluate the two portfolios using identical cash flows occurring at the same times. If you contribute to or withdraw money from your portfolio, you'll need historical price and distribution data to properly pit your portfolio against a benchmark return.

Comparing Returns Based Only on Initial Investment

If you created your portfolio with a single investment and haven't added any money to it (which might happen if you roll over a 401(k) plan into an IRA), you can compare your portfolio return with the return for a benchmark without hunting down too much information. All you need is the portfolio value at the beginning and end of the evaluation period. For the benchmark, you can use the annual returns for each year of the evaluation period.

If you make additional contributions during the evaluation period that are insignificant compared to your initial value, comparing returns based on the initial investment alone is a reasonable approximation. However, if you make significant contributions after the initial one, you must take into account cash flows as described in the section "Comparing Returns Using Cash Flows" later in this hack.

Because your portfolio has only an initial and ending value, you can use the Excel IRR function to calculate your return. The IRR function calculates the internal rate of return for a series of cash flows that occur at regular intervals, such as monthly or annually. To calculate the internal rate of return for your portfolio, specify the starting balance as the first cash flow in, enter zeros for the annual cash flows for each year of the evaluation period, and use the positive value of the ending balance for the final cash flow, as shown in Figure 8-11.

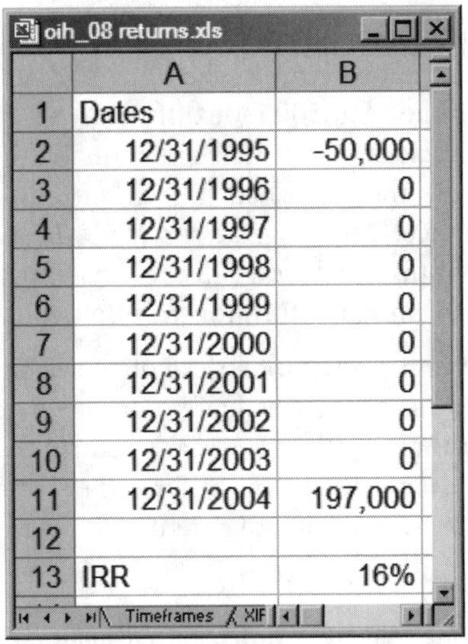

	A	B
1	Dates	
2	12/31/1995	-50,000
3	12/31/1996	0
4	12/31/1997	0
5	12/31/1998	0
6	12/31/1999	0
7	12/31/2000	0
8	12/31/2001	0
9	12/31/2002	0
10	12/31/2003	0
11	12/31/2004	197,000
12		
13	IRR	16%

Figure 8-11. Use the IRR function to calculate the return for a series of regular cash flows

Because the IRR function assumes that cash flows occur at a regular interval, it requires only the cash flow values, not the dates on which the cash flows occurred. The formula for IRR is shown in Example 8-6.

Example 8-6. The formula for IRR for a series of regular cash flows

```
IRR = IRR(B2:B11)
```

If you want to calculate the internal rate of return for a different period, you must specify the starting and ending values for the new period. Type the portfolio value for the starting date of the new period in the appropriate cell in the spreadsheet. For example, to evaluate the return for the past five years, enter the portfolio value for December 31, 1999 in cell B6 of the spreadsheet in Figure 8-11. Modify the IRR function in cell B13 so the parameter encompasses the new cash flow values, B6:B11 in this case.

To compare your portfolio to an index, the easiest approach is to use a low-cost index mutual fund. For example, the Vanguard 500 Index Fund closely matches the return of the S&P 500 index. If you're evaluating your portfolio over a period that coincides with published annual returns (such as the past ten years), you can use the published fund total return [Hack #14] from sites such as Yahoo! Finance, Morningstar, or MSN Money. However, if the period you want isn't published, you can use the annual returns for the fund to calculate the average annual return for the number of years you want.

To find the average annual return, first calculate the cumulative return over the number of years you want to evaluate. For any given year, you multiply the starting value for that year by (1 + year's return) to calculate the ending value. Because the ending value for that year is the starting value for the next year, the formula for the cumulative return for several years results in Example 8-7.

Example 8-7. Formula for cumulative return for actual annual returns

```
Cumulative return of five years of actual returns =
    (1+return1)*(1+return2)*(1+return3))*(1+return4)*(1+return5)
```

The average return for the period is the cumulative return raised to the power of 1/n, where n is the number of years of annual returns you used. The average return for five years is the fifth root of the cumulative return, as shown in Example 8-8.

Example 8-8. Formula for rolling return

```
Average return =
    ((1+return1)*(1+return2)*(1+return3)*(1+return4)*(1+return5))^(1/5) - 1
```

Subtract 1 from the return so the average return reflects only the increase in value, not the original investment.

If you store the annual returns in a column in an Excel spreadsheet such as cells B2 through B6, the PRODUCT function easily calculates the average return. The PRODUCT function multiplies a range of cells, so an Excel array formula for average return looks like the one in Example 8-9.

Example 8-9. Using the PRODUCT function to calculate average annual return

```
5-year average return = {PRODUCT(1+B2:B6)^(1/5) - 1}
```

Comparing Returns Using Cash Flows

Unfortunately, if you do contribute or withdraw significant amounts of money from your portfolio, you must compare your portfolio to an investment in the benchmark using the same cash flows. Obtaining the historical data you need for an index or even an index mutual fund takes some work and in some cases costs money. In addition to historical prices for the index on the dates of every cash flow, you must also know every index distribution (both dividend payments and capital gain distributions), when they occurred, and the reinvestment price.

Recent historical prices [Hack #17] for an index aren't too difficult to find. For example, you can download a spreadsheet (up to seven years of historical prices) from Yahoo! Finance (*http://finance.yahoo.com*). For the S&P 500 index, BigCharts.com (*http://www.bigcharts.com*) price data goes back to 1970, although you can't download the prices to a file. Type **SPX** into the Enter Symbol box and click Historical Quotes in the menu bar. Type the date for which you want a price quote and click Look Up.

Second-Guessing the Past

What if you want to compare the returns that you achieved from past investments to determine which was the better investment? Unfortunately, the need for identical cash flows makes this almost impossible. For example, if you bought the investments at different times or made different numbers of purchases in each one, the timing of the cash flows makes a comparison invalid. You're better off evaluating whether an investment produced the returns you forecasted when you purchased it and learning from your mistakes if it didn't deliver.

Obtaining information about dividend and capital gain distributions is tougher. However, you can divine distribution information in several ways, or take advantage of some online tools that provide a cash-flow-based comparison of returns:

Owning an index fund

If you've owned an index fund in a 401(k) or another account, you can extract the distribution information from your past account statements. Of course, you must figure out how much the distribution is per share and then work this value into a reinvestment calculation in your IRR spreadsheet. Honestly, you're better off spending your time honing your investment skills and managing your portfolio.

Motley Fool's My Portfolio (http://www.fool.com)

If you track your portfolio on the Motley Fool web site, the Annualized Return feature claims to evaluate your historical portfolio cash flows as if they were invested in an index such as the S&P 500. Taking advantage of this feature requires that you enter all of your portfolio transactions into your Motley Fool portfolio. In addition to some rather tedious data entry, you have to decide whether you are comfortable with your data residing with the Motley Fool from a privacy standpoint. If you are, click My Portfolio on the menu bar, and then the New Portfolio link. Follow the instructions to enter all your portfolio transactions. To add transactions at a later date, click the Edit Portfolio link on the My Portfolio page.

bivio (http://www.bivio.com)

The bivio web site offers accounting features for investment clubs or individual investors. If you subscribe to bivio's services and maintain your portfolio on their site, their Performance Benchmark report, shown in Figure 8-12, compares the return produced by the cash flows in your portfolio with the return those same cash flows would have produced in an alternative investment—any of 30 Vanguard Index Funds. You can specify a date range from as early as the first transaction in your portfolio.

See Also

For sources of distribution data (albeit at a price), check out the following web sites:

- Global Financial Data, Inc. (*http://www.globalfindata.com*) provides years of historical data and continually updated data that has been verified for accuracy. However, the price runs in the thousands.

- The Center for Research in Security (*http://gsbwww.uchicago.edu/research/crsp*) provides data subscriptions for stocks and mutual funds. Its mutual fund data, which goes back to 1962, covers more than 16,000 active funds and 8,000 that have died.

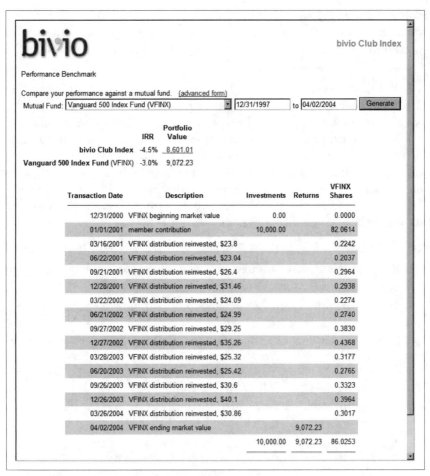

Figure 8-12. The bivio Performance Benchmark report compares your portfolio performance to the results of investing your money in any of 30 Vanguard Index Funds

Forecast Future Returns

HACK #83

The returns you might achieve using fundamental analysis depend on a company's earnings growth rate and the price you pay for the stock.

Before you purchase a stock, the challenge is to figure out what sort of return you might earn if you purchase the stock of a company at a specific price. In addition, you might want to compare the potential returns for multiple stocks to see which one best fits your portfolio. After you own a stock, reevaluating its future return from time to time can help you weed unacceptably slow growers from your portfolio. When you use fundamental analysis (see Chapter 4) to evaluate stock, the future earnings growth rate, the potential future P/E ratio, and the current price all play a part in forecasting the future return. With a current price and a potential price a number of years in the future, you can calculate the potential return, often called total return for this situation.

The P/E ratio [Hack #27] represents price divided by earnings. That means that if you have a P/E ratio and a value for earnings, you can calculate a price, which is exactly what you need to forecast future return. Unfortunately, to calculate a future price, you need an estimate of future earnings and an estimate of a future P/E ratio. With estimated this and estimated that, it's clear that your forecasts for future price and return are only as good as the estimates that you provide. By erring on the conservative side with your earnings and P/E ratio estimates, your forecast will be lower. Although the results might not seem as exciting, they are probably more attainable.

Here's how you develop a forecast for a price five years in the future:

1. Estimate the annual earnings growth rate you expect the company to achieve for the next five years.

   To estimate future earnings growth, you must know the company. Consider what has fueled its growth in the past and what is likely for the future. Successful R&D, good product pipelines, new services, cost-cutting initiatives, new stores, or acquisitions can help increase sales and earnings growth. Competition, lawsuits, expiring patents, rising costs, obsolete products all spell trouble. If you use analysts' estimates of earnings, slightly reduce those estimates, as analysts are prone to overestimate.

   As companies mature and their annual revenues grow large, they can have trouble growing at the same pace that they did in the past. If a company's growth has been slowing in recent years, be sure to lower your future expectations even further.

2. Calculate estimated future earnings five years from now using your estimated earnings growth rate.

   To calculate earnings five years in the future, increase the current earnings by your estimated future earnings growth rate for each of the five years. Example 8-10 shows the formula for calculating EPS five years out. Many investors use the EPS for the past four quarters as the current earnings. Because four quarters happen to represent twelve months, current earnings are often called EPS for the trailing twelve months, or *EPS ttm* for short. For example, a Stock Overview page at Reuters Investor (*http://www.investor.reuters.com*) provides *EPS actual ttm* in the Figures At-A-Glance section.

Example 8-10. The formula for calculating EPS in the future

```
EPS (5 years out) = EPS ttm * (1 + estimated earnings growth)5
```

Home Depot's EPS actual ttm for the quarter ending January 2004 was $1.88. If you estimate its future earnings growth rate at 10 percent a year, Home Depot's EPS five years in the future is calculated, as shown in Example 8-11.

Example 8-11. The calculation for Home Depot's future EPS

```
Home Depot EPS for 1/2009 = $1.88 * (1+.10)5 = $3.03
```

3. Choose a P/E ratio that you expect the company to carry five years from now.

   P/E ratios often cycle through overly optimistic and pessimistic phases. If P/E ratios are dropping, you might want to choose a future P/E ratio even lower than the current value. Conversely, if P/E ratios have been growing, it's safer to limit the P/E ratio to no higher than the current value. You might also use the signature P/E ratio **[Hack #36]**.

   You can view a graph of P/E ratios at MSN Money. To open Home Depot's stock page, type **HD** in the Name or Symbol box at MSN Money (*http://money.msn.com/investor/research/welcome.asp*), and click Go. Click Financial Results and Key Ratios in the navigation bar, and then click Price Ratios on the Home Depot ratios page. You'll find that its P/E ratio has ranged between 10.7 and 69.8 over the past five years, and has been trending lower the entire time. For this example, let's choose a value between the current P/E ratio, which is about 20, and the five-year low, say 15.

4. Calculate your forecast for a future price in five years by multiplying the estimated future earnings by the P/E ratio you chose, as illustrated in Example 8-12.

Example 8-12. Calculating future price

```
Future Price = EPS (5 years out) * Selected Future P/E ratio
Home Depot's Price for 1/2009 = $3.03 * 15 = $45.45
```

5. Calculate the annual return based on your forecast future price and the price at which you intend to purchase the stock.

   No one is going to force you to purchase a stock at its current price. You can calculate the return you would achieve if you buy at the current price. However, if the return is too low, you can also set a buy price and calculate the return that price would deliver. Example 8-13 shows the formula for calculating the compound annual return given the future price and the purchase price.

Example 8-13. Formula for calculating compound return from two prices

```
Annual return for next 5 years = (Future price / Purchase price)^(1/5) - 1
```

Example 8-14 calculates your annual return if you purchased Home Depot at its price as of April 2, 2004, which was $36.68.

Example 8-14. Home Depot's annual return

```
Home Depot annual return = ($45.45 / $36.68)^(1/5) - 1 = 4.38 percent
```

If you want to make sure that you achieve your minimum acceptable return, you can calculate a buy price based on the future price and your minimum return. To do this, calculate the present value using the formula in Example 8-15.

Example 8-15. The formula for calculating present value based on future value and return

```
Present Value (PV) = Future value / (1 + return)^5
```

If your minimum acceptable return is 12 percent, Home Depot's buy price is calculated in Example 8-16.

Example 8-16. Home Depot's buy price to return 12 percent

```
Home Depot Buy Price = $45.45 / (1 + .12)^5 = $25.79
```

HACK #84 Compare Returns for Alternative Investments

Converting different types of investment into the same form of compound-interest problem makes comparisons easy.

Financial calculations all revolve around the same set of parameters: present value, future value, interest or return rate, number of periods, and payment. With any four of these parameters, you can solve for the fifth, which means that with a few qualifications you can turn any type of investment into an apple and then compare all the apples to see which one is the best for your situation. To make the most meaningful comparisons with investments, the number of periods and the payment must be the same for each alternative.

Whether you calculate financial measures by hand or use a spreadsheet, the parameters are the same. If you use Excel for finance, the IRR (internal rate of return), XIRR (internal rate of return for irregular cash flows), PV (present value), FV (future value),and PMT (payment) functions all use or solve for the following parameters in one form or another:

Rate

The interest or investment rate per period. For example, if you are evaluating the annual growth for a stock, the rate is the growth for one year.

Nper

> The total number of payment periods in an annuity. If you are evaluating the annual growth of a stock that you held for five years, Nper is 5.

PV

> The cash value at the beginning of the evaluation period.

Pmt

> The payment made each period, which must remain the same for each period. IRR and XIRR use an array of values instead of the payment parameter so that the amount of each contribution or withdrawal can vary. However, if you compare IRR for different alternatives, the arrays of values must be identical for each alternative.

FV

> The cash value at the end of the evaluation period.

Comparing One-Time Investments

If you plan to contribute a chunk of money at one point in time and want to select the best investment, you can choose the variable to calculate based on your investment situation. For example, if you need $100,000 ten years from now, comparing the present value of different investments can tell you which investment requires the least amount of money up front. If you have a fixed amount of money to invest, you can compare the future value or the compound annual return.

> The rate that you calculate goes by a long list of aliases. When you're solving for the rate, it's often referred to as the *discount rate*. However, it's also known as the internal rate of return, compound annual growth rate, APY, and the equivalent rate of return.

Example 8-17 shows the formula for calculating the return (by whatever name) given the future and present prices.

Example 8-17. Formula for calculating return from two prices

```
Discount rate = (Future price / Purchase price)^(1/n) - 1
```

Suppose you have $10,000 to invest, and you have a choice between two investments: a five-year bond with a 5 percent yield and an investment your mechanic offered that pays you $18,000 in five years. Assuming you are actually willing to invest with your mechanic and risk losing both your money and a good mechanic, how do you evaluate these two investments? One approach is to compare their returns. The bond is easy. The return is the same as the bond's yield: 5 percent. Example 8-18 calculates the return for your mechanic's deal using the formula.

Example 8-18. The return for an investment given present and future value

```
Discount rate (return) = ($18,000/$10,000)1/5 - 1 = 12.47 percent
```

So, your mechanic's deal looks quite a bit better than the bond based on return alone. However, if you consider the risks involved, the deals might look completely different. To learn how to incorporate levels of risk into your evaluations, refer to the next section, "Decision Making with Risk."

Example 8-19 demonstrates the comparison of two investments using future value.

Example 8-19. Formula for calculating future value for two investments

```
Future value (mechanic) = $18,000
Future value (bond) = $10,000 * (1 + .05)5 = $12,762.81
```

Decision Making with Risk

In the previous section, you evaluated two potential investments: one riskier than the other, which might affect the return you achieve. You can use risk management tools to place investments of different levels of risk on a level playing field. One such tool is known as *expected value*, which multiplies the future value of an investment by the probability of achiev ng that value. The lower the probability of achieving a value is, the lower its expected value. For example, an investment with a future value of $10,000 and a 90 percent probability of occurring has an expected value of $9,000.

For different investments with different levels of risk, you can calculate an expected value for each investment. An investor who is totally rational picks the highest expected value. However, being completely rational might be harder than you think. For example, suppose someone told you that you could have a million dollars, no question asked, or you could flip a coin and receive two million dollars for heads and zip, zilch, nada for tails. Which would you pick? Well, a million dollars multiplied by 100 percent probability is a million dollars. Two million dollars multiplied by a 50 percent probability is one million dollars. Both alternatives have an *expected value* of one million dollars, so being completely rational, either one would be the same, right? However, risk-averse investors would probably pick the one million sure bet. Risk takers might prefer to go for the chance at two million dollars.

The challenge with incorporating risk into your evaluations is determining the probability to assign to an investment. Modern portfolio theory goes into great detail evaluating risks and probabilities [Hack #37], but you can start

---

with a simpler approach. For instance, let's compare the bond and the mechanic's investment taking risk into account. Suppose that the bond is the highest quality you can get, and you will keep the money in the bond until it matures. If the chance of default is 1 percent, the probability of achieving your return with the bond is 99 percent. The mechanic is another story. If two of your friends lost money with the mechanic and one of your friends made money, the calculated probability of achieving your return based on this unrealistically small sampling is 33 percent. By multiplying the investment returns by the investment probabilities, Table 8-7 shows the results of comparing the expected value of these two investments. Although the bond offers a lower return than the mechanic's investment, its expected value in risk terms is higher. Therefore, only the true risk taker would go for the mechanic's deal.

Table 8-7. Expected values of two mutually exclusive investments

Return (percent)	Probability	Expected value (percent)
5.0	.99	4.95
12.47	.33	4.11

Comparing Investments with Multiple Cash Flows

You might want to evaluate an investment in which you contribute regularly and end up with a set final amount. One such example is the return from a whole life insurance policy in which you pay premiums (contributions) and receive a cash value in addition to the death benefit. You also might use this calculation to figure out whether owning a house would be a better investment than buying stock. In both of these situations, the cash flows occur at regular intervals—the monthly contributions to a stock investment and the mortgage payment for the house.

Suppose you want to figure out whether it would be better to invest in an S&P 500 Index Fund or buy a house as an investment property. Evaluating an investment property is a rather complicated business, but I'll simplify it here to illustrate the basic principle. Let's assume that you're considering this investment for ten years and that the stock mutual fund will provide a long-term average annual return of 11 percent.

To compare the investment property to the fund, you must convert your down payment, expenses, and estimated value when you sell into an internal rate of return. Figure 8-13 provides a simplified example of this type of evaluation. The initial cash flow for the investment property (cell D1) is the sum of the down payment (cell B1) and the closing costs (cell B2) to purchase the house, $42,000.

	A	B	C	D
			oih_08 returns.xls	
1	Down payment	$30,000	Initial Outlay	-$42,000
2	Closing costs	$12,000	Annual payments	-$1,000
3	Annual Expense	$1,000		-$1,000
4	Net on sale	$222,000		-$1,000
5				-$1,000
6				-$1,000
7				-$1,000
8				-$1,000
9				-$1,000
10				-$1,000
11				-$1,000
12			Value at sale	$222,000
13			IRR	15%

Figure 8-13. Use IRR on the cash flows into an investment property to calculate the internal rate of return

For simplicity, this example assumes that most of the expenses are covered by rent paid by tenants, resulting in an annual cash flow of $1,000, which appears in cells D2 through D11. When the investment property is sold, the final value is the net amount from the sale of the house (cell D12). By calculating the internal rate of return for these cash flows, the return for the investment property is 15 percent a year.

The house provides an annual compound return of 15 percent. To compare this to an investment in the S&P 500 index, you can approximate the index's potential return by using its long-term average annual return (11 percent). With the assumptions used in this example, the house is a better investment than the S&P 500 Index Fund. However, you can't predict the future. If the housing market performed poorly and you couldn't sell the house for what you expected, and the stock market performed better than average, the S&P 500 index could outperform the real estate investment.

HACK #85 Assess Portfolio Quality

In investing, quality not only can keep you out of trouble, but it can improve the returns you achieve as well.

Some investors look to make a fast buck by buying *turnaround stories*—companies that have fallen on hard times but have a decent chance to make a comeback. However, some of the most successful long-term investors, such as Benjamin Graham and Warren Buffett, have looked to quality companies to build portfolios of long-term investments. Warren Buffett's mentor and the father of value investing Benjamin Graham said, "For the vast majority of common stocks, the average relationship between price and earnings will reflect the quality and growth of the issue." In investing, quality means consistency, strength, and growth, as well as those intangible measures that you simply know when you see them. Fortunately, most of the characteristics of financial quality are quantifiable, so you can rate company quality to improve your portfolio and increase your investment success.

How to Recognize Quality

Benjamin Graham believed that growth and quality drive price and earnings. From that, he asserted that quality growth companies sell at higher P/E ratios than those of lower quality and slower growth rates. The following measures summarize the elements Graham considered to be influences on P/E ratios [Hack #27] and therefore signs of quality:

- Strong historical sales and EPS growth [Hack #26] that compares favorably to the growth rates of competitors
- Consistency of historical EPS, which is also an indication of quality of management
- Strong historical and forecast profit margins that compare favorably to the margins of competitors
- Ongoing financial strength that compares favorably to that of competitors
- Consistent payout and growth of dividends
- Competence and depth of the management team that produces company results
- Positive business outlook in the company's competitive position and for the future of the industry to which it belongs

Although the last two items in the list are more subjective, most of these elements are quantifiable in one way or another. And by evaluating a company and its industry and then assigning a rating to the competence of the management team and positive competitive factors, you can include them in your overall quality rating.

Measuring Quality

There's no right answer for how to measure quality. For example, Benjamin Graham placed a great deal of emphasis on dividends, because dividend yields greater than 5 percent were typical in his day. Today, many quality companies still pay dividends and work hard to continually increase their dividend payout. However, many others don't pay dividends at all and instead reinvest their earnings to fund further growth. You can choose to include or exclude dividends as a measure based on whether you prefer to receive dividends or would rather see faster company growth.

Here's an example of an approach to measuring quality that takes into account most of Graham's elements. To make the quality measure easy to comprehend, this example normalizes values so that 100 is the highest quality and 1 is the lowest. A variety of sources provide industry averages and company grades [Hacks #19, #20, and #23]. The spreadsheet in Figure 8-14 uses numbers from Reuters Investor stock pages to calculate company and industry average performance.

	A	B	C	D	E
1		Company	Industry	Quality measures	Values
2	*Quantitative measures*				
3	5-year sales growth	16.49	16.52	Growth	49.9
4	EPS predictability	0.97		Consistent EPS	97.0
5	5-year pre-tax profit margin	9.8	9.05	Profit margin	54.1
6	*Financial Strength*			Financial strength	82.6
7	Current ratio	1.4	1.46		
8	Debt to equity ratio	0.04	0.15		
9	Interest coverage	110.42	17.21		
10	*Qualitative measures*				
11	Management rating	90		Management	90
12	Business outlook rating	85		Business outlook	85
13					
14				**Overall Quality Grade**	76.5

Sheet1 / Sheet2 / Sheet3 /

Figure 8-14. Calculate a quality rating for a stock using company and industry average values

In Figure 8-14, quality of growth (cell E3) compares a company's historical sales to the average for the industry. For example, a company that grows at the industry average receives 50 points. Companies that grow above the industry average receive more points up to a maximum of 100. The Excel formula in Example 8-20 calculates this growth measure of quality.

Example 8-20. An Excel formula for calculating growth quality
```
Quality of Growth (cell E3) = MIN((B3/C3)*50,100)
```

The calculation works as follows:

1. To calculate the ratio of a company's growth rate to the industry average, divide the five-year company sales growth (cell B3) by the five-year industry average sales growth (cell C3). For example, when the company and industry average sales are the same, the ratio equals 1.

2. To normalize the measure, multiply by 50. When the growth ratio equals 1, the quality measure equals 50.

3. To limit the quality of growth points to 100, use the Excel MIN function, which takes the smaller of the two numbers you provide. If a company grows more than twice as fast as the industry average, the quality of growth measure caps at 100.

Consistency of EPS

You can calculate the consistency of EPS (cell E4) using R-Squared [Hack #35] and enter the result in cell B4. Consistency in and of itself is a sign of quality. To show consistency as a percentage, cell E4 multiplies the R-Squared result by 100. Another source for consistency is the Value Line stock pages [Hack #20], which include a measure of Earnings Predictability that ranges between 0, totally unpredictable, and 100, totally predictable. If you use Value Line, you can enter the value directly in cell E4.

Quality of profitability

Quality of profitability (cell E5) compares a company's historical pre-tax profit margin to the average for the industry. Similar to quality of growth, a company that matches the industry average receives 50 points, whereas companies that grow above the industry average receive more points up to a maximum of 100. The Excel formula in Example 8-21 calculates this measure of profitability quality.

Example 8-21. An Excel formula for calculating quality of profitability

```
Quality of Profitability (cell E5) = MIN((B5/C5)*50,100)
```

Financial strength

Financial strength (cell D6) comprises several financial measures and is much like a credit rating. If you use Value Line data, it's simple to use the Financial Strength rating that Value Line assigns. However, in this example, financial strength [Hack #29] is a composite rating of a company's current ratio, debt to equity ratio, and interest coverage. To calculate this composite, each financial strength ratio receives a maximum of 100 points, as shown in Example 8-22. Then, the sum of the three ratings is divided by 3 so that the financial strength quality rating can be no more than 100.

Example 8-22. Formulas for financial strength quality

```
Current ratio quality = MIN((B7/C7)*50,100)
Debt to equity quality = IF(B8 = 0,100,MIN((C8/B8)*50,100))
Interest coverage quality = MIN((B9/C9)*50,100)
Financial strength quality (cell E6) =
   (Current ratio quality + Debt to equity quality
   + Interest coverage quality) / 3
```

Qualitative measures

> As you evaluate a company, you often develop an opinion about the qualitative characteristics of the company. For example, if management produces consistent results despite ups and downs in the industry, you will view the management team in a positive light. Or, you might reward a company that not only invests significant money in research and development, but has a high success rate for the new products it introduces. You can grade companies based on your gut feeling for measures such as these, or you can omit these measures to keep the quality rating as objective as possible.

Using Quality Measures

Portfolio management represents an ongoing effort to reduce risk, increase quality, and increase the returns for your investment portfolio. As you evaluate stocks to add, remove, or exchange in your portfolio, you can use your quality measure in several ways:

Minimum guideline

> When you consider a stock for your portfolio, be sure that its quality measure is above a minimum value you choose. For example, you might require stocks to carry a minimum quality value of 60, so that they are all above average in quality.

Compare two stocks

> If you evaluate two stocks with similar potential returns, you can compare their quality measures to decide which one is the best for your portfolio.

Replace stock

> As you evaluate stocks to try to improve your portfolio, you can replace stocks with ones that have higher quality and similar returns.

Sell stock

> If a company's rating begins to fall, look for a stock that offers the same return and a quality measure that is equal to or better than the original.

Flag Fundamental Sell Signals
#86
The reasons to sell are often the opposite of why you bought.

You might sell an investment for any number of reasons that have nothing to do with what the investment has done. If you need money, you might decide to sell some shares of stock whether it has performed well or poorly. As time passes, your asset allocation [Hack #74] might become unbalanced, so you sell some of your winners to boost the percentage of the lagging assets. In your ongoing efforts to improve the quality of your portfolio [Hack #85], you might decide to replace a perfectly good stock with one that happens to be even better.

However, to protect your portfolio, you also want to watch for the signs of deterioration in your holdings—sell signals. Technical analysts set up their rules for exiting a trade to limit the risk in their portfolios, as introduced in Chapter 5. Fundamental investors consider fundamental measures in their evaluations, as described in Chapter 4. When running the defensive plays in your portfolio, a checklist of your fundamental buying guidelines makes spotting sell signals easier.

Some sell signals represent serious deterioration in the growth and quality of a company. However, a company not living up to your expectations is just as serious. Your checklist for selling will depend on the type of company you are following and the measures you use for evaluations. However, the following measures are a good starting point for your sell signal checklist:

Sales and EPS growth [Hack #26]
> Slowing growth doesn't have to be a death knell for stock in your portfolio. If you consider that a company's growth might slow during your stock study, your investment might be just fine. However, your decision to buy a company using fundamental analysis usually has sales and EPS growth as one of its underpinnings. If the company growth slows well below the rate you projected, your potential return is at risk and it might be time to look for another investment.

Profit margin [Hack #32]
> Profit margins represent the percentage of money a company keeps from what it earns. Declining profit margins are often an early warning sign of lower earnings in the future, whether the cause is increased competition and lower prices, increased costs, or other factors.

Return on equity [Hack #30]
> Return on equity (ROE) is the return that management produces using shareholders' equity in the company. A declining ROE or one that drops below the industry average ROE is an early warning sign that you are not receiving a sufficient return on your equity in the company and it might be time to seek another investment.

Other fundamentals [Hacks #29 and #31]
> Other fundamental measures can predict problems. For example, deteriorating measures, such as increasing inventories, receivables, and debt, or decreasing cash flow from the same levels of revenue are signs of trouble. To see a spreadsheet that calculates financial ratios and points out good and bad results, read "Find the Best Free Excel Tools for Fundamental Analysis" [Hack #41].

Relative value [Hack #27]
> Relative value is a ratio that shows the current premium or discount for a stock compared to what investors have paid over the past five years.

When relative value gets excessively high, chances are good that the stock price will fall to more reasonable levels. Many investors consider relative value over 150 percent (1.5) to be overvalued.

Total return [Hack #83]

One of the key factors in the decision to buy a company is often the total return you expect to receive from your investment. Although you might purchase a company with a lower total return to manage your portfolio risk, you want to achieve a level of return with your portfolio and each investment must support that goal. If the total return that an investment is likely to produce drops below your target for the company, another investment might be better for your portfolio. The total return might drop because the company's growth rates have declined or because the price has skyrocketed. Either way, the potential for higher price decreases.

Management and business outlook

Evaluate the factors that affect the business and how management has responded to them. A down economy typically affects all competitors, but savvy management might take advantage of this to acquire weaker competitors and increase its market share. Expanding costs, poor product pipelines, shrinking market share, and declining product quality all point to management that isn't solving the challenges that face the company.

Figure 8-15 provides one example of a spreadsheet that highlights potential sell signals [Hack #78]. Columns I and J include the estimated growth rates for the company in the portfolio. If the quarterly growth rates (columns E, F, and H) and the EPS growth rate for the last twelve months (column G) are less than the estimated rates, Excel highlights the cells in pink.

				% CHANGE				Est. Growth Rate	
	Shares	Name	Ticker	Qtrly Sales	Qtrly PTP	ttm EPS	Qtrly EPS	Sales	EPS
11	500.0	HOME DEPOT INC	HD	5.8%	5.1%	14.4%	8.3%	10.0%	9.2%
12	750.0	SYNOVUS FINANCIAL CP	SNV	5.6%	9.6%	10.2%	6.5%	13.0%	13.0%
13	700.0	Lincare Holdings	LNCR	21.3%	24.1%	27.0%	34.1%	20.0%	20.0%
14	400.0	SUNGARD DATA SYSTEMS	SDS	21.9%	30.0%	26.0%	26.9%	16.0%	16.0%
15	600.0	LOWES COS	LOW	23.5%	nmf	28.7%	30.2%	20.0%	18.0%

Figure 8-15. An Excel spreadsheet can highlight sell signals

The evaluation shown in Figure 8-15 represents a situation at one point in time. If you want to evaluate these companies, you must compare the current results before you decide on a stock.

CHAPTER NINE

Financial Planning
Hacks 87–100

With self-service becoming a business mantra, we become more responsible for our financial futures every day. Just consider the decline of company-funded pension plans and the popularity of employee-funded 401(k) programs. However, there's a lot more to planning your finances than choosing and managing your investments. In fact, the topic of financial planning could fill a book of its own.

Although this chapter merely scratches the surface, choosing the right financial products and services offers plenty of rewards. With good financial planning, you can save hundreds of thousands of dollars over a lifetime. Whether you invest those savings to make money or use them to have some fun, the time you spend on personal finance provides attractive returns. On the other hand, living life without a financial plan can lead to unacceptable results—surviving to retirement only to realize you have to live with your kids.

With a computer and an Internet connection, there's no excuse for letting your financial planning lapse. As you'll learn in this chapter, you can research financial products at your convenience and take all the time you want to make your decisions. In addition, by using the Web for your financial needs, you can obtain more services than you can get offline, often at better prices. Comparison shopping for loans, insurance, investments, or toasters is easy and fast; you can find the best deals in a matter of minutes.

It's true that some web sites and services lose points when it comes to customer support. If you want serious handholding, consider the quality of a company's customer service and technical support before signing up for a low-cost online service. However, web services become easier and more dependable every day. The big players in the financial arena offer tremendous online services that are easy to use despite being fully automated. If you run into a transaction that their site can't handle, they typically offer telephone services as a backup, although you might pay an additional fee.

Choose the Right Type of Account

The type of account that's right for you depends on the services you want, the returns you expect, and, in most cases, the taxes you would rather not pay.

Financial accounts boil down to savings accounts and investment accounts, but it's hard to believe that when you look at the variety of accounts that financial companies offer. Savings options typically offer a trade-off between interest rate, safety of your principal, and access to your cash. Investment accounts boil down to accounts that provide only investment services and accounts that combine your investing and banking needs into one. The rest of the account options all stem from taxes or an investor's desire to avoid them. Although the options are numerous, the right account is usually easy to spot once you know what to look for. If this hack doesn't answer your questions, financial companies include helpful information on their web sites as well. In most cases, you can also talk to one of the company's customer service representatives, who will be happy to help you make the right decision in exchange for your new or additional business.

Types of Savings Accounts

In the broadest sense of the word, the accounts that hold your stocks and other investments are savings accounts, because you're saving money and then growing it to satisfy your financial goals. But that's not what we're talking about here. A savings account in most circles means an account that pays interest on the money you deposit. Savings accounts are perfect for stashing money you need in the near future—the amount you deposit is relatively safe and you earn some return on your money. However, savings accounts are not the place for long-term savings, because inflation [Hack #37] will consume any return that you receive and then some.

To choose the right type of savings account, you must first decide the relative importance of three characteristics of savings accounts:

Insured deposits
> Money in savings accounts is safer than money invested in stocks and bonds. However, banks do go under from time to time. For the ultimate in safety of your savings, go with an account that is insured by the Federal Deposit Insurance Corporation (FDIC). If the bank defaults, your deposits up to $100,000 are covered by this federal agency.

Access to your money
> The easier it is to get to your money, the lower the interest rate you receive.

Interest rate

Obviously, you'd like to get the highest interest you can. After filtering your options based on the importance of insured deposits and easy access, you can choose the account that offers the best interest rate [Hack #1].

Table 9-1 summarizes the features of each type of savings account.

Table 9-1. The lowdown on savings account options

Type of savings account	FDIC insured?	Access	Interest rate
NOW account	Yes	This is a checking account that pays interest. Withdraw money at any time by writing checks.	Minimal; fees for this type of account might consume any interest you earn
Deposit savings account	Yes	Withdraw money at any time by submitting a withdrawal slip or transferring money to a checking account.	Low
Money market deposit account	Yes	Limited number of transactions per month and a minimum balance requirement.	Higher than deposit savings account
Money market fund	No	Mutual fund with which you can withdraw money by writing a check or transferring money to another account. Might have limits on number of transactions monthly and require a minimum balance.	Higher than money market deposit account
Certificate of deposit (CD)	Yes	Withdraw principal and interest at maturity date. Penalty for early withdrawal.	Depends on time to maturity and institution

For unlimited access to your money, choose a NOW account or a deposit savings account, but don't expect much in the interest rate department. Use these accounts for a few months' worth of emergency funds or to earn a little interest on money before you pay your bills.

Money market accounts and money market funds are suitable for a few months of emergency funds. They're great for stashing cash until you decide where to invest it or to set some cash aside while waiting for an investment opportunity to present itself.

To earn the highest interest rate for a fixed duration, most often your choice is a CD that matures when you need the money. For example, if you want the best interest rate on funds you've earmarked for your twentieth anniversary vacation in five years, purchase a five-year CD (or you could opt to purchase a bond with a 5-year duration [Hack #80]). However, you must be sure that you won't want the money before the maturity date, as the penalties for early withdrawal are steep.

Types of Investment Accounts

Creating meaningful growth in your nest egg requires investing. Sheltering your savings and earnings from taxes creates more meaningful growth, because you get to keep all of your money to invest and it compounds as quickly as possible. The variety of choices in investment accounts stems from the services clients want, the types of investments you can own, and the continually expanding options for sheltering investments from taxes.

A brokerage account at its most basic enables you to invest your money. With bare-bones investment accounts, you transfer money from another account by depositing a check or wiring funds and then you use that money to buy something.

Many financial institutions offer *cash management accounts*, which wrap investing and other financial services into one. With these accounts, cash produced by investing transactions, such as cash dividends or sales of stock, are swept into a money market fund. To access the cash in the account, customers typically receive check-writing privileges and a debit card. These services often come with a minimum balance to open the account, minimum amounts on checks such as $250, and lower interest rates on the money market fund.

> Margin accounts enable you to use the cash and investments in your account as collateral for a line of credit, which you can use in turn to purchase more investments. However, because you pay interest on that line of credit, you must earn a higher return to make the process worthwhile. It's far better to work harder to save more money to invest than to take risks investing on margin.

However, you might choose a particular financial institution and a specific type of account that it offers depending on the types of investments you buy and the services you want:

Mutual funds from one mutual fund family
    A brokerage account with that fund family makes it easy to buy any fund within the fund family and exchange money between funds.

Mutual funds from several companies
    In this situation, it's easier to manage your portfolio by setting up an account with a one-stop-shop brokerage. For example, Charles Schwab offers their OneSource service, in which you can purchase more than

1,000 mutual funds from a variety of fund families with no loads and no transaction fees. Other funds are available as well, but you'll pay a small fee to purchase them.

Funds, stocks, bonds, and more

One-stop-shop brokerages also are the best choice when you invest in more than mutual funds. If you purchase stocks and bonds, evaluate the commissions for purchasing those investments for each brokerage [Hack #89]. If you invest in other types of investments, such as options, make sure that the brokerage you choose handles those.

> No one says you can keep only one investment account. You can use one account for low-cost mutual fund investing and another account for stocks and bonds. In addition, you might use multiple brokerage accounts to obtain low commissions from one account and superior research services at another.

Tax-Advantaged Accounts

Whether you're saving for retirement [Hack #96] or college [Hacks #91, #92, and #93] you need all the help you can get. The U.S. and state governments aren't completely heartless: several types of tax-advantaged accounts help you save money for college or retirement. However, determining whether an account is right for you can be as difficult as reading the instructions for IRS forms. Here are some simplified descriptions of your options and how they can help:

Traditional IRA

Anyone with earned income can contribute to a traditional IRA. Contributions up to $3,500 in 2004 might be tax deductible depending on your level of income. Taxes on earnings are deferred until you withdraw funds. Penalties apply for withdrawals before age 59 1/2. If you've maxed out your 401(k) contributions and want to save more for retirement, the tax deferral on earnings helps your investments compound faster.

> Minors with earned income can start saving for retirement with a Custodial IRA, established as a traditional or Roth IRA. A parent or guardian manages the IRA for the child, and turns the account over when the child becomes an adult (based on state law, not the child's maturity level).

Roth IRA

Although contributions to a Roth IRA are not tax-deductible, you can contribute after you reach age 70; there's no mandatory annual distribution; you can withdraw your contributions at any time without paying taxes or penalties; and you can withdraw earnings tax-free after the age of 59 1/2. A Roth IRA is a perfect way to save for your later years in retirement, because you can keep your money compounding in the account as long as you want.

Rollover, Roth conversion, and inherited IRAs

Most brokerages offer special accounts for converting or transferring retirement assets into IRA accounts. Rollover accounts are designed specifically for funds transferred from 401(k) or other employer-sponsored retirement plans. If you convert a traditional IRA or a rollover IRA to a Roth IRA, you must pay taxes on the tax-deferred contributions you've already made to the original account. A beneficiary of an IRA can deposit the funds into an inherited IRA to keep the assets tax-deferred until the IRS requires distribution of the assets. Consulting a tax advisor about inherited IRAs is worthwhile, because the tax rules for inherited IRAs are complex.

SEP-IRA

The simplified employee pension IRA is the easiest way to set up a pension plan for a small business or for yourself if you are self-employed. You can contribute up to 25 percent of your income each year to a maximum of $41,000 in 2004. Even with a 401(k) at your job, you can set up a SEP-IRA for a side business.

Education savings account

Investments in these accounts grow tax-deferred. Withdrawals are tax-free if used for qualified educational expenses. The adult who creates the account manages the assets until the child turns 18, at which point the adult can transfer ownership of the account to the child.

529 College savings plan

Investments grow tax-deferred. Withdrawals are tax-free if used for qualified educational expenses. The person who contributes to the account is the owner, who can name another family member as the beneficiary.

To learn more about college saving options, read "Let Me Count the Ways to Save for College" [Hack #92] and "A College Savings Plan in Every State" [Hack #93].

HACK #88 Choose an Online Broker

Online brokers offer the convenience of investing wearing your robe and slippers, but first you have to choose the right combination of services and costs.

In the past, brokerages all provided full service: in-house research, investment information, and a broker who, in theory, understood your financial objectives and recommended investments that fit. Today, brokerages come in all shapes and sizes. The old-style full-service option still offers deluxe treatment and hefty commissions, although online services often reduce your costs and increase the lavishness of the treatment you receive. Discount brokers offer fewer services and lower commissions, sometimes as little as 10 percent of what you would pay for full service. Deep discount brokers execute orders for bargain-basement prices, but you shouldn't expect much more. No matter which type of brokerage you choose, the Web has reduced commissions, increased the services you receive, and made choosing an online broker more difficult. Here's a guide to what you need to know.

A Rundown on Online Brokerage Features

Before you can choose an online broker, you must learn about the features that are available and decide how important each one is to you. Only then can you choose the best fit from what online brokers have to offer.

Has the brokerage performed on the up and up?
> Anything that has to do with money attracts the occasional financial hi-jinks. The first step in evaluating a brokerage (and an individual broker for that matter) is to ensure that the record of the brokerage or broker is clean. The National Association of Securities Dealers (NASD) offers a disclosure program NASD BrokerCheck (*http://www.nasdr.com/2000. asp*) that discloses information such as employment history, felony charges and convictions, consumer complaints, and other unseemly events.

How much money does it take to open an account?
> Minimum amounts to open an account range from zero to more than $15,000. If you're just getting started, look for brokerages that require no minimum balance. Some brokerages, particularly mutual fund companies, waive their minimum if you sign up for an automatic monthly investment plan.

What types of investments does the brokerage handle?
> Brokerages buy and sell stocks. No worries about that. However, most investors end up with at least one mutual fund. If you use mutual funds in your investment plan, consider a brokerage supermarket that offers mutual funds from many fund families with little or no transaction fees. (Fund companies pay the brokerage for access to a larger market.) Most brokerages handle other types of investments, such as bonds, options, foreign stocks, penny stocks, and IPOs, but some don't offer online trading for them. If you invest in those types of investments, check for

the availability of online trading and be sure to check the commissions and fees, as they can be high.

> To trade options, you'll have to sign up specifically for an account that includes options trading. Typically, brokerages ask you additional questions to evaluate whether options are suitable for your investment experience. However, these questions are more for the brokerage's protection, because they don't want to cover your losses.

Is there more than online access?

Some brokers offer only online access. This limitation can be risky if your Internet access drops or disappears due to snow or power outages, or the brokerage has trouble with its web site. Ideally, look for brokerages that offer online and telephone access at a minimum. However, keep in mind that telephone or face-to-face trades usually cost more than their online counterparts.

How reliable is trade execution when the market is busy?

Everyone wants her orders and order cancellations processed quickly and accurately, whether it's a meal at a restaurant or a stock trade. Timely order processing is particularly important with stocks, because you might miss the purchase or sales price you want. When the market is swamped with heavy trading volume, brokerage firms can get inundated with orders. A brokerage's web site can slow to a crawl and make it almost impossible to place a trade. Check to see whether the brokerage extends the online commission rate to a telephone order if you can't log into its web site.

What services does the brokerage offer?

Online brokers offer additional services that you might want, such as easy access to market news, research, free real-time quotes, investment alerts [Hack #24], cash management accounts [Hack #87], online banking, margin accounts, after-hours trading [Hack #55], automatic fund transfers, local offices, and integration with a personal finance application, such as Quicken or MS Money. If you always reinvest dividends, save on commissions by looking for a brokerage that automatically reinvests dividends and fractional shares at no charge.

> Some deep discount brokers skimp on tax information, so make sure that the brokerage you choose provides the tax documentation you want.

How is customer service?

Life is too short to fight poor customer service. In addition, if you spend your time on hold, you won't have time to wring the best return out of your investments. Whether you want someone to hold your hand or you could teach Warren Buffett a thing or two, your brokerage should provide prompt and polite service that ends with satisfactory results. Read in the next section "Find Your Perfect Broker" for online reviews that identify whether a broker provides the level of support you want. Call a prospective brokerage several times to check their responsiveness and quality of service before signing up.

How much do trades cost?

Trades can cost anywhere from a few dollars to more than $100, depending on the brokerage and your choice of online, touch-tone, or broker-assisted ordering. In addition, brokerages often charge different amounts for market orders versus limit orders. Some brokers offer additional discounts to investors who trade frequently. Commissions can vary depending on the number of shares and whether a stock is listed on an exchange or over the counter. You can look for an online broker whose commissions are reasonable whether online or by phone, market or limit, infrequent or daily, or you can read "Pick the Best Broker for Your Trading Style" [Hack #89] to work out the costs in detail.

What other fees are there?

Brokerages can offset lower commission by charging fees for other services, such as account maintenance, wire transfers, issuing a stock certificate, sending a copy of an account statement, and even closing your account. If a brokerage charges an account maintenance fee, check if it waives the fee when your balance reaches a specific dollar amount or you trade a number of times a year. If you use services that come with additional fees, add those to a quantitative evaluation of costs [Hack #89].

Find Your Perfect Broker

Try one or more of the following online reviews and comparison tools to help you find the brokerages that meet your needs:

Forbes Best of the Web—Brokers (http://www.forbes.com/bow/b2c/ category.jhtml?id=5)

Forbes reviews almost three dozen of the best-known, full-service, and discount brokers. Charles Schwab (*http://www.schwab.com*) wins the Forbes Favorite award, while five others were picked as Forbes Best of the Web winners. However, your needs might differ from Forbes' criteria, so don't dismiss the also-rans.

Investing in DRIPs

So why pay a broker at all? Truth is, you can buy stocks directly from many companies through their dividend reinvestment plans (DRIPs). To open a DRIP, you usually need only one share of company stock. After that, you can often buy additional shares of stock, paying little or no commission, and the company reinvests your dividends in your name without charging any fees or commissions. However, you can't specify the day on which the company buys or sells your shares for you, so these plans are best when you intend to buy for the long term.

Optional cash purchases (OCP) or direct stock purchase (DSP) options enable you to make additional purchases on a regular schedule, such as the last day of the month or the quarter. You send in a check before the purchase date; the company purchases shares for you; and then you receive account statements showing your transactions and account balance. To learn more about these programs, read the free online book on the DRIP Central web site (*http://www.dripcentral.com*).

About.com—Best Online Trading Web Sites (http://mutualfunds.about.com/cs/brokerrankings/a/onlinebrokers.htm?terms=online+brokers)
> About.com uses Internet data from Jupiter Media Matrix to evaluate online trading sites with measures such as the amount of time someone spends on the brokerage web site, the number of repeat visitors and customers, and how loyal customers are.

SmartMoney.com—Is Your Broker Right For You? (http://www.smartmoney.com/brokers)
> SmartMoney grades basic discount brokers, premium discount brokers, and full-service brokers, using tables that compare measures, such as minimum opening balance, quality of service, costs, research, investment products, and trade-execution quality. For help deciding which category of brokerage is right for you, click the What's Your Type link under the In the 2003 Broker Survey heading.

The Motley Fool—Compare Brokers tool (http://www.fool.com/dbc/dbc.htm)
> Select the Compare Brokers tab in the Broker Center menu bar to view a comprehensive comparison of four popular brokerage houses: Ameritrade, ShareBuilder, HARRISdirect, and TD Waterhouse. If the ones you're considering are in the list, great! If not, this table is a good example for building your own evaluation tool.

If you have a lot of requirements, you can get the best of both worlds using two brokerages! If you own an IRA account with a significant balance in mutual funds that you hold for the long haul, transfer your IRA account to a brokerage with great research and recommendation services regardless of the commissions it charges—as long as you stick to your mutual funds, you'll never see a commission, but you can use the research. Then, you can open a brokerage account for small, monthly investments with a brokerage with no minimum balance, low commissions, free dividend reinvestments, but no research services.

Pick the Best Broker for Your Trading Style

Commissions and fees can take a big bite out of your investment returns, so you should consider your typical trading patterns to determine the most cost-effective brokerage.

Every time you buy or sell an investment, you pay brokerage commissions. If you trade frequently or make purchases with only a few dollars, commissions can consume a big percentage of your returns. It makes sense to find the brokerage that executes your trades at the best possible price, but commission schedules are a complicated business. Brokerages charge different commissions based on a number of criteria. It's almost impossible to capture all the subtleties of brokerage commissions, because each company calculates commissions a little differently. However, you can build a spreadsheet to estimate your annual brokerage commissions based on the methods and frequency of your trades.

Brokerages often charge different commissions depending on whether you place your trades online, use a touch-tone phone system, or speak to a broker. In some cases, market orders cost less than limit orders [Hack #54]. Many brokerages offer discounted commissions for investors who trade frequently—typically a minimum of 72 trades a year. For trades that represent a large number of shares or high dollar values, commissions are often calculated using a minimum commission plus a small percentage of the trade amount. In addition, bond and option commissions have their own schedule of fees. In many cases, brokerages charge the same minimum commission whether you buy one or nine bonds, and only switch to a sliding scale when you reach ten bonds or options contracts.

Estimating Commissions

The spreadsheet in Figure 9-1 offers a rudimentary comparison of the commissions you might pay to different brokerages. The calculations take into account the number of market and limit orders you estimate that you make in a typical year (cells B2 and B3), the number of bonds and options contracts you might purchase (cells B5 and B6), and the percentage of trades you place online (cell E2), using a touch-tone phone system (cell E3), or speaking directly to a broker (cell E4).

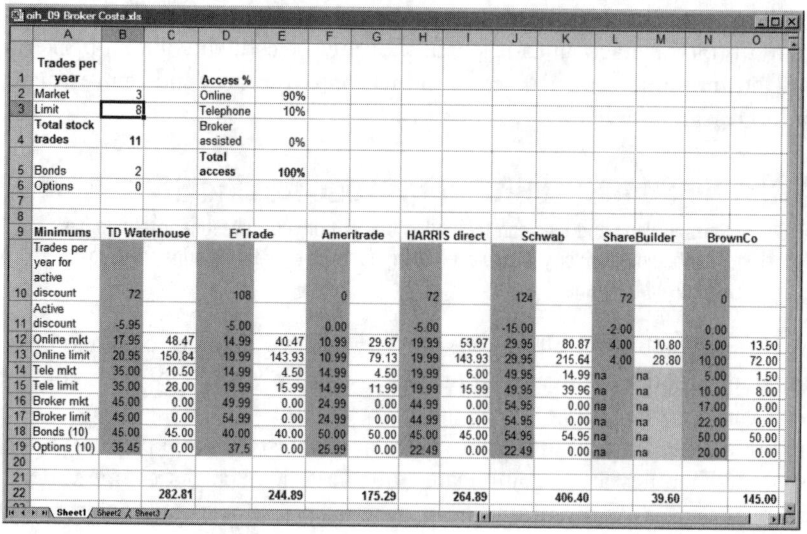

	A	B	C	D	E	F	G	H	I	J	K	L	M	N	O
1	Trades per year			Access %											
2	Market	3		Online	90%										
3	Limit	8		Telephone	10%										
4	Total stock trades	11		Broker assisted	0%										
5	Bonds	2		Total access	100%										
6	Options	0													
7															
8															
9	Minimums	TD Waterhouse		E*Trade		Ameritrade		HARRIS direct		Schwab		ShareBuilder		BrownCo	
10	Trades per year for active discount	72		108		0		72		124		72		0	
11	Active discount	-5.95		-5.00		0.00		-5.00		-15.00		-2.00		0.00	
12	Online mkt	17.95	48.47	14.99	40.47	10.99	29.67	19.99	53.97	29.95	80.87	4.00	10.80	5.00	13.50
13	Online limit	20.95	150.84	19.99	143.93	10.99	79.13	19.99	143.93	29.95	215.64	4.00	28.80	10.00	72.00
14	Tele mkt	35.00	10.50	14.99	4.50	14.99	4.50	19.99	6.00	49.95	14.99	na	na	5.00	1.50
15	Tele limit	35.00	28.00	19.99	15.99	14.99	11.99	19.99	15.99	49.95	39.96	na	na	10.00	8.00
16	Broker mkt	45.00	0.00	49.99	0.00	24.99	0.00	44.99	0.00	54.95	0.00	na	na	17.00	0.00
17	Broker limit	45.00	0.00	54.99	0.00	24.99	0.00	44.99	0.00	54.95	0.00	na	na	22.00	0.00
18	Bonds (10)	45.00	45.00	40.00	40.00	50.00	50.00	45.00	45.00	54.95	54.95	na	na	50.00	50.00
19	Options (10)	35.45	0.00	37.5	0.00	25.99	0.00	22.49	0.00	22.49	0.00	na	na	20.00	0.00
20															
21															
22			282.81		244.89		175.29		264.89		406.40		39.60		145.00

Figure 9-1. Create a spreadsheet to determine which brokerage's commission schedule works for you

The spreadsheet displays na (not applicable) in the value cells and highlights the cells with red if a brokerage doesn't handle a type of trade or a type of investment, as in the case of ShareBuilder [Hack #57], which offers only online trades and only for stocks. If you like a service the brokerage provides, such as ShareBuilder's ultralow commissions for trades placed on Tuesdays, you can set up accounts with two brokers.

This spreadsheet oversimplifies the calculations for active trader discounts, because it compares the total annual trades you estimate to the annual number of trades required by a brokerage. Unfortunately, most brokerages determine the active trader discount quarterly, so the commissions shown in the spreadsheet might be lower than the ones you pay.

To get an idea of how to build formulas to calculate commissions, dissect the one for online limit orders. The formula in Example 9-1 uses nested `IF` functions to incorporate the active trader discount and to display na if the brokerage doesn't handle the trade type.

Example 9-1. A formula to estimate commissions for online limit orders

```
online limit commission paid (cell C13)
     =IF(B13="na","na",IF(total<B$10,B13,B13+B$11)*limit_num*online)
```

The outer IF function in Example 9-1 checks whether the commission rate for the brokerage is na. If it is, the function propagates na to the cell that represents the commission paid (C13). Otherwise, the commission you pay is based on the number of trades and the charge for the type of trade and access.

The IF function in Example 9-2 calculates the commission rate for the third parameter in Example 9-1. It checks whether the total number of stock trades is less than the active trader minimum (cell B10). If the number of trades is less than the minimum, the function selects the standard commission rate (cell B13). Otherwise, it adds the active trader discount (cell B11) to the standard commission rate.

Example 9-2. The IF function for calculating the commission rate

```
commission rate = IF(total<B$10,B13,B13+B$11)
```

The formula in Example 9-3 summarizes the calculation for the third parameters of the IF function in Example 9-1. It multiplies the commission rate by the number of trades for the type of trade and by the percentage of trades performed using the type of access. The cells for the number of trades that you estimate use named ranges. The named range for cell B2 is market_num. The named range for cell B3 is limit_num. Likewise, the percentages for types of access use named ranges: cell E2 is online, cell E3 is telephone, and cell E4 is broker.

Example 9-3. Multiplying the commission by the trade and access type

```
commission paid = commission rate * limit_num * online
```

Bond and option commissions typically fall into one of three categories:

Zero
If you don't purchase any bonds or options, of course you won't pay any commission.

Minimum
Many brokerages charge a minimum for ten or fewer bond or option contracts. You pay the same amount whether you buy one or ten.

By number
After ten bonds or options, you pay a dollar amount per bond or contract.

To accomplish this rate schedule, the bond and option commission formula looks like the one in Example 9-4. Whether you purchase zero bonds or more than ten bonds, the commission you pay is equal to the commission rate per bond multiplied by the number of bonds. However, if the number of bonds is between zero and ten, you pay the minimum. The interior IF function uses a nested OR function to check for a number of bonds equal to zero or greater than ten. In this spreadsheet, the commission equals the commission rate for a block of ten bonds multiplied by the number of bonds and then divided by ten to obtain the commission per bond. If the brokerages that you are considering calculate their commissions using another formula, you'll have to modify the formulas in the spreadsheet cells accordingly.

Example 9-4. A formula for calculating both the minimum commission and a commission by number of bonds or options

```
bond commission (cell C18)
    =IF(B18="na","na",IF(OR(bond_num=0,bond_num>10),B18*bond_num/10,B18))
```

Choosing the Best Deal

Unless you can accurately predict how many trades you will make of each type and then accurately model the commission calculations for each brokerage you evaluate, it's impossible to compare commissions to the penny. Even a spreadsheet provides only a rough guide to your expenses. In addition, you'll notice that several of the brokerages in Figure 9-1 charge similar commissions. So, how do you put this information to use? It depends on how you trade.

If you place only four trades each for $10,000, the difference between BrownCo ($40) and Schwab ($119.80) is only $79.80—a mere 2/10 of a percent of the dollars that you're investing. In this case, the commission rates aren't a concern. Choose the broker that offers the services you want.

However, if you are just starting out and want to invest a few dollars each month in several different stocks, most of the commissions would overwhelm the dollars invested. As illustrated in Figure 9-2, an investor who places 6 market orders a month for a total of 72 trades in a year can face a huge difference in commissions. By buying companies on a regular schedule with Share-Builder, the investor pays only $152 in commission. BrownCo charges a very reasonable $400 for trades placed whenever you want. At the other end, the investor would pay $2,276 to Schwab for those 72 market orders.

When you trade somewhere in between these two examples and all the brokerages in your spreadsheet satisfy your service requirements, look for the brokerage with the lowest total commission. In this case, it's a good idea to add a few more rows to the spreadsheet to account for fees for maintenance, transferring assets, and issuing certificates. In some cases, high ancillary fees offset low commissions.

	A	B	C	D	E	F	G	H	I	J	K	L	M	N	O
1	Trades per year			Access %											
2	Market	72		Online	100%										
3	Limit	8		Telephone	0%										
4	Total stock trades	80		Broker assisted	0%										
5	Bonds	2		Total access	100%										
6	Options	0													
7															
8															
9	Minimums	TD Waterhouse		E*Trade		Ameritrade		HARRIS direct		Schwab		ShareBuilder		BrownCo	
10	Trades per year for active discount	72		108		0		72		124		72		0	
11	Active discount	-5.95		-5.00		0.00		-5.00		-15.00		-2.00		0.00	
12	Online mkt	17.95	864.00	14.99	1079.28	10.99	791.28	19.99	1079.28	29.95	2156.40	4.00	144.00	5.00	360.00
13	Online limit	20.95	120.00	19.99	159.92	10.99	87.92	19.99	119.92	29.95	239.60	4.00	16.00	10.00	80.00
14	Tele mkt	35.00	0.00	14.99	0.00	14.99	0.00	19.99	0.00	49.95	0.00	na	na	5.00	0.00
15	Tele limit	35.00	0.00	19.99	0.00	14.99	0.00	19.99	0.00	49.95	0.00	na	na	10.00	0.00
16	Broker mkt	45.00	0.00	49.99	0.00	24.99	0.00	44.99	0.00	54.95	0.00	na	na	17.00	0.00
17	Broker limit	45.00	0.00	54.99	0.00	24.99	0.00	44.99	0.00	54.95	0.00	na	na	22.00	0.00
18	Bonds (10)	45.00	45.00	40.00	40.00	50.00	50.00	45.00	45.00	54.95	54.95	na	na	50.00	50.00
19	Options (10)	35.45	0.00	37.5	0.00	25.99	0.00	22.49	0.00	22.49	0.00	na	na	20.00	0.00
20															
21															
22			1029.00		1279.20		929.20		1244.20		2450.95		160.00		490.00

Sheet1 / Sheet2 / Sheet3 /

Figure 9-2. Finding the winner when you trade frequently

Save Up for Something Good

HACK #90

By planning ahead and regularly saving money in the right types of investments, you can have the money you need when you need it.

You just became a proud parent of adorable twin girls. As you try to get them back to sleep in the middle of the night, you begin to think about how much money you're going to need 18 years from now for college tuition. If you happen to have a pile of money sitting around, you can invest it now and let investment return do most of the savings work for you. If you aren't so fortunate—join the club—investing a fixed amount each month and letting the nest egg grow until it's time to take the money out is the next best thing. With Excel functions, you can figure out how big a nest egg you can incubate with the money you can afford each month, or you can calculate how much you need to save each month to achieve a specific amount by your target date.

Determining the results of a savings plan deals with the time value of money. The results you achieve depend on when you put money in, when you plan to take the money out, and the interest rate or investment return you earn. For savings, use one of the following calculations for the time value of money, which are shown with their official financial names so you can impress your friends:

Single-payment compound amount

Calculates how much money you'll have in the future if you invest a lump sum today at a specific investment rate and let it compound for the number of periods until you want the money. For example, if you know the amount you have to invest, the annual rate, and the number of years until you want your money, you can calculate the amount you'll have that number of years in the future.

Equal-payment series compound amount

Calculates how much money you'll have in the future if you invest a fixed amount every period at a specific investment rate. For example, if you know the amount you have to invest each month, the monthly rate you receive on your investments, and the number of months until you want your money, you can calculate the amount you'll have that number of months in the future.

Equal-payment series sinking fund

Calculates the fixed amount you must invest every period given a specific investment rate to reach your goal in the future. For example, if you know the amount you want in the future, the annual rate you receive on your investments, and the number of years until you want your money, you can calculate the amount you must invest each year to reach your future goal.

Fortunately, mathematicians have already figured out all the equations for these calculations and Excel provides built-in functions for them. However, you still have two assignments:

- You must know which types of investments are appropriate for the amount of time you have to invest.

- You must understand the time value of money calculations to provide the right parameters to the Excel functions.

Choosing the Right Investment

Picking the right investment for a savings plan is more art than science, because it requires a balance between return and your tolerance for risk. When you have a decade or more to save, you can use higher-risk investments such as stocks, because you have time to recover from price drops. As your timeframe grows shorter, you want progressively safer investments, so price drops don't undo your hard savings work.

Don't be lured into buying ultrasafe investments when you're saving for the long term. Inflation erodes the purchasing power of your money, so investments that are safe from investment risk—the risk of a stock or bond going south—are still subject to inflation risk. In addition, college tuition is increasing at a frightening rate, in some cases 20 percent a year. To save for college, you should start as early as you can and take advantage of the higher returns that stocks can provide.

You can use Table 9-2 as a guideline for investments suitable for varying savings timeframes. Although the table includes sample rates of return, conditions change constantly. You can find the going rates for certificates of deposit (CDs), money market accounts, and savings accounts [Hack #1] at *http:// www.bankrate.com*. Yahoo! Finance is a good source for bond yields based on maturity and quality (*http://bonds.yahoo.com/rates.html*).

Table 9-2. Pick savings investments based on your timeframe.

Savings timeframe	Type of investment	Approximate annual return
Less than one year	CDs and Treasury securities of less than one year duration, money market accounts, money market funds	0.8 – 1.6 percent
One to five years	Short-term (one- to five-year) CDs and Treasury securities, zero-coupon bonds maturing at your target date	1.6 – 3.8 percent
Five to seven years	Series EE savings bonds, long-term CDs, zero-coupon Treasury securities	1.6 – 3.8 percent
More than seven years	Stocks, stock mutual funds	10 – 12 percent

Some savings investments offer tax advantages that can result in a higher effective return. For example, Treasury security interest is taxed at the federal level but not by states or cities. The interest on Series EE savings bonds might not be taxed at all, but you must hold them for five years to earn the full interest rate.

Calculating the Time Value of Money

To calculate the time value of money in any of its incarnations, you need three pieces of information: the number of periods until your goal, the interest rate (or rate of return), and a dollar value that depends on what you want to calculate. If you decide to look up the formulas for these calculations, you must know the financial names for the parameters used or results calculated:

present value (P)

> The amount of money you have today. When you contribute a lump sum at the beginning, that value is the present value. When you contribute a lump sum, the typical convention is to show this value as negative, which represents money coming out of your pocket and into your investment.

future value (F)

> The amount of money you want or will have in the future. If you enter the present value and/or the amount as negative numbers, the future value is positive, which represents the money coming into your pocket from your investment.

amount (A)

> The amount of money paid each period. If you know how much you can afford to contribute, you enter this as a parameter. If you want to know how much you must save each month, you calculate for this value. When you contribute an amount, the typical convention is to show this value as negative, which represents money coming out of your pocket and into your investment.

number of periods (n)

> The number of periods (typically months) you wait until you want to spend your savings.

interest rate (i)

> The interest rate you receive each period.

> If you are investing a lump sum or adding funds once a year, the number of periods is the same as the number of years until you want to spend your savings, and the interest rate is the annual return for your chosen investment. However, most people prefer to put some money away each month. When you do this, the number of periods is the number of months until you want to spend your money, and the interest rate is the annual return divided by 12—in effect, the monthly interest rate.

How much will you have if you invest a lump sum today? The single-payment compound amount calculates how much money you'll have in the future by investing a lump sum today. In financial terms, you're calculating the future value (F) given a present value (P), a number of periods (n) and an interest rate (i). You use the Excel Future Value function (FV) for this calculation. Because you won't invest a monthly amount, the payment parameter is 0, as shown in Example 9-5.

Example 9-5. Calculating savings from investing a lump sum

```
=FV(interest rate,number of periods,0,present value,type)
```

The fourth parameter in the FV function is the number 0 or 1, where 0 indicates an investment at the end of the period, and 1 is an investment at the beginning of the period. Excel assumes 0 if you omit the parameter. To make the most of compounding, these examples assume that you make investments at the beginning of the period.

For example, the formula in Example 9-6 shows the calculation for your savings five years from now when you invest $1,000 up front in an investment that pays an annual rate of 6 percent, compounded monthly.

Example 9-6. An example of calculating the savings from a lump sum investment

```
=FV(.06/12, 5*12, 0, -1000, 1)
```

How much will you have if you invest some money each month? The equal-payment series compound amount calculates how much money you'll have in the future by investing an amount each period. You calculate the future value (F) given a payment (A for amount), a number of periods (n) and an interest rate (i). Once again, you use the FV function, but in this case, present value is the parameter set to 0 and the payment parameter is how much you plan to save each month. To calculate the result of investing $100 each month for five years, use the formula in Example 9-7.

Example 9-7. An example of calculating the savings from a monthly contribution

```
=FV(.06/12, 5*12, -100, 0, 1)
```

If you plan to invest a lump sum in addition to a monthly contribution, enter your monthly contribution in the third parameter and the value for the lump sum in the fourth parameter.

How much do you have to invest each month to reach your target? To figure out how much you have to save each month to reach a specific savings goal, use the equal-payment series sinking fund, in which you calculate the payment (A for amount) given a future value (F), a number of periods (n) and an interest rate (i). For this calculation, use the PMT function, shown in Example 9-8.

Example 9-8. The PMT function calculates the monthly amount you need to reach a target

```
=PMT(interest rate,number of periods,present value,future value,type)
```

If you plan to invest some money up front, type that value in the present value parameter. Type your savings goal amount in the future value parameter. For example, the function and parameters in Example 9-9 calculate how much you must save each month at a 6 percent annual interest rate compounded monthly to save $12,000 five years from now.

Example 9-9. An example of calculating the monthly contribution to reach a goal

```
=PMT(.06/12, 5*12, 0, 12000, 1)
```

For this example, you have to save $171.14 a month to amass $12,000 five years from now. Because the future value in Example 9-9 is entered as a positive number (money coming into your pocket), the result of the PMT function is a negative number showing the money coming out of your pocket into savings.

HACK #91 Up, Up, and Away: The Cost of College

With college costs soaring out of sight, putting your kid through college without putting yourself in the poorhouse requires some financial homework.

For parents, the numbers are hair-raising. Like an out-of-control Mack truck, college costs increase every year at a blistering pace, and the increase actually accelerated in 2003. At the same time that college tuition is skyrocketing, a college education influences future earning power more than ever. If little Suzy can't afford to go to college, she'll earn $1,000,000 less than the average college graduate during her lifetime. So what can you do to ensure that your kids go to college without sacrificing the rest of your financial goals? Start planning as early as possible [Hack #90] and start by figuring out how much college is likely to cost. If the numbers seem impossibly high, don't worry—there are a number of cost-saving strategies you can try.

The first step to calculating the cost of college is to understand the enemy— tuition is only the beginning. Before you start to build a college savings plan, make sure you add up the costs for each of the following college expenses:

Tuition
    A lump sum or per-credit-hour charge for educational instruction.

Fees
    Vary depending on the college and your child's major. There are some fees that all students must pay, such as student activity fees, but others are optional.

Room
    Varies depending on whether a student lives on or off campus. Some colleges require all students or all freshmen to live on campus.

Board

> Meal plans for students choosing to eat on campus. Most schools offer meal plan options.

Books and supplies

> Course materials, including books, study guides, and lab workbooks.

Transportation and travel

> The cost of commuting from home to school. For commuters, these expenses include insurance, car maintenance, and parking; for resident students living away from home, these include holiday travel.

Medical expenses

> Most students remain on their parent's insurance while attending college, but there could be some extra expenses.

Personal expenses

> As your budding scholars see it, this covers their spending money for frills, such as laundry and phone charges, and for essentials like pizza and DVDs.

> Don't forget about pre-college expenses, which might include application fees, campus visits, testing fees, testing prep fees, moving costs if your kid lives on campus, new clothes, furniture, and other supplies.

The good news is that there are colleges for every budget, so anyone can afford a college education. There's a huge difference in cost between community colleges, four-year public universities, and four-year private universities. Table 9-3 lists average costs according to the College Board for tuition, fees, room, and board for the 2003–2004 school year.

Table 9-3. Average college costs for the 2003–2004 school year from the College Board

Type of school	Tuition and fees	Room and board	Total
Community college	$1,905	0	$1,905
Four-year public	$4,694	$5,942	$10,636
Four-year private	$19,710	$7,144	$26,854

Although costs for community college and four-year public college run far less than those for private school, the costs at these less expensive alternatives are rising the fastest. Tuition rose at community colleges by an average of 13.8 percent, versus 6 percent at four-year private colleges. Students at four-year public universities are hit the hardest—legislators pinched by falling revenues cut education budgets, which resulted in tuition increasing at an average annual rate of 14.1 percent. Students at the University of Missouri swallowed increases of 19.8 percent; their neighbors at Kansas State University took a bigger hit with hikes of 25.1 percent in 2002 and 20.3 percent in 2003. Historically, college cost inflation has outpaced the general cost of living, running between 5 to 8 percent a year. When it's time to prepare a savings plan, count on annual increases at least this high going forward.

> Resist the temptation to cut back on your retirement savings to send your kids to college. Save for college, but make retirement savings your priority. Your children have a lifetime of earnings ahead of them and can afford to take on some debt to finance college. You only have so many years to save for retirement, and your kids won't relish the idea of supporting you in your penury, so put your retirement first.

The Actual Costs

By now, you might be throwing your hands up in the air and kissing the idea of paying for college goodbye. Take heart; paying for college isn't that bad. The big secret is that few actually pay these outrageous amounts, especially the full freight on a four-year private school. Only 8 percent of all college students attend schools with tuition of $24,000 or more. Most college students—nearly 70 percent—face tuition bills of $8,000 per year. Parents typically pay one-third of college expenses from savings, another third from current income, and the last third from parent or student loans. You can choose from a number of online calculators to figure out how much college will cost and how to save to meet the expense, as demonstrated by the College Board's College Cost calculator in Figure 9-3. Some calculators estimate expected financial aid, college living expenses, and loan repayment amounts.

Table 9-4 reviews the best college savings web sites and calculators.

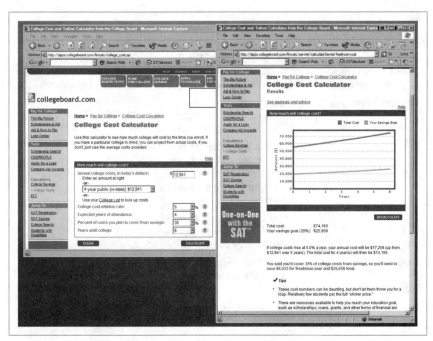

Figure 9-3. The College Board web site shows how much college will cost and what it will take to pay for it

Table 9-4. Online college calculators

Web site	Best calculators	Comments
College Board (*http://www.collegeboard.com/pay*) Click the Calculators link under the Tools heading.	College Cost—Calculates the cost of freshman year as well as the four-year total using current costs and college inflation. College Savings—Calculates the value of your college savings when college begins based on current savings and monthly contributions. Parent Debt—Calculates the amount you could borrow for each year of college without endangering your ability to repay your loans.	This is the best college cost calculator with explanations for each of the variables you enter, analysis of the results of the calculator, and suggestions for increasing your saving success.

Table 9-4. Online college calculators (continued)

Web site	Best calculators	Comments
Motley Fool (*http://www.fool.com/calcs/calculators.htm*) Click the College link.	Value of Higher Education—Estimates the additional earning power of education. College Living Expenses—Estimates annual expenses for books, personal costs, and travel. Expenses Before College—Estimates the costs for exams, college visits, and fixed costs such as furniture, moving, and a computer. Meal Plan Options—Compares the cost per meal for a meal plan to out-of-pocket meal costs.	These calculators help students and parents budget for expenses. Although the calculators use typical costs, you must enter the likely costs for your child's college.
FinAid (*http://www.finaid.org/calculators*)	Tuition Model—Explains why tuition increases faster than inflation. Loan Advisors—Estimates debt amounts parents or students can afford. Expected Family Contribution and Financial Aid—Estimates the amount of money parents and students are expected to contribute for college.	Calculating financial aid and expected family contributions is a complicated business. For the best results, read the caveats and instructions before filling out the calculator entries.
Saving for College (*http://www.savingforcollege.com*) Select the College Planning Resources tab, and then click the Calculators link.	College Savings—Uses a database of college tuition so you can determine the costs for a specific college, including in-state and out-of-state tuition. College Aid—Estimates the cost of college and qualification for financial aid.	The College Savings calculator helps you hone your savings plan if you have your heart set on a specific school, especially if it's expensive. The College Aid calculator can make adjustments for family circumstances and reevaluate your eligibility for financial aid.

Table 9-4. Online college calculators (continued)

Web site	Best calculators	Comments
Educational Services Foundation at (*http://www.esfweb.com*)	Cost of College—Provides information about how much college might cost and how to plan for it.	The Savings Calculator is best used with data for specific colleges.
The links are available on the home page.	Savings—Calculates whether your current savings plan gets the job done.	
	Loan Repayment—Provides helpful hints about repaying college loans.	
	Repayment—Determines the monthly payment and number of years to repay the loan.	

Quicken 2004 features a college cost calculator that projects future college costs and interfaces with your college savings account information.

If money is tight, consider these cost-saving strategies:

- Start your child off with two years of community college.
- Have your child get a head start on accumulating college credits by taking advanced placement classes or actually enrolling in college classes through the local high school. By placing out of college classes, your child earns credits toward graduation without paying tuition for those classes.

I know someone who earned a couple of bachelor degrees with credits to spare. When he enrolled in a prestigious business graduate school 20 years ago, when tuition was much less than it is now, he placed out of over $20,000 worth of classes.

- Thoroughly investigate financial aid options. For the 2003 and 2004 school year, more than $105 billion in financial aid was available to college students.
- If you're fired, downsized, or hit other financial obstacles after your child is enrolled, ask the college about emergency financial aid or loans.
- If your heart is set on an expensive private school, make sure that it's a much better option than your state university by checking the U.S. News college ratings at *http://www.usnews.com/usnews/edu/college/cohome.htm*.

- Consider military scholarships if you're truly strapped and your child has an interest in a military education. These scholarships are particularly helpful for education in careers such as medicine or law, which require extensive and *expensive* postgraduate education.

See Also

- *Meeting College Costs: What You Need to Know Before Your Child & Your Money Leave Home* (College Board)
- *J.K. Lasser's Winning Ways to Save for College* (John Wiley & Sons)

—*Amy Crane*

Let Me Count the Ways to Save for College

#92 Who says the government isn't on your side? Federal law and state savings
programs provide liberal tax breaks and multiple ways to save for college.

For parents with kids destined for college, the 2001 Tax Relief Act was like the best Christmas and birthday presents rolled into one. A sweet deal to start with, college savings plans got even sweeter. Now, you can save money for college through a Section 529 Plan and withdraw money tax-free through 2010. Legislation enhanced Coverdell Savings Accounts, raising contribution limits and relaxing rules. Take advantage of these college savings options to make the most of your college savings:

Section 529 prepaid tuition plan
> Sponsored by states and some private colleges, you prepay future tuition and fees at today's prices. The cost depends on the age of the child enrolled.

> Before you sign up for a Section 529 prepaid tuition plan, ask some hard questions about the health of the plan. Some states have cut off or raised the cost of enrollment in prepaid plans due to declining investment results and spiraling tuition costs. If the plan you use goes belly-up and can't meet its obligations, you might lose the money you contributed and have to start over.
>
> In addition, this type of plan might lock your child into a school that he doesn't want to attend.

Section 529 college savings plan
> Sponsored by states, you invest in a mutual fund-like account [Hack #93]. Results depend on the performance of your investments, and money can be spent at any college in the country.

Coverdell savings account
> Formerly known as an Education IRA, this is a custodial account set up for a child at a financial institution. Contributions are limited to $2,000 per year.

Uniform Gifts to Minors (UGTM) account
> A custodial account set up for the benefit of a child. Money can be used for any purpose and there are no contribution limits.

Taxable Investment Account
> By investing in their own names outside of special accounts, parents retain total control of the money, and there are no limits on contributions, although they are subject to taxes.

Choosing the right college savings plan revolves around four crucial issues:

- Control
- Taxes
- Financial aid
- Plan contribution limits

Control is a hot button for many parents, who envision the ultimate nightmare scenario, in which a child turns 18 and empties the college savings account to buy a Ferrari. For Uniform Gifts to Minors accounts, control reverts to the child at age 18. With Section 529 plans and Coverdell savings accounts, control remains in the hands of the parent or adult who established the account. The most flexible option, for both investment options and eventual use of the money, is a taxable mutual fund or other investment account in the parents' names.

To minimize taxes, pick a Section 529 plan or a Coverdell savings account. Contributions grow tax-free at the federal level; states differ in their tax treatment for these accounts. Distributions are also tax-free for Coverdell accounts and are tax-free at least through 2010 for Section 529 plans. For Uniform Gift to Minors accounts, tax treatment depends on the child's age. For children younger than 14, the first $750 of annual income (interest, dividends, and capital gains) is tax-free and the next $750 is taxed at 10 percent. Income in excess of $1,500 is taxed at the parents' higher rate. For kids older than 14, all income is taxed at the child's rate. For taxable investment accounts, see the capital gains, dividends, and interest rules outlined in "The Taxman Cometh for Your Fund Returns" **[Hack #62]**.

The sun will set on the tax-free status of Section 529 plans in 2011, unless it is extended. Under this sunset provision, Section 529 plans will retain their tax-deferred status, but all gains will be taxed when withdrawn. Experts predict that Congress will extend the tax break, but there are no guarantees.

Government and college financial aid formulas assess each family's ability to pay for college. Current rules favor assets held in the parents' names and penalize assets held in a child's name [Hack #95]. Assets in a child's name could reduce a student's ability to qualify for financial aid. Section 529 college savings plans, Coverdell savings accounts, and taxable investment accounts held in the parents' names are designated parental assets. Current rules classify Section 529 prepaid tuition plans and Uniform Gifts to Minors accounts as student assets.

Coverdell savings accounts allow annual contributions of $2,000 for people whose modified adjusted gross income is below $190,000 for joint filers and below $95,000 for single filers. The sky's the limit for most Section 529 plans with many allowing contributions in excess of $200,000. There are no limits on Uniform Gifts to Minor accounts or on taxable investment accounts.

If your kid goes to private school, you can use Coverdell savings account money to pay for tuition, fees, tutoring, books, supplies, and equipment. Want a new computer for the whole family? That qualifies as a Coverdell expense, as do private school uniforms, travel, and other school-related expenses. However, if you can afford such expenses out of pocket, think twice before raiding college savings accounts.

Table 9-5 summarizes control, tax treatment, financial aid, and contribution limits for each type of college savings plan.

Table 9-5. Features of different types of college savings plans

Type of plan	Controlled by	Tax treatment	Financial aid	Contribution
Prepaid 529	Parent	Earnings are tax-deferred; withdrawals are tax-free through 2010.	High impact; assessed as the child's asset.	Depends on the plan
Savings 529	Parent	Earnings are tax-deferred; withdrawals are tax-free through 2010.	Low impact; assessed as a parental asset.	Depends on the plan

Table 9-5. *Features of different types of college savings plans (continued)*

Type of plan	Controlled by	Tax treatment	Financial aid	Contribution
Coverdell	Parent	Earnings are tax-deferred; withdrawals are tax-free.	Recently changed from child's asset to parental asset.	$2,000 per year
UGTM	Parent until child reaches age 18	Taxed at child's lower rate.	High impact; assessed as the child's asset.	No limit
Taxable account	Parent	Taxed at parent's rate.	Low impact; assessed as a parental asset.	No limit

Well-heeled grandparents can reap significant estate planning benefits by funding Section 529 college savings accounts. Current laws limit contributions to $11,000 per year for each contributor, but a special rule allows five years of contributions in one year.

See Also

- You can find a comprehensive guide to financial aid issues and a college savings plan checklist at *http://www.finaid.org/savings/checklist.phtml.*

—Amy Crane

HACK #93 A College Savings Plan in Every State

Cut through the confusing array of Section 529 college savings plans by focusing on state tax breaks, investing options, and costs.

Section 529 college savings plans [Hack #92] are almost too much of a good thing. State Treasurers have run amok, sponsoring plan after plan. In Nevada, parents face seven choices. Parents are free to invest in any state plan offered, if they can decipher the maze of different spending rules, contribution limits, investment options, and fees. Compounding the confusion, financial advisors have jumped into the fray, offering advisor versions of college savings plans. It's actually easier to choose a Section 529 plan than you might think. Online tools help you understand your choices and select the best plan for you and your child.

To select a college savings plan, you must make three decisions:

- Enroll in a plan directly or through a financial advisor
- Invest in state or out of state
- Choose by type of investment option

Your first decision is whether to go it alone or hire a financial advisor [Hack #99]. An advisor can sort through the options for you, but you pay for that help in more ways than one. When you buy a plan through an advisor, you pay commissions as well as higher ongoing expenses [Hack #59], which cut into your investment returns. Bottom line, you'll have less to pay for college. To keep advisor costs under control, look for a fee-based financial planner. Not only do these planners charge a fixed fee for their services, they are less tempted to boost their income by recommending plans that pay them higher commissions. One source for financial advisors with expertise in college savings plans is the Find a 529Pro tool at the Saving For College web site: *http://www.savingforcollege.com/college_planning_resources/find_a_529_pro*.

Every state now offers at least one college savings plan. Whether your state's plan is the best savings plan for you to use depends on a couple of factors. The best in-state plans offer state tax deductions for contributions and tax exemptions for savings plan earnings that pay for college. Some states impose income limits on eligibility for tax deductions on contributions, while other states provide no deduction at all. Although earnings withdrawn from 529 plans are tax-free at the federal level through 2010, states differ in their treatment of these withdrawals. Some states also slap tax penalties on the earnings from out-of-state plans.

Investment options are another can of worms. Early on, investment options were painfully limited. Now, the opposite is true. Plans increase investment options on a regular basis, resulting in a confusing mix of choices. Each state selects mutual fund companies or other investment providers to manage the money invested in their plans. Vanguard and TIAA-CREF, the large retirement plan provider for teachers, are two of the biggest players in the college savings plan market. However, be wary of any manager embroiled in the mutual fund scandal. Under federal law, you can switch plans and investments only once a year.

Most investment options represent one of three forms: stable value, single fund, or age-based:

Stable value option
> Appeals to investors wary of market volatility and to those with children close to college age. However, don't count on much growth from a stable value plan because they pay a fixed interest rate that changes

every year based on market interest rates. These rates beat inflation—but not by much—and won't grow your money for the long-term. In addition, because college costs typically grow faster than inflation, stable value plans might hurt more than they help if you start saving early.

Single fund option

Offers a menu of funds from various fund families. With these plans, it's up to you to choose the right types of investments to balance risk and return [Hack #94]. If you go the single-fund route, diversify your money in a few different funds with varying investment objectives. Change the allocation of investments to lower investment risk as your child gets closer to college age. A steep decline in the market as your child heads to college could devastate your college nest egg.

Age-based plan

Helps parents balance return and risk. Age-based plans are typically a mix of stock, bond, and stable value options. The younger your child is when you enroll, the more aggressive the investing options. As the child gets older—and closer to enrollment in college—money moves into more conservative options with less chance for investment loss. Table 9-6 show two examples of the age-based investment options offered by the Utah Educational Savings Plan (UESP) Trust.

Table 9-6. An example of an age-based plan

Age	Option 2			Option 8		
	Stocks	Bonds	Money market	Stocks	Bonds	Money market
0-3	95%	5%		80%	20%	
4-6	85%	15%		70%	30%	
8-9	75%	25%		60%	40%	
10-12	65%	35%		50%	50%	
13-15	50%	40%	10%	40%	50%	10%
16+	25%	50%	25%	30%	50%	20%
Enrollment			100%			100%

Before investing in an age-based plan, make sure it offers a sufficient mix of funds. Stock funds might invest in small, medium, large, and foreign companies; large company funds are most stable. Bond funds might invest in government or corporate bonds. Money market funds are fairly similar. Because there is tremendous variation among age-based plans, consult plan documentation for specific details.

Thinking about going back to school? Consider opening a 529 plan for yourself. Most state plans allow adults to enroll, and you'll enjoy the same tax and saving advantages as your child does. If you don't end up using the plan for yourself, you can transfer the money to your child, spouse, or grandchild.

There are a few more factors worth considering before you download an application and send in your check. Look for:

- Low minimum investment requirements (around $25 to $50 for an automatic investment plan)
- High contribution limits (above $200,000)
- Ability to easily change beneficiaries
- Few restrictions on spending for qualified higher expenses
- No-penalty rollovers to other state plans
- No time limit for withdrawals
- An informative web site with downloadable applications and account access

The best resource for sorting through college savings plans is the Saving For College web site at *http://www.savingforcollege.com*. Joe Hurley, a CPA and 529 pioneer, runs the site, which offers a five-cap rating system (that's cap as in a graduation mortarboard) that ranks the features of the various programs, a tool that helps you comparison-shop, FAQs and educational resources, and links to all state programs. Figure 9-4 shows an example of the site's 529 Evaluator tool.

See Also

- *A Guide to Understanding 529 Plans* at the College Savings Plan Network at *http://www.collegesavings.org*
- Morningstar's 529 Plan Center with data at *http://www.morningstar. com/529/529Table.html?pfsection=529* and commentary at *http://www. morningstar.com/centers/529.html?pfsection=Centers3*
- 401kid at *http://www.401kid.com* offers customized 529 plan recommendations and phone consultations with an educational planner for a membership fee of $29.95 per year. Get help enrolling in plans and online statements for an extra $70 per year.

—*Amy Crane*

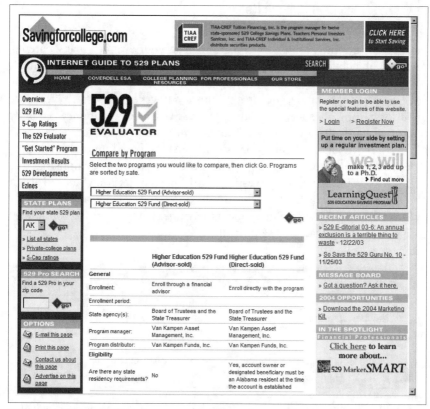

Figure 9-4. Use the 529 Evaluator to compare the features of two 529 college savings plans

Balance Risk and Return for College Costs

HACK #94

Building a college nest egg can take some time, which means that your investment strategy must change depending on where your child is on the road to college.

With college tuition soaring [Hack #91], parents who want to pay for their kids' education need as much help as they can get. Tax-advantaged education accounts [Hacks #92 and #93] are a huge help, but by far the best thing for college savings is time. By starting to save for college early, you can invest in stocks and earn returns that keep up with or exceed college tuition increases. However, stocks are risky for the short term [Hack #37], so you must move your savings into safer investments as your child gets closer to college age.

Get a Head Start on College Costs

If you're an overachiever, you can start setting money aside for college before your bundle of joy is even a glimmer in your eye. For many parents, the birth of a child is a wake-up call (even several a night for many months). As the costs of raising an infant begin to roll in, you might forget about the college costs looming decades in the future. However, these early years are great for getting ahead of the college curve. Start investing money regularly in mutual funds that own stocks. Because of the number of years you'll have to save and the higher returns that stocks or stock-based mutual funds provide, your monthly contribution can be more reasonable, as demonstrated in Figure 9-5. With 12 years of investing at a 10 percent return, you need about $350 a month to reach $100,000. If you don't start saving until five years before school and use safe investments paying 4 percent return, you'll need $1500 a month to reach the same goal.

	A	B	C	D	E
	oih_09 college monthly payment.xls				
1	Return	10%		Return	4%
2	Number of years	12		Number of years	5
3	Nest egg goal	100,000		Nest egg goal	100,000
4					
5	Monthly contribution	($358.76)		Monthly contribution	($1,503.31)
6					

Figure 9-5. The earlier you start to save, the less you have to contribute each month to reach your goal

Stock-based mutual funds are the easiest investments for this kind of savings plan. You can set up an automatic investment program, so that the mutual fund deducts your monthly contribution automatically from your checking account. When it's time to sell some of your stock investments, you simply sell the appropriate number of shares of the fund. You won't have to consider which stocks to sell or how to rebalance the stock portfolio for diversification.

To make the most of compounding, be sure to reinvest the dividends that your stocks or mutual funds distribute.

The Middle Years

The adolescent years bring a host of problems, both psychologically and financially. You're on your own interfacing with your teenager. Fortunately, the financial transformation of college savings will seem easier by comparison.

Because you don't want to lose money in the stocks in your college savings when there's little time for them to recover, the transition to safer investments begins when your child is 12 years old. The conventional advice is to start depositing new savings into safer investments, such as long-term certificates of deposit or *zero coupon treasury bonds* (also known as zero-coupon treasuries) that mature when your child heads off to college. However, if you make automatic monthly deposits to a stock fund, you could choose to continue that, and sell a chunk of your stocks or mutual funds to meet your target percentage for CDs or bonds. However, if a recession appears imminent, switch your monthly deposits to a secure savings option.

> A zero coupon bond does not pay interest during its lifetime. Instead, investors buy zero coupon bonds at a deep discount from their face value, which is the lump sum the investor receives when the bond matures. In addition to higher rates than bonds that pay interest regularly, zero coupon bonds usually carry long terms such as eight or more years, so you can purchase zero coupons that mature exactly when you need money for tuition.

By the time your child is 14, about half of your college nest egg should be in safer investments. Therefore, between ages 12 and 14, you must gradually reduce the percentage of funds invested in stocks from 100 percent to 50 percent. Realistically, you continue to reduce the percentage of money in stocks until all your college savings are safe by the time your child heads off to college.

Using CDs, traditional bonds, or zero coupon bonds for your secure savings also requires some planning. You want sufficient holdings to mature each year. In addition, if you decide to add your monthly contributions to safe investments, you could end up with numerous CDs for each contribution. Small bond purchases could kill you with minimum commissions [Hack #58]. Here's one approach to keep things simple:

1. When you transfer money from stocks to safe investments, buy a fixed-income investment that matures in time for freshman year.

2. Continue using stock transfer dollars to buy fixed-income investments that mature for freshman year up to the amount you forecast for freshman year expenses.

3. When freshman year is covered, start buying fixed-income investments that mature for sophomore year until sophomore expenses are covered. Continue this approach to cover junior and senior years.

4. When you want the monthly contribution to go into safe savings, deposit the monthly contribution in a money market account, money market fund, or savings account with a decent interest rate.

5. Twice a year, use the money in the money market to purchase fixed-income investments that mature for the college year that isn't yet covered.

Hacking the Hack

Unfortunately, the money you invest in stocks grows faster than the money in safe investments, and the monthly contributions further unbalance your plan. Trying to figure out how much money to transfer between stocks and safe havens each year might give tax preparation a run for its money as something you'd rather not do. That's why it's a good idea to create an Excel spreadsheet to help you plan your college savings program.

The spreadsheet in Figure 9-6 assumes a steady monthly contribution from the time your child is born until she graduates from college. $400 a month adds up to well over $200,000 when you save for 22 years. So, sending your child to a good, private school requires nothing more than saving the money you would spend on a cappuccino on your way to work and eating lunch at a restaurant each workday.

oih_09 college transitions.xls

	A	B	C	D	E	F	G	H	I	J	K	L
1												
2	Stock return	10%	Safe return	4%								
3	Saving years	18	Monthly contribution	-400								
4												
5	Start of Year		Stock Nest Egg	Safe Nest Egg	Total Nest Egg	Withdrawal from safe	Remaining Nest Egg	Target stock %	Target safe %	Transfer to safe	Target stock $	Target safe $
6	Age 12	-6	$110,575	$0	$110,575	$0	$110,575	85%	15%	$16,586	$93,989	$16,586
7	Age 13	-5	$108,857	$17,262	$126,119	$0	$126,119	70%	30%	$20,574	$88,283	$37,836
8	Age 14	-4	$102,554	$39,377	$141,931	$0	$141,931	50%	50%	$31,588	$70,966	$70,966
9	Age 15	-3	$83,423	$73,857	$157,280	$0	$157,280	50%	50%	$4,783	$78,640	$78,640
10	Age 16	-2	$91,901	$81,844	$173,744	$0	$173,744	45%	55%	$13,716	$78,185	$95,559
11	Age 17	-1	$91,398	$99,453	$190,851	$0	$190,851	40%	60%	$15,058	$76,340	$114,510
12	Freshman	0	$84,334	$124,065	$208,399	$50,000	$158,399	0%	100%	$84,334	$0	$158,399
13	Sophomore	1	$0	$169,741	$169,741	$55,000	$114,741	0%	100%	$0	$0	$114,741
14	Junior	2	$0	$124,305	$124,305	$60,000	$64,305	0%	100%	$0	$0	$64,305
15	Senior	3	$0	$71,814	$71,814	$66,000	$5,814	0%	100%	$0	$0	$5,814

Sheet1 / Sheet2 / Sheet3

Figure 9-6. *Calculate the money you should invest in stocks and fixed-income investments to reach your goal*

The spreadsheet uses the Future Value (FV) function to calculate how much your savings grow to over time. Example 9-10 shows the FV function calculating the result of saving $400 a month for the first 12 years. This example starts with a zero balance, so the present value parameter is zero.

Example 9-10. *The formula to calculate future value from a zero balance and monthly contributions*

```
Future Value from stocks = FV(B$2/12,(B$3+B6)*12,D$3,0,)
```

Here's how the FV function works:

```
Future Value = FV(rate,periods,payment,balance,type)
```

rate

> The interest rate per period. Because the return rate in cell B2 is an annual rate, the rate parameter in this example divides cell B2 by 12 to obtain a monthly rate.

periods

> The number of periods you plan to save. Because the function in cell C6 calculates 12 years of return (the number of years of saving in cell B3 minus the years before college in cell B6), the number of periods equals 12 multiplied by the number of years.

payment

> The monthly contribution.

balance

> Known as the present value, this is the amount of money you have at the beginning of the savings period, in this case, zero.

> For a savings plan, enter 1 as the type parameter. This calculates the future value assuming that you contribute at the beginning of each period.

When your child reaches age 12, the example switches to yearly calculations. In this example, the monthly contribution goes into stocks, so the formula for calculating the future value takes into account both monthly contributions and the balance at the beginning of each year, as shown in Example 9-11.

Example 9-11. The formula to calculate future value from an existing balance and monthly contributions

```
Future Value (cell C9) = FV(B$2/12,12,D$3,-K8,)
```

> In Example 9-11, the balance or present value is the amount of money in stocks the previous year (cell K8).

The spreadsheet performs several calculations to determine how much money you need to transfer to safe investments each year:

Safe Nest Egg

> Use the FV function to calculate the value of your safe investments at the end of a year using the safe return in cell B3. Beginning the freshman

year of college, the monthly contribution is made to safe investments, so it appears in the payment parameter in these cells.

Total Nest Egg
  The total amount of savings you have at the beginning of the year.

Withdrawal from safe
  The amount of money you must withdraw to pay for a school year. This value is zero until freshman year, and then increases by about 10 percent a year until graduation to take into account potential tuition and board increases.

Remaining Nest Egg
  The savings that remain after withdrawing money for a school year.

Target stock %
  The percentage of savings you want in stocks at the beginning of the year. This value drops each year until freshman year of college, at which point all savings should be safe.

Target safe %
  The percentage of savings in safe investments at the beginning of each year.

Transfer to safe
  The amount of money you should transfer to safe investments after any withdrawals to meet your target safe percentage. To calculate this value, subtract the amount of money in safe investments from the target safe dollars, and then add in the value of any withdrawals.

Target stock $
  The dollars you want in stock investments to meet your target stock percentage.

Target safe $
  The dollars you want in safe investments to meet your target safe percentage.

The returns you achieve don't always match your forecasts. Because the returns you supply for calculations are average annual returns, your year-to-year results almost never match your estimates. For that reason, when you get to the beginning of each year processed in your spreadsheet, replace the values for stocks and safe investments in columns C and D with the actual balances in your accounts.

HACK #95 When It's Time to Break the College Savings Piggy Bank

It takes some fancy footwork to tap college savings while maintaining your child's eligibility for financial aid, minimizing taxes on earnings, and simply making the money last.

If you're like many parents, you've cobbled together a mishmash of college savings accounts. Between gifts from grandparents, contributions to college savings accounts, and regular investments, you've amassed a respectable amount of money to pay for college. Now that the time has come to break that piggy bank open, which funds do you tap first? When you understand which savings affect taxes and eligibility for financial aid, you can call Excel to the rescue to plan your payouts.

Even if you don't think your family qualifies, it's worthwhile to fill out financial aid paperwork. Colleges recalculate financial aid eligibility each year, so your family might qualify one year, even if it didn't the previous year. Federal financial aid guidelines expect students to contribute 35 percent of their income toward college costs and parents to pony up 5.6 percent of their income. Use web-based financial aid calculators **[Hack #91]** or consult college financial aid officers to see whether you qualify. If you are close to qualifying for financial aid, you can spend your child's assets first to increase your chance of financial aid in the future. If your income and savings put you way above financial aid cut-offs, you have more flexibility for spending college money.

> It's a dream come true—your son or daughter has landed a full ride to Harvard or received an appointment to a military academy. So what the heck do you do with all your college savings? Section 529 and Coverdell savings account money can be used to pay for extras like books, travel, and foreign study. You can also transfer the money to another child in your family, yourself, or hang onto it in case you need it down the line.

Spending Assets to Qualify for Financial Aid

College and government financial aid formulas reduce financial aid drastically for students with assets in their name. To increase your child's chance of obtaining financial aid in the future, first spend down money in student assets, such as Uniform Gifts to Minors (UGTM) accounts.

1. Empty accounts categorized as a child's assets for freshman year costs, so your student might qualify for financial aid by sophomore year.

2. Next, decide whether to spend money in Section 529 college savings plans [Hack #93] or other investment savings. Some experts advise drawing on Section 529 plans last, so that they can grow tax-deferred for as long as possible. Others argue that the purpose of these savings is to pay for college and recommend using them immediately. You can compromise by adding all of your savings designated for college, dividing the total by the number of college years left, and then drawing proportionally from college and regular savings for each year.

3. If there's a gap between your college savings and expenses, dig deeper into current income or look to loans. Many colleges offer monthly payment plans to help parents manage their cash flow while paying from current income. As for loans, the typical college student graduates with debt of $19,785. The federal Stafford Loan program allows students to borrow up to $2,625 for freshman year, $3,500 for sophomore year, and $5,500 for both junior and senior years. Parents reluctant to burden their kids with excessive debt can take out a home equity loan or borrow under the federal Parent Loan for Undergraduate Students (PLUS) program.

Resist the temptation to borrow money from your 401(k) plan to pay for your child's education. If you don't repay the money on time, you face severe penalties. Besides, your retirement is too important to mortgage for any reason, even to pay for your child's college education.

The spreadsheet in Figure 9-7 shows an example of how you can spend $35,000 in savings to pay for college expenses totaling $56,031.63. Using $14,000 in Coverdell and UGTM account money immediately may reduce the assets left to pay for the last couple years but may increase a student's eligibility for financial aid as well.

Spending College Savings When Financial Aid Isn't an Issue

If your income and savings put you way above financial aid cut-offs, don't despair. Most aid is in the form of loans anyway. If you have sufficient income to pay for college expenses for the first year or two without drawing down college savings plans, do so. If not, look at your total expenses for all four years (including likely college tuition inflation) and allocate a combination of savings, current income, and loans to pay the bills. The typical parent finances their child's education from one-third savings, one-third current income, and one-third loans.

oih_09 college spending 1.xls

	A	B	C	D	E	F	G	H	I
1	College Savings	Savings when college starts	Freshman year expenses	Savings at end of first year	Sophomore year expenses	Savings at end of second year	Junior year expenses	Savings at end of third year	Senior year expenses
2									
3	Student Assets								
4	UGTM	9000.00	9000.00	0.00	0.00	0.00		0.00	
5									
6	Parent Assets								
7	Coverdell Savings Account	5000.00	4000.00	1030.00	1030.00	0.00		0.00	
8	529 Plan	13000.00		13390.00	6620.00	6973.10	6973.10	0.00	
9	Taxable Savings	8000.00		8240.00	6000.00	2307.20	2307.20	0.00	
10									
11	Debt						1052.20		11049.13
12	Current Income						4000.00		4000.00
13									
14	Total	35000.00	13000.00	22660.00	13650.00	9280.30	14332.50	0.00	15049.13
15									
16								Total debt	Total out of pocket
17								12101.33	8000.00

Sheet1 / Sheet2 / Sheet3 /

Figure 9-7. Paying expenses out of the student's assets first might help qualify for financial aid

If you have stock or mutual funds that have appreciated in value that you plan to sell to pay for college, consider giving those as gifts to your child, who can then sell them and use the proceeds to pay college expenses. The child pays taxes on the sale at his lower capital gains rate of 5 percent, much lower than a parent's long-term capital gains rate of 15 percent.

The spreadsheet in Figure 9-8 uses the same tuition and savings as in Figure 9-7, but shows how your money could grow if you pay for the first year and a half of college with a combination of cash and loans. Basically, you can pay for the last two-and-a-half years from college savings if you pay for the first year-and-a-half out of current cash flow and loans. If Congress doesn't extend the tax exemption on Section 529 funds past 2011, parents whose kids start school in 2008, 2009, or 2010 must use a different strategy. In this case, spend your Section 529 money first, and spend it before 2011 to avoid being taxed on any gains.

See Also

- Troll the Web for scholarships to reduce your costs; *http://www.fastweb. com/ib/finaid-21f* is a good place to start.
- Review loan options at *http://www.finaid.org/loans*; see the parent loan trade-off tip sheet at *http://www.finaid.org/loans/loantradeoffs.phtml*.

	B	C	D	E	F	G	H	I
1	Savings when college starts	Freshman year expenses	Savings at end of first year	Sophomore year expenses	Savings at end of second year	Junior year expenses	Savings at end of third year	Senior year expenses
2								
3								
4	9000.00	0.00	9270.00	0.00	9548.10	7805.30	1795.08	1795.08
5								
6								
7	5000.00	0.00	5150.00	0.00	5304.50	5304.50	0.00	
8	13000.00	0.00	13390.00	1000.00	12761.70	0.00	13144.55	13144.55
9	8000.00	0.00	8240.00	6400.00	1895.20	1122.70	795.68	109.50
10								
11		9500.00		2250.00			0.00	0.00
12		4000.00		4000.00			0.00	0.00
13								
14	35000.00	13500.00	36050.00	13650.00	29509.50	14232.50	15735.31	15049.13
15								
16		13000.00		13650.00		14332.50		15049.13
17								
18						Taxable Savings	Total debt	Total out of pocket
19						706.76	11750.00	8000.00
20								

Figure 9-8. *Allowing college savings plans to grow reduces the amount you have to borrow or pay out of pocket*

- Find tips on demystifying college aid awards and filling in any gaps at *http://www.collegeboard.com/pay/ways_to_pay*.

—*Amy Crane and Bonnie Biafore*

HACK #96 Save for Retirement While Still Enjoying Yourself

Online retirement planners help you find out if your current plan is working, and tell you what to do if it isn't.

If you're planning to live for years after you retire and want to have even more fun than you're having now, you must build a serious nest egg for retirement. The sooner you start saving for retirement, the easier it is, because you can take advantage of compounding and higher-return investments for your portfolio. You may be able to retire earlier than you had expected if you start saving now. If you wait too long, you'll have to scrimp before retirement to catch up or pay the price of a lower standard of living after you retire. To find out where you stand and what your next steps are, you must answer some questions and make some educated guesses. Fortunately, you can choose from a number of online retirement calculators that are far easier to understand than trying to calculate this stuff yourself.

Online Retirement Planners

You can choose from several online retirement planners to help you determine how much money you'll need to retire and whether you're on track to achieve that goal. Depending on whether you provide rough estimates or details of your financial situation, you can obtain forecasts of your retirement results. Check out these three online tools to see which one suits your needs:

Quicken.com Retirement Planner
> At *http://www.quicken.com/retirement/planner*, you can answer the questions or use built-in tools to make educated estimates about items such as life expectancy and tax rates.

CNNmoney Retirement Planner
> At *http://cgi.money.cnn.com/tools/retirementplanner/retirementplanner.jsp*, data entry is fast and easy, although you have to find most of the information on your own. In addition to telling you how much money you need, you can choose from low-risk to aggressive investment portfolios, and the tool calculates the probability that you'll achieve your investment goals.

MSN Money Retirement Planner
> At *http://money.msn.com/retire/planner.asp*, you can build a rough plan quickly and then add more information later to obtain an in-depth plan. You have to enroll to use this tool, so you must be comfortable with their privacy policy before you start.

> If you want to prepare the ultimate in thorough retirement plans, considering all your life goals, including your kids' college education, home purchases and sales, and even big vacation plans, the best tool around is the Retirement Planner included with any version of Quicken personal finance software.

What You Need to Know to Plan Your Retirement

Retirement planning is a bit more complicated than saving for a vacation. There are several factors that can affect the results of your plan and you can do no more than estimate most of them. Here are some guidelines to help you answer the questions you'll face when you use online retirement planning tools:

Estimated length of retirement
> The number of years you'll spend in retirement is possibly the biggest factor in your plan, and it's the hardest to answer. If you're like me, it's tough just to remember how old you are. You have to specify your

desired retirement age, so you might as well start with the age you would like to retire. You can always go back and change it if you have to. The real kicker is life expectancy. How do you figure out how old you'll be when you die? If you underestimate, you'll run out of money and end up on state aid—or maybe worse, living with your kids. To estimate you life expectancy based on your gender and smoker-status in the Quicken.com retirement planner, click the Estimate button on the Personal Info screen. To be safe, adjust the estimate upward if your parents, aunts, and uncles tend to live well into their 90s.

Post-retirement expenses

The next big factor in retirement planning is your desired standard of living. Most of the retirement planners ask for your current salary, the annual raise you receive, and an estimate of your annual expenses after you retire. One rule of thumb for estimating retirement expenses is 75 percent of preretirement income, the reasoning being that you stop spending money on work-related expenses such as gas, business clothes, and retirement plan contributions. In addition, your tax rate might be lower and eventually you'll be free of your mortgage payment. However, if you plan to travel the world or take up an expensive hobby like horseracing, you're better off bumping that percentage up.

You can also prepare an accurate estimate of your annual expenses by adding up your current annual expenses, subtracting the expenses you don't expect to pay when you retire, and adding new expenses for your new hobbies.

Taxes

Although the tax bite is often milder after you retire, estimating your retirement tax rate at your current level adds a small measure of safety to your retirement plan. The easiest way to calculate your tax rate is to dig out last year's tax returns. To determine your federal tax rate, divide your total tax (line 60 on IRS form 1040) by your gross income (line 22 on IRS form 1040). Your state tax rate is the state tax you pay divided by your gross income.

The Quicken.com Retirement Planner uses a combined tax rate, computed by dividing your total state and federal taxes by total income.

Inflation

Your expenses and taxes might decrease during retirement, but inflation is a parasite that eats away at your purchasing power whether you're working or have retired. For example, 3 percent annual inflation, which is the average for recent years, reduces the purchasing power of one dollar to only 41 cents over 30 years. In planning for retirement, you have to invest so your portfolio grows faster than inflation. Retirement planners use the estimated inflation rate to figure out how many inflated dollars you need for your postretirement annual expenses.

Current retirement balances and annual contributions

You can't change history, so any retirement planner you use is going to start with the retirement savings you have today. The Quicken.com Retirement Planner goes into more detail than some others. To fill out its Assets screen, you must know the following information:

Current 401(k) balance
The percentage of your salary that you contribute each year
The percentage of your contribution that your employer matches
The maximum dollar amount that your employer contributes to matching funds
Current IRA balance
Annual contribution to your IRA
Current Roth IRA balance
Annual contribution to your Roth IRA
Current balance of taxable savings earmarked for retirement
Annual contribution to taxable retirement savings

401(k) plans have been a real boon for people saving for retirement. In addition to deferring taxes on your contributions, dividends, and capital gains until you withdraw money from the account, 401(k) plans often come with company matching programs, in which your employer contributes money to match a percentage of your contributions. That's like making a 100 percent return just by putting the money in your account. If your company offers a 401(k) plan, participate at the highest percentage you can manage. If you can't hit the maximum, shoot for the maximum that your employer matches.

Contributions to IRA accounts are deductible only if your income is below a specific level. Contributions to Roth IRA accounts are not deductible at all. However, your capital gains and dividends in these accounts grow tax-deferred until you withdraw your money, so they are preferable to saving for retirement in completely taxable accounts.

Retirement benefits

You might qualify for other retirement income besides the money you save yourself—Social Security and a company pension plan being two common sources. If you're a pessimist who thinks that Social Security won't be around when you retire, you can type **0** for your estimate of annual Social Security benefits. The Quicken.com Retirement Planner includes an Estimate Benefits feature that factors your salary and the age when you plan to start collecting Social Security to calculate your annual benefits.

> If you want a more accurate estimate of your benefits based on your complete earnings history, use one of the calculators provided by the Social Security Administration at *http://www.ssa.gov/planners/calculators.htm*.

If you're lucky enough to qualify for a company pension plan, you can ask your company HR department for the annual amount you can expect. In addition, it's important to find out if there is a cost-of-living adjustment, which means that the annual income that you receive increases each year to account for increases in the cost of living.

Investment return

The final factor in retirement planning is the investment return that you expect to achieve both before and after retirement. Prior to retirement, when you have a long timeframe for investing, you can use higher-risk, higher-return investments, such as large-cap, small-cap, and international stocks. After retirement, as your timeframe for recovering from downturns shortens, you should gradually change your investment allocation [Hack #74] from higher-risk, higher-return stocks to more conservative income-producing investments, such as bonds or high-dividend paying stocks. Because of this adjustment, it's safer to estimate a lower rate of return for your portfolio after you retire. For example, the Quicken.com Retirement Planner estimates a 9 percent return for a high-risk allocation of 56 percent large-cap stocks, 21 percent small-cap stocks, and 23 percent international stocks. After retirement, a moderately risky portfolio of 41 percent bonds, 33 percent large-cap stocks, 12 percent small-cap stocks, and 14 percent international stocks will likely return 7 percent a year.

Analyzing the Results

When you finish answering the planner questions, you can see whether your plan is working. For example, the Quicken.com Retirement Planner provides a graph that shows your portfolio value increasing up to retirement and then decreasing as you use it during retirement. In some planners, you can choose whether you want to see dollar amounts in today's dollars or in dollars adjusted for the impact of inflation.

If your plan isn't working, you can modify some of your assumptions. The Quicken.com Retirement Planner includes a what-if section in which you can modify values and recalculate your plan. For example, you can choose to:

- Retire later than you had hoped
- Scale back your spending in retirement
- Boost your retirement savings
- Take on additional risk to achieve a higher investment return

I suppose you can also lower your life expectancy. However, it's tough enough to get old without having to lower your standard of living because you're living longer than you anticipated.

> Assuming higher risk in a retirement account might be all right while you're still working. If your account takes a hit and doesn't recover, you can always decide to work longer. However, after you retire, it's a good idea to keep your investment risk lower, so you don't have to sacrifice quality of life or go back to work.

HACK #97 Juggle Multiple Objectives

When you're saving for goals that occur at different times, juggling money across different types of investments takes some planning.

In most cases, your retirement savings are in accounts totally dedicated to your retirement goal. Because you probably have a pretty good idea of your retirement age, you can adjust the allocation of your retirement money without too much work [Hack #75]. The hardest part is remembering to look at all your retirement accounts as a whole. However, you might save for other goals that occur at different times—two children heading to college four years apart or start-up costs for your dream of starting a small business. You can manage each of these savings portfolios separately by creating accounts for each objective, but that could lead to an overwhelming number of accounts. A spreadsheet can help you develop one overarching allocation for the savings you need for multiple goals.

To determine an overall allocation, you must first know your allocation for each goal on its own. Allocations gradually switch to safer investments as your goal approaches. The spreadsheet in "Balance Risk and Return for College Costs" [Hack #94] calculates the distribution of money between stocks and fixed-income investments as you save and then spend a college nest egg.

If you track your allocations across additional asset categories, such as large-cap stocks, small-cap stocks, international stocks, bonds, and cash, you can add columns to your spreadsheet for each category you use.

Add a worksheet for each additional savings goal. For example, in Figure 9-9, the spreadsheet includes three worksheets: one for a child that starts college in 18 years, a second for a child that starts college in 22 years, and a third (on the Business tab) for saving the start-up costs for a small business 10 years in the future.

College 1

Start of Year		Stock Nest Egg	Safe Nest Egg	Total Nest Egg	Withdrawal from safe	Remaining Nest Egg	Target stock %	Target safe %	Transfer to safe	Target stock $	Target safe $
Stock return	10%	Safe return		4%							
Saving years	18	Monthly contribution		-200							
Age 12	-6	$55,288	$0	$55,288	$0	$55,288	85%	15%	$8,293	$46,994	$8,293
Age 13	-5	$54,428	$8,631	$63,059	$0	$63,059	70%	30%	$10,287	$44,142	$18,918
Age 14	-4	$51,277	$19,689	$70,966	$0	$70,966	50%	50%	$15,794	$35,483	$35,483
Age 15	-3	$41,711	$36,928	$78,640	$0	$78,640	50%	50%	$2,392	$39,320	$39,320
Age 16	-2	$45,950	$40,922	$86,872	$0	$86,872	45%	55%	$6,858	$39,092	$47,780
Age 17	-1	$45,699	$49,726	$95,425	$0	$95,425	40%	60%	$7,529	$38,170	$57,255
Freshman	0	$42,167	$62,032	$104,199	$25,000	$79,199	0%	100%	$42,167	$0	$79,199
Sophomore	1	$0	$84,871	$84,871	$27,000	$57,871	0%	100%	$0	$0	$57,871
Junior	2	$0	$62,673	$62,673	$30,000	$32,673	0%	100%	$0	$0	$32,673
Senior	3	$0	$36,449	$36,449	$33,000	$3,449	0%	100%	$0	$0	$3,449

College 2

Start of Year		Stock Nest Egg	Safe Nest Egg	Total Nest Egg	Withdrawal from safe	Remaining Nest Egg	Target stock %	Target safe %	Transfer to safe	Target stock $	Target safe $
Stock return	10%	Safe return		4%							
Saving years	22	Monthly contribution		-150							
Age 12	-6	$70,565	$0	$70,565	$0	$70,565	85%	15%	$10,585	$59,981	$10,585
Age 13	-5	$68,146	$11,016	$79,162	$0	$79,162	70%	30%	$12,733	$55,414	$23,749
Age 14	-4	$63,101	$24,716	$87,817	$0	$87,817	50%	50%	$19,192	$43,909	$43,909
Age 15	-3	$50,391	$45,698	$96,089	$0	$96,089	50%	50%	$2,347	$48,044	$48,044
Age 16	-2	$54,960	$50,002	$104,962	$0	$104,962	45%	55%	$7,727	$47,233	$57,729
Age 17	-1	$54,064	$60,081	$114,145	$0	$114,145	40%	60%	$8,406	$45,658	$68,487
Freshman	0	$50,439	$73,110	$123,549	$30,000	$93,549	0%	100%	$50,439	$0	$93,549
Sophomore	1	$0	$99,194	$99,194	$32,000	$67,194	0%	100%	$0	$0	$67,194
Junior	2	$0	$71,765	$71,765	$36,000	$35,765	0%	100%	$0	$0	$35,765
Senior	3	$0	$39,055	$39,055	$39,000	$55	0%	100%	$0	$0	$55

Figure 9-9. Calculate allocation separately for each goal

You might notice that the savings plan for your second child doesn't require as much of a monthly contribution. Because the savings plan for the younger child runs four years longer, you contribute less out of your pocket ($39,600 versus $43,200) but amass a larger college nest egg ($137,055 versus $118,449). To review the wonders of compounding, see "Calculate Compound Annual Rates of Growth" **[Hack #26]**.

To calculate the allocation of stocks and fixed-income investments that you need each year, create an additional worksheet and type a year label for each year in your savings plan. To get an overview of your savings for individual goals, you can create columns for dollars in stocks and fixed-income investments for each goal, as demonstrated in Figure 9-10. Columns B and C show the money in stocks and fixed-income investments for each year you save for your business. Columns D and E represent the savings for your first child's college education, while columns F and G show your second college fund. This worksheet references the cells on the individual goal worksheets, so new values appear automatically when you play what-if games on the goal worksheets.

Year	Business Stocks	Business Safe	College 1 Stocks	College 1 Safe	College 2 Stocks	College 2 Safe	Total	Stocks %	Stock $	Safe %	Safe $
1	$5,026	$0	$2,513	$0	$1,885		$9,424	100%	$9,424.18	0%	$0
2	$10,579	$0	$5,289	$0	$3,967		$19,835	100%	$19,835.19	0%	$0
3	$16,713	$0	$8,356	$0	$6,267		$31,336	100%	$31,336.37	0%	$0
4	$23,489	$0	$11,744	$0	$8,808		$44,042	100%	$44,041.87	0%	$0
5	$30,975	$0	$15,487	$0	$11,616		$58,078	100%	$58,077.80	0%	$0
6	$31,396	$7,849	$19,622	$0	$14,717		$73,583	89%	$65,734.58	11%	$7,849
7	$33,132	$14,200	$24,190	$0	$18,143		$89,665	84%	$75,465.09	16%	$14,200
8	$27,801	$27,801	$29,236	$0	$21,927		$106,765	74%	$78,964.10	26%	$27,801
9	$18,994	$44,319	$34,811	$0	$26,108		$124,231	64%	$79,912.57	36%	$44,319
10	$0	$70,101	$40,969	$0	$30,727		$141,797	51%	$71,695.74	49%	$70,101
11			$47,772	$0	$35,829		$83,601	100%	$83,601.17	0%	$0
12			$46,994	$8,293	$41,466		$96,753	91%	$88,460.12	9%	$8,293
13			$44,142	$18,918	$47,693		$110,752	83%	$91,834.16	17%	$18,918
14			$35,483	$35,483	$54,571		$125,537	72%	$90,054.16	28%	$35,483
15			$39,320	$39,320	$62,171		$140,810	72%	$101,490.46	28%	$39,320
16			$39,092	$47,780	$59,981	$10,585	$157,438	63%	$99,073.12	37%	$58,365
17			$38,170	$57,255	$55,414	$23,749	$174,588	54%	$93,583.77	46%	$81,004
18			$0	$79,199	$43,909	$43,909	$167,017	26%	$43,908.61	74%	$123,108
19			$0	$57,871	$48,044	$48,044	$153,959	31%	$48,044.38	69%	$105,915
20			$0	$32,673	$47,233	$57,729	$137,635	34%	$47,232.84	66%	$90,402
21			$0	$3,449	$45,658	$68,487	$117,593	39%	$45,657.83	61%	$71,935
22			$0	$0	$0	$93,549	$93,549	0%	$0.00	100%	$93,549
23					$0	$67,194	$67,194	0%	$0.00	100%	$67,194
24					$0	$35,765	$35,765	0%	$0.00	100%	$35,765
25					$0	$55	$55	0%	$0.00	100%	$55

College 1 / College 2 / Business / **Overall**

Figure 9-10. Aggregate your stock and fixed-income investments to determine your overall allocation needs

You might notice that the college fund columns in the overall worksheet calculate more years of savings than the goal worksheets. The college goal worksheets include only one calculation for the first several years, when all money is invested in stocks. The overall worksheet uses the FV function to calculate your college funds for each year. Then, for the years that the goal worksheets calculate (beginning in cell D12), the overall worksheet references the cells for target dollars (columns K and L on the goal worksheets).

The overall percentage for stocks in any given year is the total dollar value in stocks for the year divided by the savings total for the year. Similarly, the percentage for fixed-income investments is the fixed-income total for the year divided by the savings total. Columns I and K in Figure 9-10 show how the percentages change as savings goals grow near—for example, early on all savings are in stocks. Then, as the small business goal grows closer, the percentage in fixed-income investments increases, even though you're adding college savings at the same time. In the eleventh year, the business goal has passed, but the children are still several years from college, so your savings are back to 100 percent stocks. Once again, the percentage invested in fixed income investments increases as college grows closer, demonstrated in cells K12 through K19. K20 through K23 show why an overall allocation makes sense. As you withdraw money from savings to pay tuition for your first child, the percentage in fixed-income investments actually decreases (from 69 percent to 61 percent) instead of increasing as you might expect.

HACK #98   Get Out of Debt Before Debt Takes It Out of You

Running up too much debt can foil the best financial plans, so it pays to find out where you stand before you go too far.

Without debt, it would be tough to buy a house or your first car. Not many of us can rack up $100,000, $200,000, or more to buy a house free and clear. With debt, you can definitely have too much of a good thing. Mortgage payments, car payments, and credit card minimum payments are due every month, no matter what. If you borrow too much, you might not be able to save any money after buying food, paying taxes, and making debt payments. When things get really out of hand, you might end up borrowing money to buy food and that will simply end badly. Even if lenders are willing to loan you more money, it's a good idea to keep your debt load under control. If you find out you're over the edge of excessive debt, you can use common sense, discipline, and online tools to get back on track.

Keeping Debt in Check

When you shop for a mortgage or a car loan, lenders typically check your *debt to income ratio* to figure out how much they're willing to lend to you. Credit card companies, on the other hand, want you to run up balances on your credit cards. With rates as high as 21 percent, they rake in the dough when you maintain a balance. Paying only the minimum monthly payment on a credit card can take years to pay off the balance, and the interest you pay could end up being more than you borrowed in the first place.

So, what are these guidelines that lenders follow?

Mortgage debt to income ratio
> Lenders typically limit your monthly mortgage payment including principal, interest, property taxes, and homeowners insurance to no more than 30 percent of your gross monthly income—that's your monthly income before paying anything, including taxes and 401(k) contributions.

> You can convince lenders to loan you more than that if you can show that you've successfully handled a higher debt load. However, it's a good idea to back your debt up with higher savings so you can make your payments even if you're out of work for a while.

Total debt to income ratio
> The limit for total monthly debt payments is no more than 36 to 38 percent of your gross monthly income. Total monthly debt includes your mortgage payment, car payment, and other debt payments. Lenders estimate your monthly credit card payment as 4 percent of any outstanding balance.

Bringing Debt Back in Line

If your debt ratio is a little higher than the lenders' guidelines, you can whittle it back down with some minor adjustments to your spending. Often, you can get back on track by putting your credit card in a drawer for a while. Studies show that many people don't view credit card purchases as spending real money. Try paying cash or writing checks to bring your spending back to reality. You can also replace your credit card with a debit card, so that you have to pay it off every month.

If you can only afford to pay the minimum on your credit cards each month, you can resort to using cash advances on one card to pay another, or mailing the wrong checks to creditors to buy some time. At this point, you'll need stronger measures to get back on track. Here are some techniques to reduce your debt as quickly as possible with the minimal amount of pain:

- Pay off debts with the highest interest rate first. For example, if you carry a $5,000 balance on a credit card charging 20 percent interest, pay as much as you can afford each month on that card, while paying the minimum monthly payment on your 8 percent credit card. When the 20 percent card is completely paid, use the monthly payment you were making to start paying off the 8 percent card. When that card is completely paid, apply the monthly payment to paying off the 4 percent home equity loan.

> After your debts are paid, you can apply the monthly payment you're accustomed to dishing out now to savings.

- Stop contributing to savings until your high-interest debt is paid off. Paying off a 20 percent credit card interest by foregoing 1 percent on savings is like a guaranteed 19 percent return on your money—which is a good return even for investing in the stock market.

- If you carry a lot of debt, consider paying it off with some—but not all—of your existing savings.

> If things are really bad, you can even stop contributing to your 401(k). Because 401(k)s have other benefits, such as reducing your taxable income and employer-matching, you should halt your 401(k) contribution as a last resort.

If you want to know when you can start buying grande caramel skinny lattes on your way to work again, you can prepare a more formal debt reduction plan using the debt reduction calculator at *http://www.quicken.com/planning/debt/debt_planner*. Before you go online, search your filing cabinet to figure out how much you have in savings and identify the interest rate, outstanding balance, minimum monthly payment, and your typical monthly payment for each of your credit cards, mortgages, home equity loans, second mortgages, car loans, any other installment loans, and other debt.

After you enter the information about your debts, the planner tells you how long it will take and how much it will cost to pay off your debt on your current schedule. If you want to apply savings toward paying off your debt, select the Savings tab, type the amount of savings you want to use, and click Save/Recalculate. To find out what steps to take to make your plan happen, click Action Plan. The planner includes common-sense tips such as stop charging to credit cards, but also tells you how much to pay to each creditor each month to optimize your monthly debt payments.

On the other hand, if lack of self-discipline got you into this mess in the first place, you might want more help than the Quicken planner can provide. Debt Counselors of America is a not-for-profit organization that can help you for a small fee. You can download their publications from *http://www.dca.org* or contact them to get one-on-one help. Their One-Pay service includes working with creditors to reduce monthly payments, late fees, and interest. You make one monthly payment to DCA and they handle payments to your creditors.

HACK #99 Find a Financial Planner

Financial planners come in all shapes and sizes, so do some homework to figure out what kind you need, what services you want, and whether it's worth the cost.

The road of life is littered with financial detours. Just when you've navigated a smooth stretch, you hit a curve: funding a college education, financing a divorce, or managing an inheritance. Even if you're not faced with a big-money decision, nagging issues pop up from choosing between term and whole life insurance to the 53 investment options in your company's 401(k) plan. If you're in over your head or just want a second opinion, consider consulting with a financial planner. Although you might not find a budding Suze Orman to hold your hand, there are thousands of financial planners out there, and it's likely that one will meet your needs at a price you can afford.

First, you have to know what you want. Financial planners offer a wide variety of services, including money management, retirement planning, budget review, tax management, estate planning, and insurance analysis. Decide which services you want and whether you want an ongoing or occasional relationship with your planner. Planners offer one or more of the following services:

- Manage all your financial affairs
- Manage your investments
- Draft an overall financial plan
- Provide financial check-ups
- Give ongoing advice on all financial matters
- Offer occasional advice for specific situations

Anyone can put out a shingle and advertise that they're a financial planner. Brokers and insurance agents can call themselves financial planners, but might not provide a full range of financial planning services. To top it off, if you try to go by professional certifications, you might need a consultant just to sort through the professional designations and certifications in financial planning, insurance, money management, and accounting. Here's a rundown on who's who:

Certified Public Accountant (CPA)
> Prepares tax returns and provides advice about taxes. CPAs must have a bachelor's degree, pass an exam, obtain ongoing education, and hold a license from a state board. CPAs with the Personal Financial Specialist (PFS) also have expertise in financial planning.

Certified Financial Planner (CFP)
> Experienced and educated in the financial planning process. CFPs must pass an exam and keep up to date with continuing education credits. Beginning in 2007, all those sitting for the CFP exam must have a college degree.

Chartered Financial Analyst (CFA)
> The gold standard for financial investment advisors and analysts, CFAs must pass a three-part exam, have a college degree, work experience, and obtain ongoing education.

Chartered Property Casualty Underwriter (CPCU)
> Requires completion of ten classes with a concentration in commercial or personal insurance. CPCUs must pass a test, have work experience, and obtain ongoing continuing education credits.

Chartered Financial Consultant (ChFC)
> Requires completion of eight financial planning classes and professional experience.

> If you're in the market for a financial planner, the CFP designation is your best bet. Chartered Financial Consultants don't have to take an overall exam, and the other certifications don't deal as directly with all aspects of financial planning.

Different Strokes for Different Folks

Different types of CFPs use different compensation methods. *Commission-based* financial planners earn their fees through the commissions on financial products they sell such as stocks, bonds, mutual funds, and annuities. *Fee-only* financial planners either charge by the hour or base their fees on a percentage of the dollar value of your assets that they manage. *Fee-based* financial planners use a combination of client fees and commissions from investment products. You can determine which method of compensation you prefer using Table 9-7.

Table 9-7. Financial planner compensation methods

Payment method	Typical cost	Pros	Cons
Commissions	Front-end loads of up to 8 percent or ongoing percentages of up to 1 percent for mutual funds; commissions of $50 to $150 on the purchase or sale of stock; annual percentages for insurance agents	You don't pay fees directly out of your pocket.	Potential conflict of interest, as the planner might sell you high-cost products or trade frequently to generate more income. Often costs more than fee-only. Embedded commissions are easy to ignore.
Fee based on percent of investment assets	0.75 to 2 percent per year	You don't pay fees out of pocket and there's no conflict of interest with commission.	Cut into your returns if fee exceeds 1 percent. Might encourage planner to keep assets invested that could be employed elsewhere. Fees are paid each year.
Fee based on percentage of total client assets, which are all of your assets, such as investments, house, and retirement plan	0.75 to 2percent per year	You don't pay fees out of pocket and there's no conflict of interest with commission.	Can get very expensive; the more you own, the more you pay. Fees are paid each year.
Hourly fee	$100 to $250 per hour	You know exactly how much you'll pay. Encourages you to do your own legwork with your financial paperwork.	Planner might do unnecessary work for more income. You pay fees out of pocket.
Flat fee	$2,000 to $10,000 for a comprehensive financial plan	Gives you an overall rundown of your current financial situations with recommendations. You know exactly how much you must pay.	Expensive for a one-time snapshot of your financial situation. One or two things could change, rendering the plan obsolete.

Table 9-7. Financial planner compensation methods (continued)

Payment method	Typical cost	Pros	Cons
Yearly retainer fee	$2,000 to $10,000 per year	You know exactly how much you must pay. Removes any commission or investment asset conflict of interest.	Prohibitively expensive for all but the super-rich. Fee is paid each year.
Fee-based/mix of fees and commissions	Varies	Not all charges come out of your pocket.	Potential for commission-based conflict of interest and high fees.

Finding and Hiring a Planner

There are a couple of ways to find a compatible planner. Start with the tried-and-true method of asking friends and relatives for recommendations. Take recommendations based on long-term client-planner relationships—it means more if a friend is happy with the planner he's been with for 10 years than if someone is excited about a new planner. Seek out other recommendations from professional associates such as accountants and lawyers, and then turn to the Web. Both the Financial Planning Association (FPA)—the professional association for CFPs—at *http://www.fpanet.org/plannersearch/plannersearch. cfm* and the National Association of Personal Financial Advisors (NAPFA)—the fee-only financial planners organization—at *http://www.napfa.org* have search functions on their web sites that can help you find a planner.

The search tool for the FPA helps you find a planner near you, as shown in Figure 9-11. You can search by zip code, city, state, or within a designated radius of your zip code.

The NAPFA tool requires you to enter personal information, including your email address, before searching, and you have to specifically opt out of the organization sending your information to planners. The results are a list of all fee-only planners in your entire state, which you can then limit by zip code. You can't search out of state, which cuts down your choices if you live near a state border.

> The Securities & Exchange Commission web site at *http:// www.adviserinfo.sec.gov/IAPD/Content/IapdMain/iapd_ SiteMap.asp* can tell you if a planner or broker has ever been disciplined or investigated in addition to providing details about their client base, compensation system, and background.

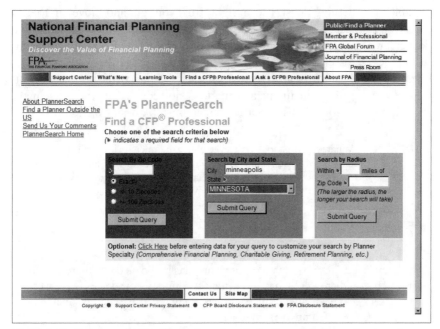

Figure 9-11. You can use FPA PlannerSearch to find a financial planner by zip code, city, state, or within a specified distance of your home

Narrow down your list of potential planners by checking out their web sites, if they offer them, for scope of services, investment approach, and fee structure. Make an initial contact by phone and ask for an initial no-fee consultation. Before you embark on the actual interview, prepare some questions. You can use questionnaire forms available online:

• The Motley Fool site (*http://www.fool.com/fa/finadvice03. htm?source=famp*) offers a financial advisor questionnaire and an advisor meeting checklist detailing which documents you should bring to your initial meeting.

• The Financial Planning Association (*http://www.fpanet.org/public/tools/ tenquestionschecklist.cfm*) has a checklist for interviewing a financial planner.

• Cambridge Advisors (*http://www.cambridgeadvisors.com/consumer/ resources/interview*) offers a worksheet that you can use to compare two planners.

In addition to answers to specific questions, stay tuned to the emotional vibes and body language of your conversation. Does the planner welcome questions? Does she explain things in a way you can understand? Is the planner someone you (and your spouse) feel comfortable with? If you're not comfortable or something doesn't seem right, trust your gut and move on; there's more than one fish in the financial planning sea. After you've settled on a particular planner, set up a meeting to work up a written agreement outlining the scope of services, a good faith cost estimate, and the responsibilities of each party. Nail down any pesky details such as the cost for phone consultations or questions on financial situations not covered in the agreement. Include a termination clause in case the relationship doesn't work out.

> Whatever you do, don't ever give a planner or broker total power over your finances. Retain the power to veto any proposed investment and insist that statements prepared by a third party are regularly mailed to your home or office.

Cheaper Advice on the Web

If you want advice and guidance, but want to keep a lid on costs, there are for-pay web sites that offer financial planning and investment advice. These web-based services are cheaper, but are also less comprehensive and personal than a relationship with a financial planner.

- The Motley Fool (*http://www.fool.com/fa/finadvice.htm?source=fanavs*) offers TMF Money Advisor subscriptions for $195 per year. The service includes phone consultations with a financial planner, an online financial planning tool that you can use and your financial planner can access, Motley Fool investing and personal finance seminars, and discussion boards.

- Morningstar (*http://www.morningstar.com/Cover/ClearFuture. html?tsection=clearfuture*) offers a more limited service, ClearFuture, for 401(k) investment advice. For $115 a year or $12.95 a month, you gain access to ClearFuture as well as Morningstar's mutual fund, stock, and personal finance analysis, tools, and information.

- Financial Engines (*http://www.financialengines.com*) isn't as comprehensive as the Motley Fool service, but offers more than Morningstar. For $149.95 a year, you receive personalized feedback on your retirement accounts, tax-deferred accounts, stock options, and financial goals. For $300 a year, you receive those services plus hands-on quarterly monitoring of your portfolio and a quarterly newsletter.

—*Amy Crane*

Build a Ladder of Fixed-Income Investments

HACK
100

Building a CD ladder provides access to your money while limiting your exposure to interest rate and inflation changes.

Do you invest in longer-term certificates of deposit to get the highest interest rate, or do you put your money in shorter-term CDs so it is more accessible even if it means settling for a lower interest rate? A strategy called *laddering* lets you have your cake and eat it too. Laddering a CD is similar to dollar-cost averaging when buying stocks or mutual funds. Managing your cash investments should be part of your overall investment portfolio strategy. The right cash management strategy can provide access to your cash when you need it while achieving higher overall returns.

The Benefits of Fixed-Income Investment Ladders

There are four main reasons to ladder your fixed-income investments:

- Obtain higher yields by investing in longer-term fixed-income vehicles
- Reduce interest rate risk, market risk, and reinvestment risk
- Structure your investments to match your goals
- Provide access to principal at regular intervals in case you need the money

A ladder is a series of investments that mature at regular, staggered intervals. For example, you might build a ladder by dividing $10,000 among five CDs such that one CD matures every year for the next five years. Once a year, you have the option of withdrawing some or all of the principal from your savings. However, if you keep the principal in CDs, your ladder is invested eventually in five five-year CDs, which typically offer higher rates than one-year CDs.

When you build a ladder, choose your fixed-income investments so that they mature when you need your money. For example, if you are retired and need annual income for living expenses, build a ladder on five-year CDs. If you need money every six months to pay tuition, invest in CDs that mature every six months. By setting up a ladder, you can access your money regularly without paying penalties for early withdrawal.

If you need money every month, you're better off with an annual ladder to keep the number of CDs manageable. You can take money out of the ladder when an investment matures and place it in a money market account for easy access until the next CD maturity date.

A CD ladder can help you manage interest rate risk. Although a ladder provides regular access to your funds, you still obtain the higher returns of longer-term investments. Although interest rates might change, the ladder averages those changes out so you achieve a steadier flow of income, instead of low income when rates are low and high income when rates are high.

> In addition, you can adjust your ladder to take advantage of trends in interest rates. When rates are low, you can build a ladder of shorter-term investments. As rates move higher, you can reinvest funds from maturing CDs at higher rates. When rates are high, you can build a ladder of longer-term investments to lock in more of your money at higher rates.

To start your CD ladder, purchase CDs that mature on a regular schedule. If you have $10,000 to invest in an annual ladder, put $2,000 each into one-, two-, three-, four-, and five-year CDs. Each year represents a rung on the ladder and, as each CD matures, you choose how to use the proceeds. When the first CD matures in one year, cash in the money you need and reinvest the remaining funds in another five-year CD.

> Most financial planners think you should have at least $25,000 for this type of five-year fixed investment plan, but you can create a ladder with $1,000 to $2,000 each year.

Laura Bruce at Bankrate.com provides an excellent example of the benefits of fixed-income investments, as demonstrated in Figure 9-12.

Investor A bought five $10,000 one-year CDs that earned $16,550 in income at the end of 6 years. Investor B invested $10,000 each into a one-, two-, three-, four-, and five-year CD and, as each CD matured, bought another $10,000 five-year CD. His six-year total income was $19,985—$3,435 more interest income over six years than Investor A received. In addition, Investor B's income stream varied only $230 annually, whereas Investor A's income varied by as much as $1,250 between the best and worst years.

—Martha Sippel

Investor A bought a $50,000 one-year CD and reinvested in one-year CDs every year thereafter at the following rates:

Investor A -- Reinvesting plan	
Year	**Rate**
Intial purchase	5.85%
End of year 1	6.10%
End of year 2	5.60%
End of year 3	5.05%
End of year 4	6.50%
End of year 5	4.00%

Investor B bought $10,000 each of a one-, two-, three-, four- and five-year CD in May 1998 and then bought $10,000 each of a five-year CD as each CD matured. The CD rates were as follows:

Investor B -- Laddered portfolio	
Initial Investment	**Buy when initial CD matures**
1 year @ 5.85%	5 years @ 7.10%
2 years @ 6.40%	5 years @ 6.20%
3 years @ 6.70%	5 years @ 5.95%
4 years @ 6.90%	5 years @ 7.20%
5 years @ 7.10%	5 years @ 5.45%

Let's compare the annual income stream generated from these two strategies.

Income comparison: Reinvesting vs. laddered portfolio							
	Year 1	**Year 2**	**Year 3**	**Year 4**	**Year 5**	**This year**	**Total income**
Investor A	$2,925	$3,050	$2,800	$2,525	$3,250	$2,000	**$16,550**
Investor B	$3,295	$3,420	$3,400	$3,190	$3,325	$3.355	**$19,985**

Figure 9-12. Bankrate provides an example of the benefits of CD ladders

Index

We'd like to hear your suggestions for improving our indexes. Send email to *index@oreilly.com*.

Y

Yahoo! Finance
  bonds, 8
  free downloads, 90
  industry average comparisons, 100
  mutual fund data, 75
  Stock Screener, 20
year-to-year results comparison, 164
yield, dividends and, 124

Z

zero coupon treasury bonds, college
  planning and, 439

Colophon

Our look is the result of reader comments, our own experimentation, and feedback from distribution channels. Distinctive covers complement our distinctive approach to technical topics, breathing personality and life into potentially dry subjects.

The items on the cover of *Online Investing Hacks* are darts. A dart is a small missile with a pointed shaft at one end and feathers at the other, and is used to play the popular game of the same name.

The game of darts is thought to have originated in England during the Middle Ages. Between periods of battle, soldiers would ward off boredom by hurling arrows at the upturned covers of wine barrels, aiming for the cork bung. As this pastime grew in popularity, the soldiers replaced the wine barrel cover with a tree's cross-section, because the natural growth-rings provided a built-in means to determine whose dart landed closest to the center.

During the winter months, soldiers spent most of their time inside, and because they couldn't throw full-sized arrows, shortened versions of the arrows were used—precursors to the modern dart.

Sarah Sherman was the production editor and the copyeditor for *Online Investing Hacks*. Emily Quill was the proofreader. Phil Dangler and Claire Cloutier provided quality control. Johnna VanHoose Dinse wrote the index.

Hanna Dyer designed the cover of this book, based on a series design by Edie Freedman. The cover image is an original photograph from Entertainment and Leisure Stockbyte CD. Emma Colby produced the cover layout with QuarkXPress 4.1 using Adobe's Helvetica Neue and ITC Garamond fonts.

David Futato designed the interior layout. This book was converted Julie Hawks to FrameMaker 5.5.6 with a format conversion tool created by Erik Ray, Jason McIntosh, Neil Walls, and Mike Sierra that uses Perl and XML technologies. The text font is Linotype Birka; the heading font is Adobe Helvetica Neue Condensed; and the code font is LucasFont's TheSans Mono Condensed. The illustrations that appear in the book were produced by Robert Romano and Jessamyn Read using Macromedia FreeHand 9 and Adobe Photoshop 6. This colophon was written by Sarah Sherman.

Need in-depth answers fast?

Related Titles Available from O'Reilly

Hacks

Amazon Hacks

BSD Hacks

Digital Photography Hacks

eBay Hacks

Excel hacks

Google Hacks

Harware Hacking Projects for Geeks

Linux Server Hacks

Mac OS X Hacks

Mac OS X Panther Hacks

Spidering Hacks

TiVo Hacks

Windows Server Hacks

Windows XP Hacks

Wireless Hacks

O'REILLY®

Our books are available at most retail and online bookstores.
To order direct: 1-800-998-9938 • *order@oreilly.com* • *www.oreilly.com*
Online editions of most O'Reilly titles are available by subscription at *safari.oreilly.com*

Keep in touch with O'Reilly

1. Download examples from our books

To find example files for a book, go to:

www.oreilly.com/catalog

select the book, and follow the "Examples" link.

2. Register your O'Reilly books

Register your book at *register.oreilly.com*

Why register your books? Once you've registered your O'Reilly books you can:

- Win O'Reilly books, T-shirts or discount coupons in our monthly drawing.
- Get special offers available only to registered O'Reilly customers.
- Get catalogs announcing new books (US and UK only).
- Get email notification of new editions of the O'Reilly books you own.

3. Join our email lists

Sign up to get topic-specific email announcements of new books and conferences, special offers, and O'Reilly Network technology newsletters at:

elists.oreilly.com

It's easy to customize your free elists subscription so you'll get exactly the O'Reilly news you want.

4. Get the latest news, tips, and tools

http://www.oreilly.com

- "Top 100 Sites on the Web"—PC Magazine
- CIO Magazine's Web Business 50 Awards

Our web site contains a library of comprehensive product information (including book excerpts and tables of contents), downloadable software, background articles, interviews with technology leaders, links to relevant sites, book cover art, and more.

5. Work for O'Reilly

Check out our web site for current employment opportunities:

jobs.oreilly.com

6. Contact us

O'Reilly & Associates
1005 Gravenstein Hwy North
Sebastopol, CA 95472 USA

TEL: 707-827-7000 or 800-998-9938
(6am to 5pm PST)

FAX: 707-829-0104

order@oreilly.com
For answers to problems regarding your order or our products.
To place a book order online, visit:

www.oreilly.com/order_new

catalog@oreilly.com
To request a copy of our latest catalog.

booktech@oreilly.com
For book content technical questions or corrections.

corporate@oreilly.com
For educational, library, government, and corporate sales.

proposals@oreilly.com
To submit new book proposals to our editors and product managers.

international@oreilly.com
For information about our international distributors or translation queries. For a list of our distributors outside of North America check out:

international.oreilly.com/distributors.html

adoption@oreilly.com
For information about academic use of O'Reilly books, visit:

academic.oreilly.com

O'REILLY®

Our books are available at most retail and online bookstores.
To order direct: 1-800-998-9938 • *order@oreilly.com* • *www.oreilly.com*
Online editions of most O'Reilly titles are available by subscription at *safari.oreilly.com*